The One Year® Praying in Faith Devotional

THE ONE YEAR®

PRAYING
in FAITH
DEVOTIONAL

*365 Daily Bible Readings on Hearing God
and Believing His Promises*

CHRIS TIEGREEN

TYNDALE
MOMENTUM®

A Tyndale nonfiction imprint

Visit Tyndale online at tyndale.com.

Visit Tyndale Momentum online at tyndalemomentum.com.

TYNDALE, Tyndale's quill logo, *Tyndale Momentum*, the Tyndale Momentum logo, and *The One Year* are registered trademarks of Tyndale House Ministries. *One Year* and The One Year logo are trademarks of Tyndale House Ministries. Tyndale Momentum is a nonfiction imprint of Tyndale House Publishers, Carol Stream, Illinois.

The One Year Praying in Faith Devotional: 365 Daily Bible Readings on Hearing God and Believing His Promises

Designed by Ron C. Kaufmann

Edited by Sarah R. Kelley

Published in association with the literary agency of Mark Sweeney & Associates, Carol Stream, Illinois.

For information about special discounts for bulk purchases, please contact Tyndale House Publishers at csresponse@tyndale.com, or call 1-855-277-9400.

ISBN 978-1-4964-4611-4

Printed in the United States of America

27	26	25	24	23	22	21
7	6	5	4	3	2	1

Introduction

YOU'VE PRAYED. You've waited. And you've wondered. You've eagerly embarked on this journey of faith, but that journey has raised a lot of questions and involved long distances between resting points. Like many Christians, you know about God's promises and you've received answers to prayer, but you've also felt as if some prayers have led nowhere. That combination of beliefs and experiences is disorienting at times. On the one hand, you live and pray with a strong conviction that God answers prayer. On the other, you aren't quite sure how it all works.

Your journey of faith, no matter how confusing it may be at times, creates a wonderful opportunity to draw closer to God and dive deeper into his Word. That's one of the purposes of growing your faith, and it's also the purpose of this devotional. These readings will help you walk out that journey with increasing insight and meaning if you've ever

- been frustrated with a shot-in-the-dark approach to prayer;
- stood in the gap between promise and fulfillment, questioning why things are taking so long;
- wondered why God can seem so close one day and so distant the next;
- felt the tension between your deep desires and his will; or
- needed daily encouragement about the challenges of prayer and the hope God offers when we bring our requests to him.

Sometimes we need a thousand assurances that God's promises are true and our prayers are effective before we believe it. Consider this devotional to be a collection of 365 of those assurances.

But it's more than just assurances and affirmations. This book is an explorer's guide to the dynamics of faith: how it works in the human heart and mind and how we can train ourselves to believe more purely, consistently, and purposefully. The readings will connect a lot of points between the thoughts and attitudes we bring into our prayers and the answers and fulfillment we receive from them.

There are many kinds of prayer. This devotional touches on adoration, thanksgiving, and confession, but it focuses primarily on requests, petitions, or supplications—not because asking is the most important kind of prayer but because it seems to be the kind we have the most questions about. We instinctively bring our longings to God and cry out to him in times of need, and we crave his responses. So these readings are centered on those prayers of faith, those times when we ask God for something specific. This devotional is not meant to be a comprehensive treatment of faith, nor a complete picture of prayer. But it does go deep into the spiritual, mental, emotional, relational, and circumstantial dynamics we experience in the prayer process.

You'll see some common themes and tensions in these pages, all of which are rooted in Scripture. For example, God tells us we can be confident that he will answer our prayers but calls us to be flexible when he doesn't—or at least when he doesn't answer them the way we expect him to. He wants to both accomplish his purposes and fulfill our desires, and learning how these two concerns merge can be both frustrating and rewarding. We experience tension between the here and now of our lives and the there-and-then of eternity, even while our prayers operate in both realms. We keep our eyes on the circumstances around us but also have to search behind the scenes, where only faith can see. We struggle to discern the difference between God's voice and our own impulses, between God's silence and God's "no," and between waiting patiently in faith and taking action in faith. We encounter mysteries and forks in the road at almost every turn.

That is the challenge, adventure, and joy of genuine prayer, and it's a significant part of our walk with God. My prayer is that this book will help you draw closer to him on all counts and at every turn. May you experience him, connect your heart to his, and receive his warm and generous responses more and more each day.

God's Heart and Ours

[Jesus said,] "If you remain in me and my words remain in you,
you may ask for anything you want, and it will be granted!" JOHN 15:7

ONE OF THE PRIMARY WAYS God accomplishes his purposes on earth is through the prayers of his people. And one of our primary motivations for prayer is the desires in our hearts. It's a remarkable dynamic, but we seem to have something of a love-hate relationship with it. On the one hand, the longings within us instinctively find a voice in our prayers; on the other, we mistrust those desires and plead for *his* will to be done. Scripture shows us, however, that God blesses our requests when they are founded on a relationship of delight with him (Psalm 37:4). And Jesus assures us that our desires are trustworthy when our lives are based on him and his words (John 15:7). As much as we may mistrust our own desires, Scripture points us back to them.

It's true that God wants our desires to align with his, but that's not the unreachable, shot-in-the-dark kind of process we sometimes think it is. Throughout Scripture, his relationship with his people suggests not a unilateral, find-my-will-or-else agenda but a blending of hearts. We were created to come close to a Father who has made himself vulnerable to the longings of his people and to absorb his desires as he cares for and works through ours. He doesn't want to accomplish his purposes arbitrarily, independent of our hopes and dreams. He wants us to dream with him.

It's a beautiful thing when our dreams intersect with God's purposes. Doors open, miracles happen, the Kingdom advances, and hearts are fulfilled. It may not always be a smooth process—sometimes it's rather disorienting, in fact—but it's good. It's how God has chosen to partner with the people he has made in his image and called to fill the world with his goodness. It's his *modus operandi* in a world being restored back to him.

God shapes the world by prayer.

E. M. BOUNDS

Why We Pray

The heavens belong to the LORD, but he has given the earth to all humanity. **PSALM 115:16**

AT THE BEGINNING, God gave human beings a responsibility to steward this planet. He did not enthrone us as autonomous kings, but he did design us to partner with him in his Kingship. Unfortunately, we squandered this enormous privilege and handed this stewardship over to unholy forces with dangerous agendas. Earth became infected with evil, and only those who were specially called seemed to recognize their role to intercede between heaven and earth. The keys God had given his people to his Kingdom were rarely used well.

But God became man in order to regain those keys and distribute them to people of faith. And today we are being remade in his image and restored to our royal stewardship of his Kingdom, with authority. Why? Because God honors his original plan. He has given us responsibility over this world, and he rarely intervenes unless we invite him. He is Lord, but we are his agents. And he has chosen not to circumvent his agents but to work through them. As landlords of his earthly holdings, we become cosigners of his decrees. We are the vehicles of his work on earth.

That's why we pray. Perhaps you see prayer as personal communication with God, a means of getting what you need from him, a conversation that draws you closer. It's that, but it's more. Many have wondered why God doesn't just go ahead and accomplish his will on his own, and this is a big part of the answer. God has chosen not to rule this world unilaterally. He designed us to be stewards at the beginning (Genesis 1:28), and we will rule with him in the end (Revelation 5:10). He has always sought people to intervene and, in the absence of a completely righteous person, became human himself in order to fulfill and restore human agency in his Kingdom (Isaiah 59:16-17). Now he has given us his own keys, reestablishing us as stewards and landlords to implement his will in this world (Matthew 16:19). One of the most effective and powerful ways to do that is through prayer.

Make that your mission. Invite God into every corner of your world. Partner with him in his answers. You are praying his Kingdom into earth.

Whether we like it or not, asking is the rule of the kingdom.

CHARLES SPURGEON

The Partnership of Prayer

The Spirit pleads for us believers in harmony with God's own will.
ROMANS 8:27

IMAGINE PRAYING TO GOD as if sitting across a table from him. As you present your requests, he looks across at you while listening to whatever is on your heart. Suddenly, you realize this is not the right setup for someone who has been completely reconciled to God and filled with his Spirit. He sees your expression and, knowing your heart already, nods in agreement. You get up, pull your chair around to his side of the table, and looking at your circumstances and the world together, you both have a conversation about the requests you were presenting a moment ago. Instead of sitting in the position of a negotiator, you are now sitting in a position of partnership. You and God are both involved in these prayers.

It is vital to hold this image or something like it in your mind when you pray. You are no longer trying to negotiate with God for a particular outcome; instead, you have been reconciled to him (2 Corinthians 5:18), and he has placed his Spirit inside of you (John 14:17; Romans 8:11). You are now in a partnership, with Jesus and the Holy Spirit interceding for you (Romans 8:26, 34) as you discuss with God his will and your desires. Though you still pray *to* him, more importantly you are praying *with* him. Knowing the difference can completely transform the nature of your prayer life.

No longer do you simply present an agenda to God and hope he stamps it with his approval. Now you can freely talk about your desires, listen for his input, let your conversations with him shape and reshape your requests, and offer those requests up, knowing they have already been vetted by the one who will ultimately carry them out. You still may not know the timing or the means, but you know the heart of the Father who helped you craft your prayers and sense agreement with him in your heart. You know his kind disposition toward your petitions and have confidence in his power to fulfill them. You and the Father, Son, and Spirit are praying as one.

Prayer is a summit meeting in the throne room of the universe.

RALPH A. HERRING

In Whose Name?

[Jesus said,] "You can ask for anything in my name, and I will do it,
so that the Son can bring glory to the Father." JOHN 14:13

SOMETHING INSIDE PULLS AT THE REINS of our prayers. *You don't deserve this*, a voice might whisper. *You haven't prayed intensely enough. You fell into sin just yesterday. This isn't really a need. Your agenda and God's are totally different. Who do you think you are, praying for such a request?* These objections make for a long internal conversation, and they limit our expectations of God. We ask for something small because we don't want to assume anything too great of him. We bargain, vow, or offer up some self-imposed conditions. We even try to do our own part because we just aren't convinced God gives as freely as our theology says he does.

All of those nagging suggestions of our own unworthiness, apathy, and irresponsibility would matter very much—*if we were praying in our own name*. But we're not, are we? We're praying in Jesus' name. As much as we insert our own histories and insufficiencies into our prayers, they really aren't relevant. After all, we aren't coming to the throne of grace clothed in our own identity. We're coming to it clothed in Jesus' identity. And that changes everything.

When you pray in Jesus' name—with his identity, righteousness, track record, and esteem—you can pray with extreme security and confidence. If he stands to inherit everything (Hebrews 1:2) and you are a coheir with him (Romans 8:16-17), then you can ask anything within his and your inheritance. Scripture never says you are partially identified with him. You are wholly, completely in him and never have to present your own ID when writing checks on his account. You'll need to do that responsibly, of course, and within the outlines of his will—but never by your own merits. That's why he tells you to pray in his name.

That's really good news. It undoes all our insufficiencies in prayer. Whether we measure up no longer matters because we are praying in the name of someone who does. Knowing that, we have every reason to pray boldly in keeping with God's purposes—as long as we are clothed in Jesus' identity and praying in his name.

A Christian has a union with Jesus Christ more noble, more intimate, and more perfect than the members of a human body have with their head.

JOHN EUDES

Prioritizing Relationship

Take delight in the LORD, and he will give you your heart's desires.
PSALM 37:4

IT'S EASY IN A DISCUSSION of faith and prayer to become focused on the objects of our faith and prayers. After all, the process of prayer involves seeking answers, waiting for something to happen, and receiving the fulfillment of promises God has given. Prayer is more than just this, of course. But Jesus often spoke of what God would do in response to our prayers, and the response isn't just a nice bonus added on to a critical spiritual discipline. Those who say the point of prayer is to change us, not get something from God, are partly right but missing something. Jesus placed emphasis on receiving answers, not on the spiritual exercise itself. That's significant.

Still, we know better than to make prayer just a transaction. God is not our vending machine, our ATM, our drive-thru window, or our microwave oven. We can't just push the right buttons and get something in return. The foundation of our lives is an intimate relationship of love with the God who created us for exactly that purpose. Everything in the Christian life—not just prayer—comes from that source. Otherwise our desires are off target and usually self-focused.

Both sides of this relationship are captured in Psalm 37:4. The idea of having the desires of our hearts fulfilled is amazing and wonderful, but what kind of desires are they? Will they be good for us or destroy us? Are they focused entirely on ourselves or on a bigger picture? Without the first part of the verse, this is a dangerous promise. But in the context of a relationship of delight, joy, intimacy, and love, it's a beautiful commitment from a generous Father.

In your life of prayer, prioritize your relationship with God. Center your life on him to the degree that he can shape your desires and trust you as he fulfills them. He delights in giving abundantly to those who understand what to do with abundance. He wants his children to be fully satisfied in his love first and then in the gifts that flow from his love. In your journey of faith and prayer, begin there, where all other blessings start to grow.

Our love for God is tested by the question of whether we seek him or his gifts.
RALPH WASHINGTON SOCKMAN

Prioritizing Presence

You know him, because he lives with you now and later will be in you.
JOHN 14:17

IMAGINE A RIDICULOUSLY WEALTHY FATHER who has two sons. One son stops by his father's office every once in a while to say hello and, at some point, asks for a bit of money to help meet some need or desire. The father usually complies but gives only as much as the son needs and does so without much pleasure. The other son spends time with his father whenever he can. He enjoys home life, sometimes goes to work with his father to help out, and makes time to pursue mutual interests together. He has needs and desires too, and he rarely hesitates to ask his father to meet them. The father almost always does—and throws in some extras with great pleasure.

What's the difference between these two sons and the way they receive from their father? They both get their needs met, and both remain solid members of the family. But one relationship is satisfying, fulfilling, and overflowing with goodwill, while the other has turned into a transactional arrangement without much heart. The father loves both sons, to be sure, but he delights in his relationship with only one of them. And because he so delights in that relationship, he is eager to give. He doesn't just react to what his son needs; he takes great joy in anticipating it, providing it, celebrating it, and even going over the top with his answers from time to time.

That's a picture of two vastly different approaches to prayer, and it should be obvious which is more satisfying to us and to God. We were made for a relationship with him that is filled with deep love, joy, and affection. That's why the Holy Spirit is given to us—God himself resides within us at the deepest levels of intimacy. When we cultivate that sense of his presence, we are cultivating the context for real prayer and faith. This is where our vision, longings, and desire for God's will are implanted and incubated in our hearts. This is what makes a life of prayer and faith fruitful and fulfilling—and what stirs the Father's joy in giving.

> Why should not every moment of our lives be a
> sort of communion with the divine love?
>
> JEAN PIERRE DE CAUSSADE

A Giving God

. . . who richly provides us with everything to enjoy.
1 TIMOTHY 6:17, ESV

MANY PEOPLE WANT TO PRAY more effectively. But we can't do so without knowing about the one we are praying to. Our perception of God is all-important, shaping everything that goes through our hearts and minds when we lift our requests to him. If we don't know he is generous by nature—one who blesses and desires to pour out his gifts on people who will appreciate them, enjoy them, and celebrate them—our faith will lie dormant in our hearts. Yes, God provides for those who hardly recognize his provision as gifts and for those who thank him but then stay away. But he delights in giving to those who draw closer to him after receiving from his hand. He loves giving to grateful, joyful recipients.

Paul addressed this dynamic of receiving in his first letter to Timothy. The "rich in this world" (6:17, NLT) should not put their trust in their riches, receiving from God and then ignoring him as if they earned what they got. But in that warning, Paul added an often-neglected phrase about God: he "richly provides us with everything to enjoy." There is no hint that the original language means "just what you need but no more," as so many of us tend to assume. No, he is not the stern father afraid of spoiling his children or the master who feels responsible only for his servants' barest needs. He is extravagant, rich, magnanimous, openhearted, and openhanded. He has already lavished us with gifts, many of which we take for granted. And he wants to pour out even more—but on the terms of faith, and in hearts that will bear the fruit of gratitude, joy, and generosity. In other words, he wants his children to be just like him, apples that don't fall far from the tree. He wants us to be openhearted and openhanded too.

Expect good things from God. Pray with awareness that he is the most generous Father ever. Ask for the sake of your enjoyment, but spread the joy. His hand opens to hearts that are open to him.

> God always has an open ear and a ready hand,
> if you have an open and ready heart.
>
> CHARLES SPURGEON

An Openhanded God

You open your hand; you satisfy the desire of every living thing.
PSALM 145:16, ESV

HAVE YOU NOTICED ALL THE ABUNDANT BLESSINGS God has given you? Many people don't. Many of us walk around for years barely recognizing the exquisite beauty of the natural world; relationships that, no matter how imperfect, give us the love and support we crave; kindhearted people who do nice things for us; relatively healthy bodies that, in spite of a few pains and doctors' visits, keep us breathing and thinking and feeling; fascinating varieties of tastes and sounds and smells; and so much more. People who have come face-to-face with death often live with a vastly heightened appreciation for each and every day. Yet we have that same opportunity without going through a crisis first. We live in a world that is filled with gifts from our God who always has an open hand.

We also live in a world that is fallen, flawed, and frustrating, and perhaps that's why we don't recognize the gifts around us. Human nature often zeroes in on whatever is wrong and needs fixing. But a heart of gratitude turns that nature around and focuses instead on the glory and beauty of our existence. Our praises orient our hearts toward the God of good things.

How does this relate to our life of faith and prayer? For one, it's knowing the God we are praying to. But it's also living with a spirit of wonder, which energizes our prayers in a way that our impression of the mundane day-to-day grind cannot. We pray eager, expectant prayers when we know this God and marvel at his creativity and generosity. Our prayers become an overflowing conversation rather than desperate pleas. They connect with the heart of the Father because they recognize who he is.

Immerse yourself in the generosity of God. Learn to recognize every single gift he has given, even if it is simply your next breath. Thank him for the people he has placed in your life, even if they rub you the wrong way at times. Enjoy today's weather, even if it's hotter, colder, or wetter than you prefer. Train your heart in the art of seeing blessings, and prayers for specific blessings will flow far more freely.

One single grateful thought raised to heaven is the most perfect prayer.

G. E. LESSING

Seek the Lord

The young lions suffer want and hunger; but those who
seek the LORD lack no good thing.   **PSALM 34:10, ESV**

MOST OF US CAN THINK OF things we lack. Some are minor details, but many are major desires—perhaps our health, the welfare of our marriage and children, our ability to get out of debt, and more. If our hearts are so inclined, we can come up with long lists of good things we lack. And many of us do have hearts so inclined. We have trained our minds well to rehearse the things we're missing out on.

But that's the problem. Minds that rehearse situations of lack and need—even serious ones—are not actually seeking the Lord. They are holding a grudge, pointing out a problem, expressing some sort of dissatisfaction with what God has given. One of the most significant and powerful goals of the Holy Spirit is to turn us toward new ways of seeing, to help us emphasize the goodness of God, to recognize how every good gift in our lives shines with his blessing. To seek the Lord is to cooperate with this transformation. Grateful hearts have done this. Complaining hearts have not.

So God urges us to seek him—not in the sense of asking him for what we need, though that's always allowed, but to truly seek *him*. He wants us to enter into his purposes, understand his ways, ask him what's on his heart today, and begin to realize all that goes into caring for our spiritual, physical, mental, emotional, and relational needs that make a simple "fix it" approach impossible. He wants us not just to approach him but to walk with him, arm in arm, with real understanding of his heart.

When we do this, we realize that in the grand scheme of things, we lack no good thing. And we are much better positioned to ask for the good things we long for. We have entered into wisdom, and wisdom colors everything in our lives, especially our prayers. It stirs up our faith, trusts in God's love, and thanks him for all he is doing on our behalf.

> The goodness of God knows how to use our disordered wishes and actions,
> often lovingly turning them to our advantage.
>
> BERNARD OF CLAIRVAUX

The Kingdom Currency

It is impossible to please God without faith. **HEBREWS 11:6**

MANY COUNTRIES TRADE EXCLUSIVELY in their own currency. When traveling to one of them, every price you see is based on the local economy; every credit card transaction will be converted into the local currency; and you cannot rely on a merchant to take your home-country cash and exchange it later. In other words, you will have to learn how to function completely within a different economy or not function at all. You have no other options if you want to buy anything.

The Kingdom of God is no different, and its currency is faith. It functions on that currency alone. Our good behavior, achievements, bargaining power, money, and status won't work there. We can use those things as statements of faith—money can be given in faith, positions can be utilized in faith, and so on—but faith itself has to be the driving force. The actions and substances in themselves are of no account. God's economy is exclusive. It's impossible to please him without faith.

We see this principle throughout Scripture. We receive salvation, our calling, answers to prayer, fruitfulness, Kingdom victories, restored relationships, and a new family all by faith. God gives us the opportunity to leverage the things of the world for eternal purposes, but we can only leverage them by faith. Nothing in his economy can be earned; his blessings can only be received. That's how his Kingdom works.

Sadly, many Kingdom citizens sow seeds of worldly currencies in the soil of the Kingdom without faith and get no lasting harvest from them. Our discipleship teaches us otherwise. Jesus calls us into an adventure of faith, and we can only experience it by letting go of the tools and treasures we used to rely on, and embracing his words and his ways. Any other effort to please God fails. He delights in those who anchor their trust in him, who use faith as a powerful currency to bring his Kingdom into this world, and who rejoice in his provision alone.

Ultimately, faith is the only key to the universe.

THOMAS MERTON

Hope and Expectation

Jesus said to the disciples, "Have faith in God." **MARK 11:22**

YOU'VE PROBABLY NOTICED a familiar dynamic in prayer. You put your praises, gratitude, requests, and petitions out there for the Lord to consider, but deep down, you feel as if answers are unlikely. You know God *can* answer, of course; you don't doubt his ability. But *will* he? That's a different question, and you have a sinking feeling he won't. Too often you see your prayers as shots in the dark that may—but probably won't—hit the target of God's will. So you pray, but without much hope. Your words say one thing, your heart another.

This may be a form of prayer, but it isn't a form of faith. Yes, you have faith in God as your source, and he's really your only hope. But is there actual hope in your prayers? Biblical hope is not wishful thinking, after all. It doesn't reflect how we might talk about our hopes for the weather or the big game this weekend. No, biblical hope is a rock-solid expectation, an anticipation of what we know is sure to come. And prayers that don't reflect that kind of hope are not filled with faith.

Jesus urged his followers to have faith in God—not just in his ability but in his goodness, favor, willingness to intervene in the lives of his people, and kind disposition toward our desires, many of which he has placed there. Faith is the key ingredient of prayer, and hope and expectancy are key ingredients of faith. In fact, you can't have a powerful prayer life without them. God will still be kind, responding often with his goodness. But a powerful prayer life is filled with the hope and expectancy of faith. That's what makes it powerful.

This is God's design. It's why Jesus said things like, "According to your faith be it done to you" (Matthew 9:29, ESV). When we stir up the expectations of our hearts—not for specific answers so much as for God's goodness and favor—things change. Answers come more freely. We see him intervene in lives, communities, and nations. And our hearts emerge victorious from the disappointment and hopelessness they once felt.

> Praying without faith is like trying to cut with a blunt knife—
> much labor expended to little purpose.
>
> **JAMES O. FRASER**

The Challenge of Faith

"You don't have enough faith," Jesus told them. "I tell you the truth,
if you had faith even as small as a mustard seed, you could say
to this mountain, 'Move from here to there,' and it would move.
Nothing would be impossible." **MATTHEW 17:20**

MAYBE I JUST DIDN'T HAVE ENOUGH FAITH. That guilty thought has plagued virtually every believer who has sincerely invested his or her heart in one of God's promises and somehow missed its fulfillment. Scripture is clear that faith is the currency of God's Kingdom, and we feel instinctively impoverished when we pray and nothing happens. A lack of response usually doesn't prompt us to step up our prayers, either. Instead, a downward cycle of unbelief can begin, weakening our expectations and undermining our faith until our prayers are little more than faint hopes.

Jesus' statement about not having enough faith has been abused by many who have placed blame for unanswered prayers on the shoulders of the one who prays. If all we need is a mustard-seed measure of faith, most of us have qualified on numerous occasions. Still, Jesus did speak these words, but not to condemn his disciples. He was contrasting the size of our faith with the size of the mountains that faith can move. Jesus was urging his followers to understand the power both of their faith and the words that flow from it. When a rock-solid confidence in the goodness of God is paired with bold statements of his will, big things happen. God rides in on the expectant declarations of those who have committed themselves to his Kingdom purposes.

Beware of limiting your prayers to whatever seems realistic. The size of the mountain is never an issue. Focus instead on the quality of your faith, what you really believe about God, and his goodness and willingness to fill your life with his favor. If a mustard-seed measure of faith can move an entire mountain that stands in the way of God's purposes, then you never need to look at the size of a problem again. Build yourself up in faith. Let your praises of God's goodness increase your expectations. Let the "yes and amen" of his promises sink into your heart. Relax and know he fights for those who love him.

Faith is blind—except upward. It is blind to impossibilities and deaf to doubt.

S. D. GORDON

Prayer's Priority

Seek first the kingdom of God and his righteousness,
and all these things will be added to you. MATTHEW 6:33, ESV

EVERYONE WHO PRAYS is asking for a kingdom to come. The question is, *whose* kingdom? We instinctively pray for our own agendas—often very legitimate, understandable requests for our lives to go well, our loved ones to be taken care of, provision in times of need, and protection in times of fear. Nothing is wrong with those prayers, but they do need to be set into a larger context. We are not called to make sure things go right in our own little world. We are called to seek the Kingdom of God—the culture of his realm and righteousness (justice, goodness, truth)—in every area of life.

On the surface, that may not change the content of our prayers much, but it will change our perspective of them. It's one thing to pray for increased provision for us to do with as we please, and it's another to pray for increased provision so we may use wealth as a Kingdom blessing. There's nothing wrong with praying for health and wellness, but that prayer gains power when we're praying to be well as vessels of Kingdom values and truths. That doesn't mean we are forbidden from praying any prayer that benefits us. God is a giver of wonderfully extravagant gifts. But the point is not just to receive a blessing. It's to see ourselves as those who have been blessed in order to bless others. We are citizens of a greater Kingdom than our own.

Pray all those prayers that are on your heart with faith and fervency. But pray them with full awareness that your highest priority in this life—the entire reason God put you on this planet—is to live out his Kingdom values, character, and ways. You are a carrier not only of the Kingdom culture but of the King. Everything you seek, even if it benefits yourself, should come in the context of your Kingdom citizenship and your longing to see his Kingdom come on earth as it is in heaven. When God's children have that perspective, he can trust them with their desires. And he adds all sorts of blessings to their Kingdom-focused prayers.

Before we can pray, "Thy kingdom come,"
we must be willing to pray, "My kingdom go."

ALAN REDPATH

An Invitation to See

Repent, for the kingdom of heaven is at hand.   MATTHEW 4:17, ESV

WHEN PEOPLE HEAR THE WORD *REPENT*, they often think of someone beating themselves up for their sins and embarking on a path of self-denial. Perhaps the word has been colored by centuries of such messages, or maybe their guilt instinct bends their thoughts in that direction. While repentance certainly does imply a turning from sin, its deeper meaning is broader and much more positive. In both Hebrew and Greek, with slightly different emphases, repentance suggests a new way of seeing and thinking that results in a new way of living. It's an invitation into a different kind of life than we have experienced.

This invitation to repent constitutes Jesus' first message in both Matthew and Mark after beginning his ministry, and it comes in the context of the Kingdom of God: The King has come, the Kingdom is right in front of you, and you'll need new eyes to see it. In order to grasp what this Kingdom is all about, you'll need to think and believe in different ways and learn to walk according to this new vision. You'll orient your life around different values, and your prayers will be focused on everything necessary for the realm of heaven to break into earth. You are entering into a new citizenship, and it changes everything.

This kind of repentance—this deeper, fuller, more inspiring meaning— transforms the way we pray. We no longer ask God just to bail us out of a problem or meet a particular need (though he will). We place our prayers in the context of Kingdom purposes: the overthrow of the enemy's brutal deception and oppression, the restoration of life and peace and wholeness in this world, the values of justice and righteousness and truth, the abundant life Jesus promised. Much more than an invitation to salvation, the gospel cries out for God's rule and reign "here and now" as well as "there and then." We don't know how to pray for such a momentous, world-shaping vision until we see it, and we can't see it until we turn from our narrow vision and embrace the King. When we do, the Kingdom advances powerfully in our lives and in this world.

The kingdom of God is where our best dreams
come from and our truest prayers.

FREDERICK BUECHNER

Your Vision of God

*Master, I knew you were a harsh man. . . . I was afraid I would lose
your money, so I hid it in the earth.*   MATTHEW 25:24-25

JESUS COMPARED THE KINGDOM OF GOD to a master who entrusted his money to three servants while he was away on a long trip. Two of the servants stewarded his money well, investing it and gaining a profitable return. The other servant was afraid of losing his money and buried it in the ground, avoiding both losses and gains. The master commended the first two stewards for their wisdom but rebuked the third harshly. Why? Because that servant, seeing his master as "a harsh man," lived in fear. His view of the master inhibited his ability to step out in faith.

Your vision of God matters. It shapes how you live, what you think, the emotions you feel, the freedom (or lack of it) you experience, the joy (or lack of it) that fills your heart, and much, much more. It also affects how you pray and the faith you bring into your prayers. If you see God as a begrudging, hard-hearted master, you will pray small, conservative, tentative prayers. If you see him as a bold investor or extravagant giver who is delighted with your creative stewardship, you will pray big prayers and expect great things.

Many Christians think they are praying to a harsh master, keeping their requests modest, pleading for crumbs from the master's table. They have forgotten the extravagance of their adoption into the royal family and pray like orphans still hoping to be welcomed in. But our Master is full of joy, able to laugh at his opposition, overflowing with favor for his beloved, passionate toward his people, zealous about his purposes, and willing to defy expectations. His words toward the rebellious and adversarial are harsh, but his words toward those who love him are always tender, inviting, and generous. So why do many who love him pray as though he might respond as an adversary? They have a false picture of his nature. They have forgotten how happy and loving he is. If you want to pray big, faith-filled prayers, adjust your vision of God. Expect great things from him, and he will commend you for your stewardship of his love.

Expect great things from God; attempt great things for God.

WILLIAM CAREY

The Generous Father

Everything I have is yours. LUKE 15:31

JESUS TOLD A MEMORABLE PARABLE about two sons. The younger son insisted on getting his inheritance early and ran off to spend it wastefully. The older son stayed home and worked faithfully, determined to stay in his father's good graces. When the wandering son finally realized his foolishness and came home, the father abandoned all dignity and ran out to meet him. He dressed his son in a fine robe, gave him a family ring, and threw a party. Meanwhile, the older son was offended at this display of attention on an irresponsible, immoral fool and refused to join the celebration. The father begged him to reconsider, offering the same generosity he had lavished on the returning son: "Everything I have is yours."

Most of us find ourselves identifying with either the younger or older brother. We have gone our own way and realized our error, or we've worked hard to please the Father without realizing the blessings before us. Neither son lost or gained his son-ship in this story; they both remained his sons all the way through. And just like these sons, we can't earn our Father's gifts or exhaust their supply. Our family relationship is not on the line. We simply need to recognize who our Father is and what he is like.

Christians who don't see the Father clearly think they either have to go their own way to be satisfied or become good enough to be rewarded. Neither fits the picture God paints of himself. His arms are open, the family inheritance is already ours to enjoy, he loves to dress us in love and acceptance and authority, and he enjoys a good celebration. All that he has is ours.

Pray with that vision of your Father. You don't need to sin to have a good time, and you don't need to work to receive his favor. The entire storehouse is there for the asking. He'll want you to ask responsibly and steward it well, but he is never stingy with his wealth. He lavishes love, joy, peace, gifts of grace, victories, and abundant life on his children. Pray for them in full confidence that he is eager to give.

In his love he clothes us, enfolds us, and embraces us;
that tender love completely surrounds us, never to leave us.

JULIAN OF NORWICH

Plant Your Prayers

If you had faith even as small as a mustard seed . . . **MATTHEW 17:20**

WE OFTEN LOOK AT PRAYERS OF FAITH as transactions. We make a request, and either the request is answered the way we hoped or it isn't. If it is, we rejoice; if it isn't, we walk away or try again later. We're content when a healthy percentage of our requests turn out in our favor.

But what if prayer isn't a transaction? What if it's a conversation in which the seeds of our desires and visions for life, many of which have been given by God, are discussed and considered and left to season for a while? What if prayer is more like planting seeds in the soil of God's Kingdom, where they are hidden for a time but have the full potential to grow, bloom, and bear fruit if someone waters them, fertilizes them, and cultivates the right conditions for them to grow? What if we've walked away from prayers God has already said yes to but in his timing—and never noticed that they were beginning to grow? What if we've neglected the process?

That's how prayers of faith are sometimes presented in Scripture—and how they tend to work out in our own lives. Jesus compared our faith to a seed. It may start out small, but over time it grows and eventually bears fruit—if we don't give up on it. In fact, the seeds of faith we sow in prayer today can shape the world for generations to come. Seeds, after all, grow into all sorts of big plants. They already have within them the DNA of what they will become. All it takes is the right environment for them to grow.

Think of your prayers as seeds, not transactions. Some may pop up overnight, but many will not bear fruit for a while. Some may only emerge from the soil of the Kingdom decades later. But they do emerge. They accomplish things that would not have happened otherwise: changing lives, advancing God's purposes through his people, and transforming the world around you. They are investments both in the now and the forever. Over time, you will see the splendor, taste the fruit, and smell the fragrances of the master Gardener's work.

> We must patiently, believingly continue in prayer until we obtain an answer.
>
> GEORGE MÜLLER

Big God, Small Mountains

You could say to this mountain, "Move from here to there,"
and it would move. **MATTHEW 17:20**

JESUS AND THREE OF HIS DISCIPLES had gone "up a high mountain" (Matthew 17:1), where he appeared in supernatural splendor along with two ancient heroes of faith. It was an amazing experience, but like many amazing experiences in life, it was followed immediately by a problem. At the foot of the mountain, a man had brought his demonically oppressed son to the other disciples for help. Though Jesus had sent his followers on a mission to cast out demons on a previous occasion (Matthew 10:8), they weren't having any success with this one. Their futility became a teaching moment, an occasion for Jesus to utter these astounding instructions about faith and words. Big mountains—and presumably the evil afflicting this boy—have to move in response to faith in God's goodness and power.

Jesus taught essentially the same lesson on a road near the Mount of Olives, where he had commanded a fig tree to wither (Matthew 21:21-22). Several mountains were visible there, but his reference to "this mountain" likely applied, contrary to the speculation of many commentators, to the nearby Herodium, a man-made eyesore that Herod the Great had created to be his palace fortress and to glorify himself. That means that both times Jesus taught this lesson on the power of faith, prayer, and words, it was in the context of evil intrusions against his people. He was arming his followers with the means to overcome whatever the enemy tries to impose on them.

The bottom line is that we should refuse to be impressed by the size of our obstacles, the tactics of the enemy, and the power of evil agendas. Jesus was not emphasizing the size of faith nearly as much as the size of God. He had just come down from a "high mountain," yet it was movable. He wanted us to see the absurdity of any perspective that makes mountains bigger than the Father. He wants us to see them as opportunities to showcase the Father's goodness, not as problems that get in the way. Far too many believers let their mountains overshadow the power and presence of God rather than seeing them as proof of what he can do. We are told to reverse that perspective by faith. When we do, mountains begin to move.

Faith expects from God what is beyond all expectation.

ANDREW MURRAY

Before All

Listen to my voice in the morning, LORD.   **PSALM 5:3**

GOD IS NOT PARTIAL TO OUR PRAYING at any particular time of the day. He is timeless, and even on this single planet, it's always morning somewhere. The idea of bringing our requests to him in the morning is not meant to be an order, a ritual, or a scheduling issue. Still, it does reflect our priorities, and for a God who asks for the firstfruits of our labors, the first of our time seems appropriate. When we set aside the first and last moments of our day to talk with him, all the time in between seems better ordered, and we are more solidly anchored in our relationship with him. Devoting our morning hours to him is a way of saying all the rest are his too.

Why is that important? Because if we don't live our lives with God as our reference point, we find ourselves wrestling with hard decisions more often, arranging our priorities with greater difficulty, and settling for circumstances that are not his will for us. And if we don't bring our requests to him early, we tend to live without expectancy. We don't go through our days with anticipation of how our morning prayers play out or how he might give answers and encouragements along the way. When we don't lay his promises out before him as gifts we've claimed, we miss opportunities to receive their fulfillment or be reminded that fulfillment is coming. If we don't set the tone for our day with him, the day may take on a very unwelcome tone. And we'll go along with it if our minds are not fixed on him.

Fix your mind, heart, prayers, and faith on God every moment of the day, but especially early in the morning. Give him the firstfruits of your time. See how your hope swells, your anticipation grows more focused, and his presence becomes more noticeable. It is far better to fit the demands of your schedule around your prayers than to try to fit your prayers around the demands of your schedule. The trajectory of your day—and of your life—will become far more satisfying.

> Let God have your first awaking thoughts. . . . Cast yourself upon him
> for the day which follows.
>
> RICHARD BAXTER

Be Patient

I bring my requests to you and wait expectantly. **PSALM 5:3**

IMAGINE PLANTING A SEED IN A GARDEN with the hopes that it will grow and be fruitful. You fertilize the soil, water the area the right amount, and expect nature to follow its course. But just to be sure, you check on the seed from time to time to make sure nature really is following its course. You brush back the soil, look for any signs of green, and celebrate when the seed begins to germinate. You then replace the soil to let the process continue. With this amount of attention, your seed is likely not to mature. After all, part of the growth process is letting things happen for a season when you can't see anything happening at all.

A prayer of faith is like that. You plant it, water it, cultivate it, and expect to see it sprout above the soil at some point. But you can't help it along. You can't examine its progress every day by digging it up and inspecting it. You can't say you trust the one who makes things grow while also trying to make him conform to your expectations. You either trust the process of faith or you don't. You trust the Gardener who breathes life into the faith of his people or you don't. Micromanaging the process kills it.

When you plant a seed of faith, do your part to cultivate it, but don't interfere with it. If you dissect it to make sure it's developing correctly, it won't. Your self-initiated involvement in the process is a hindrance to healthy growth. God may ask you to be part of the process, but he won't ask you to micromanage it. You'll have to decide: *Is this my process or his?* If it's yours, proceed at your own risk. If it's his, let it be his.

Faith is ultimately a partnership, so work as God instructs. Participate as he leads. But constantly judging whether things are happening or not—whether God is living up to his promises, and on your schedule—is not faith. It's an attempt to use God for your purposes. Learn the difference and be patient. Wait expectantly—and expect to wait.

> The Lord seems constantly to use waiting as a tool
> for bringing us the very best of his gifts.
>
> CATHERINE MARSHALL

Kingdom Prayers

[Jesus said,] "I will build my church, and all the powers
of hell will not conquer it." MATTHEW 16:18

A LOT OF GOOD THINGS are happening in the world. You wouldn't know that from news media—we're fed a constant stream of horrendous events and destructive criticism—but the Holy Spirit is moving in powerful ways. Our perception, though, is that things are getting worse and worse. And the more we let that perception settle in, the more we tend to pray defensively and fearfully. We find ourselves asking God to prevent bad things from happening more than we ask him to work powerfully to advance his Kingdom. We ask him to be a shield rather than a warrior.

There's nothing wrong with asking God to be a shield, but fear and dread are not gifts of the Spirit. They are never meant to be the energy behind our prayers. In his mercy, God certainly answers many of our fear-based prayers and provides protection and provision in response to our pleas. We can see this clearly in the Psalms; many of them begin in crisis and end with gratitude. But when our worries become the basis of our prayer life—when most of our conversations with God are filled with requests for him to prevent problems—we are emphasizing the wrong things. In many cases, we make ourselves victims and think only about how we want him to defend us from the next crisis.

Go on the offensive. One of our primary missions on this planet is to set captives free, pray God's power into enemy territory, and advance the Kingdom of God. We are to storm the prisons where powers of darkness hold their victims—to destroy the works of the evil one, just as our Master did (1 John 3:8). That begins on our knees, with expectation and faith. Prayer based on fear is necessary in a pinch. Prayer based on confidence in the mission of God should be the norm. When we are moved by his love, inspired by faith, and bold enough to ask for huge, powerful works from his hand, we begin to look past the headlines and notice what he is doing in the world. We see the Kingdom coming and the gates of hell bending to his plans.

God wants us to be victors, not victims; . . .
to overcome, not to be overwhelmed.

WILLIAM ARTHUR WARD

The Eyes of Faith

We live by believing and not by seeing.   2 CORINTHIANS 5:7

FROM THE MOMENT WE ARE BORN, we are trained to perceive reality through our physical senses. We see, hear, touch, smell, and taste the world around us, and we rely on what those senses tell us. As we age, we become aware that our senses can mislead us, that not everything is as it appears. But overall, we trust them. They are our best bet for understanding reality—at least in a material world.

From the moment we are born again, we are trained to perceive things differently. We have to learn biblical revelation to know something about God, and we have to read between the lines of our circumstances to recognize what God is doing in them. We are being called into a life of faith. This life will not demand that we ignore our physical senses; those perceptions are helpful and necessary for functioning in a physical world. But they do not lead us into eternal truth by themselves. For that, our spiritual senses need to be awakened, cultivated, and honed through time and experience to recognize the eternal environment we live in. We have to learn to base our plans, decisions, and prayers on the truth of an unseen world.

As we cultivate this faith life, it becomes beautifully, painfully clear that we are not making things up. God really does answer prayer; spiritual truths really do play out in our lives; unseen forces really do affect the world around us. Even so, we need reminders of this invisible reality at times. We have to pursue our calling to walk by faith and take initiative to see, think, feel, and walk differently than we did before.

When Paul talks about living by believing and not by seeing—walking by faith rather than sight—he means it comprehensively. This is an all-encompassing walk. To live as Kingdom citizens and experience the wonders of God, we have to think thoughts of faith, feel the assurance of faith, and talk the words of faith—not occasionally but constantly and consistently. We have to be weaned from dependence on the visible and pray behind the scenes. When we do, invisible realities enter into the visible realm and change things. Faith, rooted in ultimate truth, becomes sight.

God has made for us two kinds of eyes: those of flesh and those of faith.

JOHN CHRYSOSTOM

The Tyranny of the Tangible

*Faith shows the reality of what we hope for; it is the
evidence of things we cannot see.* **HEBREWS 11:1**

NOWHERE IN THE BIBLE are we given a comprehensive definition of faith.
God chose to reveal himself through a history of testimonies about who he is and
how he works rather than a systematic theology. But we are given some descriptions
of faith, and this remarkable verse in Hebrews is one of the clearest. Translations
vary, but the point is always that faith is reality, substance, evidence, a palpable
manifestation in the spirit of what has not yet been manifested to natural eyes. It
is an inward testimony of what is actually true, whether that truth has been made
visible in our lives yet or not. It is not wishful thinking or an up-in-the-air hope. It
is the art of knowing. It is a certainty.

That has profound implications for the way we think. When we lament the
way circumstances appear, we are not looking at a situation in faith. Our natural
tendency is to make observations and talk about how bad everything is. But while
we are focused on the visible, God is leading us on a journey of faith, rearranging
our perspectives on life and circumstances. He means to divorce us from our trust in
the visible and rivet our attention instead on the invisible—specifically, whatever he
has promised and declared to be true. He wants us to see into the spiritual realm, be
aware of his purposes and plans, and listen for his instructions. He wants us to rely
on his promises, even when all visible circumstances point in an opposite direction.

To do that, you'll need to learn to see and think differently. In any challenging
situation, ask yourself: Is my mood based on the visible or the deeper reality? Am I
placing more trust in my circumstances or in the God who is above them? Have I
learned the language of God's promises, or am I still immersed in the language of
the obvious? These are probing questions, likely to bring some discomfort, but they
are necessary. They train us, as Paul instructed, to walk by faith, not by sight. They
overthrow the tyranny of the tangible and drive us into the goodness of the Father.

> Faith tells us of things we have never seen and
> cannot come to know by our natural senses.
>
> JOHN OF THE CROSS

Faith *Is* the Evidence

*Faith shows the reality of what we hope for; it is the
evidence of things we cannot see.* **HEBREWS 11:1**

IF YOU'VE SPENT MUCH TIME PRAYING for God to do something—to provide for a need, heal an illness, overcome a problem, intervene in a relationship—you may have noticed a familiar dynamic. We tend to ask for his help and then watch very closely for evidence that he is responding. If we see some of the change we hoped for, we assume the answer was yes. If we don't, we eventually resign ourselves to his "no." We let our observations dictate our faith.

That's not how faith is meant to work. Sometimes God spends an extraordinarily long time working out his purposes. Abraham, Joseph, Moses, David, and the kingdoms of Israel and Judah experienced excruciating gaps between promise and fulfillment. And like them, in those gaps, our minds and hearts go on winding journeys of belief and doubt, certainty and confusion, questions and more questions. There's a purpose in that process, though we hardly recognize it at times. It strips us of our tendency to look for evidence that God is answering our prayers or working out his plans. We are being anchored instead in his faithfulness. We are learning to walk by faith.

Don't tamper with that process by constantly examining your surroundings for proof that God is at work. Enjoy the evidence when you see it, but understand that it is not a sign of what God will ultimately do every time. Faith doesn't look for verification. Faith *is* the verification. It's the substance of things hoped for, the reality of the eternal, the evidence of things we have not yet seen. If faith is evidence of the unseen, then straining to see undermines it. Faith is comfortable standing alone.

Faith is also patient. It does not waver with the ups and downs of situations. Our compulsion to look for evidence along the way will send our moods soaring or plummeting with every shift in circumstances. Mature faith waits confidently, regardless of what our natural eyes see. When the time is right, in God's perfect planning, we'll see what we've believed.

> Faith, mighty faith, the promise sees, and looks to that alone;
> laughs at all impossibilities and cries, "It shall be done!"
>
> CHARLES WESLEY

The Process of Faith

*Faith shows the reality of what we hope for; it is the
evidence of things we cannot see.* **HEBREWS 11:1**

ABRAHAM SPENT DECADES WAITING for the fulfillment of God's promise
of a son. In the meantime, he speculated about alternative heirs (Genesis 15:2-3);
wondered whether God meant for him to have a son through a servant rather than
his wife—and then acted on that thought (Genesis 16); and laughed at the possibility of the promise being literally fulfilled (Genesis 17:17). He never actually gave
up faith, and Paul generously wrote much later that Abraham never wavered in it
(Romans 4:20). All the while, Abraham was going through a process all people of
faith must go through: He was being weaned from the visible and forced to fix his
eyes on what is unseen. He was learning to see the spiritual reality behind the scenes.

Abraham may seem like an extraordinary example—he had an extraordinary calling, after all—but learning the dynamics of faith is a normal journey for citizens of
God's Kingdom. We are never told to invent another realm and fix our eyes on it; we
are given specific promises that force us into a choice. Will we look around to see if
a promise is real or look to the God who is faithful to believe it's real? Will we stake
our faith on visible circumstances or on what God has said? Do we have the courage
to exercise naked faith—the kind that has absolutely nothing to go on except a word
from God? Much of our journey between promise and fulfillment tests our answers
to those questions. It's one thing to say we have faith, but it's another to cling to our
faith when it is tested, stretched, pulled, pushed, and stripped of all external support.
The process can either purify our faith or kill it.

That's God's design, and we need to embrace it. Abraham was right to ask God
questions and consider whether he had actually heard him correctly. But once the
affirmation came, he had to decide: Would he believe God or believe his circumstances? He chose the former, and a nation of faith was born. As people of faith, we
follow in those footsteps. Based only on a promise, we choose to believe what we
cannot see until belief sees its reward.

Real trust in God is above circumstances and appearances.

GEORGE MÜLLER

Natural Prayer

Your Father knows exactly what you need even before you ask him!
MATTHEW 6:8

JESUS SAID GOD KNOWS EXACTLY WHAT WE NEED before we even ask. He also told us to ask. Because God is merciful and generous, he sometimes supplies our needs regardless of whether we ask, but he has not set up his Kingdom to work this way automatically. Giving us whatever we need without our asking would completely subvert the relationship. We would never realize how desperately we need to turn in his direction and seek his face. We'd think we could get by without a conversation. We would miss the purpose we were designed for—fellowship, friendship, and intimacy with God.

Not all of our conversations with God are based on asking and receiving, but for most of us, that's where they begin. We know we are fundamentally broken, so we ask for salvation. We have needs and desires for provision, protection, relationships, and more, so we ask him to take care of us. We have dreams and goals that are beyond our reach, so we ask him to help us obtain them. Somewhere along the way, we begin to worship and give thanks as we should. But our relationship usually begins with an awareness of our need. God seeks us there, we come to him on that basis, and the relationship grows.

Asking and receiving is the rule of the Kingdom, and it never becomes obsolete. In fact, it becomes a delight. We get to know our Father, he enjoys the give-and-take, we draw closer in the process, and love flourishes. We do not surprise him with our requests—he knows them beforehand—but he takes pleasure in fulfilling them according to his purposes. If we think we have to twist his arm to give us what we ask for, we have misunderstood past delays and gracious denials. But if we keep asking with the simplicity of a child making a request of his or her father, we enter into the joy of his kindness and love. We grow into his likeness and extend the same love to those around us. And we pray as naturally as he intended.

A habit of prayer is one of the surest marks of a true Christian.

J. C. RYLE

Kingdom Come

Your kingdom come, your will be done, on earth as it is in heaven.
MATTHEW 6:10, ESV

WHEN JESUS TAUGHT HIS DISCIPLES TO PRAY, he covered several broad topics—our relationship to the Father, our need for daily sustenance, the centrality of receiving and giving mercy in our lives, and the importance of resisting evil. But the petition that frames all others in this model prayer is a request for God's Kingdom to come and his will to be done on earth as it is in heaven. In everything we pray, this is the context. We orient our lives toward God's Kingdom advancing in this world.

Traditionally, the Lord's Prayer has been recited with a between-the-lines assumption that Jesus certainly must mean a future Kingdom, perhaps in his millennial reign or the heavenly realm. But Jesus clearly specifies his Kingdom come "on earth," and there is nothing in his words that implies that it must wait until generations after the disciples are gone. No, he wants all generations to be praying for the advance of his Kingdom on earth right now, in real and tangible ways. After all, the Kingdom came with the King (Matthew 4:17), and the King has not left us (Matthew 28:20; John 14:16-18). He saves, heals, delivers, and offers abundant life. He fully intends to fill the earth with his people (Matthew 24:14) and his glory (Habakkuk 2:14). He came to destroy the works of the enemy (1 John 3:8). He is on a mission, through us, to transform the world.

It's true that the Kingdom doesn't come in all its fullness until the King returns. But it is coming in the meantime because the King inhabits his people. And one of the primary ways it comes is through our prayers, just as Jesus instructed. Never hold back when praying Kingdom values into this world. Pray for abundant life, justice and mercy, restoration of lives, and the environment of heaven in the societies of earth. Expand your prayers from your visible field of influence to your community, city, nation, and world. Ask God to intervene anywhere and everywhere. Let your will and his will be one.

> The only significance of life consists in helping
> to establish the kingdom of God.
>
> LEO TOLSTOY

Call to Battle

Your will be done.   MATTHEW 6:10

MOST PEOPLE READ THIS VERSE with an implied addition to the end: "as opposed to mine." It's true that even when we strongly believe God has planted his desires within us, given specific promises about them, and told us to pray them in faith, we should still submit to his higher purposes and assume his right to redirect us. Everything we pray comes under the umbrella of his will above all other wills. But the juxtaposition of wills is not only between God's best for us and our independent impulses. It's between God's purposes and every other rival. We are praying for his will to be done over and above all else.

That means we think more comprehensively when we pray this prayer. "Your will be done (as opposed to the world's, the enemy's, the agendas of powers and rulers, the systems and processes that function against your ways, the decisions of fickle people)," and on and on we can go. We are not merely praying for God to have his own way in our lives. We are praying for his agenda to be accomplished in this world, for his purposes to be exalted above all human designs and maneuverings, for his heavenly hosts and earthly children to advance his Kingdom and purposes here and now and forever. We are honoring his ultimate desires and plans.

That turns this prayer from a submissive retreat to a rousing battle cry. It claims territory for his Kingdom in our families, churches, communities, workplaces, industries, governments, public discourses, school systems, social structures, cities, nations, regions, and our own lives. All of these areas become arenas in which this prayer can be prayed, believed, and applied. When we pray for God's will to be done, we are praying for all other wills to align with it or fall away forever. When we pray for his Kingdom to come, we are praying for rival kingdoms to go. And we pray in complete confidence that he hears and answers.

Satan dreads nothing but prayer.

SAMUEL CHADWICK

Today

Give us today the food we need. **MATTHEW 6:11**

A YOUNG MAN SPENT YEARS praying for his future—his life's work, his poten-tial mate, the children he didn't yet have, the places where God wanted him to live, and so on—with his eyes always set on the distant horizon. In fact, this young man did more than pray. He worried. He focused so obsessively on the future that he missed many of the opportunities God had given him in the present. God graciously met most of his immediate needs anyway, but this man missed out on the pleasure of asking and receiving daily requests. One day he looked back and realized he had never actually enjoyed the moment. He was always living in a time that hadn't come yet, and therefore never really living.

That story describes no one in particular but many people in general. Most of us can relate to it to some degree. We look back at the past in regret, we look to the future with anxiety, and we miss out on what God is doing in the here and now. If we noticed, we would be grateful for how he is providing and blessing our daily existence with his kindness. But we become so preoccupied with future needs that we can't enjoy today's provisions. We miss the God of today.

God gave his people training in the daily bread principle early on by feeding them manna in the wilderness and forbidding them from gathering extra to be eaten as leftovers the next day. In the prayer he taught his disciples, he reminded them of that truth—that tomorrow has enough worries of its own and our real focus is today—right now—with the needs and opportunities around us. We look at tomor-row's problems and wonder if we will have faith for them, while God looks at today and says we have all the faith we need. When the time comes for tomorrow's faith, we'll have it. But for now, we are to trust him for the needs of the day.

Feel free to plan for tomorrow, but focus on today. Live with today's faith for today's needs. God is focused on your now because that's where you are. And that's your only opportunity to experience him today.

> He that fears not the future may enjoy the present.
>
> **THOMAS FULLER**

A Culture of Grace

And forgive us our sins, as we have forgiven those who sin against us.
MATTHEW 6:12

WE PRAY WITH A SPIRIT OF GRACE. After all, grace is the foundation of our relationship with God, the environment of his Kingdom, and the basis of the gospel of redemption. All of our prayers are uttered within a relationship of love and grace, acceptance and mercy, kindness and joy. So when we ask God to forgive our sins, we are in keeping with the Kingdom we live in.

Unfortunately, we often step out of the Kingdom environment by applying judgment, criticism, grudges, and biases toward people around us. We seem comfortable with the incongruity, but if we stop to think about it, we find that we are living, thinking, and praying from divided hearts. We are applying the culture of grace to ourselves and our relationship with God but a culture of unforgiveness to others. That's not only harmful and stressful on the human soul; it blinds us to the needs God wants us to pray for and makes the prayers we do offer him exercises in hypocrisy. It puts God in the position of responding in grace to those who don't even recognize the value of it. That's a problem.

If we pray with a spirit of grace but then harden our hearts to deal with others, we are conflicted and confused. We are trying to merge two incompatible kingdoms in our own hearts, and our prayers of faith cease to flow freely. We wonder why God isn't responding, while he waits for us to demonstrate to others the same kindness that we want to receive from him. We end up with a very cluttered and obstructed prayer life.

When you pray, continue to ask for forgiveness, but take the mercy you receive and apply it to everyone around you. Your faith is based on God's grace, and you'll need to let grace flow so your faith can grow. The forgiveness God gives you and the forgiveness you extend to others—from your heart—are part of the same package, and both make your prayers pleasing to him. Choose a culture of grace in all things and make room for God's blessings to come in.

> He that cannot forgive others breaks the bridge
> over which he must pass himself.
>
> THOMAS FULLER

Living Guilt-Free

Do not lead us into temptation, but deliver us from the evil one.
MATTHEW 6:13, NKJV

MEDIEVAL MONKS WHO REALLY WANTED to test their spiritual strength would surround themselves with a feast and refuse to eat, or sleep in the presence of an undressed woman and resist the urge to touch her. Not many went to such extremes, but some felt the need to confirm that they could resist obvious temptations. They preferred to have opportunities to sin and deny them rather than to avoid temptation and think they had accomplished something.

We might find such mental gymnastics amusing, but many Christians spend an awful lot of energy trying to resist temptations rather than avoiding them in the first place. And when we fall prey to them, we blame our human weakness rather than our willingness to put ourselves in tempting positions to begin with. We forget that Jesus told us to pray not only to resist temptation but to be delivered from both temptation and the evil one altogether. We are instructed to pray for avoidance.

What does that have to do with prayer? For one thing, we can pray to be delivered from evil in complete faith that God is willing to answer and help us avoid tempting situations. And if we do face them at times, we can trust him for strength and wisdom before, during, and after. He gives us a way out, around, or through.

But this prayer is vital for faith in other areas as well. Our faith is undermined far more often by the guilt and shame that follows sin than by the sin itself. Though God never tells us we are unworthy to pray in the aftermath of failure (or any time), we assume that we are. We hold back. We pray without any conviction that God might answer because we've beaten ourselves so thoroughly with a guilty conscience. This request and the one before it—being led away from temptation and forgiven when we've fallen for it—are powerful supports for a life of faith-filled prayers. Pray them often and always trust the protecting, cleansing work of God.

> The purpose of being guilty is to bring us to Jesus. . . . If we continue to make ourselves guilty—to blame ourselves—then that is sin in itself.
>
> CORRIE TEN BOOM

Moved by Prayer

The king's heart is like a stream of water directed by the Lord;
he guides it wherever he pleases. **PROVERBS 21:1**

IN HUDSON TAYLOR'S YEARS OF PREPARATION for mission work in China, he made it a point to trust God for provision rather than asking people for it. On one occasion, he found himself without enough funds to pay his landlady, yet he wanted to prove to himself that human beings could be moved by God through prayer. Even though he could have asked the doctor to whom he was apprenticed to pay his salary, Taylor knew he would not have such access to funding sources once he was in China, considering the long travel times for correspondence in his era. So he prayed. And waited. And felt terribly embarrassed, knowing that his rent was due Saturday night and he had nothing to pay it with. He resisted the temptation to ask his employer and retreated to his room to plead with God.

On Saturday afternoon after the doctor had finished his rounds and sat down to relax, he casually asked if Taylor's salary was due again. It was, Taylor replied. The doctor apologized and wished Taylor had reminded him earlier. He had sent the week's earnings to the bank already. Late that night, the doctor returned to the office laughing. A wealthy patient had decided to pay his bill at that unusual hour rather than the following Monday. Apparently, the patient felt uneasy about it and ventured out at night to deliver it. The doctor handed the money over to Taylor—just what he needed to cover his rent.

Hudson Taylor's faith swelled at this confirmation that once on the mission field he would be able to trust God to "move the hearts of men" in response to his prayers. He never wrestled again with God's willingness to provide in a time of need. He certainly experienced times of need, but he also experienced miraculous answers to urgent prayers. He learned a powerful lesson that any of God's children can take to the bank: Our Father is aware of our needs, hears our pleas, and responds to faith that is willing to be tried, tested, stretched, pulled, pushed, and confirmed. Even when the decisions of others are involved, he honors those who trust in him.

It is possible to move men, through God, by prayer alone.

HUDSON TAYLOR

Fully Convinced

He was fully convinced that God is able to do whatever he promises.

ROMANS 4:21

AS HUDSON TAYLOR WAS COMPLETING his medical training in preparation for his mission work in China, he was doing an autopsy on a man who had died of malignant fever. Taylor had forgotten that he'd pricked his finger the night before, and even though he was very careful not to cut himself during the surgery, he began to feel sick, weak, and faint. His symptoms worsened throughout the morning, and eventually a surgeon told him that his finger prick from the night before must have allowed the infection to enter his system. The surgeon told him to get home as soon as possible and arrange his affairs because, he said, "You're a dead man."

Taylor was sure God had called him to China and told the surgeon so. Even so, he barely managed to make it home and soon after fainted from pain. Over the next few weeks, he gained strength. A doctor told him that his austere diet had conditioned him to withstand this attack on his body, and his uncle helped him eat and drink heartier food during his recovery. Taylor was weak for some time but healthier than anyone expected him to be after his infection. And he eventually sailed to China just as God had called him.

Nothing in Scripture assured Taylor he would make it to China, but his sense of calling and many confirmations through prayer were enough to convince him. His is an example of staking one's life on a word from God, even when that word looks impossible. Experts and friends gave him little chance of fulfilling his goals as a missionary, yet God's voice was the only one that mattered to him. He knew God could do whatever he promised.

When God gives you that kind of conviction, refuse to let it go. You are under no obligation to heed the voices of human beings, who even in their areas of expertise are still quite fallible. Their voices may speak louder, but God's is resolute. Learn to trust his leading, ask him for confirmation if needed, and then cling to his promises with tenacity. Whatever he has promised you, he is fully able and willing to do it.

Contrary to reason, faith regards the invisible things as already materialized.

MARTIN LUTHER

Don't Give Up

Never stop praying.   1 THESSALONIANS 5:17

IN AN AGE OF MICROWAVES, drive-thru windows, and web pages that frustrate us when they don't load within seconds, we are hardly conditioned for persistent prayer. Our expectations are increasing; our attention spans are decreasing. Scripture and past experiences remind us to endure, but we seem to have redefined endurance to mean a matter of days rather than a matter of years. We want our prayer requests to look like our online transactions—short, simple, direct, and true to the buttons we've pushed. We bring a customer-service mindset into our relationship with God.

Our minds know how flawed this attitude is, but our reflexes still insist on it. And since God is not going to conform to our culture of immediate gratification, we must retrain ourselves to thrive in a culture of planting now and harvesting later. In other words, we need to avoid distractions and remain focused in our prayers. We have to remind ourselves that prayer and belief take time and that we inherit the promises of God through faith and patience (Hebrews 6:11-12). We need to recondition ourselves with tenacity.

Perhaps Paul's words to the Thessalonians are instructing us to fill our days with prayer, to take advantage of the gaps in our schedules to lift up the needs of those around us, to breathe in and out our prayers while our minds and bodies are occupied with daily activities. That's never a bad idea. But he is just as clearly encouraging us not to give up—to maintain prayer and faith until answers come, to endure the long journey of waiting, cultivating, and refining until our prayers are ready for harvest. To do that, we will need to refuse distractions and diversions. Natural thinking causes us to pray for a few days and assume God has said no when no answer comes. Kingdom thinking understands that the silence is a call to come closer, press in, keep asking, and hang on. Until we hear a clear "no" or "not now," we are not to give up.

Spiritual fatigue is an enemy of faith. It lowers our expectations, droops our shoulders, and compels us to resign to the inevitable. But what seems inevitable to us is never inevitable to God. Never stop praying. Keep believing. And press ahead until you hear from him.

The great point is never to give up until the answer comes.

GEORGE MÜLLER

Qualified to Receive

He washed away our sins, giving us a new birth and
new life through the Holy Spirit. **TITUS 3:5**

DEEP DOWN, WE KNOW WE ARE UNWORTHY of receiving answers to our prayers. We've fallen short of God's glory, and our desires and agendas haven't always aligned with his will. We know that he doesn't owe us a single thing; on the contrary, we are indebted to him. Why would he answer any petition at all?

Of course, none of this guilt is the point, no matter how genuine it is. God knowingly made promises to imperfect people, aware in advance that the redeemed would still fall short of his glory. We are in a lifelong process of being conformed to his image, and we don't perfectly reflect him yet. Still, he fully intends to fulfill what he has said, based not on our faithfulness but on his (2 Timothy 2:13).

Even more, God has qualified us by giving us his Son's righteousness. Jesus qualifies for God's inheritance, and in him, we are coheirs of God's promises. We've been cleansed of our sins and given a right standing and a new identity before God. Through Jesus' sacrifice, we've been adopted into the royal family, and God has no intention of disowning us or cutting us out of the will. Our own sense of unworthiness is irrelevant. Our sins have not disqualified us, even if they flared up again just yesterday. God has made us worthy with the gifts and identity he has given us. The faithful Father gives to the faithful Son, and we benefit by being related.

The idea that our sins and mistakes have disqualified us from receiving God's answers is a lie. We can't ask in faith and then depend on merit. Just as we are saved by grace through faith, we live and ask by grace through faith. It's true that persistent rebellion can take us off course, distort our desires, and position us outside of God's will, but that's a matter of proximity, not qualification. Like the Prodigal Son, we are welcomed back, and we are even given the family inheritance. Ask from that identity and believe your answers will come.

Faith is extending an empty hand to God to receive his gift of grace.

A. W. PINK

Pray for Faith

God has allotted to each a measure of faith. **ROMANS 12:3**, NASB

THE BIBLE EMPHASIZES THE IMPORTANCE of faith time and again. God repeatedly told his servants to have faith and commended them when they stepped out boldly and trusted what he said. Jesus taught his followers often about faith, chastising them when they didn't believe and urging them to believe more strongly. Salvation, answers to prayer, and Kingdom victories come through faith. It is a running theme—the dominant running theme, in terms of what God expects from us—throughout the pages of his Word.

Knowing that, shouldn't we do everything we can to muster up more faith? If our prayers depend on it, then we want to strengthen it. But as much as we are encouraged simply to have faith, and as much as we long to be filled with it, we can't just wish it into being. It has to grow. And before it grows, it has to be given. Faith is a gift from God (Ephesians 2:8), a seed he plants within us, the substance of his Kingdom on earth. It's the fundamental necessity of Kingdom life, and it has to originate with the King.

That's why our first and biggest prayer each day should always be for stronger, deeper, greater faith. God has already given us the gift of faith, but this is no immutable, stagnant gift. It grows. Just as physical resistance exercises our muscles, the resistance of life exercises our faith. Our experiences and victories enlarge it. Over time, we take for granted things that were once a huge stretch for us. We become strong by believing more each day. And our prayers depend on that increase.

Many Christians spend long hours praying out of their fears and discouragements. Those prayers become significantly more powerful when filled with expectation and faith. If faith is the currency of God's Kingdom, there's hardly any point in praying without it. A vibrant, effective prayer life is saturated with faith, which comes not from our own psyche but from the God who grants it freely. Ask for that first in order to ask for everything else on your heart. The best way to increase the strength of your prayers is to ask for increasing confidence behind them.

> Ask God to work faith in you, or you will remain forever
> without faith, no matter what you wish, say, or can do.
>
> MARTIN LUTHER

What the World Needs Now

*The earnest prayer of a righteous person has great power
and produces wonderful results.* JAMES 5:16

MANY PEOPLE, INCLUDING CHRISTIANS, read the headlines or look at the troubled lives around them and lament how bad things seem to be. Our hearts break and sympathies swell for people going through hardships and pain. We wish we could help, but our resources and words often fall short. We tell them our prayers are with them—and hope that means something in the end.

It does, if we pray in faith and persistence. If we really want God's Kingdom to show up in people's lives—spiritually, mentally, emotionally, relationally, physically, and in every other way that God demonstrates his goodness—we need to spend time interceding for them. This goes beyond offering God a brief mention of their needs, though he hears and often responds to those prayers too. It requires an investment, a bit of diligence, and emotional engagement. Scripture rarely highlights casual prayers; it emphasizes heartfelt, insistent pleas. God is responsive to the love and compassion that energizes us. If we are going to change our families, churches, workplaces, communities, cities, and nations, we will have to pray. And we will need to put our hearts into it.

The world needs heartfelt prayer. Our lives are full of people who need us not only to pray, but to pray in power. We have access to the keys of God's Kingdom, and we are negligent if we don't use them. Our prayers for others are as important as the other items on our to-do lists, yet they often fall to the bottom or are forgotten altogether. We need to prioritize them—to find a few more minutes in our day, to fill our downtime with petitions to the Father, to breathe out our requests more intentionally. The seeds we plant in those moments take root and grow over time, whether we notice them growing or not. Like a financial investment that compounds throughout the years, our prayers are used by God to advance his Kingdom in human hearts and relationships. Sow them now, and anticipate the fruitfulness to come. Our earnest prayers are powerful and effective—and one of the best ways to respond to the needs around us.

The greatest thing anyone can do for God and for man is to pray.

S. D. GORDON

The Heart of God's Will

I have not stopped thanking God for you. I pray for you constantly.
EPHESIANS 1:16

ONE OF THE BEST WAYS to invest your life and relationship with God in the lives of others is to pray for them with faith and power. For anyone who has ever longed to bear fruit for God's Kingdom but not known how, that's good news. You don't need to have a degree or be in a vocational ministry; you don't even need to ask anyone's permission. The only requirement is a heart that loves, believes, and asks. You can change the world—or more accurately, God can change the world through you—right where you are.

There are some things you can do, however, to position yourself for that kind of influence. First, you may need to change your mindset on prayer—to recognize that it's more than a wish, more than a blind effort to hit the target of God's will, and more than a day or two of trying. It's an ongoing spiritual, emotional, mental investment in the lives of those you pray for, rooted in gratitude and accompanied with confident hope and expectation. Second, you'll need to have some specific requests. Sometimes those specifics will be obvious, but other times they won't. And even though God does not expect you to pray with omniscience about people's hearts and needs, he does expect your requests to fit the broad parameters of his purposes.

For that, you can't go wrong with the apostolic prayers in New Testament letters. They capture the heart of God for his people brilliantly. If you ever wonder how to pray for the people in your life, begin there. Paul's prayers in Ephesians 1:17-20 and 3:16-19, for example, call upon God to fill them with wisdom, revelation, the light of his truth, and the fullness of his presence, and to root them in the unfathomable love of Christ and the power of his resurrection. You can hardly pray anything greater than this, and you'll never need to tack an "if it's your will, Lord," to the end of it. These are life-changing requests, and they eventually bring lasting fruit. Pray them earnestly and see what God does.

> The Word of God represents all the possibilities of God
> at the disposal of true prayer.
>
> A. T. PIERSON

The Priority of Spiritual Vision

. . . asking God, the glorious Father of our LORD Jesus Christ,
to give you spiritual wisdom and insight. **EPHESIANS 1:17**

WHEN PAUL BEGAN TO DESCRIBE HIS PRAYERS for the Ephesian church, the first words from his hand were a request that they receive divine wisdom and insight—the necessary foundation for flourishing lives. God certainly welcomes requests for provision, protection, and assistance in certain situations, but the real substance of our lives comes through knowing him. This is our priority; everything else is secondary. If we encounter his goodness—if we look into the depths of his wisdom, power, and love—we are anchored in the realest reality there is. Everything else flows from this source.

Paul is praying for his readers not only to know God but to have their hearts and minds aligned with him. If God answers this prayer—and why wouldn't he fulfill something so centered in his will?—he is raising up a people who see into his heart and understand his purposes. In other words, this insightful prayer from Paul will multiply insightful prayers among other believers. It puts first things first by requesting that God's will be done and his Kingdom come on earth in the hearts and minds of human beings as it is in heaven. Those who have spiritual wisdom and insight—who have Kingdom-saturated vision—rarely need to guess God's purposes when they speak, minister, and pray. They sense what God is doing and align with it.

How might God respond if you prayed this request for yourself and the people around you day after day, month after month, year after year? What fruit would one day be harvested from these seeds? The prayer for wisdom and revelation may not feel very exciting—for some, it's like asking for what you need rather than what you want for Christmas—but it sets the stage for all other blessings. People with spiritual insight have the maturity to handle whatever other gifts God wants to give. They understand Kingdom priorities. They can be trusted with his extravagance. And they use their vision to pray confidently and expectantly into the lives of others.

> You can't get second things by putting them first. You can get
> second things only by putting first things first.
>
> C. S. LEWIS

The Certainty of His Promises

*I pray that your hearts will be flooded with light so that you can
understand the confident hope he has given to those he called—his holy
people who are his rich and glorious inheritance.* **EPHESIANS 1:18**

IMAGINE HAVING TO GUESS GOD'S DESIRES—not knowing his nature, never recognizing his purposes, perpetually wondering if your words line up with his. It would be like trying to honor a contract you've never read, straining to understand a speech spoken in another language, or accepting a gift that can't be unwrapped. You might piece things together occasionally, but not consistently or with any confidence.

We can be grateful that God has not put us in that position. In fact, he is quite clear about the gifts, blessings, and provisions he intends to give us. His promises reach every area of our lives, and he has invited us to take him at his word. He wants us to understand our inheritance in him.

Paul's prayer for the Ephesians to understand their confident hope, calling, and inheritance is a good reminder for all believers. These words can mean that as God's people we are his rich and glorious inheritance or that God has given a rich and glorious inheritance to us. In either case, God's promises are fulfilled by Jesus (2 Corinthians 1:20) and accessible to us through him. Jesus inherits all things (Hebrews 1:2), and we are coheirs with him (Romans 8:16-17). God's promises are ours to receive by faith.

Let those promises serve as the "legal" basis for your prayers. They are fundamental to our conversations with God, and asking for what he has already spoken is powerful. His promises stir up our faith and open our hearts to receive from him on a basis greater than our own leanings. They legitimize our requests and draw us into a deeper understanding of his covenant. They ring true in our hearts, confirm our faith, and help us endure until we see the answers. They are evidence of his unbreakable faithfulness in our lives.

> The purposes of God are his concealed promises;
> the promises, his revealed purposes.
>
> PHILIP HENRY

The Greatness of His Power

I also pray that you will understand the incredible greatness
of God's power for us who believe him. **EPHESIANS 1:19**

MOST CHRISTIANS HAVE at some point been intimidated by a huge problem or overwhelming situation. Many of us have even developed a remarkable ability to turn hints of potential problems into near certainties through our worries and anxieties. The possible threats grow powerful, and our faith becomes weak.

Jesus told his followers that their faith could move mountains—even a small amount of faith would be enough to move a big God to action. So when Paul prayed for the Ephesian church, he asked God to give them a clear view of his nature and their inheritance in him—his goodness and his promises—and he wanted them to understand the enormity of God's power for those who believe. He knew that praying fervently without faith is like shopping with huge needs but no money. But those who recognize God's power in addition to his goodness and promises are relentless in their prayers. Rather than seeing huge mountains and a distant God, they see a huge God and small hills. They look at their problems not as hindrances or obstacles but as platforms for God to showcase his nature and opportunities to demonstrate his work in this world. They become believers in the truest sense of the word.

People who aren't convinced that God is present, willing, and powerful pray faint prayers that are barely a step up from wishful thinking. People who have encountered the incredible greatness of God's power don't need to manufacture faith; they simply believe. Their understanding of his power leads to experience; experience leads to greater faith; greater faith leads to greater understanding and experience. God's power manifests in the lives and prayers of those who recognize how unfathomably able he actually is.

That's why this understanding of vision, promise, and power is so essential in the lives of God's people. We have to know he is good, embrace what he promises, and let ourselves be overwhelmed by his power. His Kingdom overcomes every evil agenda and every unholy fear. And the confident prayers of his people invite his Kingdom into every area of life.

The greater and more persistent your confidence in God,
the more abundantly you will receive all that you ask.

ALBERT THE GREAT

43

The Power Within

*. . . that according to the riches of his glory he may grant you to
be strengthened with power through his Spirit in your inner being,
so that Christ may dwell in your hearts through faith.*

EPHESIANS 3:16-17, ESV

WE SPEND A LOT OF TIME praying for strength. We ask God for the strength to face mountains, to pray without giving up, to exercise our spiritual gifts, and to relate to people with grace and love. We even ask him for the strength to believe.

We do need strength for all of these things, and God generously provides it. But Paul's prayer takes a deeper approach and focuses on one astonishing truth that will affect every other situation in our lives. We need strength to believe that Jesus—the real Jesus who walked the earth two millennia ago, the one through whom and for whom all things were created—is dwelling inside us. The miracle-working, truth-telling, resurrected Jesus resides in our spirit when we believe in him. Many of us live most of our days aware of that concept but not fully sensing the reality of it. Paul prays that this would become more than theory in our hearts—that we would experience Jesus ministering through us and that we would step into the presence and power he gives.

That can happen only with divine help. According to these verses, we need to be strengthened by the power of the Spirit to be able to experience the living Jesus. His presence within us is more than our natural selves can handle. We need his enabling before asking him for strength for anything else.

Think of the implications. If we believed not only that the hope and promise of Jesus live within us but that the actual presence and power of Jesus are at work within us, we would begin to grow stronger in faith and step out with more confidence. If we practiced his presence as a minute-by-minute awareness, all our thoughts and attitudes would be transformed. That's why praying this prayer for yourself and others is life changing. Believe God will answer. It's his ultimate will for every human life.

You have nothing to do in life except to live in union with Christ.

RUFUS MOSELEY

Knowing the Unknowable

. . . and to know the love of Christ that surpasses knowledge,
that you may be filled with all the fullness of God. EPHESIANS 3:19, ESV

MANY BOOKS HAVE BEEN WRITTEN about knowing God. We talk about growing in our relationship with him and knowing him better. We study his Word to see what he has done in the past and to better understand his nature, character, and ways. We want to know about him intellectually and by experience.

That's an admirable goal, and we can learn a lot about who God is by digging deep into his Word, experiencing him through life and prayer, and having a genuine relationship with him. But our normal efforts are not nearly enough, primarily because he is too big to be fully known. There is too much depth, too much variety, too much mystery. We can grow in knowledge of him, but our minds can only do so much.

That's why Paul prays that we would know the love of Christ that surpasses knowledge. This may seem contradictory; how can we know what is beyond knowledge? But this must be a divine awareness awakened within us by God himself. If the love of Christ surpasses natural knowledge, there is no way to comprehend it naturally—especially in the infinite dimensions that Paul uses to describe his love in the previous verse. We need supernatural strength to be able to grasp the breadth, length, height, and depth of his love.

When, with God's revelation and power, we begin to grasp what is beyond our capacity to comprehend, something changes inside us. We see differently and are transformed into his image (2 Corinthians 3:18). And as we are changed, we are filled with his nature. In fact, according to Paul's prayer, we are filled with the fullness of God—the infinite embodied in the finite, just as the Word became flesh so many years ago. This is a staggering thought, and one we would dare not believe if it were not revealed in the inspired Word. It's also part of a life-changing prayer God is certain to answer as we grow in believing him.

> The love of God is broader than the measures of man's mind;
> and the heart of the Eternal is most wonderfully kind.
>
> FREDERICK WILLIAM FABER

Prayers for More

*Now to him who is able to do far more abundantly than all that
we ask or think, according to the power at work within us . . .*
EPHESIANS 3:20, ESV

PERHAPS IT SEEMS ARROGANT to want to be filled with God's fullness—to move in divine wisdom, perfect love, and explosive power. From a certain perspective, this kind of praying might come across as a desire to impress, to have status, to be a superhero of faith. It just seems so . . . unrealistic.

Yet this is our calling, and it's expressed beautifully in the apostolic prayers of the New Testament. If we are to make any lasting difference in this world, what better way than to become a vessel of God's wisdom, power, and love? What greater position could we possibly be in than to pray in the name of a perfect Savior for the perfect gifts his Father has promised? And to pray not only for ourselves but for those around us—to see the work he has done *for* us and ask him to multiply it *in* us and *through* us—is at the heart of our mission. It's objective number one in the mission to advance his Kingdom on earth.

The prayers of the last few days have put us on a path toward overflowing with God's wisdom, being filled with his measureless love, and walking in his extraordinary power. As those attributes grow in our lives, we have everything we need to pray incisively according to God's purposes, be motivated by his heart, and see him respond to the faith within us. This divine life may seem distant at times, but God is able to do well beyond what we can ask or imagine—and we can imagine quite a lot. How does he do this? Through the power that works within us—the power of the Resurrection, the divine energy source, the radiance of glory implanted in everyone who believes. This is the atmosphere God has called us to walk in, and it's available by faith through his promises. It's also the center of his will for our families, churches, workplaces, schools, communities, cities, nations, and other arenas of his Kingdom. Pray in this power, this will, this abundance. You and your world will be blessed by the fullness of God.

> Your Christian life is to be a continuous proof that God works impossibilities.
>
> ANDREW MURRAY

God of Impossibilities

I am the LORD, the God of all the peoples of the world.
Is anything too hard for me? JEREMIAH 32:27

SOMETIMES WE THINK OUR PRAYERS are a stretch—that they assume too much or reach too far. We know God is good, but we also know good fathers don't spoil their children. And we're certain we need the Father's moderating hand in our lives. We don't want our requests to be too bold or unrealistic.

It's true that God wants us to be able to handle the weight of his gifts, and sometimes he measures them accordingly. But if you've ever heard that God will give you what you need but not what you want, don't believe it. He may not give you *everything* you ask for, but he is the Giver of good gifts. And some of those good gifts are extravagant. They stretch boundaries. They are not limited by human expectations or by our own sense of what we don't deserve. They aren't confined to some realm of the semi-miraculous-but-not-too-impossible. Sometimes they are exactly what we think couldn't be done.

God makes ways where there seems to have been no way. He makes pathways through the wilderness and creates rivers in wastelands (Isaiah 43:19). He can grow a garden on a garbage dump, turn ashes into beauty, and bring life out of a sealed tomb. He calls things that are not as though they are. The question is never whether God can do the impossible; it's which impossibilities does he want to do?

We can be grateful that some of those impossibilities are spelled out for us in Scripture. Being filled with God's wisdom, power, and love to the point that we overflow with his fullness is one of them. Being resurrected from death is another. Healing, deliverance, and restoration are common in the Bible. So are unexpected twists, reversals, and breakthroughs. Don't limit your prayers to spiritual normalcies— or normalcies of any kind, for that matter. Expect the new way, the river in the desert, and the impossible possibilities. Pray with unlimited vision.

Faith sees the invisible, believes the unbelievable,
and receives the impossible.

CORRIE TEN BOOM

God of Promise

Not a single one of all the good promises the LORD
had given to the family of Israel was left unfulfilled;
everything he had spoken came true. JOSHUA 21:45

EARLY IN SCRIPTURE, God established himself as a faithful keeper of promises. He followed through on his warning about eating from the wrong tree. He kept his promise to a faithful family in the midst of an earthshaking flood. He honored his covenant with once-childless Abraham and filled the world with his descendants. And he delivered his people from captivity, just as he said he would. There's a reason they were able to enter the Promised Land. It had been promised.

It wasn't always easy, and the fulfillment didn't always look as expected. Abraham waited long years for his miracle and then was painfully tested in it years later. The captives in Egypt spent four centuries there and in at least the last few decades, if not longer, were brutally enslaved. They didn't anticipate an army in hot pursuit after their deliverance or a long journey through the wilderness, either, and they complained about both. They were intimidated by the opposition in the land of inheritance and had to fight intense battles in order to finally receive it. But throughout all the journeys, trials, and battles, God never failed to keep his word. He did what he said he was going to do. He held up his end of the deal.

We'll find the same dynamic at work in our lives too. We pray in faith to receive what he has promised, and sometimes we're surprised when the answer doesn't come magically and instantly. We may complain about the battles and trials we have to go through, and there will be times when the promise takes so long to be fulfilled that our faith nearly breaks. Still, God is faithful. His promises may include conditions, but he will keep his end of the deal when we meet those conditions—and sometimes even when we don't. He makes promises because he wants to fulfill them. They are his will for us. Don't let go, even when the wait is long and the trials are intense. Everything he speaks comes true.

God is the God of promise. He keeps his word, even when that seems impossible; even when the circumstances seem to point to the opposite.

COLIN URQUHART

The Greater Promises

All these people died still believing what God had promised them. They did not receive what was promised, but they saw it all from a distance and welcomed it. They agreed that they were foreigners and nomads here on earth. **HEBREWS 11:13**

THE STORY OF ABRAHAM in Genesis assures us that he received what God had promised him—descendants who would be a worldwide blessing. Abraham waited long years and struggled to understand the promise, thought God might have one thing in mind when really he had another, and finally rejoiced over a miracle child who kept the promise alive. So what are we to think when we read in chapter 11 of Hebrews that the heroes of faith—Abraham included—died without having received what was promised to them? How is someone able to receive the promise and die without receiving it?

Contradictions in Scripture are not clear contradictions; they are tensions, divergences, variations that send us deeper into the text to understand the nuances of God's ways. In virtually every case, we can see God working at multiple levels. Abraham received a promised child, but the original promise was far greater: "a great nation" and blessing for "all the families on earth" (Genesis 12:1-3). We see only Noah and his family being spared in his generation, a near end to humanity, but then righteous remnants multiplying for generations to come. We see signs of a coming Kingdom that patriarchs, prophets, priests, and kings envisioned and even enjoyed—to a point—but could only anticipate in its fullness. We see God fulfilling his promises in seed and bud but full flowering saved for more lasting purposes.

Your testimony will be similar. You will both "see" and "not see" God's promises fulfilled in your life. You will see seeds, buds, and fruit but not the full harvest. You will need to fix one eye on his work in your generation and another on his work in generations to come. That's because the promises given to you are not just about you. They are about a greater Kingdom, and your relationship with God along with your understanding of his will for your life is only part of the whole. Live with an eternal focus. Rejoice in what he is doing now in your life. Rejoice even more over what he is doing through you for eternal blessing.

All the Holy Spirit's influences are heaven begun, glory in the seed and bud.

MATTHEW HENRY

A Child's Kingdom

*I tell you the truth, anyone who doesn't receive the Kingdom of God
like a child will never enter it.* MARK 10:15

PARENTS BROUGHT THEIR CHILDREN TO JESUS for him to touch and bless them. His disciples thought they were bothering him, but Jesus scolded the disciples for being the bother. Obviously, children should come to him, he insisted. They are most able to see Kingdom ways. They are the ones who get it.

Those who apply this passage to salvation and entering God's Kingdom aren't wrong. The innocent faith, humility, and acceptance of a child certainly characterizes our ability to receive the salvation God has promised. But there's more involved in the Kingdom than our entrance into it. The Kingdom is a comprehensive lifestyle and experience. There's no reason to read into this passage a salvation-only message. In fact, the fullness of the original language points us to a bigger picture: Anyone who doesn't *welcome and take hold of* the Kingdom of God—*in all its ways and wonders and promises*—will never *begin to experience it.* Jesus goes beyond the salvation experience; he's talking about a way of living and seeing.

That makes this childlike vision relevant not only to our acceptance of the gospel but in our ability to live it out daily. We often start out with simple faith that takes God at his word and runs with it. Somewhere along the way, we are conditioned out of that innocence through some unanswered prayer or teaching that emphasizes all the caveats and fine print on God's promises, focusing on what they don't mean rather than what they do. We realize, perhaps years later, that we have to work our way back toward simple, childlike faith again. It's hard for adults conditioned in rationalist thinking to arrive at innocent belief. It's a journey sometimes better accomplished by just choosing childlike faith rather than striving for it. We have to rebuke the rationalizations and explanations surrounding God's promises and just embrace them. Trusting God implicitly is a choice. And it's the only way to experience the joys and treasures of his Kingdom.

A child lives by faith, and his chief characteristic is freedom from care.

HANNAH WHITALL SMITH

Praying in Pictures

Look up into the sky and count the stars if you can. That's how many descendants you will have! **GENESIS 15:5**

GOD HAD TOLD ABRAHAM OF HIS PROMISE, but words don't always capture the fullness of a thought. So he gave Abraham an illustration, a metaphor of what he wanted to do. He expressed himself visually.

This happens a lot in Scripture. For all its words, the Bible is extremely visual—filled with images, visions, parables, and pictures that express what God is doing far better than words can. Prophets often looked to "see" what God was saying (literal translations of Habakkuk 2:1 and Revelation 1:12, for example). They entered into varying degrees of vision to understand his direction and ways. They used metaphors to communicate his truth to people who just weren't getting it. They learned the language of God.

We need to learn God's language too, and sometimes it consists of pictures. We often envision some future scenario—a job opportunity, a diagnosis, a longed-for child, the resolution to a complicated problem—and then try to translate that image into words when we pray. But instead of fumbling around with explanations, why not present the picture to God, who speaks that language and knows our hearts? Prayer is not dependent on the right words; we don't have to explain everything to the God who knows our hearts. We can mentally draw the picture and pray it to him. "Lord, do you see this vision I have? That's what I'm asking for." There's nothing wrong with communicating with God the same way he often communicates with us. It's powerful.

The faith of a child speaks this way too. When a budding artist brings a scrawled picture of . . . well, something . . . to his or her parents and says, "I made this for you!" there's a message in it—a heart of love, a desire to please, a sign of interests, perhaps even a hoped-for gift. If you want to have the faith of a child, this is a great way to express it. When words fail—and sometimes even when they don't—pray in pictures. The God who sees knows just what to do in response.

> Every happening, great and small, is a parable whereby God
> speaks to us, and the art of life is to get the message.
>
> MALCOLM MUGGERIDGE

Praying Positively

I tell you, you can pray for anything, and if you believe that
you've received it, it will be yours. **MARK 11:24**

WE PRAY WITH CERTAIN ATTITUDES, bringing a mixture of beliefs, assumptions, and emotions into our prayers that color them darkly or brightly. A certain spirit in our words reflects our mood, which in turn flavors our faith—or lack of it. If we look closely enough, we can probably identify it. If we look in a mirror, we may even be able to see it on our face.

This energy behind our prayers has a lot to do with faith and expectation—and therefore with answers. There may be times when you pray in an attitude of fear, despair, bitterness, or judgment, hoping God will answer but braced for the disappointment you expect to come. You want to believe, but you also want to guard your heart. That's natural. But Jesus clearly urged his disciples not to hold back, not to put boundaries around their hearts that protect them from disappointments. He told them to go ahead and believe.

The tenses in this one sentence from Jesus are fascinating. Whatever you are praying for (present tense), go ahead and believe you have received it (past tense), and it will be yours (future tense). In other words, when you pray, place your mind and heart in the future—after the answer has come—enjoying the goodness of your God and the victories he brings. In that place, it's entirely appropriate to thank him for what he has done. Once you're there, you can come back into the present and know the answer is coming. Yes, you may not know God's will perfectly; and yes, you might miss some details. Caveats aside, there's no denying Jesus' words. He clearly said to believe.

Be observant about the energy and spirit behind your prayers and determine to pray with boldness, expectation, and gratitude for whatever God will do with them. These attitudes stir up faith, a vital ingredient in any powerful life of prayer. Don't put pressure on yourself; in his mercy, God also answers desperate, fearful prayers. But greater answers come in response to faith. Pray positively, and positive answers will flow much more freely.

We block Christ's advance in our lives by failure of expectation.

WILLIAM TEMPLE

Joy before Breakthrough

Always be full of joy in the LORD. **PHILIPPIANS 4:4**

IF YOU'VE BEEN FOLLOWING GOD for a while and have set your heart on something he has promised, you know by now there's often a gap between his promises and fulfillments. *Faith* is what we do in that gap. It's the process our hearts, minds, and spirits take from point A to point B of God's will, and it can be quite the journey. That journey sometimes discourages us but always stretches us. We watch for his plan to unfold in our lives, with one eye on the evidence of what is happening and another on what is yet to come.

While we're watching, we need to remember a very important truth: Joy almost always comes before breakthrough. In fact, being aware of that truth will take our eyes off the details and turn them back toward the faithfulness of God. In other words, we turn our attention from the promise to the Promiser. That shift enables us to enjoy the moment before the answer comes. It anchors us in the goodness of our Father rather than the gifts he offers us. As much as we want to see him work out his wonderful purposes in our lives, we want even more just to know he is with us and watching over his plans. And that makes the gap between promise and fulfillment much more than just a waiting process.

Some of us spend years waiting for God's promises and purposes to be fulfilled or our prayers to be answered. We have anxious faith in our hearts. But anxious faith isn't faith at all. The questions that bounce around in our minds of whether God will work things out, whether he is on our side, whether he can really be trusted to do what he said—they all undermine trust. On good days, we can answer those questions positively. On other days, we wonder and worry and talk about believing God's promises without actually believing.

Anchor your heart in joyful, expectant faith, no matter what contradictions and closed doors you're facing. The journey of faith takes time. Fill that time with joy. Trust your Father. Rejoice always in the ways he has surrounded your life with goodness. Joy opens doors that fear and disappointment are powerless to unlock.

A holy, joyful expectancy is of the very essence of true waiting.

ANDREW MURRAY

Flip the Script

Don't worry about anything; instead, pray about everything.

PHILIPPIANS 4:6

THIS VERSE MAY COME ACROSS AS GOOD ADVICE, an uplifting word of encouragement. But it's phrased as a command: "Don't worry about anything." A simple word study confirms that anything means *anything*—that we are to be anxious for no things, nothing at all. Even when we have legitimate concerns, God gives us something to do with them. He invites us to cast our cares on him and let him deal with the details. Nowhere are we told that God gets stressed out, and nowhere are we given license to depart from his nature. When we're worried and he's not—and he never is—we are disagreeing with him. We are not taking advantage of the greatest means we have been given to change the world.

If you struggle with anxious thoughts, you may be receiving prayer prompts from God and turning them from, "Okay, Lord, here's where you want to work" into "Oh no! Look what could go wrong!" In fact, many people who wrestle with anxiety find that one of their greatest ministry gifts is intercession. They realize that all of the troublesome thoughts they have about what might happen, the dangers that lie ahead, and the things that need to be taken care of are actually the Holy Spirit encouraging them to cover their lives and the lives around them with prayer. The intensity of their former anxieties becomes the intensity of their prayers.

Your opportunities to worry are also your opportunities to exercise faith. The only difference between them is your response. It will take great mental discipline training yourself to respond out of faith rather than worry, but you will never grow in your prayer life unless you do. Perhaps you haven't seen immediate results and assume your prayers aren't doing much, though Scripture assures you they are. Or maybe you're wondering if you're supposed to do something but feel helpless because you don't know what it is. If so, flip the script on your worries. Learn to see those opportunities. Don't waste them on fear, anxiety, worry, or dread. Turn them into occasions for powerful, faith-filled petitions to God, covering your life and your world with his goodness.

Pray, and let God worry.

MARTIN LUTHER

Thanks in Advance

Do not be anxious about anything, but in everything
by prayer and supplication with thanksgiving let your
requests be made known to God. **PHILIPPIANS 4:6, ESV**

ANXIETY KILLS FAITH AND UNDERMINES PRAYERS. Most of us have experienced that. We pray in fear, hoping the protection or provision we're praying for will come, but at the same time we're overwhelmed by the possibility that it won't. Paul wrote in Ephesians that God can do "infinitely more" than we can imagine according to the "power at work within us" (3:20). That power is what energizes us. But anxiety is the wrong kind of energy. It adds no power to our faith.

What does feed our faith? Gratitude. When we thank God for the answers to our prayers—perhaps not the exact answers according to all our wished-for details, but definite answers nonetheless—we are acknowledging that he is faithful to his promises. Why not go ahead and get excited about what he is going to do? Why not praise him for his compassion, attentiveness, and faithfulness? Why wait to see if he follows through to decide whether we're going to thank him? Faith counts on an answer—in his way and in his time, of course—and trusts that it is coming.

Many would look at gratitude-in-advance as naive, delusional, or even manipulative—as if God is beholden to whatever we presume upon him. But we are not presuming anything; we are believing what he said. His promises were his idea, not ours. Obviously, we don't want to manufacture worship in order to get something from him. But we do want to take him at his word and worship him because he has given us the kind of relationship that makes that possible.

We know God is going to be good to us. That's his nature. We know he will answer prayers in some way that will be satisfying and fulfilling. That's his promise. So go ahead and add thanksgiving to your prayers of faith. Push through those self-accusations of "faking it" and press ahead until it's authentic. See how your faith swells, your expectations expand, and your relationship with God is enriched. Notice how much lighter—and less anxious—you feel. It's always appropriate to worship and give thanks to God. His goodness is just as true before prayers are answered as after.

Faith without thankfulness lacks strength and fortitude.

JOHN HENRY JOWETT

The *Shalom* of Prayer

*Then you will experience God's peace, which exceeds anything
we can understand. His peace will guard your hearts and
minds as you live in Christ Jesus.* **PHILIPPIANS 4:7**

GOD'S DESIGN FOR HIS PEOPLE is *shalom*—the peace, wholeness, fullness, and satisfaction of life that comes with living in his Kingdom. This Hebrew word for peace shows up throughout the Old Testament, even as part of the Messiah's identity as the Prince of Shalom. This rich meaning is usually behind the New Testament word translated as "peace" in the New Testament, which was written in Greek by people steeped in Hebraic thought. When Paul tells us that presenting our requests to God without anxiety and with gratitude will result in peace, he surely means the fullness of God's *shalom*. It's a satisfying place of rest.

Anxious prayers bring no peace. If the energy or emotion behind our prayers is heavy, fearful, bitter, or hopeless, we are wrestling in prayer and not believing. There's a place for that kind of prayer, to be sure—it often happens on our way to faith. And even if our wrestling doesn't lead to the peace of faith, God still often answers. He's merciful, after all, and meets us at our points of need. Desperate prayers are not inappropriate.

Still, God wants our conversations with him to be filled with faith, hope, reassurance, and peace. Many of the psalms begin in turmoil and end in gratitude because God has led the psalmist on a path toward faith and rest—that place of *shalom* in the inward spirit. He works best when we're at rest—when we have released our burdens to him. Scripture is filled with battles that were won when his people worshiped, believed, and trusted. Sometimes they fought in faith; sometimes they didn't even have to fight at all. Releasing the responsibility of a problem to God, with gratitude and praise, invites him into it. Knowing that fills our hearts with the *shalom* of the Kingdom, the fullness of peace in our lives.

"Let go and let God" is a trite saying, but trite doesn't always mean untrue. Don't abdicate your role in his plans, but do relinquish your anxiety about it. Trust him to carry the weight of his promises. Let the peace that exceeds understanding fill your heart and mind.

Worry is an intrusion into God's providence.

JOHN HAGGAI

Strengthen Your Core

*You, beloved, building yourselves up in your most holy faith and
praying in the Holy Spirit, keep yourselves in the love of God, waiting
for the mercy of our Lord Jesus Christ that leads to eternal life.*

JUDE 1:20-21, ESV

IT'S A COMMON SIGHT AT THE GYM: guys who show up in the spring to prep themselves for beach season. They go for the heavy weights and strain to build up their arms, shoulders, and chests, since those are the muscles that impress. The problem is that focusing on visible power without first building up the core—those hidden muscles that support everything else and hold it all in balance—can result in strain and injury. Going straight for bulk results in bodies that can't handle the weight of their own gains.

That's true in the spirit, too. Many people seek a life of powerful prayer because they want power. That's understandable. We love to see "results," and sometimes that's all we focus on. But when our prayers only seek visible and impressive outcomes—when we go for miracles and divine interventions in our circumstances—we risk gains we can't sustain. We pray for power without first having the character and wisdom needed to know which answers to pray for. We end up with low levels of spiritual maturity that can't handle the weight of our calling.

That's why, in both the gym and our prayer lives, it's wise to target the core first—to build up our innermost being. Then we can proceed with wisdom, discernment, and character from which powerful prayers flow. It's why Paul prayed for inner strength in order to be able to handle Christ within (Ephesians 3:16-17). It's also why some people rise to high positions but then crash and burn because of character failures. If we really want spiritual influence, and if we really want to connect with the heart of the Father on important matters in this world, we'll need to be strengthened in the character, faith, wisdom, and purity of our inner selves. One of the best ways to grow in effective prayers for others is to pray for ourselves, that we would grow in spiritual strength. The world needs people who pray such prayers. Their faith knows how to lift up the weight of its problems to God.

Christian character grows in the secret place of prayer.

SAMUEL ZWEMER

A Kingdom Mind

I want you to understand what really matters. **PHILIPPIANS 1:10**

IF WE ARE GOING TO SEE WITH KINGDOM VISION, we will have to retrain our minds. Our thought patterns, after all, have been shaped by worldly ways and negative influences from day one. We've been well trained in flawed relational dynamics, distorted perceptions, and degrading earthly values. Much of this has been modeled for us by well-intentioned but imperfect human beings, and much of it has been embraced by our own willful and self-oriented hearts. We need to learn new patterns, and they won't come easily. Like water flowing down a mountainside, our habitual thoughts have dug deep trenches in our brains. And neurologists have confirmed how difficult it can be to establish new pathways. The old thought-threads in our brains perceive new threads as threats and actually seek to subdue and suppress them. If we want lasting change, we will have to be stubbornly persistent. Willfulness is not always a bad thing. We will have to insist—again and again and again—on godly ways of thinking.

Immersion in Scripture is one way to do that. We have to marinate in the Word for it to infuse us with truth and vision. When we do, we see how great people of faith—like Paul with his relentless joy—responded to the situations around them with hope rather than discouragement, faith rather than fear, positive rather than negative expectations, and love rather than bitterness and strife. The more we absorb these response patterns, the more we begin to walk in them. We start to think in new ways. We learn the language of the Kingdom. We find that we thrive in a culture of gratitude, faith, hope, and love. We begin to defy our old thinking, and whole new possibilities open up in front of us.

If you want to radically reorient your prayer life, insist on this process of change. These are skills that will upgrade your vision and faith, without which prayers seem empty and powerless. Immerse yourself in the Word, and wherever possible, surround yourself with faith-filled people. Give your mind permission to think outside of its limited, negative, earthbound ways. Those thoughts no longer serve you well. A Kingdom mind will change you forever.

Hope is the power of being cheerful in circumstances
which we know to be desperate.

G. K. CHESTERTON

Always Positive

I will continue to rejoice. **PHILIPPIANS 1:18**

WHAT HAPPENS TO YOUR THOUGHTS when circumstances shift in unexpected ways? Do you tend to view that shift as a threat to your hopes and expectations, or do you understand it as part of what God is doing to work out the hopes and expectations you've prayed for? Do you default to the mindset of *This is going wrong* or *This is going right*? Do you live in fear or faith?

It's not unusual for those of us trained in worldly ways of thinking to default to the negative—to interpret events through a lens of disappointment, to assume that whatever happens is evidence that God is not answering our prayers rather than evidence that he is. Yes, those events may appear threatening, but Scripture is full of examples of negative turns that were actually positive progress. What do we believe when a situation shifts? Does our faith rise or fall? What do our thoughts say about God?

Paul had plenty of opportunities to see his circumstances in a negative light. He easily could have spun them toward despair. Instead, he was relentless in his view that whatever happened, it would work out for his good and God's glory (Romans 8:28). In the first chapter of Philippians alone, he saw his confinement in Rome as an opportunity to influence people in high places; he rejoiced that the self-centered preaching of rivals was still getting the name of Jesus out there; and he saw himself in a no-lose situation as the possibility of death approached. Would he remain in the flesh and have opportunity to bear more fruit or would he die and go to be with Jesus? In his eyes, either option was a win. He refused to let any suspicion of God's purposes, any thought of God's neglect, or any possibility of unanswered prayer creep into his mind. He insisted on rejoicing because he knew—with absolute conviction—that God was doing good things, no matter how those things appeared on the surface.

That's Kingdom thinking, and we will falter in prayer and faith if we don't embrace it. Saturate your life in joy, regardless of how things look. God is on the move, even when he seems to be still. Whether or not you see it, he is working out all things for your good and his glory.

Hope can see heaven through the thickest clouds.

THOMAS BENTON BROOKS

Claim What He Names

The LORD said . . . "You have seen well, for I am watching
over my word to perform it." **JEREMIAH 1:12, ESV**

MANY CHRISTIANS TAKE AN EXCLUSIVE "not my will, but yours" approach to prayer (Luke 22:42, ESV) without any awareness that God cares about their own desires. Others take Jesus' promise that "you may ask for anything you want" (John 15:7), and they run with it regardless of God's purposes and plans. Somewhere in between is a middle ground that recognizes the fullness of what Scripture says. Yes, we need to defer to God's will above all else; and yes, God does, in fact, urge us to ask according to the desires within us. But prayer is neither a formula for selfless automatons nor a formula for getting stuff. It's a conversation within a real relationship between God and his people.

As you seek balance, go ahead and acknowledge that prayer has a name-it-claim-it dynamic—but not in the presumptuous sense so commonly preached in some ministries. We can't just name whatever we want and claim it. We can, however, claim what God has already named. We need a word from him—some direction, some promise, some "yes" to our desire. We first let God name it; then we can claim it. That's where prayer takes off. He sets the boundaries that fit his Kingdom purposes, and then we enter into those boundaries with desires rooted in the context of his Word and ways. He answers our truest, deepest prayers—and even many that weren't entirely necessary, simply because he's a good and generous Father.

The good news is that Scripture is full of his promises, and if you are engaged in a community of faith, you have plenty of people around you who will remind you of them. You will begin to recognize when God is speaking at critical moments to assure you of his plans and desires. You will hear his *yes* to whatever prayers he intends to answer through the pages of Scripture, in the preaching and counsel and conversations of believers, and in the symbolic language of faith you have developed with him over time. When that yes comes, believe it. Pray it. Hold on to it. God's promises come alive in the hearts of those who cling to what he has said.

Pleading the promises of God is the whole secret of prayer.

MARTYN LLOYD-JONES

Honor the Testimonies

*If the LORD is with us, why has all this happened to us? And where are
all the miracles our ancestors told us about?* JUDGES 6:13

*BAD THINGS HAPPEN TO GOOD PEOPLE. . . . Thousands prayed for her, yet
she still died. . . . That man's ministry has seen many miracles, yet his own son is sick. . . .*
Somewhere behind the scenes of our faith is this running commentary on whatever faith has not accomplished—what God has not done, answers that have not
come, disappointments the faithful have experienced. Though God has often done
wonderful, powerful works in response to prayer, the exceptions seem to ring truer.
They undermine our faith.

These are counter-testimonies, enemies of faith, the stories of worst-case scenarios, the echoes of "yes, but" that seem to grow louder the closer we come to pure
faith. When we entertain them, our faith weakens. Testimonies of what God has
done carry great power because they bring his past goodness into the present, stir up
our faith, and prophesy of possibilities to come. When we focus on testimonies of his
goodness, we grow more confident in asking. But the human mind and influences of
darkness come against such testimonies because they don't pass the test of empirical
data. They don't happen one hundred percent of the time. The counter-testimonies
destroy our confidence, convince us our circumstances will be among the exceptions,
and turn our prayers into wishful thinking.

Whatever it takes, don't let that happen. Insist on God's goodness, regardless of
what visible evidence seems to suggest. Whatever you steep your thoughts in is generally what you are most likely to experience. So if you're steeping your thoughts in
the exceptions or the problems or the counter-testimonies of what God hasn't done,
you are much less likely to experience the answer to your prayers. Your faith—in this
case, a negative kind of faith in non-answers—may very well be rewarded, to your
disappointment. The faith God is looking for is always based on who he is and what
he has done. Honoring testimonies of his answers multiplies them in our own lives.
Steep your thoughts in them, and your faith—true Kingdom faith—will cultivate a
life full of God's answers.

The ringing testimony of the Christian faith is that God is able.

MARTIN LUTHER KING

False Answers

"Now's your opportunity!" David's men whispered to him. "Today the Lord is telling you, 'I will certainly put your enemy into your power, to do with as you wish.'" **1 SAMUEL 24:4**

DAVID HAD A GOLDEN OPPORTUNITY to kill Saul. It would have fulfilled David's calling and God's promise and ended his long, tumultuous exile on the run. From all appearances, the moment was a godsend. But David would have had to dishonor the currently anointed king in order to become the future anointed king. He would have had to defy God's character to enter into God's promise.

That's a sure sign of compromise—a watering down of the promise, a temptation to circumvent God's ways in order to get to God's goals. Jesus later faced an even more egregious alternative when he was tempted in the wilderness. The adversary promised him the kingdoms of the world (Matthew 4:8-10)—something already implicit in the Messiah's inheritance (Psalm 2:8). We are often presented with such alternatives, compromises, and distractions in response to our prayers. Sometimes they look a lot like God's answer; sometimes they are transparently manipulative or sinful. In any case, they are shortcuts to fulfillment and enemies of faith. They work against us even while appearing to work for us.

We can be confident that God's answers to our prayers of faith will be consistent with his character and ways. Even when they seem scandalous—the promise of the Messiah was fulfilled through an ostensibly illegitimate pregnancy, for example—at their core, they will fit his true nature. His goodness is at the heart of every promise, and even when the journey seems difficult, it comes without compromise. The answer will not stir up second-guessing or feel less than fulfilling. It will align with his faithfulness and satisfy the desire that prompted the prayer in the first place.

Remember that as you hold on to the promises God has given you. He does not give substandard gifts through backhanded means. His fulfillments may seem sudden, but he does not take shortcuts. Stay true to your faith. Refuse the less-than alternatives. Believe that God answers in the fullness of what he has promised.

He will be infinitely merciful to our repeated failures;
I know no promise that he will accept a deliberate compromise.

C. S. LEWIS

A God of Details

How precious are your thoughts about me, O God.
They cannot be numbered! I can't even count them;
they outnumber the grains of sand! **PSALM 139:17-18**

SOME PEOPLE ARE RELUCTANT TO "BOTHER" GOD with small things. Others resist asking him for "too much." We want our prayers to be just the right size—too big to deal with on our own but not so big as to seem presumptuous. We forget how intricately involved God is in every detail of our lives.

God is everywhere, even in those details, and he has invited us into a comprehensive relationship. He is already aware of everything. He watches over our lying down and rising up, our comings and goings, our hopes and fears, our needs and wants. He wants us to understand the importance of "small beginnings" (Zechariah 4:10) and to see every mountain as minuscule compared to him (Mark 11:22-23). He wants us to have God-sized vision—more expansive than any telescopic view and more intricate than any microscopic view. He doesn't want us to agonize over details or massive problems. He wants us to bring those details and problems to him instead. He saves, empowers, and restores much more thoroughly than we can imagine.

Kingdom thoughts allow for no hesitations, no barriers between our prayers and God's attention. They conform to his character, to be sure, but they place no other limits on our conversations with him. So go ahead and "bother" God with the small things, and go ahead with your audacious requests. Have the kinds of conversations that are welcomed in intimate partnerships. Talk to him about minor inconveniences—your need to find a decent parking space, that awkward moment in your conversation with a friend, the annoying problem at work, and more. Talk to him about major challenges—your most impossible desires, your most enduring problems, and more. Your life is more than these things, but your relationship with God should encompass all of them. He calls you a friend (John 15:15; James 2:23), and you have every reason to act like one.

The great tragedy of life is not unanswered prayer but unoffered prayer.

F. B. MEYER

Between God and Us

When trouble strikes, you lose heart. You are terrified
when it touches you. **JOB 4:5**

JOB WAS DESPONDENT OVER HIS LOSSES and cursed the day he was born. He had tried to be a man of integrity and live in faith, but his righteousness had apparently failed. He began comparing those who lived uprightly with those who lived recklessly, and the rewards and consequences that came, but he was beginning to notice that patterns don't always hold true. And after much anguish, his friend's response hit Job where he was most vulnerable: his rapidly eroding hope.

Without realizing it, we often base our prayers of faith on something other than faith—expectations that God will reward our upright lives with good things. Over time, however, we begin noticing that the pattern doesn't always hold. So we adopt a new pattern: prayers accompanied by nagging little thoughts of fine print and conditions, fears that every promise comes with some divine legalese or caveat somewhere else in Scripture that undermines its full effect. And our old thought patterns can find plenty of evidence for those subversive fears. Bad things really do happen to good people. People with great faith really do have diseases that don't get healed, children who struggle, financial setbacks, and broken relationships. All the praying in the world didn't fix things for them, did it? The more we look at other people's evidence, the more our faith fades.

Kingdom thinking doesn't look at other people's evidence that way. It allows our faith to be stirred up by their victories, but it doesn't buy into negative examples. It is always biased toward God's goodness, faithfulness, and hope. We don't live in denial of a fallen, broken world, but we focus on the upward call of Kingdom fulfillment—the story God is writing in *our* lives according to *our* faith. We can't afford to read his promises through the lens of disappointments, whether ours or others'. We have to read them through the lens of his character. When we do, we choose hope and joy, not fear. We leave disappointment behind and celebrate whatever he is doing for us, in us, and through us. We pray in faith with eyes only on his purposes for our lives.

His love in times past forbids me to think He'll leave me at last in trouble to sink.

JOHN NEWTON

The Language of Hope

I pray that God, the source of hope, will fill you completely with joy and peace because you trust in him. Then you will overflow with confident hope through the power of the Holy Spirit. **ROMANS 15:13**

THE LANGUAGE OF COMPLAINT is in vogue. The people who are considered most insightful are those who criticize. The people who come across as most discerning are those who express cynicism and skepticism about everyone and everything. The people who are most "real" are those who readily point out how bad things are and how victimized they feel. And while there's nothing wrong with being honest about feelings, the point of immersing ourselves in biblical truth is to rise above those perspectives and see the big picture. Negativity may be trending, but it isn't helpful. And it certainly isn't how God thinks.

A Kingdom mind is hopeful because it aligns with God. God is not wringing his hands over any situation on earth and wondering how he'll manage it. There is no problem that has him stumped, no lack that exceeds his resources, no mistake so far out of bounds that it's irredeemable. While many of God's people focus on whatever God hasn't done yet, God is focused on what he has promised and what he plans to do. He sees the end from the beginning (Isaiah 41:26; 46:10), and it never leaves him scratching his head. He is filled with hope because he sees the future and knows his goodness will reign. That's hope. And the God of hope will fill us with it as we believe.

Human nature gravitates toward the glass-half-empty, or even the glass-only-one-percent-empty. We tend to focus on the problem areas of our lives, and our words follow. But fallen human nature does not cultivate a fertile environment for prayer and faith. The Spirit who overflows in our hearts does. He fills us with joy and peace in believing because we were designed for such things. Learn to speak his language—words of hope—regardless of what your natural eyes see, and you will grow in the trust that empowers meaningful, earthmoving conversations with God.

Our life is grounded in faith, with hope and love besides.

JULIAN OF NORWICH

The Power of Love

If I didn't love others, I would have gained nothing.

1 CORINTHIANS 13:3

PAUL WROTE A LOT about powerful spiritual gifts, mountain-moving faith, and sacrificial service that advances God's Kingdom on earth. And he exemplified a ministry of strong words and miraculous works in his efforts to spread the good news of the Kingdom throughout the ancient world. But all of those words and works would have counted for nothing, he said, if love had not been behind them. Of faith, hope, and love, the last is the greatest (1 Corinthians 13:13). In fact, faith and hope are rooted in and can only bear fruit in the soil of love.

That tells us a lot about the mindset behind our prayers. We often ask God to do amazing things because we need to feel fulfilled, to be somebody, to be pulled out of a desperate situation, to prove a point, to fulfill our responsibilities as praying people, or even to accomplish his will. None of these motives disqualifies us from praying, but if love is not ultimately behind our prayers—if it is not the energy or the driving force that moves us to pray—we will often be disappointed over our fruitlessness. It isn't because God doesn't honor faith, hope, or the purposes of his Kingdom; it's that faith, hope, and the purposes of his Kingdom are rooted in his nature, which is fundamentally love. Nowhere are we told that God is faith, hope, or righteousness (though he is certainly faithful, hopeful, and righteous). But we are told that God is love (1 John 4:8, 16). It's who he is by nature. So if our prayers are going to be rooted in his nature, they must be rooted in, saturated in, and driven by love.

That is not a burdensome condition, but it does require us to change the way we think—to "repent" into a Kingdom worldview that seeks no advancement that isn't thoroughly loving. Our hearts need to shift their focus from our *agenda* for people, no matter how spiritual it is, to our deep *compassion* for them. When this replaces the nervous, fearful, desperate, needy, power-focused, pseudo-spiritual energy behind our prayers, the atmosphere of the Kingdom in our lives becomes much more fruitful. Our prayers begin to flourish in a climate of love.

He who is filled with love is filled with God himself.

AUGUSTINE

Unnatural Vision

We have stopped evaluating others from a human point of view.
2 CORINTHIANS 5:16

WE LOVE TO CATEGORIZE PEOPLE. It's rarely intentional and usually subconscious. We have a tendency to size people up according to first impressions and how their words, behaviors, and attitudes fit into our past experiences. Sometimes those mental responses are positive, but they can also be negative, judgmental, and even condemning. We form or resist relationships based on instinct.

Sometimes when we think we are being a good judge of character, we are really seeing people according to their past and/or their present, which is not at all their whole story. A Kingdom mind looks ahead. It can envision a shepherd boy like David, marginalized even by his family, becoming a mighty, passionate, God-loving king. It can look at a zealous, murderous finger-pointer like Saul and see an apostle like Paul. It can absorb past offenses, look past annoying characteristics, and even understand a heart steeped in bitterness, anger, or hopelessness in order to see the image of God within. No matter how obscured that image is, no matter how quirky or grating or socially awkward someone's behavior appears, there is a treasure inside, a measure of divine worth that is loved by the heart of God. Connecting with his heart gives us that kind of love too. We learn to see people for who they can become rather than for who they have been or now seem to be.

You can't pray for people well without this Kingdom perspective. If you're focused on sin, depravity, shortcomings, offenses, or even just a few oddities, you won't be able to call out the treasures God has placed in a person or have faith for more than what you see. Jesus came not to condemn but to save (John 3:17); our prayers must come from the same spirit and be aligned with the same mission. Whatever it takes, we have to look past the visible to see the invisible—to live (and pray) by faith, not by sight (2 Corinthians 5:7). Only then can we expect God to move in response to our requests to reach into people's hearts, work in their lives, and bring them into the purposes he has for them.

> The grace of God does not find men fit for salvation but makes them so.
>
> **AUGUSTINE**

Sacred Mental Space

Let God transform you into a new person by changing the way you think. Then you will learn to know God's will for you, which is good and pleasing and perfect. ROMANS 12:2

YOUR MIND IS SACRED SPACE. You may see it as a processor of neutral thoughts, the place where you weigh pros and cons and make decisions, where your dreams and desires reside next to all your insecurities and anxieties. But as part of the temple of your body, your mind is meant to be a dwelling place for God. The endless stream of thoughts passing through your brain does not belong to you alone. It should not go off in directions that do not fit the nature, character, and wisdom of God. He wants to occupy the throne of your thinking.

That's why it's so important to rid your mind of unworthy fears, ambitions, judgments, and other attitudes that don't align with the Spirit. Entertaining such contradictions is like hosting guests in your home who have nothing in common and clash awkwardly in every conversation. Thoughts born from fear, bitterness, and pride are inhospitable to the Spirit. If we want to enjoy his company, we need to uninvite his opponents.

Perhaps you haven't realized how connected your thought life is to your prayers, but both are part of the same spiritual package—your life as God sees it. When you pray, you aren't just offering up words or putting in a request; you are presenting yourself in your new identity, your whole being—with all your dreams, desires, and purposes. You are conversing in the context of loving the Lord with all your heart, soul, strength, and mind. Your prayer life flows directly out of your mental universe.

That means your mental universe—and therefore your prayer life—needs to align with God's nature. We're told that we have access to the mind of Christ (1 Corinthians 2:16). Why would we fill the hard drive in our heads with anything else? Treat your mind as a holy and sacred space, invite God alone to write his thoughts into it, and then pray your heart out. Watch to see what God does with the invitation. Those who make room for him find him eager to enter in and move in partnership with them.

Think through me, thoughts of God.

AMY CARMICHAEL

Becoming Fearless

Don't be troubled or afraid. JOHN 14:27

SOME PEOPLE ARE NATURALLY FEARLESS. But the rest of us have little difficulty imagining a worrisome possibility, creating unwanted scenarios around it, and letting that dangerous outcome swell in our minds until it seems almost inevitable. Quite unintentionally, we know how to cultivate our fears and lie awake imagining them. And because our mental space is the shaper of our prayers, we end up with a dark and distorted list of requests for God to deal with.

If prayer is like planting seeds, then fear is one of the hardest soils to till. It's appropriate and important to pray when we're afraid, of course; many of the psalms begin that way. We can bring our hearts and minds to God in any condition. But it's also important to let the Spirit of God move us from fearful to faith-filled prayers— to agree with rather than rebut his promises, to let our hearts loosen their death grip on our own security and trust God to secure us, to relinquish our worst-case scenarios to his best-laid plans. Fruitful prayers are born of faith, hope, and love— especially love—and fear is an enemy to each of these and the fruitfulness they bring. It distorts our vision, undermines our faith, casts a negative light on everything God has said, and kills our compassion with self-protecting responses. In other words, it turns us inward, away from the light of God and into the darkest corners of our old-nature lives.

It is often said that the most frequent command in the Bible is "do not fear" (in variously worded phrases). It was spoken before big battles, great miracles, intimidating assignments, and generally unsettling circumstances. Jesus repeated it to his disciples the night before his crucifixion, assuring them that in spite of the tumultuous events ahead, they were rooted in a Kingdom and a peace that were greater and deeper than the world could ever give. A Kingdom mind always moves in that direction—away from troubled thoughts and toward the possibilities, promises, and purposes of God. He would not have told us to be fearless if our fears were well-founded. In light of his wisdom, power, and love, they aren't. Prayers steeped in that confidence become living, moving testimonies to his goodness.

Victory over fear is the first spiritual duty of man.

NIKOLAI BERDYAEV

Single-Minded

Everything else is worthless when compared with the infinite value of knowing Christ Jesus my LORD.   **PHILIPPIANS 3:8**

PERHAPS YOUR PRAYER LIFE FEELS SCATTERED—an attempt to cover each member of your family, church, and workplace; your health and finances; the upcoming items on your to-do list; the ministries and missionaries serving around the world; the nations that need a profound move of God; the victims of tragedies in the day's headlines; and more. These are good prayers, and they are all part of our lives and world that God is concerned with too. But in the overwhelming lists and categories, amid all the items you can probably never get to on a normal day, remember where your life is anchored. Remember the overarching category. See your life and your concerns as a single entity—a mission to know Jesus and see his Kingdom come in increasing measure.

That does not remove any of the above items from your prayer list, but it does bring them under one all-embracing concern. The life of prayer is a single-minded pursuit, not a to-do list. It begins and ends in relationship with God; everything else flows from that relationship. A Kingdom mind learns to see family, work, health, finances, ministry, and daily needs and concerns as part of an overall mission in this world that can be summed up in a single prayer: "Lord, your Kingdom come, your will be done here, now, on earth, just as it is in heaven." In reality, you are praying heaven's truths, values, power, and love into your situations on earth. There is nothing greater you can pray. It is all-inclusive; everything else is just a more specific detail.

Summary prayers can keep us focused. When we pray them because we are too busy or lazy to get specific, they are weak. When we pray them because we are fully aware that God's mission in this world through us is ultimately a single pursuit, they are powerful. The difference is in the relationship. When our single-minded pursuit is to know God, we begin to pray the things on his heart. When we pray the things on his heart, his heart is moved. His Kingdom comes through those who seek him above all.

The seed is choked in our souls whenever Christ is not our all in all.

CHARLES SPURGEON

A Here-and-Now God

I am confident I will see the LORD's goodness while
I am here in the land of the living. **PSALM 27:13**

"ENDURE NOW; ENJOY LATER." That seems to be the perspective many Christians take on life. It's reinforced in theologies that have been birthed or emphasized in times of persecution or other difficult circumstances, it ran strong in the first few centuries of the church, and it was common in medieval and Reformation teaching. Life is hard, and the joys of heaven await.

Jesus taught his disciples that they would have trouble in this world but to be of good cheer because he had overcome the world (John 16:33). It's a profound truth that keeps our focus on eternity. But he didn't say that we would *only* have trouble in this world or that he would overcome the world one day but not yet, without any fulfillment in the meantime. No, he said he had already overcome the world, and he invited his followers into the overcoming. We may continue to experience some contradictions to the Kingdom of God, but we also continue to experience its blessings among us. That's because when the King left, he didn't actually leave. He promised to be with us always (Matthew 28:20). He sent his Spirit to be with us and in us (John 14:16-21). The idea that life is drudgery here on earth but we have a glorious heaven to look forward to has hints of truth, but it isn't the full picture. We are promised plenty of joys and advances now.

A Kingdom-oriented mind refuses to defer all the good stuff until after the King's return. It's true that the Kingdom will come in its fullness then, but glimpses and tastes of it are already here. We are in the in-between, when expecting too much or too little before the Second Coming are both theological mistakes. If we err on one side, it needs to be on the side of expecting too much. Faith always leans toward moving mountains rather than hills. God's promises for prayer always seem to stretch our current experience. If it is God's nature to give good gifts (James 1:17), we are not reaching beyond his nature to ask for them. With the optimism of David's hope in today's verse, we seek heaven's realities in our lives today.

He never tires of giving.

TERESA OF AVILA

The "Yes" of God

All of God's promises have been fulfilled in Christ
with a resounding "Yes!" **2 CORINTHIANS 1:20**

WE COME TO GOD'S PROMISES with many questions, concerns about meeting his conditions, wariness about the precise context of his words, and suspicions of theological fine print behind them. Does the promise apply to us? Does the situation fit? Have we done everything we can to qualify for it? All of these questions create uncertainty and undermine our faith. And all of them are legitimate if we are praying in our own name. But because we are praying in Jesus' name—i.e., from his own identity—then these questions are redirected toward him. And he is worthy of every fulfillment of God's promises without qualification.

This liberating, motivating truth is included in Paul's statement about Jesus being the "yes" and "amen" of God's promises. They all apply to him, and we are in him. Gone is the fear that we might not qualify. Gone is the disorienting search for context to figure out whether God's goodness applies to us or someone else. Gone is the question of whether all the conditions have been met. If a promise was meant for God's people at a certain place and time, and God's people ultimately find their identity in Jesus, then it was meant for all who are in Jesus. If it was conditional on obedience to the law or some deeper standard of righteousness, and Jesus fulfilled the law and all righteousness, then it is meant for all who are in Jesus. If it is part of the inheritance of the Son, then it is part of the inheritance of those who are in the Son. We receive whatever Jesus stands to inherit (Romans 8:17), and he inherits everything (Hebrews 1:2).

Jesus is the "yes" of God to all our needs. That doesn't mean we need nothing but Christ—no food, no protection, no fulfillment or satisfaction. It means that our needs are answered by him, in him, and through him. He is the mediator of God's provision in every area of our lives, and we only need to add an "amen" in faith. We don't have to twist God's arm when we pray. We can assume he is on our side because he is in Jesus, who is in us, fulfilling all of his Word.

Jesus Christ is God's everything for man's total needs.

RICHARD HALVERSON

The Prayer in Heaven

He is sitting in the place of honor at God's
right hand, pleading for us. **ROMANS 8:34**

NOT MANY PEOPLE REALIZE that Jesus is praying for us, but it's true. He is at the throne of God interceding—praying, substituting his own qualifications for ours, and advocating for us before the Father. So is the Holy Spirit (Romans 8:26-27). They are both having a conversation with the Father about what is good for us, what we need, what our purpose is (and has been from the foundation of the world), what challenges and obstacles we face, how we find our identity in Christ, and how we have believed and continue to believe. There is no discord in this conversation; it is "in harmony with God's own will" (verse 27). It is a divine summit meeting on the state and direction of our lives, leading toward the best outcome for us now and forever.

That's an amazing thought, but even more amazing is the invitation we've been given to enter into this conversation. The Trinity is not talking behind our backs. We are welcomed into the discussion. Our prayers are integral to God's purposes for us, and the Father, Son, and Spirit enjoy hearing them. We can't manipulate God to do what we want, but we can freely express our desires and discuss what's on our hearts. We can also ask what's on his heart. As we grow in understanding of his desires, our prayers are deepened, enriched, sometimes redirected, and always more fulfilling. In powerful agreement, we align them with the divine conversation going on. We come boldly to this throne of grace (Hebrews 4:16).

You have been given a relationship with the Father, the Son, and the Holy Spirit, and relationships involve communication. You are therefore able to join this conversation as an interested party. It may take some time to get used to it, but do get used to it. Don't barge in with a list of demands; ask God for some context. Relax and listen. Like a person arriving late to a meeting, try to get a sense of what's going on before speaking up. Then speak up. Envision the Kingdom, pray for its increase, and influence your world by entering the court of your King.

If I could hear Christ praying for me . . . I would not fear a million enemies.

ROBERT MURRAY M'CHEYNE

Blessings Already Ours

All praise to God, the Father of our LORD Jesus Christ, who has
blessed us with every spiritual blessing in the heavenly realms
because we are united with Christ. **EPHESIANS 1:3**

THE FIRST CHAPTER OF EPHESIANS is one of the most encouraging, uplifting passages in all of Scripture. It presents God's plan from ages past to love us, choose us, adopt us, bless us, seal us in his Spirit, and give us an inheritance. It includes a deep and powerful prayer for our ability to understand and receive all he has given. And all of these blessings are expressed with one very fascinating characteristic: They are in the past tense.

That's important. God has already blessed us with every spiritual blessing in Christ. He has already chosen, adopted, forgiven, and redeemed us. He has already unveiled the mystery of his will and guaranteed our inheritance. In other words, many of the assurances and promises we pray for have already been given.

But our prayers often follow a common trajectory: We ask for something God has already promised or given, see a lack of evidence for that particular thing, and continue to ask as though it has not yet come. We long for the things of his Kingdom he has already given us and pray from a place of insecurity, as though we are not yet fully blessed children of God. But faith takes God at his word. If, for example, he has already given us the power of the Holy Spirit, instead of looking at our powerlessness and then pleading for more power, we can look at the promise first and foremost and thank him for the gift. Then any hint of power from the Holy Spirit, no matter how small, becomes an occasion for huge celebration. We cultivate a spirit of worship and gratitude around the things God has done, and before long we realize how present those things are becoming in our lives.

We are not waiting for God to give certain gifts; he is waiting for us to celebrate them, unwrap them, try them out, and grow in them, giving thanks every step of the way. An eye for lack never sees what is there; an eye for fulfillment sees it a mile away. And whatever faith truly sees, faith then brings into our experience.

It is unbelief that prevents our minds from soaring into the celestial city
and walking by faith with God across the golden streets.

A. W. TOZER

Resisting the *Why*

This happened so the power of God could be seen in him. JOHN 9:3

THE DISCIPLES ASKED A VERY COMMON QUESTION. They wanted to know the *why* behind a blind man's circumstances. It's a natural impulse, and sometimes it becomes one of the strongest themes in our prayers. We don't just want God to fix things; we want to know why they happened to begin with. We want to make sense out of whatever is going on in our lives.

Not many people get an answer to that question, at least not immediately. The disciples didn't get a full explanation at all. Jesus simply told them that God was going to glorify himself in that man's life. God is not opposed to our questions, of course, but he has bigger and better ones in mind. Whenever we go through trials and challenges, he doesn't want us obsessing over the reasons they came or what we did to deserve them. He wants us to turn our attention toward him.

Doing so leads to those bigger and better questions. *How do you want to show yourself in this situation, Lord? How are you using this problem to display your character? What side of your nature do you want to reveal here?* These questions raise our perspective and invite God to intervene, sometimes in dramatic ways. Virtually every problem we go through has the potential to be a platform for a revelation of God. Our challenges highlight something about his nature—his love, compassion, kindness, wisdom, power, protection, provision, deliverance, healing, and more. Biblically, the most difficult situations were the greatest stages for his glory. Our lives can set the stage for his glory too.

In fact, that's how we turn our *whys* into prayers. We don't need to understand everything that happens in our lives. Some things will remain hidden until the veil is lifted from our natural eyes. But we aren't called to understand God nearly as much as we are called to trust him. He loves our intellect, but he wants our loyalty more. When we give it—when we get past our inward focus and ask how he wants to reveal himself in our crisis—things begin to change. He meets us there and shows us who he is.

He who perseveres makes every difficulty an advancement and every contest a victory.

CHARLES CALEB COLTON

Resisting the *When*

How long, O LORD, must I call for help?   HABAKKUK 1:2

FAITH AND PATIENCE ARE ALMOST ALWAYS two sides of the same coin, and we often find ourselves in the gap between receiving a promise and experiencing its fulfillment. Sometimes that gap can be excruciatingly long. We ask a lot of questions during those waits. *How long until you answer, Lord? When are you going to fulfill your promise? Did I misunderstand it?* Though we know prayer isn't a formula—we don't get answers from God the same way we make a withdrawal at a drive-thru ATM—we're still a bit disappointed it doesn't work that way. We just don't know how long we can wait or why we even have to.

Asking God *when* is a natural response, but like our questions about *why*, it is rarely answered on our schedule. God is doing a lot of important work in the process, and he doesn't sacrifice thoroughness for the sake of speed. That is painfully clear in the lives of many biblical heroes of faith: Abraham, Joseph, the enslaved Israelites in Egypt, David, many of the prophets, exiles in Babylon, and entire segments of the church through long periods of persecution. Even now, we wait for Jesus' return with the assurance that God is not slow in keeping his promise (2 Peter 3:9). We have to persevere in faith.

God will let us in on what he is doing, however. Many of his promises begin with a vision of something specific, and we are invited to take hold of that vision by faith. Our faith may be tried and tested, pushed and pulled, stretched and strained, but that is by design. We either give up or draw closer to God. He uses the process to cultivate our relationship with him.

Recognize the difference between passing time and waiting patiently. There's nothing godly about enduring when you have no choice—everyone does that— but enduring without anxiety or complaint requires spiritual maturity. Persevering faith—the kind that trusts God in the process and expects his goodness in the end— obtains his promises. Those who abandon the *when* and fix their eyes on God are sustained by and rewarded for their faith.

The ability to wait, and stay, and press belongs
essentially to our intercourse with God.

E. M. BOUNDS

Never a Formula

When you pray, go away by yourself, shut the door behind
you, and pray to your Father in private. Then your Father,
who sees everything, will reward you. MATTHEW 6:6

WE OFTEN TALK ABOUT PRAYER as if it's powerful in itself. We say it can accomplish great things, and we talk about having a powerful prayer life. We aren't wrong; Scripture gives us plenty of promises about the power of prayer. But they are all in the context of a relationship. We don't just pray; we pray to our Father. We don't just intercede; we intercede between human beings and the God who loves them. We don't just come up with random petitions; we pray what the Holy Spirit has laid on our hearts. And we don't simply pray from our own identity; we pray in Jesus' name, clothed with his Spirit, asking in the context of his mission to redeem and restore lives, families, cities, and nations. We have to remember that we aren't just talking to the air or declaring words of faith as if they are magic. A Kingdom mind is always in conversation with the Trinity.

Remember that faith is not a formula. It's part of a relational bond. Praying is not just a matter of having the right attitude so you can get what you want (though it will produce the right attitude, and you will get much of what you want, in some form or another). Nor is it a way to manipulate the universe, which magical thinking aims to do. It is a way to partner with God to advance his Kingdom, along with all its wonderful manifestations and blessings, in this world. We are doing more than trying to make things right. We are preparing a highway for the King of glory, serving as ambassadors of his realm while we live in another, furthering his agenda—very broadly interpreted—in our own lives, the lives of those around us, and the rest of this world that he loves so much. In that sense, prayer is an act of love, a communication of hearts that are ultimately on the same page. Make it personal. Be aware of his presence in every detail of your life. The Father who sees in secret is always there.

Prayer is an effort to lay hold of God himself, the author of life.

SUNDAR SINGH

Thirsty Faith

*I remember the days of old. I ponder all your great works and think
about what you have done. I lift my hands to you in prayer. I thirst
for you as parched land thirsts for rain.* **PSALM 143:5-6**

THE MORAVIANS BEGAN a century-long prayer movement for God's intervention in world affairs, prompting (by many accounts) the modern missions movement
and representing a new era of connecting with God and his purposes in this world.
It began with a move of the Holy Spirit that restored unity in a fractured fellowship
and continued with intense prayer for God's intervention in the affairs of human
beings. Moravians were acutely aware of God's works in Scripture, and they called
those works into the present with constant petitions. They prayed the days of Acts
into the early modern era.

Throughout history, plenty of believers have trusted God casually for their protection, provision, and progress. That isn't insignificant; it counts as faith. But casual
faith is a low level of trust that makes assumptions about God and puts him in the
background of our lives. He isn't opposed to a calm spirit; we are called to rest in him.
But when believers pour out their hearts, cry out to him for his presence or wisdom
or love, and hunger in the depths of their being for any hints of his kindness, he
seems to come rushing in with a ready answer. He responds to those who seek him
with hearts desperate for a response.

Search the Scriptures for God's greatest works and then plead for them earnestly.
Lift your hands in prayer in continuation of the prayers that were answered long
ago. Do not resist the hunger and thirst that make you uncomfortable; they are
signs of the Holy Spirit at work, invitations for the God of miracles and missions to
enter into your life now, a recognition that he is inviting you—and everyone who
believes—into more. The days of old are not a closed book; they are opening hearts
to what God can do. Believe his works then, ask for them now, and receive them in
gratitude. Your hunger and thirst will be satisfied, and the rains of glory and grace
will come down. God is revisiting and reviving old works as new works today.

Lord, revive your church and begin with me.

A CHINESE CHRISTIAN

Night and Day

Let us offer through Jesus a continual sacrifice of praise to God,
proclaiming our allegiance to his name. **HEBREWS 13:15**

WHILE STILL IN SCHOOL, Count Nikolaus von Zinzendorf and his friends established what they called the Order of the Mustard Seed—a spiritual "knighthood" under a covenant of radical service to Jesus. Over the years, that covenant influenced everything Zinzendorf did, the Moravian refugees gathered on his lands, and the prayer movement grew out of it. The Moravians became perhaps the first Protestants to send missionaries to distant lands, and they started a round-the-clock prayer watch in 1727 that continued for the next hundred years. Only eternity will tell how much this group of believers influenced the course of history.

Other round-the-clock prayer movements have been started in recent times, and we can appreciate the heart behind them. Just as King David, the man after God's own heart, took the Ark of the Covenant to Jerusalem, established the Tabernacle there, and set up priests and worshipers to minister continually before the Lord (1 Chronicles 16); just as Paul urged believers to pray without ceasing, at all times and in every situation (Ephesians 6:18; 1 Thessalonians 5:17); and just as the writer of Hebrews called for a continual sacrifice of praise; many modern believers have seen the importance of prayer and worship in shaping lives, the community of believers, and the societies we are called to influence. History has demonstrated God's powerful responses to those who seek him constantly.

No single person is called to pray around the clock. Our bodies were designed for sleep, and we are called to work, relate to family and friends, eat, and enjoy other activities. But the upward and inward interaction between our spirit and God's can become as natural as breathing, which we do around the clock. Our prayers of faith can become like a heartbeat, always present, sometimes noticeable, and completely normal for those alive in him. Whenever your heart feels the inclination to bring God into the margins of your day—through prayer, worship music, celebration, and gratitude—it's appropriate to honor that impulse. He is with us—and our prayers of faith can connect with him—every moment of every night and day.

Prayer should be the key of the day and the lock of the night.

THOMAS FULLER

Praying in His Image

You must have the same attitude that Christ Jesus had.

PHILIPPIANS 2:5

ON HER WAY TO CHINA IN THE 1920s, Isobel Kuhn was told by a well-known Bible teacher that "all the scum of [her] nature [would] rise to the top" when she got to her field of ministry.[1] Isobel wasn't aware of much scum within her, but she kept that warning in mind. A couple of years later, when she moved to a remote area with her husband and discovered that the women she would be ministering to were covered with lice and fleas, that warning became clear. She did not want to feel revulsion for people she had come to love, so she prayed a prayer of faith: for God to make the souls of these women more important to her than any superficial concern.

God answered that prayer. Kuhn soon found herself hardly noticing the lice and fleas, drawn in love to the women and their spiritual needs. She had prayed to see people as Jesus sees them, to no longer regard others according to the opinions of fallen human nature (2 Corinthians 5:16), and her prayer was perfectly in line with God's will for her and all of us. We are being conformed into the image of Jesus so we can see as he sees, love as he loves, have compassion as he did, be disturbed about the things that disturbed him, and pray as he prayed. In fact, that's the true orientation of the entire journey of faith and life of prayer we're called to. We are not asking for God to give us things independently of his nature. We are asking to enter into his love, purposes, promises, and life. We pray as human beings who have been united with him and are becoming like him in every way.

We hardly need to wonder if God is going to answer a prayer to conform us more to his image. That's his stated purpose for us even from the beginning. And the more he fulfills those desires and prayers, the more we find ourselves praying from desires that line up with his. Our hearts become increasingly moved by love, our prayers begin to sound a lot like his, and our faith becomes increasingly fruitful.

> Nearness to Christ, intimacy with him, assimilation to his character—
> these are the elements of a ministry of power.
>
> **HORATIUS BONAR**

The Art of Vision

We don't look at the troubles we can see now; rather, we fix our gaze
on things that cannot be seen. **2 CORINTHIANS 4:18**

THE MORE TIME YOU SPEND IN GOD'S PRESENCE, the more you will strangely, surprisingly find yourself filled with increasing vision. Sometimes a sense of vision will come up within you and grow through your desire to seek it out. You will have ideas, and you may wonder if they are God's or yours. But since you are united with him in Christ and in fellowship with him in your spirit, it doesn't necessarily matter. You are being conformed to his image, and he is imparting his desires and purposes into you. Over time, you begin to see in ways that look a lot like his Kingdom.

Cultivating vision is an art. There are no formulas, systems, or step-by-step programs that will do it for you, though a certain amount of intentionality, discipline, and practice will help. It begins and ends in relationship as you open your heart to God, ask to hear from him and see through his eyes, and learn to discern and receive whatever he gives. You'll need to let your mind think creatively and sometimes respond to things in your heart that may not make sense at first. After all, the Bible is filled with God-given instructions that defied logic. We are being conformed to the image of a creative God; thinking outside the box is part of the journey. Vision very often requires the heart of a poet or an explorer.

If you feel frustrated in your desire to cultivate vision, remember that it involves seeing what is unseen. Yes, you will be confronted by troubles that are so up front and present that they seem to rule your world. But faith looks beyond those circumstances. No matter how awkward it may feel to do so—at times, you may think it's just wishful thinking—it's necessary. It's the only way to connect with God and see what he is doing through your life, prayers, and faith. Your vision will toughen your skin and stretch your faith; after all, you are anchoring yourself in an unseen realm. You're gazing at it with eyes of the Spirit until it is finally revealed.

Vision is the art of seeing things invisible.

JONATHAN SWIFT

What Matters Most

*The things we see now will soon be gone, but the things
we cannot see will last forever.* **2 CORINTHIANS 4:18**

PAUL WROTE THIS WHILE DEFENDING HIS MINISTRY and reminding
the Corinthians of the glories of the new covenant. The "things we see now" refers to
the hardships and struggles he and other believers were going through, and it applies
to every transient thing in this life—our bodies, homes, income, entertainment. But
it is a particularly powerful statement about our troubles. We fix our eyes on the
unseen because the seen doesn't last. We cultivate our vision because we long to look
into eternity and shape our own (and others') experiences of it. We desire to pray
for what matters most.

Too many people are absorbed in the *next thing*—what they need in their daily
life to make it better, bigger, smoother, and more exciting. And there's certainly nothing wrong with praying about that needed raise, that next vacation, that better job,
or that crazy upcoming schedule. God is concerned with all our concerns; he wants
us to share what's on our hearts. But our hearts need to be expanded sometimes to
include the fundamental needs of this world, the brokenness of the people around us,
the emptiness of lives filled with things that don't ultimately matter, the disorienta-
tion of a world gone astray. We need to live with eternal perspectives.

Above all, anchor your prayers in eternity. Root them in your relationship with
a God who is looking at the big picture. Orient them around the things that matter
most. Prioritize those dreams and longings and then leave the remaining space for
those daily matters of comfort and convenience. Whether the people in your world
realize it or not, they need someone talking to the Father about the gaping holes in
their lives and the shape of their eternal experience. They need advocates before the
throne, friends in high places, intercessors standing between them and the God who
loves them and longs to be recognized by them. They need you to see the things that
last forever and pray that their eyes would be opened to see them too.

The only way to get our values right is . . . to see things not
in the light of time, but in the light of eternity.

WILLIAM BARCLAY

Pray Big Prayers

Anything is possible if a person believes. **MARK 9:23**

GOD WANTS US TO DREAM BIG DREAMS and pray big prayers. But he doesn't want us to cultivate those dreams and prayers independently. He doesn't give us wonderful promises about faith for us to go our own way, praying our whims and satisfying our self-centered agendas. All of his promises come in the context of accomplishing his purposes in our lives, on this planet, for the growth of his Kingdom, and ultimately for his glory. But while some people may interpret that context narrowly—as only spiritual, for ministry, never for ourselves——we come to realize there's a middle ground. God's Kingdom is broadly defined, reaching into every corner of our lives. He does want to give good gifts and pour out his blessings, especially on those who can be trusted with them because they have set their hearts on him above all.

So we pray boldly, realizing that God wants us to learn the power of faith—or more precisely, his power through our faith—to accomplish great things. We were designed with that longing, and no one has ever been able to uproot it from the human psyche. Our longing for the transcendent remains because we were made in the image of God and are now being fully restored in it. There's no reason to shy away from it. God has always had big plans and grand visions, and we are being drawn into them. He is zealous about thorough redemption and restoration, and our ambitious faith simply aligns with his desires. In dying with Christ, we have stepped into a supernatural life of resurrection and power. The realm that was once beyond us now opens in front of us. And we are called to keep pressing in.

Don't be afraid of audacious faith. Let it fill you, possess you, and overwhelm you. Dream big dreams, open your eyes to God-sized visions, and pray fearlessly. Acknowledge your own limitations, then ask to enter into God's limitless reach. Join the adventure with him. Embrace the power and glory of the Resurrection in every area of your life, and pray it into other lives too.

I do not want merely to possess faith; I want a faith that possesses me.

CHARLES KINGSLEY

Is He Willing?

Moved with compassion, Jesus reached out and touched him.
"I am willing," he said. "Be healed!" **MARK 1:41**

WE USUALLY CARRY two big *ifs* into our prayers—*if* God can and *if* God will. The former is answered easily enough; we know God can do anything. But the latter isn't so simple. God has given us confidence for those times we are praying according to his will (1 John 5:14-15), and Jesus gave us the supreme example of praying for God's will instead of our own (Luke 22:42). His instructions to pray for God's will to be done (Matthew 6:10) then become an ever-present question in the back of our minds. *Am I praying according to God's will?* If we aren't sure that we are, we may feel as though our prayer won't matter and lose heart.

But God's will is much broader than most of us think. He has generous plans for our lives, and he allows for our desires to blend with his purposes. Jesus told his friends to pray for "anything you want" (John 15:7) because he knew their desires would overlap with his. A well-known psalm assures us that those who delight in God can have the desires of their hearts, which are both given and fulfilled by him (Psalm 37:4). God is not bent on pigeonholing us into a narrowly defined plan, refusing to answer any prayer until it hits the exact center of his purposes. He already knows how to weave our mistakes into his overall plan, and he does the same with our desires. He is willing to inspire them, shape them, or even accommodate them to fit his work in this world.

A concerned father asked Jesus to help, "if you can" (Mark 9:22). Of course he could! Jesus said that "if" is not even a question. But a leper said, "If you are will-ing, you can heal me and make me clean." (Mark 1:40). Jesus gave the same positive response. Yes, he is willing. That question is settled too. He demonstrated throughout his ministry that he was willing, never turning away a request to heal, deliver, or save. He invites us to come to him, fully aware of his generous heart, and ask.

God never made a promise that was too good to be true.

D. L. MOODY

The Aroma of Prayer

They held gold bowls filled with incense, which are
the prayers of God's people.   **REVELATION 5:8**

THE DRAMATIC SCENE SURROUNDING GOD'S THRONE in the book of
Revelation includes twenty-four elders and "four living beings" with multiple eyes,
wings, and faces. Each elder and creature was holding a harp and a bowl. The bowls
were filled with incense, an image of sweet-smelling pleasure meant to be deeply
inhaled. That incense represents the prayers of the saints—the petitions, pleas, and
offerings of praise we bring to God. We breathe them out; he breathes them in. It's
a remarkable picture of something far more powerful than words.

Those prayers are later offered along with "much incense" on the golden altar before
the throne (8:3, ESV). With fire from the altar added, the prayers are hurled to earth,
where spectacular things happen. We get the impression that our prayers reach a tipping point, becoming an aromatic offering to God and returning to earth with holy
fire. Something happens to them in the hands of angels and the worshipful atmosphere
of heaven. God turns them into powerful instruments of his work on earth.

That ought to be encouraging. We don't see what happens to our prayers when
they leave our mouths or hearts, but apparently they build up and overflow with elec-
trifying results. They may take time—bowls are a reservoir, after all, a holding tank
awaiting further use—and we may not understand why. We repeat them with the
persistence of faith and multiply them in the fellowship of faith. We make concerted
and persistent petitions. But according to the highly colorful and symbolic language
of prophetic revelation, they are being held for a time. Only at God's bidding is the
bowl poured out on the altar and fire falls.

Whatever the reason, take heart. Envision your repeated prayers as filling up a
bowlful of power and praise. Know that they are a sweet aroma to your Father on his
throne. Don't give up on them; let them build. In the fullness of time, when God is
ready to answer, they will be highly valued and powerfully used. They are an act of
worship that gives God great pleasure.

> The pure prayer that ascends from a faithful heart will be
> like incense rising from a hallowed altar.
>
> AUGUSTINE

Say It

*God . . . gives life to the dead and calls into existence
the things that do not exist.* **ROMANS 4:17**, ESV

HUMAN BEINGS TALK A LOT. We rarely hesitate to use the mouths God has given us. But what are we using them for—to talk about our rough day, the problems we have, the things people should have done but didn't, and so on? We think we're just sharing our feelings and inviting sympathetic responses. But what if more is going on? If the God who has made us in his image calls into existence things that do not exist, perhaps we also have the capacity—to a degree—to call into existence things that do not exist. Perhaps our words mean much more than we think they do.

In fact, some passages in the Bible suggest that our tongues are quite powerful, having the ability to speak life and death into the people and situations around us. This is no magic trick, of course; if our words could conjure up whatever we wished for, we'd speak a lot of things into being. But what if, over the course of time, our words had the ability to prophesy truth and declare reality into the world around us? What if we have been given the responsibility of declaring truth again and again and reinforcing it in our lives? What if God has endowed our words with power?

He has, according to Scripture, and though we could debate how far to take this verbal ministry, our words are at least supposed to line up with our faith, and our faith tends to line up with our words. That being true, we have an opportunity to speak life and truth to our world.

Don't waste that opportunity on the obvious, declaring what your natural eyes see. Anyone can do that, and it simply entrenches visible reality in your life. Instead, call things that are not as though they are. Declare what you see with eyes of faith. When you do, you bring the promises and purposes of God into the world, the unseen and hoped for (Hebrews 11:1) into the realm of the seen and experienced. Our words bridge the gap between the invisible and the visible and invite God's plans into our lives.

Take my lips, and let them be filled with messages from Thee.

FRANCES HAVERGAL

Talk to Your Mountains

*I tell you the truth, you can say to this mountain, "May you be
lifted up and thrown into the sea," and it will happen.* **MARK 11:23**

YOU'VE ENCOUNTERED MOUNTAINS. They stand in your way, seem
immovable, and threaten to thwart God's purposes for your life. Still, Jesus said to
speak to them in faith. He pointed to a specific mountain—likely Herod's palace, a
man-made mountain representing the ways of this world—and told his disciples such
monstrosities could be cast into the sea. All it would take is faith and words, the same
kind of commands God spoke at Creation with every "Let there be . . ." According
to Jesus, we were designed with a capacity to issue orders in his name.

Most of us haven't experienced the fullness of that promise. Then again, most
of us haven't tried, at least not with persistence. Few of us have really explored the
certainty of faith that is aligned with God's purposes and spoken it over our mountains as Jesus did when he calmed storms and commanded healing. But that doesn't
mean we shouldn't believe it's possible. If Jesus said we have this ability, then it means
something. We have every reason, even the obligation as his followers, to find out
what this kind of certainty looks like.

As you explore the meaning of Jesus' promise, learn to be very intentional about
cultivating your faith and then lining up your words with it. Don't just think what
you believe; speak it out. You don't have to broadcast your expectations to everyone
you meet, but you should at least make sure your conversations are consistent with
the things you are praying for. When we pray one thing and then utter negative
words about the possibility later, we are betraying our own beliefs. The life of faith
aligns our vision with our faith and words and actions. The synchronization is
powerful. The more we bring every element of our faith life together, the more we
find out just how powerful it can be. And the more we see unyielding mountains
beginning to move.

Prayer is a powerful thing, for God has bound and tied himself thereto.

MARTIN LUTHER

Without a Doubt

*You must really believe it will happen and have
no doubt in your heart.*   **MARK 11:23**

VIRTUALLY ALL CHRISTIANS have had the experience of praying for something and not seeing it come to pass. Yet most Christians can also recall very few times praying for something with every fiber of their being and declaring it to be true with absolute certainty. Is there a connection between these two statements? Probably. Jesus didn't just talk about faith as an idea and treat it as wishful thinking. Neither did he refer to it generally as a system of thought or belief in God's existence. He spoke as if faith were a substance, just as Hebrews 11:1 does—a reality, something concrete, a certainty in the spirit about things in the unseen realm. And as Jesus and his disciples stood in front of the withered fig tree that he had cursed the day before, he told them that speaking to their mountains would not accomplish anything unless they had no doubt.

Far too many Christians beat themselves up for not having enough faith when they pray for a person's healing and that person remains sick, or for being ineffective in ministry though they have worked and believed the best they could. After all, this same Jesus who spoke about the importance of having no doubt was quite generous earlier with a man who said he believed but then asked Jesus to help his unbelief (Mark 9:24). Still, there is power in living, speaking, and acting with absolute certainty in what we believe and what God is doing in the spiritual realm. Prayers are answered. Mountains move. God loves that kind of confidence and has wired his world and his people to move forward in it. Creation is rigged in favor of faith.

Learn to discern the difference between presumption and faith. When you know you're walking in faith, do it all the way. Root out those little voices of unbelief, those hints of doubt that question whether you really know your God. Pray for faith to believe, and then pray for the thing you're believing for. You were created to move mountains—and circumstances and people—by the certainty in your spirit.

Turn from your doubts with horror, as you would from blasphemy.

HANNAH WHITALL SMITH

Irrelevant Details

Caleb tried to quiet the people as they stood before Moses. "Let's go at once to take the land," he said. "We can certainly conquer it!"
NUMBERS 13:30

GOD HAD TOLD MOSES to send spies into the Promised Land to scout it out. So Moses gave twelve men specific instructions, which included gathering information but *nothing* about trying to assess whether entering the land was doable. Nevertheless, all but two came back with a negative report, spreading fear about how the people in the land were big and hostile and the towns were fortified. Sure, the land was fruitful and pleasant, but what good would that be if it couldn't be conquered? The ten discouraging spies had forgotten that the Promised Land had already been promised to them. They lost sight of their assignment and instead questioned God's ability to fulfill his words. After all they had seen in the Exodus, they still didn't get it. They became the prime example of what not to do and how not to respond to a promise from God.

Two men, Caleb and Joshua, had a different spirit. They didn't doubt God's willingness, since he had given the promise in the first place, and they didn't question his ability to do what he had said. God was both willing and able, and that was enough. It didn't matter how big the people were, how strong the city walls were, or how contentious some of their past run-ins with these people had been. When God gives a promise, none of the details matter to the heart of faith. The mind has no business questioning what God has said he is going to do. The responsibility is on him to carry it out, and a follower's responsibility is simply to believe and follow.

We forget that sometimes. The words of the serpent in Eden echo in our minds: "Did God really say . . . ?" (Genesis 3:1). Sometimes we convince ourselves he didn't. Sometimes we still believe he did but convince ourselves that there are extenuating circumstances, details that make the promise untrue, things perhaps God hadn't accounted for. That was the perspective of the ten skeptical spies, and we must refuse it. When God promises something, it's a promise. Believe it, live it, and move forward—no matter what you see in the land ahead.

The ultimate ground of faith and knowledge is confidence in God.
CHARLES HODGE

Conditioned on Faith

[The LORD said,] "Not one of these people will ever enter that land. . . .
None of those who have treated me with contempt will ever see it."
NUMBERS 14:22-23

GOD'S PEOPLE HAD BEEN DELIVERED from severe oppression in Egypt through a dramatic rescue involving deadly plagues, a pursuing army, and a miraculously parted sea. God gave them food and drink in a barren and dry wilderness, protected them from attacks, and sent them in the direction of their land of promise. The entire objective centered on serving and worshiping God and having a place of their own. But when the time came to enter the land, they didn't worship or believe the place could be their own. In spite of all they had seen, almost all of the Hebrew people implicitly assumed God could not fulfill his promise.

That attitude tends to develop in our lives in subtle ways. Few believers, then or now, would directly state that God can't fulfill his promises, but our thoughts and actions essentially make that case against him. We pray for direction and assurances, and we receive them clearly, yet we still talk about obstacles and challenges that could make our situations impossible. We read of "great and precious promises" (2 Peter 1:4) and follow them up with "yes, but . . . ," as if God's promises are contingent on circumstances or "realistic" possibilities. We list pros and cons even after he has given us guidance, as if any pros or cons make a difference in how he guides. We undermine our own faith without even realizing we're doing it.

That attitude has devastating repercussions. Many of God's promises are conditional, and faith is usually the primary condition. When he has given a clear promise or clear direction, none of the details we see have anything to do with whether that promise or direction is true. When we talk and act as if they do, we are, from God's perspective, treating him "with contempt." He takes it personally. As his followers, our job is to prioritize what he has said above all else—above giant obstacles, impossible defenses, or any other lie standing in the way of our promised land. His word trumps all others, and when we attach our faith to it, problems and obstacles must bow before his will.

All unbelief is the belief of a lie.

HORATIUS BONAR

A Different Attitude

[The LORD said,] "My servant Caleb has a different attitude
than the others have. He has remained loyal to me, so I will bring
him into the land he explored. His descendants will possess
their full share of that land." **NUMBERS 14:24**

CALEB AND JOSHUA WERE THE ONLY TWO SPIES of the twelve who
believed in the promise—or at least who believed that it wasn't contingent on
whether they could defeat giants and destroy their city walls. In other words, they
believed God could fulfill his word regardless of what circumstances looked like.
And for that, they were commended. They were also given entrance to this land forty
years later—Joshua as the leader and Caleb as an old but vigorous man of faith. In
fact, Caleb was positively singled out for having a "different attitude," a spirit that
energized him to follow God fully. He entered into the land because he believed.

That's how faith is rewarded. Centuries later, the writer of Hebrews urged his
congregation of Jewish Christians to persist in their faith and not fall away from the
promises God had given them in Christ. He wrote about the Israelites' time in the
wilderness, when many of God's people were skeptical of his power and fell away.
He told them not to let their hearts be hardened—a process that makes us resistant
to faith—but to press ahead and believe. He assured them that the way to inherit
God's promises is through "faith and endurance" (Hebrews 6:12). Or, to describe it
like Caleb, through maintaining a different spirit from the people around us.

Faith does not conform to the world's ways or people's expectations. If we want to
be people of faith who inherit God's promises—who actually enter into the promised
lands he has laid before us—we will have to maintain a different attitude. That means
when people talk pessimistically, we don't join in. When headlines scream about the
crises that are coming, we envision a hope and a glorious future. When our own
hearts get discouraged, we find ways to strengthen them in the Lord. We persist in
swimming upstream, against the culture, and into the promises of God. Because in
the end, faith wins and God is pleased with it.

Faith is the victory! Oh, glorious victory that overcomes the world.

JOHN H. YATES

Suddenly

Pharaoh said to Joseph, "See, I have set you over all the land of Egypt." **GENESIS 41:41,** ESV

JOSEPH HAD WAITED YEARS for God to fulfill his promises to him. He had been told of future glory, but everything that happened from that moment forward seemed to send him in the opposite direction—into an existence with no glory at all. Sold into slavery, imprisoned unjustly, and forgotten by those who promised to put in a good word for him, Joseph was in a place of little hope.

He surely must have wondered why nothing had worked out. Yet while Joseph was seemingly moving away from God's purposes for him, he was actually moving toward them. When the time came, he was elevated from prison to Pharaoh's court in a single day. The promise—or at least the early evidence of it—was suddenly fulfilled. His prayers had certainly been heard long before, but only after years of waiting did he receive any indication of God answering. All he had was an old promise and trust that God was with him.

That's often how God's promises and our faith work together. They break through suddenly. With God, of course, *suddenlies* are years in the making, but to us they appear out of the blue. They sometimes break into our experience long after we first prayed and possibly even after we've forgotten we prayed. They show up when we least expect them—even though by faith we are supposed to be expecting them. They remind us that prayers are like seeds that sometimes grow up imperceptibly and then bloom overnight.

Don't get discouraged by the waiting. Remember that we inherit God's promises by faith and patience (Hebrews 6:12). The blessings of his Kingdom usually grow before they appear, like bowls being slowly filled with incense. The answers come both suddenly and in the fullness of time, long in the making and yet surprising when finally made. He has not forgotten any promise he's ever given, and many of your prayers are still on his heart to fulfill. In one way or another, in this age or the age to come, you will be satisfied.

The permanence of God's character guarantees the fulfillment of his promises.

A. W. PINK

Righteous Faith

The Scriptures tell us, "Abraham believed God, and God counted him as righteous because of his faith." **ROMANS 4:3**

ABRAHAM IS THE FATHER OF FAITH, the biblical template for what it looks like to receive a promise from God, believe it, and wait it out until fulfillment comes. His story is more complicated than it often seems in our retellings, but in many cases his life gives us a model to follow. God had told Abraham something specific, and a journey of faith began.

God still gives promises, of course. Important promises are threaded throughout the pages of Scripture, and we who believe stake our lives on them. There are people who insist that all of God's promises in Christ are about a spiritual salvation and nothing else or that every promise God gives must be identified in a specific chapter and verse—that personal promises are a thing of the past and only general ones remain. It's true that his promises fit within the wonderful, overarching story of redemption, and that biblical promises are anchor points he uses as foundations for everything we believe. But Abraham was declared righteous for receiving a promise about something other than spiritual salvation: a child. His promise fit within a larger context of God's plan of revealing himself through a chosen people, establishing his Kingdom, restoring this world to his original design, and reigning forever with all who have believed in him. But it was personal. He was declared righteous for something other than believing a general redemptive plan.

Our promises will fit that larger context too. But like Abraham's, they include matters both of the spirit and of practical daily life. They are oriented toward God's overall purposes for us, but they incorporate lots of personal and experiential steps along the way. Our dreams, desires, and prayers need to fit into the big picture, but the fulfillment of them still involves personal touches from God in our here-and-now life. Will we seek them out and believe them? That's the journey of faith. We interact with a God who walks with us personally, guiding us into his will. Righteous are those who believe him.

> God is the great reality. . . . His promises are real
> and glorious, beyond our wildest dreams.
>
> J. B. PHILLIPS

Promises Received

The promise is received by faith. **ROMANS 4:16**

GOD GIVES MANY PROMISES IN SCRIPTURE—promises for salvation, prayer, spiritual strength, relationships, children, health, material blessing, the battles we face, the presence and power of his Spirit, and much more. So why aren't more people experiencing them? Why is so much of our theology built around exceptions and conditions to these promises rather than their fulfillment? Why do we so often wonder what we're missing?

We forget that promises are of no use unless they are received. And the only way to receive God's promises is by faith. We can only experience what we actually believe we will experience. That doesn't mean God's promises are magic, and it doesn't mean that everyone who prays for health and isn't healed, or who prays for protection and has an accident, was lacking in faith. No theology condensed to fit a human brain is big enough to explain everything that happens. But we do know that those who stake their faith on what God has said will find his promises working their way into their experience far more often than those who can't get past the doubts and questioning. Radical faith tends to result in radical testimonies; waiting for God to do whatever he will do generally doesn't.

The bottom line is that God's promises are invitations to step more fully and boldly into our relationship with him. They will stretch us, the adventure may last a while, and we will need to remain in dialogue with him. But God did not give his promises for us to see them as faint hopes. He gave them to us to base our journey on. They are cues for direction, encouragement for trying times, rallying points for persistence, and ultimately testimonies of his faithfulness. Abraham spent years in questioning, receiving further clarification, and setting his eyes on visual illustrations God had given him. He and his wife both laughed as the time neared. But they ended up anchoring their hopes in what God had said, and it happened. When we anchor our hopes there too, we find him faithful. The fruit of his promises fills our lives according to the seeds of faith we have allowed into our hearts.

Faith is to believe what you do not see;
the reward for this faith is to see what you believe.

AUGUSTINE

Against All Hope

Even when there was no reason for hope, Abraham kept hoping.

ROMANS 4:18

GOD PROMISED ABRAHAM DESCENDANTS when he and his wife were already at an unreasonable age to have children. Then God waited another twenty-five years before doing anything about it. On the surface, that seems cruel. God could have fulfilled the promise right away or waited to tell Abraham about it days before the time of fulfillment, sparing him all those years of painful anticipation. But Abraham was given something to envision, plan on, hope for, and wait for—for two and a half decades. We can hardly fault him for wrestling, for the questions he asked during the process, for the ways he wondered how the promise was to be fulfilled. After all, God had not told him up front how it would happen. Why not assume other culturally appropriate ways of fulfillment? Abraham did, and he was wrong. He simply had to wait, question whether he had been faithful enough, get stretched beyond belief, and then come back to what God had said. He went through an excruciating process.

That's quite a disorienting position, yet God puts us in it often. He gives us promises, hopes, visions, dreams, a quiet "yes" to our prayers—and then waits. Sometimes those promises take years, decades, possibly even generations to fulfill. They rarely play out right away.

You may find yourself in the awkward position of having a "yes" from God while living long seasons in an apparent "no." You'll have a choice to make. Are you going to reason your way out of the yes, question whether you've been disqualified from receiving it somewhere along the way, or simply lose heart? Or are you going to choose hope anyway? Against all hope, Abraham chose hope. When believing became difficult, he still believed. He did question, and he did have some ups and downs. But they were all part of the journey of faith. Long delays and adverse circumstances are part of that journey because that's how God gives us eyes for eternity and conforms us to Kingdom ways. Know that, reconcile your heart with it, and then choose hope. Even against all hope, believe.

When a train goes through a tunnel and it gets dark, you don't throw away your ticket and jump off. You sit still and trust the engineer.

CORRIE TEN BOOM

Unwavering Faith

Abraham never wavered in believing God's promise. In fact, his faith grew stronger, and in this he brought glory to God. **ROMANS 4:20**

ABRAHAM RECEIVED AN ASTOUNDING PROMISE—he and his offspring would be made into a great nation (Genesis 12:1-3). But years went by, and Abraham began to wonder how the promise would be fulfilled. Would it be through a servant, as inheritance customs often worked? No, God told him it would be through his own offspring (Genesis 15:4). Would it be through his wife's servant—another customary way of keeping inheritance in the family? No, it would be through Abraham's own wife, well past her prime, a miracle beyond reasonable expectation (Genesis 16:1-3; 17:15-16). Abraham laughed (Genesis 17:17), and when the promise was just a year from fulfillment, Sarah laughed too (Genesis 18:9-12). It was absurd, after all. Who would believe it? But Abraham and Sarah received into their hearts what God had spoken, and he followed through by giving them a son.

Later biblical testimonies call this winding, up-and-down journey of faith "not wavering." From our standpoint, Abraham and Sarah seemed to waver quite a bit. At one point, they had so given up their expectations that they laughed at the idea that they might be fulfilled. But God judges human faith not by the detours it took during the journey but by where it ended up. Did it last? That's unwavering faith. It persists no matter how much it is assaulted by visible evidence and may even grow stronger the more unlikely fulfillment seems. God's assessment of faith like that is that it is as solid and pure as gold that has been tried and purged by fire.

If you endure in faith, you will run into similar dynamics at times. Not every faith experience is so demanding, but some are. At times, you may grow discouraged by how weak and faltering your faith seems to be. Never mind your own assessment; God is more focused on where your faith arrives than where it travels in the middle chapters of your story. He is purifying something precious, drawing you closer in the meantime, and anticipating a joyful end. Anticipate it with him, and your faith will be called unwavering.

It is when the answer to prayer does not come . . .
that the trial of faith, more precious than gold, takes place.

ANDREW MURRAY

Tested Faith

Until what he had said came to pass, the word of the LORD tested him.

PSALM 105:19, ESV

ABRAHAM'S GREAT-GRANDSON JOSEPH experienced a similar gap between receiving a promise and seeing its fulfillment, but Joseph faced much more adverse circumstances. God had given him dreams of one day being in a position of authority and his brothers bowing down to him. But Joseph unwisely shared those dreams with his brothers, who were already jealous of him. Not long afterward, they threw him into the bottom of a pit and then sold him to a caravan passing by. Joseph ended up in slavery in Egypt, was later falsely accused of a crime, and seemed to have been forgotten in prison well over a decade after God's promise had been given. Everything seemed to be going in the opposite direction of fulfillment.

But everything was actually moving *toward* fulfillment. Joseph simply couldn't have known it based on visible circumstances. He was left to wonder. Had he made an unredeemable mistake in telling his brothers his dreams? Had he disqualified himself somehow? Had God reneged on the promise? Was it ever a promise to begin with or just a random dream? When a promise has been planted in our spirit, these questions and more inevitably swirl around in our hearts and minds. We think they demonstrate a lack of faith, but they are part of the process. Our faith is being stretched, pulled, bent, pressed, and turned in all sorts of directions, seemingly ready to break but also being prepared to endure and eventually break through. Faith that is tested is faith that stands strong. That's what the Kingdom is built on.

Like Joseph, you may find that the fulfillment of your promise looks very different from what you could have imagined. You may also find yourself in some really dark places along the way. It's fine to ask God questions in those dark seasons; this is a time of drawing close to him and learning to discern his voice. He may even rearrange your expectations while keeping the promise intact. Follow him on that journey. Let yourself be stretched, no matter how uncomfortable it feels. The word of the Lord is being rooted deeply into your spirit, where it was designed to flourish.

The body has two eyes, but the soul must have but one.

WILLIAM SECKER

Praying from Victory

He disarmed the spiritual rulers and authorities. He shamed them
publicly by his victory over them on the cross. **COLOSSIANS 2:15**

MANY CHRISTIANS HAVE BEEN TRAINED TO PRAY as if trying to obtain a victory in their petitions. That isn't a wrong perspective; many victories are won on our knees. But neither is it the whole story. In fact, one of the reasons we pray in Jesus' name is that he has already won the victory. He isn't trying to become the King; he already is. And we aren't trying to gain a victory in our relationship with him; we can simply enter into the victory he has already gained. Our prayers are not trying to establish a new truth; they are anchored in the truth of what already is. We just need to claim his victory rather than plead for it.

This is one of many examples of our call to Kingdom thinking. There's a reason we're told to renew our minds; we have to learn to think like members of a royal priesthood. If we want to inherit the Kingdom of God—not simply experience salvation but the full range of Kingdom realities—we have to train ourselves to think in Kingdom ways. That means praying often *from* victory rather than *for* it.

Learn to shift from prayers of wishful thinking to prayers of victory. Pray with full knowledge that the battle has already been won. You will be praying into effect a victory that is already real but simply needs to be made manifest. Jesus gave us the basis for this kind of prayer when he declared his death and resurrection as the time when Satan would be cast out (John 12:31). He disarmed spiritual adversaries and authorities. He handed the keys of the Kingdom to his followers. He told us to pray in his name—the name of the victor who is seated above every other authority and power. We are there with him, in victory, with petitions on our lips. We pray as those whose answers have already been won.

We tread the road the saints above with shouts of triumph trod. . . .
The faith by which they conquered death is still our shining shield.

JOHN H. YATES

Powerless and Powerful

We are powerless against this mighty army that is about to attack us.
We do not know what to do, but we are looking to you for help.

2 CHRONICLES 20:12

KING JEHOSHAPHAT AND THE PEOPLE OF JUDAH were surrounded by a coalition of armies. They were sitting ducks, powerless against a force that vastly outnumbered them. But instead of surrendering or losing heart and waiting for defeat, they cried out to God. Jehoshaphat expressed their vulnerability—and their faith—perfectly: "We are powerless. . . . We don't know what to do, but we are looking to you for help."

That may not seem like the best place to be, but it's an extremely strong position. Those worries that cause us to lose sleep may do a number on our sense of security, but they actually put us right where we need to be—if we let them. They take us into the fortress of our Father, where he has promised to protect us. He doesn't necessarily shield us from every battle, and we don't always win in the short term. But we do always overcome. In the end, we are supported and strengthened by the God who promised to defend us.

If you've ever wondered what to do with your concerns—how to move from saying you have faith to actually having it—this is it. It's one thing to know he is watching out for you, but it's another to actually trust him to do so. Simply expressing your worries to God may help in the moment, but not for long. Actively declaring your own insufficiency while honoring God for his complete sufficiency begins a shift in your mind. Trust begins to grow. Faith begins to flourish. The inner condition of the heart begins to strengthen as the knowledge and presence of God fills it. Your worries begin to wither and die.

Everyone wants that, but few know how to get there. Your starting point is to stop trying to be self-reliant and to begin owning up to your weaknesses. Then step into God's strength. Tell him the next step is up to him. You may have to take it, but that's his call. He already knows the solution. Invite him into the problem. Our powerlessness is a perfect match for his power.

The way to grow strong in Christ is to become weak in yourself.

CHARLES SPURGEON

Responsibly Not Responsible

*Don't be discouraged by this mighty army, for the battle
is not yours, but God's.* **2 CHRONICLES 20:15**

THE PEOPLE OF JUDAH HAD GATHERED at the Temple in Jerusalem to fast and pray for deliverance. That's not always what happens when God's people get together in the midst of adversity. Sometimes they complain, lament, share their fears, and cultivate a spirit of dread. But this group had gathered to seek God—and God spoke. A prophetic voice pierced the air with an encouraging word: *Don't be afraid, don't get discouraged, and don't own the battle. It's not yours; it belongs to God.*

Relinquishing your battles to God can be a difficult process. *Saying* you are giving them to him is not difficult. Actually letting go of them is. But when you turn your battles over to God, they are no longer on your to-do list. God may still ask you to be involved, but the responsibility of victory is on him. He's calling the shots, and he owns the outcome. The burden is no longer on your shoulders. You can relinquish the weight of it to him.

That may feel irresponsible, but it's actually liberating, and God has fully authorized this freedom. It's never a mistake to give him leadership in your life. You are more irresponsible when you try to handle on your own the things he has promised to carry. Moses told the Israelites to stand still and see God deliver them through the parted sea; God told David when and when not to go into battle; and Jesus accomplished salvation for us. In this case, God told Jehoshaphat that this battle was not the king's or army's responsibility. You have every reason to follow the same pattern and let him fight for you. In your actions, you may need to put yourself on the battlefield. In your spirit, you can rest completely in him.

Turn your battles over to God and then disown them. Yes, you'll still be interested in the outcome, but you won't have to make sure it happens. Your Father is fighting for you while you keep your eyes and heart on him. There is no better position to be in. He may allow battles to come, but he never loses the ones we've given to him.

The more we depend on God, the more dependable we find he is.

CLIFF RICHARD

Worshipful War

At the very moment they began to sing and give praise, the LORD
caused the armies of Ammon, Moab, and Mount Seir to start
fighting among themselves. **2 CHRONICLES 20:22**

IT HAD TO GO AGAINST EVERY INSTINCT of the kingdom's warriors. No one sends the worship choir into battle ahead of the soldiers. Such a bizarre tactic is an open admission of vulnerability, an invitation for the enemy to gain the upper hand. It could have been seen as an act of suicide. But instead it was an expression of priorities and a statement of faith. When Jehoshaphat sent singers into the battlefield, he was trusting what God had said. The people were willing to put that trust on the line.

Our anxieties, fears, and doubts are powerful. They take control of our lives and choke the attitudes of the Kingdom out of us. It's hard to grow faith, hope, love, and joy in a stressed, discouraged heart. We let our mental soundtracks play the same worrisome suggestions over and over again, and gratitude for our blessings rarely comes to mind. Worshiping is the last thing we feel like doing in a season of adversity.

Yet these are the attitudes that transform us from within and change the atmosphere around us. When we send the "singers" out first in our lives, right into the midst of adversity, we are making a statement of faith: God is our priority, we worship him above all else, and our battles are no longer ours. We are choosing no longer to see our problems as big and our God as small; we are flipping the script in our hearts and staking our welfare on his ability to handle everything. We are believing he is greater than our fears.

One of the best ways to live an overcoming lifestyle in the journey of faith is to worship God in the area of your fears, doubts, anxieties, and needs. If you are in a financial crisis, worship God for his ability to provide. When you are in pain, worship him for his healing touch. If it's truly worship, it's not manipulation. It's a declaration of faith that changes our lives on two fronts: the condition of our hearts and the situations we face. God enters into the worship, and our transformation begins.

A life in thankfulness releases the glory of God.

BENGT SUNDBERG

Another Climate Change

*Should I not have concern for the great city of Nineveh, in which there
are more than a hundred and twenty thousand people who cannot
tell their right hand from their left?* **JONAH 4:11,** NIV

EVAN ROBERTS HAD LONG PRAYED for a move of God in Wales, even as a
youth. When he preached at a series of meetings in 1905 at the age of twenty-seven,
things began to happen. Social problems and vices greatly diminished, and court
dockets rapidly reduced. People gathered with expectancy. Many publicly confessed
their sins, and conversions multiplied into the tens of thousands in what became
known as the Welsh revival. An entire region was changed, and the revival influenced
many other cities and regions around the world.

God is able to change the spiritual atmosphere of entire cities and regions through
the prayers and service of his people. God changed the city of Nineveh through a
call to repentance, even after his prophet, Jonah, initially resisted giving the message. Through prayer and fasting, the evil agenda of Haman was turned into a great
opportunity and promotion for the Jews of ancient Persia in the book of Esther.
Peter healed a man in Lydda, and seemingly the entire city turned to the Lord (Acts
9:32-35). And countries like South Korea, provinces in China, cities in the United
States, regions of Africa, and many other places have seen revival in response to
concerted prayer. Through acts of faithfulness, backed in most cases by the prayers
of his people, God has transformed vast spiritual climates to be more open to him.

We can pray for our cities and regions knowing that God has compassion for
them. Sometimes such prayers go on for years before we see their fruit, but we can
trace virtually every mass spiritual awakening in history to small groups of believers who prayed intensely and persistently for God to move in their areas. Moments
of breakthrough often come with simple acts of obedience and declarations of the
Good News as catalysts, but those breakthroughs have been long in the making. God
moves human hearts, human prayers call out for God's intervention, and power falls.
Whenever we lament the condition of our world, we must pray diligently for God
to move in it.

Secret prayer is the springtime of life.

EVAN ROBERTS

The Strength of Joy

Don't be dejected and sad, for the joy of the LORD is your strength!

NEHEMIAH 8:10

WHEN THE JEWS WHO HAD BEEN EXILED throughout the kingdom of Persia returned to Jerusalem, it took decades to rebuild. More than a century after the city was destroyed, the walls were completed, and the community rededicated itself to God's law. But when the law was read at the dedication ceremony—it had to be interpreted for many who no longer understood Hebrew—the people began to weep. They were overcome with regret for having fallen so far from God's standards. They realized how much they had lost, to the extent that Nehemiah had to remind them of what they had gained. Regret is not a Kingdom value; the joy of the Lord was their strength.

We live in a Kingdom of joy and thrive only when we allow joy to become our dominant attitude. We shouldn't put on a fake smile to falsely present how spiritual we are; that's hypocrisy. But becoming like God, we learn to have joy even while we work, solve problems, or grieve. We root ourselves in the ultimate certainties of the Kingdom. We bless our enemies with joy, pray for difficult situations with joy, enter into our battles with joy, think about tomorrow with joy, and do everything else we need to do with hearts full of rejoicing and praise. In fact, we have to if we want to experience the climate of the Kingdom in our lives. This is what it's all about.

It's wonderful when the evidence of God's work is easy to see in our lives—when our prayers are answered, he supernaturally intervenes, and we feel the fullness and abundance of his *shalom*. But if we're searching for those things with hearts full of frustration, discouragement, bitterness, regret, and doubt, we may have to wait a long time. The climate of the Kingdom is joy, and the fruit of the Kingdom depends on it.

As you pray, pursue joy. Saturate your life in it. Let your faith be rooted in its rich soil and see what grows. It's room temperature in God's Kingdom, regardless of what your outward circumstances look like. Your life, your prayers, and your faith flourish because the joy of the Lord is your strength.

Joy is the serious business of heaven.

C. S. LEWIS

The God of Hope

"I know the plans I have for you," says the LORD. "They are plans
for good and not for disaster, to give you a future and a hope."
JEREMIAH 29:11

IMAGINE TALKING WITH GOD about a really discouraging problem and suddenly hearing his audible voice agreeing with you: *"Yes, this one is challenging. I'm not sure what to do about it. It's beyond me."* Absurd, right? God is never discouraged, never hopeless, never at a loss for a solution. He sees the end of things from their beginning, he knows every option, and he opens doors and makes a way where there seemed to be no way at all. He never wrings his hands over a problem, and he never loses heart.

That may seem obvious to us. Not many who believe in God would suggest he gets stressed out like we do. But if he is full of hope, certainty, solutions, and redemptive ways, what are we suggesting when we are full of discouragement, uncertainty, and anxiety? If God is never discouraged over our lives and we are, aren't we disagreeing with him? Something in our perspective is not lining up with his. It makes little sense to believe in a God of hope and continue to feel hopeless.

We can take comfort in the fact that if we saw God's perspective at any given moment, we would be greatly encouraged. If he knows the good plans he has for us, then getting a glimpse of those plans—or even trusting in them while they remain unseen—would relieve all our concerns. We could be sure our prayers are accomplishing something in the spirit and moving him to intervene. We could know the outcome is something we will celebrate. We could embrace the hope he gives us without second-guessing it.

Go ahead and do that. Choose not to be discouraged. Admit that you don't see the whole picture and agree with God that if you did, you would recognize how good it is. Hope is not based on understanding how everything works out. It's trusting that it does. He is the God of hope. You can live with the expectation of his goodness in every area of your life.

Everything that is done in the world is done by hope.

MARTIN LUTHER

Stubborn Faith

"Dear woman," Jesus said to her, "your faith is great. Your request is granted." And her daughter was instantly healed. **MATTHEW 15:28**

A GENTILE WOMAN PLEADED WITH JESUS to help her tormented daughter, and the compassionate Son of God did not say a word. Even in the face of her cries, he kept his silence. The disciples, bothered by her persistence, tried to send her away. She would have been the only person in the Gospels who came to Jesus for healing or deliverance and didn't receive it.

Jesus eventually reminded the woman of his immediate mission—to save the lost sheep of Israel—and that she wasn't part of it. But she was not deterred and kept pleading. He told her bluntly that Gentiles were considered dogs—a common term Jews used for non-Jews. And rather than objecting, she accepted the label. She pressed in. She had a need, and he was the only one who could address it. Finally Jesus answered, but not with a rebuke. He called her "dear" and commended her for her faith.

How could Jesus be silent in the face of a desperate plea? Why did he take so long to answer? We often ask such questions, and the answer is probably similar to the answer we see in this story: Jesus lets the drama of faith play out. Real faith persists through impossibilities, obstacles, objections, or even insults. Real faith recognizes God's nature against all visible circumstances and says, "I know who you are. I know you're good, even if I can't see your goodness right now." Real faith endures until the answer comes. And what once looked like God's reluctance turns out to be his compassion. He was waiting for outward evidence of our unwavering trust.

The prayer of faith is not easily turned away. It may be bothersome to the people who hear it. But God invites it. Like a neighbor banging on a door at midnight (Luke 11:5-8), a woman pestering a judge (Luke 18:1-5), or a Gentile insisting on the goodness of a Jewish Messiah, keep on asking, seeking, and knocking. Good things come to those who won't be persuaded that God is silent, distant, or unmoving. Stubborn faith is rewarded with his blessing.

> Battering the gates of heaven with storms of prayer.
>
> ALFRED TENNYSON

Faith That Persists

One day Jesus told his disciples a story to show that they
should always pray and never give up.   LUKE 18:1

JESUS TOLD A PARABLE about a widow and an unjust judge. She wanted justice—rightness, goodness, the fullness of God's will in an adverse situation—and the judge ignored her. But she kept pestering him until he relented. He wasn't concerned about her situation; he just wanted her to stop. Her persistence led him to act in her favor in the end.

God isn't an unjust judge, and he doesn't ignore our requests. Still, this hypothetical situation illustrates a need for persistence in our prayers. Where we might think we are pestering God, Jesus says to go ahead and pester him. Where we might think we are presuming on his goodness, Jesus says to go ahead and presume. And where we might wonder why God doesn't answer after a first request, Jesus says to cry out day and night. These attitudes—these persistent, enduring, even pesky approaches to our Father—are called faith. And Jesus wonders if he will find it on earth when he returns.

The whole point of Jesus' parable was to encourage his disciples to "always pray and never give up." Like the Gentile woman in Matthew 15 who kept asking Jesus to heal her daughter, we are urged to look past silences, apparent rejections, the raised eyebrows of people around us, and the seeming inappropriateness of our requests to see the God who is encouraging us to come closer and deeper into his will and open arms. He never promises he will answer our prayers exactly as we envision them. But he does promise to answer them. His goal fits very well with ours. We both want to see his purposes, his goodness, and the fullness of his will established on earth—even in the details of our lives.

People living in a microwave society are not conditioned for such persistence, but it's a dynamic of God's Kingdom in this world. Embrace it and exercise it. Keep pressing in. Allow God to shape your prayers, but don't just let go of them. They demonstrate the kind of faith he loves to reward.

> Persistent praying never faints or grows weary. . . . It declines
> to rise from its knees until an answer is received.
>
> E. M. BOUNDS

Breakthrough Within

Then your salvation will come like the dawn. . . . When you call,
the LORD will answer. "Yes, I am here," he will quickly reply.
Remove the heavy yoke of oppression. **ISAIAH 58:8-9**

ISAIAH WROTE TO PEOPLE who were praying, fasting, and pleading with God for a breakthrough in their circumstances. They asked God to take action but only from a distance, "pretending" they wanted to be close with him (58:2). In other words, they were focusing on the appearance of their relationship with God rather than on the relationship itself. But Isaiah pointed them toward inner change that would result in outward change. He brought them in line with their true identity as children of God and how that identity should play out in the world.

Isaiah was addressing a specific situation, but a larger principle was at work, and it applies to our prayers too. We are often looking to God for a breakthrough in faith, some movement on a promise or desire he has said yes to. But just because God has given his approval doesn't mean everything is ready to unfold. We never have to earn his gifts, but we do have to position ourselves for them. Like a father who won't hand over the keys of the car until his son or daughter has learned how to drive, God rarely brings us into the next season of faith and growth until we're prepared to handle it. The breakthrough we hope for is very often germinating inside us, preparing for its outward display.

If you've been waiting for God to fulfill a desire and are wondering why he's hesitating, you need to know that he is as interested in the outcome as you are. He is always excited about fulfilling the callings he has put in your heart. But internal breakthroughs almost always precede external ones, and fulfilling your inward calling is of most importance. He is rooting your heart in something other than the circumstances you hope for. Let your heart grow in the directions he has called. Delight in him and anticipate his goodness. Let the dawn break within you before it appears to the outside world.

> To want all that God wants . . . this is the kingdom of God.
>
> FRANÇOIS FÉNELON

Always God's Will

Always be joyful. Never stop praying. Be thankful in all circumstances,
for this is God's will for you who belong to Christ Jesus.

1 THESSALONIANS 5:16-18

MULTITUDES WRESTLE WITH FINDING God's will for their lives—where to go, what to do, who to be in relationship with, how to make a lasting difference in a needy world. These are important questions, of course, and God is eager to walk with us as we seek out the answers. He promises his wisdom and guidance. But we're missing something if we seek God's specific will for future direction without stopping and paying attention to the direction he has already clearly revealed. If we truly want to know his will for our lives, it begins here: "Always be joyful. Never stop praying. Be thankful in all circumstances." This is the climate of his Kingdom every moment of every day, and it's where he wants us to live.

Why is this important? Because prayer and faith flourish in a climate of joy and gratitude. That's why Paul sandwiches prayer between these twin attitudes of celebration in this verse. It's one thing to never stop praying out of despair, urgency, neediness, unworthiness, and lack. It's another to never stop praying out of joy, hope, gratitude, security, and fullness. God may graciously answer our desperate prayers, but he enters into our joyful and hopeful prayers with his presence. These prayers recognize who he is and what his Kingdom is like, and he joins the celebration.

If you've ever wondered whether it's realistic to give thanks in all circumstances and experience joy in the trials of life, here's the answer. God wouldn't tell us to do it if it couldn't be done. He has given us complete assurance that we can trust in him to guard our lives and provide for our needs. We are not immune from pain, but regardless of our experience, we can be sure we will never find ourselves beyond his reach. All of our experiences, mistakes, and pain are redeemable. We already know everything works out for our good and there is glory in the end. Prayer and faith flourish in hearts that choose to dwell in that assurance now, joyfully giving thanks.

> Joy flows right on through trouble. . . . It is an unceasing
> fountain bubbling up in the heart.
>
> D. L. MOODY

Envisioning Reality

Where there is no prophetic vision the people cast off restraint,
but blessed is he who keeps the law. PROVERBS 29:18, ESV

MEDIEVAL MONKS CONTEMPLATED THEMSELVES, their world, and God's Kingdom with two sets of senses: the physical and spiritual. They wrote of physical sight, sound, taste, touch, and smell but usually as prompts for corresponding spiritual senses. They sought to see, hear, taste, touch, and smell spiritually and talked about their spiritual vision as priority above all. They cultivated spiritual eyes so they could see eternal truths.

In a sense, that's what faith is—seeing with spiritual eyes. But faith is only part of our vision, which gives us a context for what we will believe and ask for in prayer. Proverbs 29:18 is not always easy to interpret, but at the very least it tells us that a life of vision—an understanding of what God is doing and where he is leading—keeps us on track. It points us in the right direction. God may adjust our vision from time to time, but he always wants us to have one. Jesus lived with vision; he went to the Cross because he knew God's purposes and saw the joy ahead of him (Hebrews 12:2). Paul lived with vision—an often adjusted one as far as his travels were concerned—and kept moving forward throughout his ministry to reach the Gentile world. The great leaders and prophets of Scripture were given the gift of spiritual sight, and they anchored their lives on what they saw. Why? Because vision not only shapes our lives; it shapes the world.

Never underestimate the power of your vision. Ask for it, cultivate it, refine it, saturate yourself in it, be motivated by it, but most of all, live it. Create your personal mission statement by envisioning your character, purpose, and work. Your vision will serve as a prophetic sense of destiny to drive you and draw you deeper and further into God's will for your life. It will tell you how to pray and empower your prayers with faith, expectation, and the certainty of divine hope. It will keep you anchored in the invisible realm and establish you as a vessel of eternal truth.

When God gives a vision, transact business
on that line, no matter what it costs.

OSWALD CHAMBERS

APRIL 18

The True You

You are a chosen people. You are royal priests, a holy nation, God's
very own possession. As a result, you can show others the goodness
of God, for he called you out of the darkness into his wonderful light.
1 PETER 2:9

IF YOU'VE EVER WATCHED KIDS playing sports, you've probably noticed an interesting phenomenon. They take on the characteristics of their favorite athlete—his or her demeanor, gestures, and attitude. It's human nature; we grow into the image of things we love and the models that have made an impression on us. It's easier to see in children, but it's true for all of us—we become what we behold.

Young athletes don't always become the stars they envision being, but they do develop the competitive and overcoming spirit they've seen in their heroes. A sense of identity has powerful effects, shaping almost everything about us. That's why our spiritual lives are absolutely dependent on the spiritual identity we've embraced. If we've envisioned ourselves as always being weak, sinful, incapable, and destined for futility, we will probably live out that vision. If we want to be fruitful for the Kingdom but are steeped in old and unfruitful thought patterns, we are cultivating conflicting visions. If we long for God to answer our prayers of faith but can't get past the memories of unanswered prayers in our hearts, our vision is compromised. If we know who we really are—chosen, beloved, a royal priesthood, God's own possession, called by his name and imbued with his character—we will grow into that vision. It all depends on what we see.

That's why Paul's letters usually begin with statements and blessings of identity before ever getting to the instructions. New instructions and inspiration have little effect when superimposed on old, false identities. You are a constantly renewed person, and old things have passed away (2 Corinthians 5:17). Above all else, cultivate the true you—not the one you feel, but the one God has revealed—and make it your foundational vision. You will grow into it, base your prayers and faith on it, and live powerfully from the eternal truth of what God has done.

> When we are born again, we all have visions, if we are
> spiritual at all, of what Jesus wants us to be.
> OSWALD CHAMBERS

Bold Visions

Your sons and daughters will prophesy. Your young men will
see visions, and your old men will dream dreams. ACTS 2:17

ON THE DAY OF PENTECOST, when some of the first believers in Jesus were gathered in one place, the Holy Spirit came upon them dramatically with visible signs and powerful effects. This outpouring created a scene that was a little difficult to interpret—the Spirit is good at that—so Peter offered some context. He quoted from the prophet Joel and implied that the "last days" had begun. The old and young, male and female, were entering into a new era of inspiration that by implication continues to this day: We dream dreams and have visions. We are granted insights from the Holy Spirit into what God is doing and how we can be part of it. We are participants in his Kingdom coming on earth.

Scripture is clear that we are to have a strong, motivating, life-shaping vision of our own identity in Christ as God's chosen and beloved people. Understanding who we are always precedes what we are called to do. Actions flow out of identity, so it's vital to be saturated in our true identity, to steep ourselves in God's love and be healed from past emotional and spiritual wounds. But we are also called to do things, and those things come out of the vision, dreams, and inspiration God has placed within us. If we are born of his Spirit, we have his Spirit's mission. We see through spiritual eyes. God gets things done by putting his heart and his desires inside of his people.

Knowing who you are is foundational in the life of faith. Seeing what God is calling you to do is the overflow. That vision involves big-picture purposes as well as the day-to-day protection and provision you need from him. It involves you and your loved ones and the larger world around you. In order to enter into a full, vibrant, powerful life of prayer and faith, you will need to learn to dream dreams and see visions. And you will need to let them drive you into the throne room of grace, where bold dreams and visions are validated, refined, and empowered.

When the Spirit of God comes into a man, he gives him a worldwide outlook.

OSWALD CHAMBERS

Single-Visioned

When you ask him, be sure that your faith is in God alone. Do not waver, for a person with divided loyalty is as unsettled as a wave of the sea that is blown and tossed by the wind. JAMES 1:6

JAMES HAS HARSH WORDS for double-mindedness. Most biblical writers do. In some cases, they are referring to split loyalties between God and the world, mixed priorities that pull us in two directions at once. Here James is referring to the prayer of faith—in this case a prayer for wisdom. Double-mindedness calls God's promise into question and undermines any expectation of receiving it. The literal translation is "two-souled," a person wavering between two expectations. *Will God give this or won't he? Is this promise valid or not? Can I expect him to come through or not?* It's a back-and-forth questioning of God's willingness to answer a prayer and provide what he's promised, and we find ourselves caught between the two extremes in many situations in life.

It's okay to question whether your vision for a specific situation is on target or not. That's part of our relationship with the God who has called us into his purposes. He wants us to sort out these situations. But that's not the same as having a clear vision and questioning it every time the situation changes, letting what's visible assert its authority over our faith, rising and falling with the waves of circumstance. No, we are to be anchored in eternal truths, our hopes fixed on what is unseen with eyes of flesh but seen with eyes of the spirit. When God promises something, all contrary evidence and objections are irrelevant. What matters is what he has said.

When God has given you vision for a certain area of your life, feel free to have plenty of conversations with him to confirm it, refine it, clarify it, and adjust it. But don't doubt it or blend it with competing visions. We are called to be single-minded people who move forward on the revelation he has given, not on the pros and cons of worldly circumstances. The words of God are truth. Fix your vision on them and pursue them without wavering.

Believe your beliefs and doubt your doubts; do not make the mistake of doubting your beliefs and believing your doubts.

CHARLES F. DEEMS

Agents of the Kingdom

*Indeed, the Sovereign LORD never does anything until he reveals
his plans to his servants the prophets.*   **AMOS 3:7**

AMOS WAS PROPHESYING TO ISRAEL about its injustices, and his message
about God's willingness to reveal his will to human beings is enlightening. He tells
us that God's preference is to say what he's going to do before he does it. Perhaps his
arrangement with human beings as stewards of this planet necessitates our prayers
before he intervenes, or maybe he just wants us to be aware of what's going on. Either
way, he rarely acts unilaterally. He calls us into partnership with him to know, see,
pray, tell, and act. He fills our eyes with visions of his will.

If God did that with selected messengers before the outpouring of his Spirit, how
much more could he do it in an age of filling all his people with dreams and visions?
We are constantly hearing God's purposes in our hearts, minds, and conversations
but usually without recognizing them as such. The question is rarely whether we are
hearing God's voice; it's whether we are recognizing his voice. He has equipped us
to sense his purposes in our lives and our world, and he is calling us to pray those
purposes by faith into real-life experience. We are agents of the Kingdom agenda.

If that doesn't give meaning to your days, nothing will. Your job as an ambassador of God's Kingdom is to sense his purposes and, by faith, pray them into being.
Be ready to speak and act as part of the answer to your own prayers, but your first
role is to intercede for human beings while being rooted in the heart of your Father.
Envision his will, believe he has revealed it for a reason, and enter into the process of
calling it into life on earth. You have been given ears to hear in order to know your
God and shape history. Your prayers are divinely sown seeds, appointed vessels for
changing this world.

> There is hardly ever a complete silence in our soul.
> God is whispering to us well nigh incessantly.
>
> FREDERICK WILLIAM FABER

Listening Prayer

I will climb up to my watchtower and stand at my guardpost.
There I will wait to see what the LORD says and how he
will answer my complaint. **HABAKKUK 2:1**

HABAKKUK COMPLAINED TO GOD about his plan to send an ungodly nation against Judah, and he wanted answers. God complied. It doesn't always work that way; we have many questions that God doesn't necessarily address. But he does invite us into an ongoing conversation with him and can handle our questions and confusion. He may remain silent about certain issues, but in general he tells us to ask.

But Habakkuk did more than ask. He positioned himself to hear and "see" what God would say. Habakkuk was quite aware that God often speaks in pictures. He was willing to isolate himself for a time of listening, and he remained there until God spoke. People don't do that unless they expect God to say something. Habakkuk trusted that God would eventually make his will and wisdom known.

That's a vital assurance to have as we pray in faith. Early in our spiritual growth, we may simply pour out to God whatever is on our hearts, hoping some of our prayers hit the mark. But over time, we learn to pray with God, listening for revelation from him in order to pray in sync with his purposes. It's one thing to ask God to do something; it's another to hear what he wants to do and then ask with assurance that he will do it. One approach results in scattershot prayers; the other establishes highly targeted requests. We can easily imagine which is more fruitful.

As you cultivate your spiritual vision, don't forget to ask God—with full expectation that he will answer—what his heart is on a given matter. Spend some time listening for direction in prayer. Station yourself on your watchtower, and don't give up until the answer comes. When it does, pray it with all your heart and with the conviction that God would not have guided you there if he didn't have every intention of fulfilling your request. He delights in satisfying the hearts of those who have sought to know his.

> The whole science of the saints consists in
> finding out and following the will of God.
>
> ISIDORE OF SEVILLE

Seemingly Slow

Still the vision awaits its appointed time; it hastens to the end—
it will not lie. If it seems slow, wait for it; it will surely come;
it will not delay. **HABAKKUK 2:3**, ESV

IT'S BOTH FASCINATING AND ALARMING how often this thought—*If it seems slow*—comes up in the life of faith. God is able to do things extremely quickly when he wants to. He can suddenly turn the tables on evil, open or close a door, and solve a problem we've been wrestling with for years. Of course, he has foreseen it all from the beginning; nothing is actually sudden to him. God has had all of eternity to lay the groundwork for his plans. But from our point of reference, he can act quickly. And, from that same point of reference, we are discouraged when he does not.

We are well-acquainted with slow processes of faith. As beings who have only so many decades to work out our earthly journey, we easily grow frustrated with the plans of a timeless God. But this is how he works. He can be excruciatingly thorough in preparing our situations and hearts for the appointed fulfillment. Generations, even centuries, passed before the prophesied Savior came in the fullness of time. Nearly two millennia have passed since he said he was coming again and since Peter assured us that God is not slow in keeping his promises (2 Peter 3:9). What may seem long to us is normal for God.

That gives us plenty of opportunity to exercise faith. Habakkuk was told that his vision would hasten until fulfillment, that it was not a lie, that even if it seemed like it was delayed, it wasn't delayed. There's a reason Scripture gives us such examples and assurances. We have to be told that our perceptions are not entirely accurate—that God is at work even when we don't see him working. The good news is those assurances come with the promise that God is more than capable of accomplishing his will. When he gives a vision, it does not lie. His promises are certainties. Faith-filled hearts are trained in patience, and faith will most certainly become sight at the appointed time.

> When the dream in our heart is one that God has planted there . . .
> all of the spiritual resources of the universe are released to help us.
> CATHERINE MARSHALL

Destroying Strongholds

*We use God's mighty weapons, not worldly weapons, to knock down
the strongholds of human reasoning and to destroy false arguments.*

2 CORINTHIANS 10:4

PAUL WAS WAGING A SPIRITUAL BATTLE about the legitimacy of his ministry, and some of his opponents—rivals who perhaps cast him as an unconvincing, unpolished preacher—were confusing the issue with false arguments and human reasoning. As he addressed his apostolic authority, he gave us profound truths we can apply to our own minds. After all, that's where many of our spiritual battles take place. We are sometimes troubled with faithless thoughts. We entertain questions that provoke fear, worry, discouragement, disappointment, and bitterness. These attitudes war against our faith, undermine our prayers, and undo our hope. If we want to have the kind of faith that prevails in the spiritual realm, we will have to learn to be ruthless with these thoughts.

That can't be done with human reasoning. The false arguments in our minds are every bit the spiritual battle Paul faced in his ministry. We have to use God's weapons against them. We ground ourselves in the revelation he has given; we stake our faith on his promises alone; we filter out distortions and shadows that weaken our expectation of his goodness. God's weapons overcome human logic and visible evidence. There will be times when we have to choose between a revelation from God and the reasoning of our minds. "This is what God said" is a solid fortress.

Learn to recognize any thought that does not align with God's perspective and cut it off. Be ruthless. Don't try to explain it, understand it, reason with it, or accommodate it. If it isn't God's thought, dispense with it. Talk with him about what's true and what isn't; there's nothing wrong with clarifying his purposes. But don't compromise his truth about your identity, calling, or the vision he has given you. Whatever sharpens the sight of faith is good; whatever doesn't, isn't. Build your strongholds on the goodness of his nature and the promises he has given his people, and the false, destructive strongholds that have presumed against your faith will lose their power.

> Almighty God, give us grace that we may cast away the works
> of darkness and put upon us the armor of light.
>
> BOOK OF COMMON PRAYER

Seeing God

We destroy every proud obstacle that keeps people from knowing God.
2 CORINTHIANS 10:5

JUST AS PAUL TOOK A STRONG STANCE against reasonings and arguments that hindered knowledge of God, we need to take a strong stance against every obstacle in our own hearts and minds. We are not born knowing the ways of God, and we are brought up in a world that often opposes them. Our minds need to be retrained. We need to learn new ways to see.

How do you see God? Your vision of him will affect every area of your life, especially your prayers of faith. If you see him as someone whose arm needs to be twisted, who needs to be given some reason to be on your side or take up your concerns, you will pray as a beggar, perhaps even as an adversary, constantly trying to convince him to give you what you long for. If you see him as a hard master, you will go to great lengths to get his attention, seek his favors, and justify your requests. But if you see him as a kind, generous keeper of promises who is constantly inviting you into partnership, where your longings and his purposes intersect, you will run into his presence and set your heart on his faithfulness. Those are vastly different attitudes of prayer, and they lead to vastly different ends. Only one will be satisfying to you and your Father.

Destroy every obstacle that comes against that partnership—that seeks to distort it, cast a shadow over it, twist it into a negotiation, or color it into anything other than what God designed it to be. You do not need to bargain with God or change his mind toward you; Jesus has already accomplished all, bridging any and all gaps between you and your Father. You have access to the knowledge of his will, the mind of Christ, and the Spirit he has placed within you. Every obstacle to intimacy with him is intruding on a sacred relationship. Get rid of it. Insist on the simplicity and joy of knowing him and trusting him with innocent, childlike faith. Your prayers will flow from a grateful heart and be filled with life.

> What comes to our minds when we think about God
> is the most important thing about us.
>
> A. W. TOZER

Praying from a Clear Conscience

*If we confess our sins, he is faithful and just to forgive us our sins
and to cleanse us from all unrighteousness.*   **1 JOHN 1:9, ESV**

AN OLD PARADIGM of Christian spirituality—one common throughout the Middle Ages and even in many strains of Protestantism—assumes that every sin disqualifies you just a little bit more from having your prayers answered. It's based on a false belief that we can earn our status with God and on the true belief that sin and rebellion obscure God's will for our lives. But for those who find their identity in Jesus and have been thoroughly cleansed by him, our merit is no longer relevant. Our prayers are based on his righteousness and standing before God, not our own. We have nothing left to earn.

Still, sin does hinder our prayers by altering our perception of ourselves, which in turn undermines our faith. The issue is not how God see us; he looks at us through the lens of Jesus. Nor is the issue our sin itself. The issue is faith, and guilt and shame undo it. Our biggest problem with self-perception is not our sin but the guilt and shame we attach to it. We forget how thoroughly we have been cleansed, how righteous we are in Christ. Our guilt and shame lead us to think that our works have something to do with our spiritual status.

If you don't see yourself as having been cleansed; if the weight of sin and failure hang over your head; if you carry burdens and feel stuck in the mire of worldliness, you probably won't pray with much faith. Whether God sees you this way or not isn't the point. (He doesn't.) The point is that when your heart doesn't feel free, you don't pray freely. When you don't see yourself as faithful, or cleansed of unfaithfulness, you won't pray with much faith. How you see God is the most important aspect of your prayer life, but how you see yourself is the next most important. Confession sets you up to experience the cleansing he has already given you and to see yourself as he does—free from guilt and shame. Pray from that place always and let God's view of you fill you with confident faith.

> God has cast our confessed sins into the depths of the sea,
> and he's even put a "No Fishing" sign over the spot.
>
> D. L. MOODY

Sharing the Divine Nature

*Because of his glory and excellence, he has given us great and
precious promises. These are the promises that enable you
to share his divine nature.* **2 PETER 1:4**

MANY CHRISTIANS ARE INFECTED WITH *I'm just a worm* theology—a
self-focus constantly reminding us of how unworthy we are in God's sight and how
depraved we remain. There's nothing wrong with reflecting on the enormity of God's
grace, of course; our sinful background is what we've been saved from. But there's
nothing in Scripture that suggests that we remain in an unworthy, sinful, depraved
state, nothing that tells us to linger on what we've been saved *from* without moving into what we've been saved *for.* Even some of the most troublesome believers in
Scripture, the church at Corinth, are called saints, "holy ones," those already made
holy by Jesus (1 Corinthians 1:2). We are beloved, treasured, and sanctified, even
when we don't act like it. We have been given extraordinary promises that allow us
to share in God's divine nature.

As we've seen, our self-perception has everything to do with how we pray. Those
who remain acutely sin-conscious, as though their sin is greater than the transforming grace they've been given, tend to pray weakly, timidly, and without much expectation. Those who recognize the magnificent privilege and status they've been given
through Jesus and fully identify with him will come boldly into the throne room
of grace. But the fact that we've been given promises enabling us to share in God's
divine nature points us even further into the importance of praying those promises
into our experience. If sharing in God's divine nature empowers our prayers, then we
need to pray we would fully understand what it means to share in his divine nature.
We need to soak in the identity we've been given. Those great and precious promises
need to become our experience in every area of life.

Pray to know who you are so you can then pray for others from your divine
identity. Daily ask God what the supernatural life looks like in you, and step into it
in every way he leads. Don't let his great and precious promises fall to the ground.
Take them in, and live, breathe, and pray from your new divine nature.

All the resources of the Godhead are at our disposal.

JONATHAN GOFORTH

Already Given

Make every effort to respond to God's promises. **2 PETER 1:5**

IMAGINE A PARENT GIVING A CHILD a wonderfully wrapped gift. The child gets excited, thinks about what is inside, and anticipates the joy of opening it. But before long, the child wonders if it's really true and starts asking if there's anything beneath the wrapping—again and again. Day after day, the child asks for something already given, and the parent has to keep pointing back to the promise. In fact, the parent has to remind the child that this gift has been available from the moment it was presented. Still, the child waits, hopes, and asks that it be true—even when it already is.

That's how many of us approach the promises of God, especially those related to the divine power he has given us for living a godly, supernaturally enabled, transformational life. We ask for wisdom, even though he has already given us the mind of Christ. We ask for greater love, even though he has filled us with the Spirit of love. All of the fruits of the Holy Spirit are ours, yet we strain for them, plead for them, and resist entering into them. We spend much of our prayer time asking for things that have already been promised, already been given, and are already available for the taking. We simply need to learn how to respond.

Responding to God's promises means entering into them. Some of them may be for one day down the road, but most are for now. Savor them, turn them over in your mind, believe they are true. Imagine what it's like to exercise them, then go out and exercise them. Yes, you'll stumble along the way—every child learning a new thing is clumsy with it at first—but it makes no sense to give up on a promise from God. He has given us a new nature, a clean slate, transformed ways of seeing and thinking, life-giving relationships, extraordinary promises for prayer and faith, and his presence within us. Asking for those things only prolongs the wait. Instead, believe and receive. Step out in faith. Live the new life you've been promised.

Every promise God has ever made finds its fulfillment in Jesus.

JONI EARECKSON TADA

Truly He Promised

I tell you the truth, if you have faith and don't doubt . . .
MATTHEW 21:21

JESUS SOMETIMES PRECEDED HIS TEACHINGS about prayer and faith with an emphatic phrase: "I tell you the truth" or "Truly I say to you" or, in the old King James, "Verily, verily." All of Jesus' words are true, of course, and he hardly needs to add extra force to his promises. But this is like saying, "Really, I promise, this is as sure as it gets." When he puts the "amen" in front of a statement, the next words out of his mouth deserve extra attention.

Here Jesus emphasizes the importance of having faith without doubting. And while we may agree with this in our minds, our hearts sigh at the thought. *If only*, we think, realizing that our best efforts at mustering up faith—pure faith with no doubt mixed in—seem to fall short. We want to believe without question, but we often have questions. We want to have absolute assurance, but lingering alternatives bounce around in our minds. Every *what if* and *if only* we can imagine show up at inopportune moments in our faith journey. How does Jesus expect us to arrive at this pure, unblemished faith?

Perhaps that's where our prayers need to begin—not with the object or desire we are praying for but with the faith he gives us to believe it's God's will. He will tell us if it isn't, of course, but he will also tell us if it is. And if he gives us that inward assurance—if faith is something he works into our hearts rather than something we muster up on our own—we can rest there, fully confident that his promise is being fulfilled.

Make that your goal. Pray for the faith to believe, and then, as the Holy Spirit leads, go ahead and enter into the answered prayer as if you are already there. Inwardly live in that answer, thanking God for it and sensing the fulfillment, before the answer enters into your outward circumstances. Your doubts need to be answered before your prayers are, so take them to God. Let him cultivate your assurance, and then rest in it. Truly, he has said that you can.

> The promises of God are just as good as ready money any day.
>
> BILLY BRAY

By Faith

It was by faith.   **HEBREWS 11:4**

THE WRITER OF HEBREWS BUILT HIS ENTIRE LETTER around one major point: that enduring faith is the entryway into the promises of God. He wrote primarily to Jewish believers who were tempted to fall away from their faith, to give up on what they had started, to question the validity of this gospel and how it fit with their heritage. So he reminded them of their long history with God, the nature of the covenant and priesthood God had established with them, and the ways of God in getting his people from point A to point B on their journey. The bottom line was that the journey has always been based on faith, always required patient endurance, and always come with great hardships and great rewards. He gives numerous examples—a section we now call the "hall of faith" in chapter 11. Again and again, God's calling has involved stepping out in belief of what has been promised but remains unseen.

Fourteen sentences in this single chapter begin with the phrase "It was by faith . . ." The examples that follow demonstrate what normal people who believed God were able to do. They experienced miracles, great victories, and fulfilled promises. They experienced hardships, too—ridicule, persecution, extreme circumstances, excruciating waits. But the impossibilities they faced became possible because of faith. When people believed, God responded.

Faith is a really big deal in Scripture. It is such an uncompromising theme that the writer of this letter says, amid all the impossibilities that must bow to God, one impossibility remains: pleasing him without faith (11:6). Knowing God exists is not enough, though it's a great start. We are called to live in such a way that invisible realities open up before us as we take steps of faith. We work in partnership with God to bring about what is not yet seen, as we walk with him to establish his Kingdom in this world. We bank our lives on what we do not yet see, and eventually we see. That's our new normal, as strange as it seems to watching eyes. When we have finished our journey, God should be able to look back over our lives and say, "It was by faith."

Only he who can see the invisible can do the impossible.

FRANK GAINES

Audacious Prayer

Let us come boldly to the throne of our gracious God. **HEBREWS 4:16**

PERHAPS YOU HAVE HEARD the following quotes: "Attempt something so great for God that unless he intervenes, it is destined for failure." "If your vision isn't keeping you awake at night, it isn't big enough." These quotes express a common thought in the life of faith: There's no need for faith in anything that we can accomplish on our own. The object of our faith must be beyond us for us to see God at work in it.

The other side of that equation is that God usually requires something of us as evidence of our faith—some action or response that puts feet to what we believe. Somewhere in between those two extremes—whatever is attainable entirely by human effort and whatever is so beyond us that we can do nothing to help—is a middle ground of partnership, an intersection between our need and God's provision, a small investment on our part multiplied by God's enormous increase. Like the fishes and loaves Jesus expanded into a meal for thousands, we offer what we have. But what we need is vastly more. We are virtually helpless at the throne of grace.

That's actually a good place to be. Helplessness is a prerequisite for the greatest miracles of God. In fact, we are invited to come into that place with empty hands and bold hearts. It makes little sense to approach an infinite God with tiny requests. Impossibilities do a much better job of honoring him. We are to ask big, believe big, and expect big. That's his will for our lives of faith and prayer.

Don't be afraid of asking too much from God. Don't ask presumptuously or selfishly, of course; that's the wrong spirit. But there's a difference between the wrong spirit and the wrong size, and we never need to worry about the latter. God welcomes extravagant, audacious visions. He is more than happy to adjust them to his purposes. But he will never downsize them to be more manageable. He is able to answer our biggest, boldest prayers.

> Large asking and large expectation on our part honor God.
>
> A. L. STONE

Come Boldly

There we will receive his mercy, and we will find grace
to help us when we need it most.   **HEBREWS 4:16**

MANY PEOPLE SEE THE THRONE OF GOD as one of judgment, the seat of someone with an unbending will, a place of impermeable glory that incorporates no human agendas. But Scripture emphasizes his throne as one of grace, a place of compassion and help, where a Father has paid an extravagant price for his children to come rushing in without hindrance. His presence is where our deepest, highest, most personal needs and desires are met.

That means our journey of faith should always lead us there first. His throne is not a place where we will hear, "How dare you ask such a thing!" or "Sorry, your faith just doesn't measure up." We will not be informed of how unqualified or undeserving we are, how far off the mark our prayers have strayed, or how inappropriately we are standing where others grovel. We may be gently redirected and reshaped, patiently instructed, and compassionately told to wait, but we will not be summarily dismissed. Our prayers will not be shot down. We have been invited before God, not merely to show up but to enter boldly. His throne is a place of encouragement.

You need to remember that in your prayer life. There will be days when you wonder how long you must wait or whether God has even heard you. As your faith is being stretched, pulled, strained, pressed, and nearly broken, you will need to rely on the grace of your Father to give you an encouraging word, point you to some sign of his working, and surround you with supportive fellowship. You will need seasons of refreshing that only grace can bring.

Ask for them. Don't be afraid to tell your Father when you need some encouragement to stoke the fires of faith. Don't act as if he has left you alone in this journey. Let him help you along. He not only waits for the time of fulfillment; he will walk with you all the way there. Boldly bring your faith before him, and boldly ask him for the grace to sustain it. He is always willing to meet you where you need him most.

He rides at ease whom the grace of God carries.

THOMAS À KEMPIS

Taste and See

Taste and see that the LORD is good. Oh, the joys of those who take refuge in him! **PSALM 34:8**

DAVID FOUND HIMSELF IN PHILISTINE TERRITORY after fleeing Saul's court and his irrational wrath. The Philistine king's officers recognized him, and David could have been in just as much danger there. So he feigned madness before the king and was kicked out, escaping to hide in a cave—not typically circumstances a person would expect to celebrate. But David had trained his heart to see God's goodness, and he wrote a psalm about it. He urged all who would read it, even these three thousand years later, to find their joy in the nature of God.

David could have told us to imagine how good God might be. He could have expounded on his theology of divine beneficence or given us hypothetical platitudes about God's nature. He could have suggested we think of our best moments and single them out as the rare exceptions of God's favor. Instead, he put it all on the table and invited us to taste and see. "Test the evidence," he was saying. To him, all the evidence pointed to an extravagantly generous God.

While many people imagine the best of life's experiences as their baseline and then lament everything that falls short, David (at least at this point in his life) saw survival as his baseline and celebrated everything that rose above it. The first approach undermines faith and anticipation of God's goodness; the latter builds faith and anticipation. Many of us spend quite a bit of time thinking God hasn't provided for all our needs, when actually he has a different definition of *need* than we do. Still, God goes well beyond it in his dealings with us. When we understand this, we grow in faith and expectation. We pray increasingly confident prayers, never assuming too much but also never hoping too little. We bank our lives on the fact of God's goodness and being able to experience it in the here and now. We have tasted and seen, and we are sure we will taste and see even more.

> God is not merely good, but goodness.
>
> C. S. LEWIS

Good and Perfect Gifts

Whatever is good and perfect is a gift coming down
to us from God our Father. JAMES 1:17

SOME PEOPLE HAVE A STRANGE NOTION of the good things in life. They see God as a depriver of what's really fun, enjoyable, and extravagant. It comes from long-held theologies that rightly emphasize the importance of inner fulfillment, simple devotion, and avoiding luxury and self-indulgence that distracts the spirit. But it can also paint God as an austere Master who gives only what is needed and no more—like a cranky great uncle who gives only school supplies for a birthday or a trainer who is always pushing greens and grains and never offering a treat. Like the White Witch of Narnia, this God governs a landscape where it is always winter but never Christmas. It's a distorted view of his nature and sends us looking elsewhere for anything more than basic rations. It doesn't recognize the good and perfect gifts he has already given.

To a much larger degree than we might imagine, our future experience of God's good gifts depends on our past appreciation of them. It isn't as if he withholds his goodness out of pettiness, waiting impatiently for a "thank you." The issue is a matter of our own hearts and what's good for them. If we aren't living in awareness of his bounty with gratitude for what he has done, we will take his future blessings and run with them, using them in self-centered and unhealthy ways (which is why theologies of deprivation have thrived). We will wrench them out of the relationship and handle them as our own assets. In other words, his good gifts might drive us further from his heart.

That's the opposite of his purposes in giving them. There's a right way to receive, and it begins with hearts thoroughly saturated, immersed, and overflowing with appreciation. The soil of a heart so conditioned is fertile ground for receiving God's gifts—for praying and believing with confidence, for trusting in his goodness, for stewarding the increases he brings. Appreciative, joyful hearts are mature hearts that can handle God's extravagance. Prepare yourself by cultivating yours. Pray, knowing that your Father loves to give good and perfect gifts from above.

God is all that is good, in my sight, and the goodness that everything has is his.

JULIAN OF NORWICH

Endure to the End

David was now in great danger because all his men were
very bitter about losing their sons and daughters, and
they began to talk of stoning him. 1 SAMUEL 30:6

DAVID WAS IN A PREDICAMENT. He had taken refuge with the Philistines, Israel's enemy, to avoid Saul's unreasonable wrath, and now the Philistines were about to go to battle against Saul's armies. Would David have to fight against his friends—and against the king he had twice refused to kill—or would he distance himself from the Philistines and provoke their wrath too? Thankfully, God spared him from that dilemma; the Philistine commanders didn't trust him enough to bring him into battle with them. But then David faced another crisis. After he and his men returned home, they found their camp had been raided by the Amalekites, and their wives, children, and possessions were gone. His own men—keenly aware that he twice could have killed Saul and ended their seemingly endless exile—were furious. They wanted to stone him. They were tired of being on the run and facing life-threatening dangers day after day after day.

Such is the journey on the way to God's calling. It can test and stretch and press us in excruciating ways. Few of us will ever face the physical dangers David did, but the spiritual battles can be just as intense. David's testing reached a climax at this point; these were the last big dilemmas and battles of faith he faced before the promise of his kingship was fulfilled. But they came at the end of a very long, arduous process. Most of us can endure a brief intense time of testing. Not many of us can go from test to test for years without being tempted to drop our hopes, prayers, and calling. But the faith journey stretches beyond our strength, and if we want to receive what God has in store for us, we will have to walk it out to the end.

Your journey of faith will likely take you through some deep valleys, and while there, you may feel like giving up. Don't. Sometimes the greatest victories are just on the other side of them. They are often the last stage in a long process of enduring. God will carry you through them if you will cling to him and his word to the end.

We conquer not in any brilliant fashion; we conquer by continuing.

GEORGE MATHESON

127

Your Source of Strength

But David found strength in the LORD his God.   1 SAMUEL 30:6

IN DAVID'S DARKEST MOMENT between the promise God gave him and its fulfillment years later, he had nowhere to turn. Even his own men, mighty warriors and steadfast friends, wanted to kill him for putting their lives on the line for such an unreasonably long time. So David turned to God and found his strength there. We don't know what he thought or prayed in that moment (some of the psalms about similar crises he faced may give us a clue), but his connection with God and spiritual refreshment happened at just the right time. He was able to ask for and receive God's guidance, and he won back all that the raiders had taken. God restored David's heart, and then David restored what he and his men had lost.

We can't have consistent faith without knowing how to find our strength in God. We have to become settled in unsettled seasons and circumstances. We will be bombarded with global and national crises that pop up frequently, with situations and circumstances that scream contradictions to God's will for our lives, with people's perspectives and commentaries that undermine our faith, and with our own inner turmoil and questions that undermine it even more. Nowhere in Scripture are we promised a smooth ride. In fact, Jesus promised just the opposite (John 16:33). But he also promised that he had overcome and that we would overcome too through him. That's where we can find our strength—in the promises, encouragement, and spiritual resources flowing into our lives and from the Holy Spirit within us. We participate in all of God's victories by clinging to and resting in him.

Remember that the next time you face a crisis of faith, whether it comes from outside sources or deep within. There may be plenty of people in your life to encourage you in rough times. But as in David's life, those same friends may intensify the rough times, even when they don't intend to. You'll have to find your strength in a more dependable source, be refreshed, and let God open your ears to his voice. Only he has the power to carry you through to the end.

> Prayer has a mighty power to sustain the soul
> in every season of its distress and sorrow.
>
> CHARLES SPURGEON

The Testimony of Worry

Give all your worries and cares to God, for he cares about you.

1 PETER 5:7

THERE'S A REASON SCRIPTURE OVERFLOWS with encouragements and commands telling us not to fear, worry, be anxious, or be alarmed. Fallen human beings who can't see God with natural eyes are prone to all these troublesome attitudes. Sometimes we lie awake at night thinking about how a problem will be resolved. Sometimes we envision problems that aren't even problems yet. They are possibilities, not certainties, but we find it difficult not to think about what we would do if or when they appear. Our minds have been well trained in magnifying the *whys* and *what ifs* of life. We are masters at turning hints and hunches into horrible situations, and we might even wonder if the God who has promised to take care of us actually will.

So God assures us time and again that he will. He has promised that he will deliver us out of all our troubles (Psalm 34:19). His goal is to turn our trials of faith into testimonies of his faithfulness. No matter how multiplied and unyielding our difficulties may be, they must yield to him. When we cast our faith onto him, we enter into his power over them. We become overcomers. That's the story he has assigned to those who love and believe in him.

Worry is a false testimony. It is negative faith—the belief in something that opposes God's will and conviction that whatever we go through will not work out for our good. People of faith simply must replace those worrisome thoughts with the assurance that God carries our burdens and delivers us. All the "do not fear" and "be anxious for nothing" commands in Scripture are not just encouraging pats on the back. They are warnings against a very unhealthy mental habit that can negatively affect our future. In reality, our future is in his hands. He has promised this. And he wants to replace every false testimony with the certainty of his goodness.

The future is as bright as the promises of God.

ADONIRAM JUDSON

The Security of Love

Perfect love expels all fear.   1 JOHN 4:18

GOD IS LOVE, John wrote in his first epistle, assuring his readers they had nothing to fear in judgment because "love expels all fear." It's a wonderfully encouraging verse, but many of us apply it only to our eternal destiny at the end of the age. In reality, we fear smaller judgments throughout our lives of faith. It's where some of our deepest worries, anxieties, and doubts come from. We think that if we'd been good enough or had enough faith, bad things wouldn't be happening and we wouldn't be going through the same intensity of trials and adversity. Our fears and doubts are rooted in the idea of having to go through something rather than around it—and that going through it won't be as miraculous, redeeming, or fulfilling as avoiding it altogether. Of course, it makes little sense to apply God's love to Judgment Day but not to the rest of our lives, as if our smaller, daily fears are reasonable. His love applies everywhere, in every situation throughout our entire lives.

What are we saying about God when we worry? We are accusing him of not being concerned for us, of not being on our side, of not having our best interests in mind, of possibly losing control of the world around us or at least not caring enough to orchestrate it. The subtle accusations are many, and we would hardly admit to them. But our worry is actually emotional slander against the God who has repeatedly promised that he has overcome the world, will deliver us from our troubles, and works all things together for our good. We are questioning how—and whether—his love works.

It can be extremely difficult to break that mental habit—our thought patterns run strong and deep—but we have to form new habits to think in Kingdom ways. We have to embrace hope, assume God's kindness toward us regardless of what we see, and let his peace rule in our hearts. He tells us not to worry because he knows we have no reason to do so. He promised.

> Be assured, if you walk with him and look to him and
> expect help from him, he will never fail you.
>
> GEORGE MÜLLER

Pester Him

*If you keep knocking long enough, he will get up and give you whatever
you need because of your shameless persistence.* **LUKE 11:8**

JESUS TOLD A PARABLE about being a pesky neighbor who repeatedly knocks
on a neighbor's door at midnight to ask for some bread to feed a visiting friend. It's a
strange and unlikely scenario, but it makes for a vivid picture. It compares our prayers
to requests that should have been handled before midnight; to inopportune moments
of need; and to persistent and even annoying demands. It doesn't paint a flattering
picture of the petitioner either, but his persistence gets the job done.

Of course, in our own prayers, God is not annoyed by our requests, doesn't need
to be woken up, and is glad to answer us for reasons other than "shameless persistence." As with the unjust judge who gives a nagging widow what she wants just to
get rid of her (Luke 18:1-5), Jesus is not trying to paint an accurate picture of God
here. He makes a rather different point: the importance of praying with urgency and
persistence. In the latter parable, the point was to "pray and never give up" (18:1).
In this one, the message is similar: Don't feel shame about your "shameless" prayers.
Keep at it. Praying persistently does not mean remembering to mention something
to God from time to time. It means banging on a door passionately and tenaciously
until the answer comes. Whether we understand it or not, it's part of the deal. Our
relationship with God and our role as a steward of his Kingdom on earth allow plenty
of room for boldness. We are like soldiers on the front lines who have no option of
giving up before the battle is won.

When you know who God is, you can "pester" him—or, as the passage goes on
to say, you can keep on asking, seeking, and knocking until God answers what was
asked, provides what was sought, and opens the door that was closed. Uncertainty
about his goodness, patience, and love will undermine that resolve. Knowing his
character, his purposes, and his invitation strengthens it. Bold, persistent prayers are
welcomed prayers, and when the time is right, they will be answered.

> Some people think God does not like to be troubled with our constant
> coming and asking. The way to trouble God is not to come at all.
>
> D. L. MOODY

Pray for Yourself

Keep on asking, and you will receive what you ask for. Keep on seeking, and you will find. Keep on knocking, and the door will be opened to you. For everyone who asks, receives. Everyone who seeks, finds. And to everyone who knocks, the door will be opened. LUKE 11:9-10

AS YOU'VE GROWN IN FAITH, you've likely realized that your prayer life is bigger than your immediate concerns. God cares for your troubles, of course, but you fit within a larger purpose: the advancement of his Kingdom on earth. Your relationship with him is personal, but it's larger than you are. You are meant to spill over into the world around you. You are called to be a fount of life, love, faith, joy, peace, wisdom, and comfort for the people you know. God pours all of his blessings into you for two purposes: for you to experience them yourself and for others to experience them in you. You are a carrier of his Kingdom.

It's extremely important, then, to pray for yourself. You can pray diligently and zealously for others, but if those prayers are coming from a leaky vessel that is not overflowing with the wisdom, power, and love of God—if they aren't saturated in faith and purpose—then they are not as effective and empowered as they could be. Just as flight attendants tell us before takeoff, it's important to tend to our own oxygen masks before helping others with theirs. If our prayers aren't flowing from ongoing experiences with the goodness of God, they aren't nearly as likely to impart those experiences to others.

As we've seen, praying in power is not a matter of earning or deserving answers to our prayers, but it can be a matter of positioning—of stepping into the authority we have been given to pray in Jesus' name. We need encounters with the goodness of God because they stir up our faith and cultivate expectancy. When we keep on asking, keep on seeking, and keep on knocking for God to fill our lives with the Holy Spirit and the wisdom, power, and love he promises, we begin to embody the things we are praying for in others. We become vessels that carry the blessings and power of God. And that is worth prioritizing in our prayers every day.

God longs to make something supernatural of us.

ANDREW MURRAY

Spirit-Breathed Prayer

If you sinful people know how to give good gifts to your children,
how much more will your heavenly Father give the Holy Spirit
to those who ask him. **LUKE 11:13**

MANY PEOPLE FIXATE on the object of their prayers: *Am I asking for the right things? Is this the will of God? Do my prayers line up with his purposes?* These are not bad questions, but they are all focused on prayer itself, as if saying the right words secures the answer. But what if the real issue is not so much the words that flow from our hearts when we pray but our hearts themselves? What if our desires are not the key nearly so much as the mechanism that desires them? What if we haven't gone deep enough in aligning our prayers with God?

God has a remedy for any disconnect we might feel between our prayers and his purposes. He is focused not on tweaking our wants but on overhauling our "wanter." One of the most significant prayer initiatives we can have is to ask for inner transformation—for his Spirit to invade our spirit to such a degree that our prayers are initiated by him, through him, and for him. When our petitions are saturated in the Holy Spirit, we don't have to wonder if they are aligned with the heart of God. They come from his heart to start with, and we are simply voicing them. The impulse to add "if it's your will" grows fainter when we know God is inspiring our spirit and planting his will within.

Jesus assured his followers that the Father gives the Holy Spirit to those who ask him. Some Christians love to debate what it means for him to "give the Spirit." They question whether he means new birth, his constant presence, or an empowering experience, and never realize that any prayer for deeper, stronger, more powerful experiences with the Holy Spirit is always appropriate in any situation. Whether you already "have" the Spirit is not the issue. The important thing is whether you are relying on him and being inspired by him. If you are in need of more Spirit-driven, Spirit-directed, and Spirit-empowered prayer, ask and keep on asking—and trust God to fill you with prayers he longs to answer.

Prayer is the breathing in of the Holy Spirit.

SUNDAR SINGH

The Gift of Faith

A spiritual gift is given to each of us so we can help each other....
The same Spirit gives great faith. 1 CORINTHIANS 12:7, 9

PAUL WROTE OFTEN ABOUT SPIRITUAL GIFTS, sometimes in general terms and other times with specific lists that itemize certain gifts. As with so many spiritual attributes, every believer has a measure of these gifts. We are called to have wisdom, give generously, share our faith, and so on. But the Holy Spirit magnifies different gifts in different people. And one of those gifts is faith, the ability to believe God in extraordinary measure, to be filled with certain expectation of visions and callings being fulfilled. Some people seem to be able to believe more easily than others.

That's not me, many people think, assuming they would know about their gift of faith if they already had it. But don't be so sure. A gift from God is not a static, permanent, unyielding decision from above. Rarely does Scripture suggest that either you have it or you don't. In fact, in just a few paragraphs, Paul urges the Corinthians to eagerly desire—literally "covet"—every spiritual gift (14:1), implying that we can get some we don't already have. The fullness of his language there suggests that we should set our hearts on these gifts, be jealous for them (not *against* other believers but *for* the gifts themselves), and eagerly anticipate them in our own lives. Sure, there will be a few he has given that direct the course of our service in the body of Christ, but all are available in some measure for those who seek them. And as vital as faith is in the Kingdom of God, it should be one we desire in ever-increasing measure. We can grow in this gift. And as we steward it well, God pours out even more for our greater growth.

Make it a point to seek that gift daily. You can't muster up faith on your own, but the more deeply and closely you fellowship with the Holy Spirit, the more his gifts fill you and empower you. Spend time with him and see how they grow. Ask for them. Receive the capacity to believe what he says. Count on him to give great faith.

A man cannot have faith without asking; neither can he ask it without faith.

EDWARD MARBURY

Immersed in the Spirit

Be filled with the Holy Spirit, singing psalms and hymns and spiritual songs among yourselves, and making music to the Lord in your hearts.

EPHESIANS 5:18-19

SCRIPTURE GIVES US BEAUTIFUL DESCRIPTIONS of the benefits and blessings of our relationship with God through his Spirit. It lists spiritual gifts and fruit, creating a composite picture of who we are called to be. But a lack of faith, love, patience, or any other gift or fruit of the Spirit should not send us looking for more. These gifts are not compartments of the spiritual life or components we can pick and choose from a buffet line. Instead, we should spend more time fellowshipping with the source. We don't need more gifts. We need more Spirit.

Of course, we already have full access to the Holy Spirit, and in reality, we can't get *more* of him. But we can draw closer, go deeper, and have more experiences with him. Just as a husband or wife can't get more married but can have more of each other in time, love, and intimacy, we can't become any more born of the Spirit than we already are. But we can certainly become more saturated in his presence and filled with his power. The key to the spiritual life is not spirituality. It's the Spirit himself. He is the manifestation of every aspect of our relationship with God on earth.

That's vital for our journeys and adventures of prayer and faith. The Holy Spirit plants seeds in our hearts—promises from God's Word, visions of his purposes, callings he has given us to fulfill. The only way those seeds grow is by fellowshipping with him, the deep intimacy of knowing and loving him. All of life is birthed in intimacy, and our faith comes alive and is nurtured in his presence. We birth the things of the Spirit in our hearts to the degree that we know and love him. The greatest thing we can do for our prayers of faith is to be filled with him and let his will and words grow, bloom, and bear lasting fruit.

To possess a Spirit-indwelt mind is the Christian's privilege under grace.

A. W. TOZER

A Spirit-Filled Mind

Let the Spirit renew your thoughts and attitudes. **EPHESIANS 4:23**

PERHAPS YOU'VE NOTICED a fascinating phenomenon in your own wandering thoughts—the ability to have deep spiritual insights and inspirations one moment and the tendency to completely undo them the next. Our thought patterns are a contorted web of trails, some leading to wonderful places and others to barren wastelands. Mentally and emotionally, we are mixed bags, capable of spiritual heights and unspiritual depths almost simultaneously. It's hard for faith to flourish in such an environment—every time it reaches toward the light and begins to emerge, the rocks and thorns of our internal wilderness seem to assert their supremacy again. Neuroscientists tell us that new thought patterns and habits face such obstacles, and they last only through persistence, repetition, and necessity. If we are going to think in new ways and reach greater heights of faith, we will need a thorough spiritual transformation.

But if the key to nurturing seeds of faith is being immersed in the Holy Spirit, growing in fellowship with him, and being saturated in the glories and gifts of his presence, then we have to learn to notice our thoughts and attitudes that compete with him. It is impossible to think spiritual things consistently while also holding on to unspiritual thought patterns. We inevitably have impulses that contradict the Spirit's nature from time to time, but we can't afford to nurture those contradictions. As much as possible, our minds need to merge with his. What goes on in our heads needs to match the flow of his wisdom, power, and love. We can't afford to entertain the lies and distractions—anything the Spirit hasn't inspired—in our inward lives.

Let your thoughts become pure—not with some hyperspiritual definition of purity so common in medieval deprivations or puritanical admonitions (after all, God has given us some wonderful physical and material gifts), but with a single focus on the Spirit's influence in your life. Embrace both the fullness of God's *yes* to abundant life and his *no* to everything that steals, kills, and destroys. In fact, if your *yes* is big enough, then your *no* to all competitors becomes easy. Dive fully into fellowship with the Holy Spirit. Embrace his influence, and your thoughts and attitudes will turn toward faith in every corner of your life.

May the mind of Christ my Savior live in me from day to day.

KATE B. WILKINSON

Praying from the Spirit

Pray in the power of the Holy Spirit.   JUDE 1:20

YOU CAN PRAY ANYWHERE—that is a fundamental truth of the spiritual life. Praying is not dependent on your location, at least physically. But it may be dependent on your location spiritually. It matters whether you are praying from a place of faith, trust, rest, rebellion, confusion, desperation, victimization, or distorted identities. God invites us to talk to him anytime, but when we are praying from a place that is contrary to the Holy Spirit's nature and influence, his answers will be focused on lifting us out of those perceptions. When we are praying in the Spirit, though—when our spirit is aligned with his wisdom, power, and love—there is nothing remedial for him to focus on. His Kingdom is advancing for us, in us, and through us.

That's one reason Jude urged his readers to build one another up in faith by praying in the power of the Spirit. Literally he says to "pray in the Spirit"—from intense fellowship that is motivated, inspired, and empowered by God's work within us. Believers debate whether "in the Spirit" refers to the deep groanings of Romans 8:26, the unknown languages of 1 Corinthians 14:14, or something else, but the bottom line is that we are called to pray prayers that originate in God's heart, are inspired by our communion with him, are endorsed by his wisdom and zeal, and are carried out in his strength. This is no futile, tentative prayer life but a divine appointment in another realm, a conversation in the heavenly throne room. As stewards of God's Kingdom on earth, we are invited here to add our human voice and agency to the Kingdom agenda. That's a powerful position for asking.

If you need the Holy Spirit to pull you out of the depths, pray your heart out and believe he will answer you in power. But seek more than that. Aim to pray from your position in him and his presence in you. Pray for power from on high above all else. There is no better place from which to voice your requests.

> Where there is much prayer, there will be much of the Spirit;
> where there is much of the Spirit, there will be ever-increasing prayer.
>
> ANDREW MURRAY

Ask for a Word

Take heart, men, for I believe God that it will be just as it was told me.
ACTS 27:25, NKJV

PAUL WAS ON HIS WAY TO ROME in a ship destined for disaster. He knew that from the beginning. He had warned the helmsman that things wouldn't turn out well. But even though Paul had foreseen a violent storm, he was not able to assure his fellow passengers that their lives would be spared until he heard from God. And once God revealed the outcome of their safety and survival, Paul counted on it. He declared it boldly. He rode out the remainder of the terrifying storm without being terrified because he had confidence in what God had said.

You will need that kind of confidence to weather your storms. Otherwise, every shift in the winds of circumstance will shake and rattle your faith. You may not need to speak out as boldly as Paul did—God's words to you may not necessitate warnings and assurances to others—but you will need to cling to whatever he has revealed to preserve your own experience of it. And the only way to do that is to begin your adventures of faith by asking him what to pray for and listening for his answers. You can't cling to a word from him unless you've received one.

There's a huge difference between praying for God to do what you think is good and praying for him to do what he said. Sometimes a general prayer based on your understanding is fine, but sometimes you'll need to hear from him first. Mine his Word for his promises. Ask him for direction, just as if you were seeking him for a major decision. Ask how to pray and then pray how he leads. That does two things: It aligns your prayers with what he is doing in the situation, and it solidifies your faith so you can pray confidently. After all, if he has given direction, he has done so for a reason. You know he is planning to respond. When you align your prayers with his will, you can weather any storm with the confidence that he will accomplish it. You can plant your faith on the word that was planted in you and trust that it will be just as he said.

> The voice of God, having once fully penetrated the heart,
> becomes strong as the tempest and loud as the thunder.
>
> **IGNATIUS OF LOYOLA**

Don't Give In

Don't you think God will surely give justice to his chosen people
who cry out to him day and night?   **LUKE 18:7**

SOMETIMES YOU HEAR GOD CLEARLY or see his direction so plainly spelled out in Scripture that you know you are praying according to his will. Still, nothing is happening. He seems not to be answering. The contradictions to his will persist—broken relationships, bad choices, evil aggressors, injustices that violate his Kingdom—and they are damaging lives. Eventually, you resign yourself to the mystery of unanswered prayer, concluding that your prayers must not be in his will. Even though they clearly are.

That's exactly the kind of situation that prompted Jesus to tell his disciples parables about persisting in prayer. In the parable of the relentless widow and the unjust judge in Luke 18, Luke spells out Jesus' purpose up front: "to show that they should always pray and never give up" (verse 1). No matter what answer or lack of an answer we have gotten; no matter how long the unjust situation has persisted; no matter how many times we have already prayed the same thing; we are to keep crying out for justice, rightness, and truth. In every situation, we are to pray for God's Kingdom to come and his will to be done on earth as it is in heaven—and never stop. For whatever reason, this is how God has chosen to work. We ask, he answers, and his will is done. Sometimes it is just done long after the asking begins.

Never resign yourself to things that are not God's will. Adjust your requests, if needed. Learn to see his will in unexpected situations; sometimes he gets really creative with the people and circumstances he works with. Always pray with a certain amount of flexibility for him to accomplish his will unconventionally. But don't give in. Far too many prayer projects have been left unfinished, with answers hanging like nearly ripe fruit from a tree, while God's will remains undone. One of the greatest character traits you can develop is tenacity in pursuing God's purposes on earth. Apply it to your family, church, school, workplace, community, city, and beyond. He authorized relentless prayers, so pray them boldly—day and night until God brings justice into your world.

Nothing great was ever done without much enduring.

CATHERINE OF SIENA

Ignore the Reports

For forty days, every morning and evening, the Philistine
champion strutted in front of the Israelite army.   1 SAMUEL 17:16

THE STORY OF GOLIATH goes into a lot of detail about his apparent invincibility. Long before the chapter ever mentions God, and even before it mentions David visiting the front lines, we read of Goliath's size, the weight and materials of his armor, the enormity of his weapon, his relentless taunts, and the fear and dread of Israel's warriors as the imposing enemy shouted, strutted, and dared them to respond. God's people were terrified and paralyzed. All they could see was the near certainty of defeat.

Our prayers often face such obstacles that mock us every time we pray—not giants with swords and spears, but mountains that just won't move, enormous odds stacked against us, unwanted situations that seem inevitable. We hear taunts and reports from the enemy camp: *Your prayers aren't going to be answered. This situation is too big. Obviously nothing is going to change. You are powerless against this enemy.* And on and on. Just as God is not mentioned in the story of Goliath until David finally brings him up, God seems irrelevant to our situation until we come to our senses and faith kicks in. We have to be reminded that faith is the assurance of things *not* seen, not the validation of what is already in plain sight.

In your life of faith, you need to learn to ignore reports from the enemy camp. Listening to those reports to see if God is accomplishing what he has promised honors the visible evidence more than the promise. It refocuses your vision, moving it from the faithfulness of God to the tyranny of circumstances, which is always discouraging. If God has assured you of an answer to prayer, no negative turn of events, no disappointing words, and no defiance from those involved have anything to do with the answer. Only what God has said matters. The taunts of the enemy, the obstacle, the adversity, and your own inner doubts are not the final authority. God is, and he is faithful to keep his word.

> Are we not bound to exercise the utmost confidence, and have a felt and strong assurance of mind, that what is promised shall come to pass?
>
> CHARLES FINNEY

Fullness of Life

*[Jesus said,] "The thief's purpose is to steal and kill and destroy.
My purpose is to give them a rich and satisfying life."* **JOHN 10:10**

FROM THE EARLIEST POST–NEW TESTAMENT TIMES, many Christians have been taught to pray against themselves. Interpreting Jesus' call to deny ourselves (Matthew 16:24) as a prohibition of pleasure, satisfaction, and fullness, they have prayed for complete self-abnegation, enduring hardship not for the sake of the gospel but simply for the sake of hardship. It's true that we are called to reject self-centeredness and rebellious wills, but what about the rich aspects of our lives that fit the image of God and align with his design? What about the desires the Holy Spirit puts within us? A wholesale rejection of self throws it all away. In other words, some Christians throughout history have made the thief's job easy by stealing, killing, and destroying themselves and deferring all abundant, satisfying life to a distant age.

But Jesus came to give us a rich and satisfying life now and forever—abundant, whole, and fulfilling—which means we have every reason, even the mandate, to pray for it. His words don't give us license to turn the promise of abundant life into a mission of self-indulgence or adversity-avoidance, but they do mean we can pray for spiritual, mental, emotional, physical, and relational healing; for protection and provision, and the grace to handle hardship when protection and provision are lacking; and for restoration of everything in our lives and the lives of others that has been stolen, killed, and destroyed. If Jesus came to undo the works of the enemy (1 John 3:8), then we can certainly pray that the enemy's works be undone. And we can do it with confidence and zeal.

Your prayer life is not simply a wish list of things you want God to do but a vision of his Kingdom. Whatever doesn't fit the Kingdom is a result of the Fall and a work of the thief. Aim your prayers there. Your mission in life as a follower of Jesus is to bring things into alignment with Kingdom design—to live, work, and pray for restoration. Your faith is an agent of abundant life for yourself and others. It's why the Savior came.

> The more seriously we take the future promise of God's kingdom, the more unbearable will be the contradictions of that promise which we meet in the present.
>
> JÜRGEN MOLTMANN

Positioned for Grace

*God saved you by his grace when you believed. And you can't take
credit for this; it is a gift from God. Salvation is not a reward for
the good things we have done, so none of us can boast about it.*

EPHESIANS 2:8-9

WE HAVE ENTERED INTO A KINGDOM OF GRACE. Those of us who have
been immersed in the gospel of grace alone through faith alone are trained well in the
idea that we bring nothing to the table in God's Kingdom. We can't earn our salvation or answers to prayer. We can't bargain with God, merit his favor, or impress him
with works. Our salvation, sanctification, fruitfulness in ministry, and answers to
prayer are all given through his grace, and we dare not mix any self-effort into them.

That doctrine, thoroughly supported by Scripture, has blinded us to some other
considerations, however. We've become so resistant to bargaining with God or trying to earn his favor that we've forgotten the importance of positioning ourselves
to receive what he wants to give. It's true that we can't earn answers to our prayers,
but our maturity is not a matter of earning. We don't entrust our children with an
inheritance when they are spendthrifts; we don't give them the family business when
they have no business sense; and we don't hand over the car keys when they haven't
learned how to drive or demonstrated any sense of responsibility. All of these could
be gifts of pure grace that no child could merit, but he or she does need to become
mature enough to be able to handle them. So we wait. We help them grow. We withhold our gifts until the moment those gifts will bless them instead of ruining them.
We try to be wise in how we give our gifts of grace.

God is infinitely wise, so he often withholds his answers to our prayers until we
are ready for them—by his definition of *ready*. In the meantime, position yourself
well. Grow into the size of your desires while you are waiting for them to be fulfilled.
Don't try to earn them, but do prepare yourself to handle them. Grace pours into
your life according to your capacity to carry it.

Prayer is the means by which we obtain all the graces that rain down
upon us from the divine fountain of goodness and love.

LORENZO SCUPOLI

Redirected Worship

Pull down your father's altar to Baal, and cut down the Asherah pole
standing beside it. Then build an altar to the LORD your God here.

JUDGES 6:25-26

GOD GAVE GIDEON, A VERY INSECURE ISRAELITE, a mission to overthrow an oppressor. "Go with the strength you have," he said (Judges 6:14), though Gideon was convinced he didn't have any. The fact that God was sending him should have been enough to persuade Gideon that victory was certain, but it wasn't. The mission would require a lot of faith, and Gideon needed his to be revived, nurtured, and strengthened before he had the nerve to take God's word into battle.

We find ourselves in that situation often—theoretically believing in God's power (Gideon was well aware of past miracles) but hardly expecting it to apply to our own lives in the here and now. We have faith that God *can* do anything, but we don't necessarily have the faith that God *will* do something. Like Gideon, we need our faith restored, activated, and turned from past glories into present applications. We need to believe the God we believe in.

The first step in that resurrection of faith is a resurrection of worship. Gideon's great adventure of faith began with instructions to tear down the family's idolatrous altar and replace it with an altar to God. When we are worshiping the wrong things—when our attention is constantly directed elsewhere and we are drawing our energy and life from temporary fixes rather than the eternal source—our faith breaks. It's impossible to root our faith in God when we are investing our hearts in other things. Gideon had wondered why the Lord didn't seem to be with Israel, yet local worship practices provided a clear answer: Israel wasn't with the Lord. As the deliverer, Gideon would have to get his own priorities right before he could deliver. His faith had to turn toward truth. So does ours.

Anchor your whole self in God before you try to anchor your faith in him. Saturate yourself in worship, where God's presence and power become easy to see. A heart fixed on him begins to believe, and faith leads to victories he has promised.

> The issue of faith is not so much whether we believe in God,
> but whether we believe the God we believe in.
>
> R. C. SPROUL

Ask for Help

If you are truly going to use me to rescue Israel as
you promised, prove it to me. JUDGES 6:36-37

WHEN GOD SAYS SOMETHING, it's true. There's no need to question it. But Gideon wanted to be sure. Maybe he thought the encounter with the angel of God's presence had been an illusion, or maybe he had a flawed view of God and wondered if God might pull the rug out from under him. More likely, he was so uncertain of his worthiness that he disqualified himself from the possibility of victory. After all, armies were gathering. Perhaps it hadn't occurred to him that it's impossible to be victorious if you don't have a battle to begin with. He needed confirmation that things were still headed in the right direction.

Many of us wouldn't have the nerve to question God's integrity by asking, "If you're going to do what you said . . ." Nevertheless, Gideon asked—twice—and God patiently answered both times. Of course God would do what he said; that's his nature. And he had no problem giving Gideon multiple assurances that this mission was going to work out in a really good way.

Our adventures of faith often come with a lot of questions, and we're usually more subtle than Gideon in dealing with them. We rarely ask God to prove he's being honest, but we do question whether we have heard him correctly, taken steps to position ourselves for his answers, disqualified ourselves somewhere along the way, and applied his promises as they were intended. We bounce back and forth between "I don't measure up!" and "It isn't about measuring up." Or between "I'm standing on faith" and "I think I'm being presumptuous." Or between "I know what God said!" and "Did God really say that?" In those vague territories, feel free to ask God for guidance, assurance, encouragement, and confirmation. Keep the dialogue going; he has not sent you on your way with a past promise and no presence. Talk to him about it and let him speak to you whenever he chooses. His silence may test your faith at times; his voice will eventually come through to confirm it.

There is a living God. . . . He means what he says
and will do all he has promised.

HUDSON TAYLOR

When It's Time to Get Up

When Gideon heard the dream and its interpretation, he bowed in worship before the LORD. Then he returned to the Israelite camp and shouted, "Get up! For the LORD has given you victory." **JUDGES 7:15**

GOD HAD GIVEN GIDEON MULTIPLE ASSURANCES of victory, of prayers and promises answered, yet Gideon was still uncertain when the time for battle came. Yes, God had promised success, but when? How? In what sequence of events? While it's good to be in sync with God's processes, Gideon was a little too preoccupied with the details. Still, God gave him a final assurance—words from the enemy camp of Gideon's impending success. It was "go time."

Your adventures of faith will almost certainly lead up to a "go time." Sometimes God fulfills his purposes while we wait, but more often he concludes our time of waiting with a call to enter into the process itself—to go to battle, step out in faith, be the catalyst we've been waiting for. Like Gideon, we'll need to be careful; too many believers have tried to force God's hand by acting when they shouldn't have. But don't misunderstand; there is a time to act. Faith without works, as James insisted, is hardly faith. At some point, under God's direction, we will likely be called to move.

The good thing is that God is willing to give us guidance for when the time is right. When he does, Gideon's response is a good one for us to follow: to bow down in worship and declare that the time for victory has come. Many of our prayers involve long periods of waiting, but the moment of crisis calls for a different response. Like Gideon, we "get up" and choose to walk in victory. We pass through the parted waters. We overcome the obstacles. We enter into the Promised Land. We engage in battles. We claim the promise God has given. And we give thanks.

Watch for those moments. Don't rush them; wait attentively. But when the time comes, get up. Your faith looks to him in hope, but also in partnership. Recognize when the Lord has given you victory.

> You honor Jesus when you act in faith on his Word.
>
> EDWIN COLE

Refuse to Be Moved

There were troops, horses, and chariots everywhere. "Oh, sir,
what will we do now?" the young man cried to Elisha. **2 KINGS 6:15**

ELISHA'S SERVANT COULD SEE ONLY ADVERSARIES, and they were very real. But they weren't the ultimate reality. Like the rest of us, he was used to living by sight. Our minds have been well trained in interpreting visible circumstances as truth. We look at what is happening around us and take it at face value.

That's a rookie mistake in the life of faith. We hear a report, encounter a setback, experience adversity, and get discouraged that things are going in the wrong direction. But in matters of faith, the wrong direction is often the right direction, just as we've seen with Joseph, who seemed to be sent in the opposite direction of his dreams on multiple occasions but was actually headed toward them the entire way. We have a financial crisis and wonder why God isn't providing for us; we get lab results and wonder why he isn't healing us; we're halted at a closed door and wonder why he hasn't opened it. All the while, God may be leading us into that important phase of the journey in which we have nothing but our faith to stand on. The life of faith is a constant process of taking our eyes off of appearances and fixing them on God and his words. Our visible circumstances are not the truth of a situation.

This is not the same as living in denial, except in the sense of denying appearances that are contrary to what God has said. It is not the same as living in a fantasy world, indulging in wishful thinking we've come up with on our own. We don't just make up the reality we want to have. Faith means anchoring ourselves to God's promises, to the truths he has told us in his word, to the vision, purpose, and calling he has given us, and rejecting any outward appearance that contradicts these truths. We have to decide where we are going to fix our gaze and then refuse to be distracted by circumstances and visible discouragements. People may think we're escaping reality. According to God, we're walking straight into it.

> Seeing is not believing. Seeing is seeing. Believing is
> being confident without seeing.
>
> G. CAMPBELL MORGAN

Truth Behind the Scenes

Then Elisha prayed, "O LORD, open
his eyes and let him see!" **2 KINGS 6:17**

ELISHA'S SERVANT HAD ONLY SEEN the troops, horses, and chariots of the enemy coming against him and his unarmed master. But when Elisha prayed for God to open the young man's eyes, he suddenly saw a vast army of horses and chariots of fire, an altogether different sort of power. Where the young servant might have prayed desperately for survival (if he had gotten that far in his panic), he could now think in terms of total victory. His entire mood and perspective changed.

Often our prayer is for God to grant the things we have asked for. We have our eyes fixed on the problem and our hopes fixed on a solution. But better focus precedes that outcome-centered prayer. A higher priority is to pray that God would open our eyes and let us see—that our faith would be strong before visible answers come. If faith is the "reality of what we hope for," the evidence and assurance of what remains unseen (Hebrews 11:1), then it's really important to have faith up front. Otherwise prayer will feel (and often be) powerless. A lot is riding on our vision.

Human nature defaults to relying on what we see. Faith comes through a changed nature that defaults to the real story behind the scenes. Even if we aren't sure what that story is yet, we know it's there, and we can go searching for it. We can ask God to reveal it. We can pray for our eyes to open so we can see it. Then we establish ourselves in that spiritual vision and live in defiance of the natural one. We cannot live the life of faith while being focused on what the rest of the world calls reality. We can only live it by stripping away the surface view and unveiling what's behind it.

Practice the art of envisioning the help that is on your side. Ask God for revelations of it—insights and assurances of the help that is there and the solution he wants to provide. Train your eyes to see behind the scenes from the start. Great victories are won for, by, and through people who have stationed themselves in the realm where real power lies.

Faith is the sight of the inward eye.

ALEXANDER MACLAREN

Always and Everywhere

Pray in the Spirit at all times and on every occasion.
Stay alert and be persistent in your prayers for
all believers everywhere. **EPHESIANS 6:18**

PAUL HAD JUST WRITTEN a powerful passage to the Ephesians on the spiritual battles we face, drawing imagery from Isaiah and Roman soldiers to call attention to the nature of the fight and our need to prepare. Our spiritual armor and weapons are sufficient, but we have to wear and wield them in a Holy Spirit–saturated context. So just when we think this visual passage is winding down, Paul reaches the climax: The spiritual battle is above all a matter of prayer.

Unfortunately, there is a paragraph break in many Bible translations between the passage on armor and the passage on praying, and most readers who enjoy envisioning spiritual armor tend to tune out at obligatory admonitions to pray. *Of course, we're supposed to pray,* they think. *We've heard that before.* But if the purpose of this vivid illustration was to lead up to this instruction, it must be more than obligatory. It's imperative. This is critical to our lives and the people we pray for.

Perhaps that explains the sweeping nature of Paul's words. We are to pray at *all* times on *every* occasion, persistently praying for *all* believers *everywhere*. If we ever thought we could cruise through life, if we ever wished for a carefree existence, we were greatly mistaken. God gives us seasons of rest and refreshing, to be sure, and he never wants us to be stressed out. But he does want us to be alert. The spiritual welfare of the people in our sphere of influence depends on it.

Take these words to heart. Let Paul's inclusive appeal ring in your ears throughout each day. You have not been called to develop a type A spirituality, but you do have moments of downtime you can fill with prayers and petitions. Your fellowship with other believers should pulsate with prayer whenever you meet. Rest in the Spirit, but be diligent in listening for the appeals he is making through you. As individuals and churches, we are on a relentless mission that is driven and supported by our requests to our Father in heaven.

Prayer meetings are the throbbing machinery of the church.

CHARLES SPURGEON

Weapons of War

Put on every piece of God's armor so you will be able to
resist the enemy in the time of evil. **EPHESIANS 6:13**

THERE'S A REASON FOR THE WARNING not to bring up religion and politics at dinner parties. They are polarizing issues that highlight differences more than commonalities, and we can avoid speaking of them when we choose. But at a deeper level, spiritual battles rage around us, and we can't smooth them over so easily. Spiritual truth has always been a matter of contention. Jesus was clear that people would split over him (Matthew 10:34-36). God's Kingdom is always contested in this world.

Whatever illusions of neutrality we had when we embarked on the Christian life, whatever dreams we had of everything turning out well for us, we soon realized instead that we landed in the middle of a battle. The conflict may be expressed through human beings, but that's not where it originates. We are in the front lines of a cosmic war. We have to choose whether to stand firm or flee, and efforts to flee are generally futile. We are in this until God takes us out or Jesus returns in final victory.

That's the bad news. The good news is that we have nothing to fear. The victory has already been won. Fighting continues, and we do have to enforce the victory, but the outcome is not in doubt. The enemy resists the Kingdom of God, but we keep advancing, and the gates of hell cannot prevail against it. But we have to move forward.

For your current mission, you have been given a remarkable set of armor. It is spiritual, so you have to wear it spiritually, and the only way to do that is through spiritual resources like worship, prayer, and faith. That means you have to learn to see it, count on it, apply it, and believe it is doing something in the invisible realm. Prayer then becomes a vital necessity—your communication between headquarters and the front, your lifeline to your source of strength. You are "special forces" in the Kingdom of God, and your world is depending on you. Learn to envision your armor and sword and refuse to go through any day without praying from the certainty of your security and victory in God.

Prayer is a strong wall and fortress of the church; it is a good Christian weapon.

MARTIN LUTHER

Faith Against the World

Hold up the shield of faith to stop the fiery arrows of the devil.
EPHESIANS 6:16

YOU'VE PROBABLY REALIZED BY NOW that the fallen world is stacked against your faith. The creativity and power of God are written into creation, and the human heart longs for a connection with him, so the basic upward call is clear to those with eyes to see it. But moving in that direction isn't easy. Biblical truth is presented in myriad ways with multiple interpretations and emphases and sometimes with distorted motives. It's real, but it can become muddled, even in your own heart and mind. And as you've surely noticed, your faith has no shortage of opponents who would love to see it disappear.

The good news is that you don't have to counter every argument, explain every mystery, answer every question, undo every attack, or even respond to much of what is said. You don't have to master the ways of God or figure out how to grow spiritually. You'll need to embrace his wisdom, power, and love, but you don't have to try to become omniscient or omnipotent. You simply need to keep responding in faith.

Still, the Christian walk often seems like an uphill climb because of the ways of the world. If you've ever wondered why it's so hard to have faith about certain things, this is it. Faith is powerful in the spiritual war, and it will be resisted every step of the way. It quenches flaming arrows and neutralizes enemy strategies. It is absolutely central to everything in the Kingdom of God.

That means that your prayers, work, relationships, and other areas of life need to be accompanied by faith. Faith brings God's words and power into any situation. Spiritual enemies of God hate it. You have to learn to thrive on it. By faith, you cling to what God has said, and when you do, his words remain inviolable in your life. Faith quenches lies about God and his promises, contradictions to his plans and purposes, and strategies against his Kingdom. Hold up that shield constantly, and never underestimate its strength. Your prayers, works, words, and life become astonishingly powerful under its protection.

Once we attain to a real faith, all the forces of hell are impotent to annul it.

J. O. FRASER

Plead His Promises

Take the sword of the Spirit, which is the word of God.
EPHESIANS 6:17

WHEN YOU FIRST EMBRACE a promise from God, you might think that's the end of the story. He said it, you believe it, it's a done deal. In a sense that's true, but you'll likely run into some obstacles along the way. You'll wrestle with internal doubts about whether you're understanding his promise correctly, with external forces that tell you this is not how life really works, with temptations that would have you give up or compromise, and with lies that say you're wrong and shame you for it. Before long, you're stuck in spiritual mud, caught by spiritual thorns, and dumped in a spiritual ditch. You feel like you can't move forward, can't go back, and can't give in. You are in a spiritual limbo where once-powerful promises seem to wither away.

The promises are still powerful, of course. God doesn't speak things that grow weaker over time. But our faith can grow weaker, and we can begin to wonder where God is in the situation. The problem is not God, or even that our faith was misguided. It's our neglect of the sharp, penetrating weapon we've been given for our spiritual battles. We need to take up the sword of the Spirit, the words God has spoken into our hearts.

You'll find some expression of those words somewhere in Scripture, even if they first came to you through an inner conviction, timely counsel from another believer, or the voice of the Spirit when you were praying. Look for them, embrace them, memorize them, and rehearse them again and again. Sometimes the only thing lacking in faith is a remembrance of the living Word and an active use of it in conversations and prayers. Sometimes you just have to wage war using the promises God has given you.

Learn those promises and take them into battle. Take them into your prayer closet too. You won't wage war against God there, but you will use your sword against everything that opposes his truth. As you do, lies and contradictions will lose their power, doubts will give way to faith, and God will honor your trust in his integrity. His promises will come alive again in your heart.

Learn to plead the promises of God!

AMBROSE WHALEY

Till Victory Appears

He always prays earnestly for you, asking God to make you strong and
perfect, fully confident that you are following the whole will of God.
I can assure you that he prays hard for you. **COLOSSIANS 4:12-13**

THE COLOSSIANS SEEMED TO KNOW many people close to Paul, and he had important pieces of news to share with them. One was about a member of their own fellowship, Epaphras, who had visited Paul and perhaps prompted this letter. So what did Paul want to share about this friend? That he prayed for them. Hard.

In fact, Paul wrote that Epaphras prayed "earnestly"—employing a Greek word that's used to describe deep struggles or intense wrestling matches, the same word from which we get the word *agonize*. Epaphras wasn't in agony for the Colossians— that would take the connotation too far—but Paul does imply that the intensity of his prayers reflected the spiritual battle for Colossian souls. Epaphras wanted these believers to grow in maturity, to become strong in the faith, to know the will of God and pursue it fully. Nothing in Paul's words or Epaphras's desires suggests a casual kind of prayer lifted up on behalf of his friends. No, he wrestled. His prayers were somehow part of a critical battle in the Kingdom.

That's sometimes how prayer works. Generally we fill our prayers with worship, joy, gratitude, and an expectant heart, but our requests and issues are rarely light-hearted. Our conversations with God can grow intense, not because he is opposed to us but because it is absolutely imperative that we reach a place of faith where we follow through to victory. We may not understand why things are difficult or over-whelming, but they are. Communication between the front lines and headquarters happens in the heat of battle, and sometimes the needs are urgent. We cannot afford to engage casually and unemotionally.

The Holy Spirit will prompt you in those times. When he does, fully engage. Wrestle in whatever way is necessary. Pray with urgency and insistent, immediate, unrelenting faith. Significant battles are won when ready warriors answer the call and press in until victory comes.

> I have known persons to pray for hours, till their strength was all exhausted with the agony of their minds. Such prayers prevailed with God.
>
> **CHARLES FINNEY**

Devoted to Prayer

Devote yourselves to prayer with an alert mind and a thankful heart.

COLOSSIANS 4:2

JEREMIAH LANPHIER WAS CONCERNED for the souls of businessmen around him. In fact, he prayed for them every day during the noon hour. Eventually he wondered if others might like to join him, so he started a regular weekday prayer meeting during the lunch hour when businesses were closed. He passed out fliers— the most immediate way to reach large numbers of people in 1850s New York—and invited many to come. But at the time of the first meeting, no one had shown up. Only a few straggled in during the hour, and only a few of those agreed to try again the next week and the next. But within six months, more than 10,000 men were gathering for prayer. Revivals with hundreds of conversions began to break out nearby and then further away. A spiritual movement had begun.

Similar stories are told of other prayer movements—the Moravian movement, revivals in China and Korea, and many others. In fact, history has been shaped by unknown prayer warriors even more profoundly than by the famous names and faces we put in our textbooks. That's because history's actors perform their scenes on a stage governed by a Playwright and his stagehands. When he responds to the prayers of his people, tides turn and trends give way to the currents of his Kingdom. He is building something magnificent through the prayers and faith of Kingdom citizens.

Because of your connection to the source of life, you have more influence in this world than you have yet imagined. You may never be recognized for that power or even see its effects yourself. But people with eyes of faith know the potential and take advantage of it. Like Jeremiah Lanphier and many before and since, they believe that crying out to God for his purposes is much more powerful than trying to forge our own. A life devoted to prayer changes the course of history and blesses a world that resists its own Creator. It puts you in a position of authority no matter how little earthly power you hold. And it makes you a partner with God in his mission to rescue, redeem, and restore the lives of many.

Every great movement of God can be traced to a kneeling figure.

D. L. MOODY

Changing History

One day as these men were worshiping the Lord and fasting,
the Holy Spirit said, "Appoint Barnabas and Saul for the
special work to which I have called them." **ACTS 13:2**

THE MORAVIANS BEGAN A PRAYER MOVEMENT in the 1720s that lasted more than a century. Out of their dedication to corporate prayer came some of the first drops of a gushing stream we now know as the modern missions movement. God prompted some of them to go to the Caribbean islands to minister to slaves, and though the work was difficult and many died, a sense of responsibility for the unevangelized world began to spread within Protestant circles. Over the next two centuries and beyond, many Christians would dedicate their lives sacrificially for all to hear the good news of the Kingdom.

Things happen when we bring no agenda to God other than worshiping him. That's what the leaders in Antioch seemed to be doing. The literal sense of today's verse is that they were ministering to the Lord rather than asking him to minister to them. When we focus on worship, we are entering into the environment of heaven, where worship fills everything all the time. We cannot help being changed in that environment. God's voice and his purposes become clearer. Divine thoughts begin to flow. The Holy Spirit speaks. And in the case of Paul and Barnabas, the Moravians, and many other people and groups who have encountered God in worship, things change. Plans unfold. World history takes a different turn.

One of the greatest things you can do for this world is to enter into the heavenly environment by worshiping God. Nowhere are you more aligned with truth and in sync with the created universe. You may be tempted at times to worship him in order to get something, but that isn't worship. Come to him without any agenda other than loving him and anticipating his goodness—somehow, in some way, at some time of his choosing. The more you immerse yourself in his praises, the more you will carry the aroma of heaven with you. You may hear his voice or sense his purpose. And this world will undoubtedly be the better for it.

The worship of God is not a rule of safety—it is an adventure of the spirit.

ALFRED NORTH WHITEHEAD

Ones Who Intercede

He saw that there was no man, and wondered that there was no one to intercede. **ISAIAH 59:16,** ESV

"WHY DOESN'T GOD DO SOMETHING?" Most people have asked this question at some point in their faith journey when confronted with difficulties. We long for him to intervene in situations that seem to beg for intervention. We pray and wait, hoping he will do something to resolve those situations. Meanwhile, according to certain passages in the Prophets, God is looking at us and saying, "Why don't they do something?"

Isaiah described injustices going on around him that, not surprisingly, sound very similar to what we see in our world today. People were groping for justice and righteousness, and God "saw it, and it displeased him" (verse 15, ESV). God certainly didn't expect his people to do everything themselves—to accomplish miracles and to establish his Kingdom in their own power. But he did call them to live out Kingdom values. But they neglected his covenant, and society was in a mess. Though he "wondered that there was no one to intercede," he nevertheless brought salvation himself. He became the intercessor he was looking for.

There's a profound principle in this prophetic observation: God is looking for human beings to intercede. He assigned us to be stewards of his creation (Genesis 1:26-28) and agents on earth who ask for his intervention, who stand between heaven and earth and mediate his blessings to this planet. In fact, this seems to be why God became man rather than simply saving us from afar. If he set up the world to be under human stewardship, and there were no righteous humans to fulfill that purpose, he would have to become the righteous human he was looking for. Since he redeems us and fills us with his Spirit, we can now be the intercessors we were called to be.

Make the most of that position. Be the heavenly agent on earth who invites God's action into our affairs. Live as a mediator in the gap, a conductor of his presence into the world around you. Be the answer to your question of why nothing is happening. Pray for God's wisdom, power, and love—and embody them however you can.

God does nothing on earth except in answer to believing prayer.

JOHN WESLEY

The First Resort

All the believers devoted themselves . . . to prayer. **ACTS 2:42**

"ALL WE CAN DO NOW IS PRAY." It's often a statement of resignation, the last words we say before giving up, a desperate plea in a desperate situation after all other recourse has been attempted. Human nature tends to default to self-reliance, which means that whenever we face a problem, need, or crisis, we immediately do everything we can to deal with it ourselves. Some people pray along the way; others hardly think about prayer until all other options run out. But we have to become spiritually minded people to default to prayer in the first place. Otherwise, it becomes our last resort.

Think of the message that conveys. When prayer is nothing more than a last resort, we use God to fill in the gaps of our own abilities, as if human effort is primary and God is our supplement. He becomes our backup plan. But when we saturate our lives in prayer, covering every situation with a request to know God's will and be empowered to carry it out, he becomes the priority and we become his helpers. Prayer up front acknowledges that God is up front—that he is the driving force in our lives. The difference between the two approaches tells us a lot about how we see God, ourselves, and our world. Where we place prayer in our priorities says something about where God fits in our lives.

God is gracious to answer prayers of last resort, even if they relegate him to last-resort status. But we are designed to begin, continue, and end with prayer in everything—in stewarding our families, carrying out our business, relating to others, living out the gospel, and influencing the world. Prayer is not only for those critical moments of relational, health, and financial concerns but for constant communication with our source of life at all times. It should pervade our lives more than the food we eat and the air we breathe. A life saturated in prayer may face no fewer problems than a life without it, but they are different problems and managed in entirely different ways, filled with purpose and fruitfulness—and with God involved every step of the way.

We need more Christians for whom prayer is the first resort, not the last.

JOHN BLANCHARD

Ask Early and Often

If you need wisdom, ask our generous God, and he will give
it to you. He will not rebuke you for asking. **JAMES 1:5**

ONE OF THE MOST PERSISTENT THEMES throughout the Bible is that God will guide us if we let him. He directs our steps and delights in the details of our lives (Psalm 37:23); he shows us which path to take when we seek his will and refuse to rely on our own understanding (Proverbs 3:5-6); he opens a way through the waters (Isaiah 43:16); and he promises that his plans for us are good (Jeremiah 29:11). From beginning to end, he has a plan for us, and he extends a certain latitude within that plan for us to exercise the choices he gives us. But in spite of all the wonderful promises about his guidance in our lives, many believing Christians still seem to lack direction. Why? Because we don't always ask.

Perhaps it's more accurate to say we tend to ask only when we reach a moment of decision, a fork in the road that prompts us to pray while we're weighing the pros and cons. But that's a remedial kind of prayer, a plea for momentary wisdom, a request for a transaction rather than a lifestyle—like asking him to take the wheel only when we've lost control of the car. But asking God for an understanding of his will should be a way of life from the start. He'll step in at any moment, but sometimes not with the immediate information we crave. When we invite him into our decision-making, he comes to lay a foundation, and that takes time. When we ask him into a deadline-driven decision, time is limited. We may have already missed an opportunity to understand his purposes.

It's never too early to ask God for wisdom. He is eager to guide us, even to show us things we will face down the road (Jeremiah 33:3). At any point, he is willing to steer our lives in the right direction—and sooner is always better.

Is prayer your steering wheel or your spare tire?

CORRIE TEN BOOM

Feelings of Faith

Jesus was sleeping at the back of the boat with his head on a cushion.
MARK 4:38

A STORM WAS RAGING, the disciples were panicking, and Jesus slept. That's hard to do on Galilean fishing boats. They weren't very big, and with twelve men along for the ride, it couldn't have been a relaxing environment even on the calmest of days. But this day wasn't calm at all—both outside in the weather and inside the disciples' hearts. High waves broke into the boat, it filled with water, Jesus' friends were terrified, and he was having a quiet little nap.

Faith itself is not an emotion, but it is accompanied by many. It embraces peace and calm, quiet resolve, expectant joy, even the zeal of the Lord, and it rejects fear, panic, dread, discouragement, and other volatile moods that undermine its power. In fact, we can be sure that if we are in panic mode, we are not in faith; and if we are in faith, we cannot be in panic mode. Our emotions play a significant role in how our faith develops and what it looks like to others. They are symptoms for diagnosing the condition of our spiritual health.

If we are praying "in faith" for God to do something and are still worried about or discouraged over the situation, signs suggest that we don't really believe. If we really believe God is going to do something good or trust him to work things out, we tend to get happy about it in advance. Our faith affects our emotional state, and our emotional state affects our faith—which is why it is so vital to cultivate a climate of worship, gratitude, peace, and joy in our hearts and homes *even before God has answered.* Jesus was able to sleep in the boat because he knew he was on a mission from God. He surely had to be alert to enemy resistance, but he didn't have to worry about whether the Father would take care of him along the way. He recognized God's plan and trusted him to watch over it. Faith gives rest to a restless heart, even as the storms of life rage.

> God incarnate is the end of fear, and the heart that realizes that
> he is in the midst . . . will be quiet in the midst of alarm.
>
> F. B. MEYER

A Different Way to Care

Teacher, don't you care that we're going to drown? **MARK 4:38**

THE DISCIPLES WERE EXTREMELY BOTHERED by the storm that threatened to overwhelm their small boat. And the longer Jesus slept, the more they were bothered by him, as well. After all, it looked like he didn't care about the catastrophe. His peace made him appear irresponsible. He wasn't doing anything to help; he was just being passive. Everyone else seemed to understand the call to action, but Jesus remained motionless.

That's often how it is in the life of faith. The emotions that come from our trust in God—peace, joy, relief, rest, contentment—can make us look irresponsible. Our peace can actually provoke conflict. When we don't get as stirred into a panic as the people around us do, we appear unconcerned. When we don't jump into action at every perceived threat, we seem inactive in a time of need. People think the calmness we have comes not from faith but from a cold heart. We are accused of not caring.

The truth of the matter is that we care a lot, but we've turned our cares over to God and trust him to intervene. We do want to be responsible, and we'll do whatever we can to help. But ultimately, the responsibility is on God, and we have to believe him even when others are pressing us to act out of stress, fear, and panic. We trust that he is working out all things for the good of those who love him (Romans 8:28) and has solutions for every problem we face. We learn to recognize that most people's sense of urgency does not line up with his priorities. Jesus rarely reacted to human urgencies and never panicked. As those being conformed to his image, that should be our outlook too. That does *not* mean we are to be lazy or irresponsible. It does mean, however, that our approach to life is not driven by fear or weighed down by heavy burdens and overwhelming demands. Our care, concern, and compassion are clothed in trust and fully at rest in the one who cares for every detail of our lives.

Never be afraid to trust an unknown future to a known God.

CORRIE TEN BOOM

Calming the Storm Inside

Why are you afraid? Do you still have no faith? MARK 4:40

IT'S NORMAL TO BE AFRAID in the midst of a terrifying, boat-tossing, wave-crashing storm. Human physiology and emotions were designed for self-protection, and when our safety is threatened, fear provokes action. Yet Jesus asked his followers why they were so afraid—why, in light of the greater truth of God's presence and love, they reacted more strongly to the situation they saw with their eyes. From a fallen human perspective, the fear seems obvious, thoroughly based in reality. From heaven's perspective, it isn't reality at all—or at least not the reality that matters most.

Jesus was able to sleep in the boat and calm the storm because the peace inside him was stronger than the storm outside. Our inner environment always trumps our outer environment if we let it; the spiritual realities of this world are stronger and more significant than natural forces. Sure, natural forces can overturn a boat or cover us with thundering waves, but they don't rule our destiny or dictate our relationship with God, and they don't defy his promises and purposes. Yet we so often let the natural environment dictate our inner condition, as if the circumstances we see are bigger and stronger than God's words to us. We seem to think the situations we face are greater than God's plan.

They aren't. God has a plan for us, and trusting him is a necessary part of carrying it out. Faith in God is powerful because God himself is powerful. When we conform to the image of the worried, stressed, insecure, panicking people around us, we are moving in the wrong direction. We must conform instead to Jesus, the Prince of Peace. The way we handle our worries at any given moment tells us volumes about what we think of God. If they are calmed by the voice of faith, we are becoming like Jesus and growing into God's purposes. If they are not, something needs to change. And we have the tools for that—the example and the will to stand up, speak to the storms with confidence, and tell them to be at peace. Those words have power, and they strengthen the peace inside of us to become greater than the storms outside.

The cure of fear is faith.

NORMAN VINCENT PEALE

Desperate Prayers

Hannah was in deep anguish, crying bitterly
as she prayed to the LORD. **1 SAMUEL 1:10**

HANNAH WAS DESPERATE FOR A CHILD and prayed her heart out. She even made a deal with God—not always a good idea, but this one served his purposes. At a time when righteous servants were lacking, she would dedicate her child to his service if he gave her one. And when she went to the Tabernacle to make this vow, she prayed so passionately and intensely that the priest thought she was drunk. Discovering her true purpose and her fervent petition before the Lord, he blessed her to receive whatever she had asked for. And she went home with the assurance of faith.

God answers desperate prayers. We see that more than once in Scripture. It's evident in the Exodus, when his people cried out for deliverance; in the period of the judges, when his people repeatedly begged for his intervention in situations they had created through their own idolatry; in the Psalms, when David and others were in desperate situations and pleaded with God for rescue; in the books of the prophets, when Israel and Judah were being disciplined for their sin and turning their backs on God; in Acts, when Peter was in prison and the believers gathered to pray all night for his release; in Revelation, when saints and martyrs cry out for justice; and in plenty of situations in between. But desperation alone, though it moves God's heart, does not prompt his response. Hannah received not because she was desperate but because she went home believing. Her faith was part of her process.

God takes pity on the oppressed, the hurting, the brokenhearted, the weak, and the vulnerable. We are invited to come to him in any condition and pour out our hearts, even as passionately and incoherently as Hannah seemed to be doing when the priest thought she was drunk. But somewhere along the way, faith becomes part of the equation. The pleas of the desperate turn into trust in the Father who loves them. Many psalms begin in crisis but end in praise, even before God has intervened. Some people let desperation drive them from God; others let it drive them into his presence. Hannah did the latter and received the blessing she longed for.

Prayer is love in need appealing to love in power.
JAMES MOFFATT

Emotions in Sync

Then she went back and began to eat again,
and she was no longer sad. 1 SAMUEL 1:18

MANY CHRISTIANS HAVE BEEN TOLD that emotions belong in the back seat of their lives, that feelings should never be allowed to steer us away from truth. There's some truth to that, but emotions are absolutely essential for bonding with an emotional God, and they are accurate indicators of what we really believe. If our hearts are in turmoil, then we are not confident that things are going to work out for our good or according to our prayers; if our hearts are at peace, then we are trusting and resting in God's good purposes for our lives. What we feel is like the light on the dashboard that tells us what's going on inside the engine. And if our feelings are out of sorts, we know to look under the hood.

One moment, Hannah was deeply distressed and pleading with God for help. The next moment, "she was no longer sad." The only thing that happened between those two moments was the blessing she received from a priest for God to grant what she had requested. Based on nothing more, her heart shifted from tumult to calm, from worry to relief, from distress to rest. She simply believed what he said. She apparently wasn't confident that God would answer her prayers merely because she prayed them; she was confident only in the confirmation that came from one of God's servants. She heard the confirming word and counted on it.

Hannah's emotions affected her faith, and then her faith affected her emotions. There is no lesson in this passage about getting rid of emotions and living by robotic adherence to truth. No, we are told repeatedly throughout Scripture that God has compassion, joy, delight, zeal, anger, jealousy, and grief. They are holy emotions, to be sure, but they are feelings nonetheless. We live by faith not by stripping our emotional lives away but by synchronizing them with God's heart. And when we take his promises to be true, we can rest in them, delight in them, and rejoice. Hannah did, and she was able to go home and eat again, waiting expectantly for God to fulfill his Word.

> Faith is . . . such an inward and felt assurance and hearty and joyful embracing of truth, as to produce corresponding feeling and action, and to exclude doubt.
>
> CHARLES FINNEY

The Feelings of Jesus

God knows how much I love you and long for you with
the tender compassion of Christ Jesus. **PHILIPPIANS 1:8**

PHILIPPIANS IS AN EMOTIONAL LETTER, and Paul was not shy about expressing what he felt. In some letters, he expressed anger and frustration, but this one is full of joy. And not just any joy but the joy that comes from confidence in who God is and what he is doing, even when we don't know exactly what that is. The only way to get that kind of joy is through fellowship with the Holy Spirit, who lives within every believer and shares with us the emotions of God. As we are being conformed to God in our minds and wills, we ought also to be conforming to his feelings about everything—people, sin, his plans for the world, and more. Then we begin to sense a love and compassion coming from beyond ourselves.

That's how Paul expressed his affection for the Philippian believers. He longed for and loved them "with the tender compassion of Christ." He was motivated by the perspective and feelings of the Spirit of Christ within him, thoroughly feeling the love and joy as his own, but also knowing it was in sync with the love and joy of God. His heart had merged with the Lord's, and he expressed his/their feelings openly and often.

The more we grow in intimacy with the Lord, the less we are able to distinguish between his heart and ours. That's how it is in any loving relationship; as our lives merge with someone else's, we often take on their desires and feelings, and they take on ours. It's hard to know where we begin and the other ends, and vice versa. In our relationship with Jesus, we begin to think as he thinks, feel as he feels, long for the things he longs for, and have the same motivations, compassions, angers, jealousies, joys, and more. His heart and our hearts beat as one. That's a remarkably fruitful condition for praying for his will—and ours (though we can hardly tell the difference)—to be done.

> When men are animated by the love of Christ they feel united, and the needs, sufferings, and joys of others are felt as their own.
>
> JOHN XXIII

When Love Prays

I pray that your love will overflow more and more, and that you will keep on growing in knowledge and understanding. **PHILIPPIANS 1:9**

PAUL HAD JUST TOLD BELIEVERS in the Philippian church how he longed for them with the tender compassion of Jesus. But as we know, love doesn't just sit there. It is moved to action, and very often that action is prayer. So Paul immediately told the Philippians how he had been praying for them—how the compassion of Jesus filling his heart had come out in his words, faith, and spiritual power. He prayed that their love would grow more and more (as his had), and that their knowledge and understanding would increase. He wanted them to see the King and the Kingdom as clearly as they could because that's the most loving thing we can hope for in someone else's life.

The fact that Paul's prayers were motivated by love—specifically by "tender compassion" (verse 8)—is significant. We should never pray just for the sake of praying or even for the sake of making things right, accomplishing godly goals and purposes, or getting our needs met. Our prayers are to flow from a fountain of love because that is the foundation and fundamental truth of who God is (1 John 4:9, 16). Our prayers have to connect with God at this point; otherwise, they are pointless. As Paul wrote in 1 Corinthians 13, all of our activity is fruitless apart from love.

The good news is that prayer is especially fruitful when motivated by love—far more so than if we pray because we want to see miracles, experience God's power, satisfy the needs and longings in our hearts, or have our spiritual status validated. None of those desires are necessarily wrong; they just aren't the highest priority. Instead, when we are driven to pray for ourselves and the people around us because our hearts overflow with love for God and others—because our compassion moves us, as it so often moved Jesus—we are moving in sync with God's Spirit. Our prayers carry his DNA within them. His love—and ours—becomes the reason, the purpose, and the outcome of the things we pray.

We are never nearer to Christ than when we find ourselves lost in a holy amazement at his unspeakable love.

JOHN OWEN

Jealous Prayers

The LORD Almighty says: "I am very jealous for Zion;
I am burning with jealousy for her." **ZECHARIAH 8:2,** NIV

MOST OF US HAVE A HARD TIME thinking of God as jealous. We see jealousy as petty, volatile, and unbefitting an eternal, sovereign God who holds the entire universe in his hands. But in spite of our objections, God applies the term to himself. He even says his *name* is jealous (Exodus 34:14). He has a pure, zealous love for his people and grieves when that love is rejected—especially in favor of lesser loves (and all loves are less than his). He portrays himself repeatedly through prophets as a most worthy lover who is often betrayed by adulterous people. These are not the words of a dispassionate God.

It makes sense, if we think about it. Jealousy is a natural by-product of love. After all, if we say we love someone intensely yet don't seem to care when that person rejects us for someone else, do we really love that intensely? If God is love, then he cannot be a God without jealousy. He longs for the affections of his people, and he wants their affections to prioritize him above all else. It has to be that way. It's the way love works.

What does that have to do with our prayers and faith? Everything. If God burns with jealousy for the love of his people, our prayers should also burn to put love—ours and others'—in its proper place. It's one thing to pray for people to enter into a relationship with God; it's another to pray that they would passionately adore him. One scratches the surface; the other pierces the heart. And since this intensity of love is God's purpose for everyone called to enter into his Kingdom, we can pray it with the utmost faith. We can pray with the jealous heart of God for those he loves—that his Spirit would pursue them zealously and that their hearts would unfold before him, softening and opening to receive all he has for them. This is the heartbeat of his Kingdom and the most direct way to align our hearts with his Spirit. And it invites his Kingdom powerfully into our world.

> There is no human wreckage, lying in the ooze of the deepest sea
> of iniquity, that God's deep love cannot reach and redeem.
>
> JOHN HENRY JOWETT

Heartfelt Prayer

He looked around at them angrily and was deeply
saddened by their hard hearts. **MARK 3:5**

JESUS WENT INTO A SYNAGOGUE on the Sabbath and noticed a man with a deformed hand. He knew his opponents were watching to see whether he would violate the law (as they interpreted it) to heal the man or resist compassion to uphold the law. They knew his tendency and were waiting for the opportunity to use it as proof that someone who played fast and loose with God's standards could not be from God. The problem was that they had completely missed what God's standards really were.

In this moment, with everyone watching to see whether the compassionate Savior would behave compassionately, Jesus let the dramatic pause linger a bit longer. As it did, he looked at them with anger, saddened by their hard hearts. There was a time when pictures and films rarely portrayed Jesus with such emotions—some showed him as always serious, with a faraway gaze in his eyes—but according to the Gospels, those emotions were there. He was frequently moved with compassion (Matthew 9:36; 14:14; Mark 6:34); he reacted harshly to commercial exploitation of worship (Matthew 21:12; John 2:15); he prayed with anguish, loud crying, and tears (Luke 22:44; Hebrews 5:7); and he was driven to the cross by the anticipation of joy (Hebrews 12:2). We do not follow an unemotional Savior.

Just as you seek to conform your thoughts and your will to Jesus, also conform your emotions to his. Don't let feelings determine your truth, but by all means, let them fuel your prayers and move you to action. That balance is difficult for many, but it fits his example. Your goal as his follower is to seek his purposes, think his thoughts, and feel his heartbeat, lining yourself up with him however you can. You have help in this; his Spirit lives within you and will influence and shape you to whatever degree you yield to his work. But you also have people and situations around you that will prompt emotional responses constantly. Don't avoid those responses; lean into them and align them with God. His heart will feed your prayers, your prayers will move his heart, and he will accomplish his work through you.

The impulse to prayer within our hearts is evidence
that Christ is urging our claims in heaven.

AUGUSTUS HOPKINS STRONG

The Testimony of Faith

*Abram believed the LORD, and the LORD counted him
as righteous because of his faith.* **GENESIS 15:6**

ABRAHAM'S JOURNEY OF FAITH was filled with missteps. Though he and Sarah were childless, God promised to make a great nation of him, but he really didn't say how. At some point, Abraham began to wonder what part he was to play in this process—how much of it was up to God and how much of it was up to him. God hadn't given him instructions, and he didn't specify which woman would carry his children. He left a lot of blanks for Abraham to fill in, and Abraham created a mess with them. Years later, when the fulfillment of the promise seemed overdue, God reiterated it, and Abraham laughed. Then Sarah laughed and even lied about laughing. Eventually, the child of promise was born.

Interestingly, when the New Testament tells the story of Abraham and Sarah's faith, it leaves out all the missteps (Romans 4:18-22; Hebrews 11:8-12). It focuses only on the faith that surfaced at times in the process. That's because from God's point of view, our entire journey of faith is defined by our moments of belief and where we end up. All the things we tend to focus on—the misunderstandings, mistakes, sins, and regrets—are washed away in the testimony of fulfillment. Never mind that Abraham questioned, meddled, laughed, and made decisions that still divide the Promised Land today. He believed, and God considered him righteous.

That's your testimony too. You may go through all kinds of ups and downs in your faith, wondering how God is going to fulfill his promises to you, taking on more or less responsibility than you should, narrowing down the specifics of his plan, saying and thinking the wrong things, losing heart when things take too long, and generally waiting it out without knowing the details you want to know. But if you once believed, and if you end up believing when the time for fulfillment has come, that's faith, no matter what else happened along the way. His testimony of your process will not include those regrettable moments of unbelief. If you survive this journey with faith intact, you are an example of faith for the ages. And God considers that righteousness.

Faith in God will always be crowned.

WILLIAM S. PLUMER

The Focus of Faith

Let us run with endurance the race God has set before us.
We do this by keeping our eyes on Jesus, the champion who
initiates and perfects our faith. **HEBREWS 12:1-2**

HEBREWS 11 IS A WONDERFULLY ENCOURAGING CHAPTER about great heroes of faith. We read of their bold actions that were based on nothing but a promise from God, their steadfast insistence on his words, their vision of the greater "city" he is building, their endurance through adversity and persecution, and the great rewards that far outweighed any costs they suffered. We read with admiration, letting the author's repeated declarations that it was all "by faith" sink deeper into our hearts. And then we go back into the Old Testament and read the stories of these heroes and realize a very startling fact: Most of them were extremely flawed people.

Yes, our heroes of faith were a mess. Many of them came from dysfunctional families and passed on their dysfunctions to future generations. They made lots of mistakes and ended up with lots of regrets. They sometimes said the wrong things, did the wrong things, and got mixed up with the wrong people. Some were victims of horrible offenses; others perpetrated horrible offenses. They lived from day to day and year to year with moments of great faith but also seasons of wandering and wondering in between. In other words, they were human—very much like us.

Perhaps that's why the writer of Hebrews follows up this glowing list of heroes of faith with encouragement that applies to all of us: We are to lay aside everything that weighs us down—our sins, to be sure, but also our regrets, our obsession with "getting it right," and our doubts—and run the race with endurance. How? By fixing our gaze on Jesus. Instead of focusing on the messes in our journey of faith, we are to focus on the one who ran the race perfectly and the fulfillment he accomplishes— just as the writer of this letter did in chapter 11. When we gaze at our flaws, our obstacles, or the race itself, we falter. When we gaze at the inspiration of our faith, the champion who leads us on, we endure to the end and win.

Fight the good fight with all thy might;
Christ is thy strength, and Christ thy right.

J. S. B. MONSELL

A Model for Asking

[Jesus said,] "You haven't done this before. Ask, using my name, and you will receive, and you will have abundant joy." **JOHN 16:24**

JAMES O. FRASER, MISSIONARY TO THE LISU OF CHINA in the early twentieth century, developed much of his prayer life from a fascinating contemporary illustration. At the time, the Canadian government offered incentives for British citizens to emigrate to Canada and claim territory in the west. Plenty of territory was waiting to be cultivated; all that was needed were people who would boldly come, accept the conditions of the government, claim as much land as they could reasonably cultivate, commit to care for the land, and then be faithful to work it. It was an open invitation to spread out and steward resources for the benefit of the realm.

That's a lot like prayer. We have an open invitation from God to ask and receive—to claim territory for his Kingdom. But sometimes there are conditions, especially when we are praying for fruitful Kingdom lives. We ask specifically, we commit to steward the gift faithfully, we enter into what we've been promised, and then we cultivate what we've been given. We receive it as a gift of grace, but we also participate in the process and continue to partner with God in managing it, just as in the original commission to humanity (Genesis 1:26-28). It's how God has chosen to expand his Kingdom and entrust it in the hands of those who represent him well.

That's what we really want, isn't it? We search for purpose and meaning, and we want our work to last. Some people may end up passing their days frivolously, but nearly every human being has longed for lasting fruit, for a life that matters in the long run, for truth and love to operate effectively in us. Jesus promises that to his followers, and he urges us to pray toward that end. So pray with that kind of definition and commitment. Understand the terms of God's promises—that his gifts are free, but once given must be handled with care. Develop a vision for the territory of your calling and ask God for it. Then take definite steps, by faith, to enter in.

The crowning wonder of [God's] scheme is that he entrusted it to men.
HENRY DRUMMOND

Deep Faith

Let your roots grow down into him, and let your lives be built on him.
Then your faith will grow strong in the truth you were taught,
and you will overflow with thankfulness. **COLOSSIANS 2:7**

THE FIRST PSALM PICTURES BELIEVERS as trees planted by streams of water. Their roots grow deep into the soil, and they bear fruit with the seasons. Paul recalls this image in his letter to the Colossians and encourages them to let their roots grow deep into Christ, the one who promised rivers of living water flowing from within. When we do, our faith grows strong. And when our faith grows strong, spiritual truths and realities become visible. We overflow with thankfulness.

There's a lot going on in that simple image—a process of investing our hearts and minds in the truth of who Jesus is and what he said; growth in our abiding, life-drawing relationship with him; and a lifestyle of fruitfulness in certain seasons. Our lives of faith are like seeds planted in the ground, and in the right conditions they grow into something rich, nourishing, powerful, and strong. But it takes time. Trees and roots don't grow overnight. Fountains of thankfulness aren't just turned on and off like a faucet. Seeds of faith—both our general faith in Jesus and our specific faith in the promises, callings, and purposes he has given us—have to mature. We have not embarked on a magical, instantaneous process.

Learning to live with the expectation of God's goodness in response to our faith on the one hand and the long view toward full maturity in whatever he has planted on the other takes some balancing. But both sides of that faith equation are impor-tant. It's a lifestyle from beginning to end, comprehensive in nature. Prayers of faith sometimes look like simple transactions, but they usually only appear that way in people who are thoroughly saturated in the ways of God's Kingdom over time. We love instant miracles like the ones Jesus did, but we often forget they came in the context of a deep, rich life of prayer on isolated mountains and within inner rooms. If we want that kind of harvest, we need that kind of planting season. In time, the harvest comes.

Spiritual growth consists most in the growth of the root, which is out of sight.
MATTHEW HENRY

170

Under Authority

Just say the word from where you are, and my servant will be healed.

MATTHEW 8:8

A ROMAN CENTURION APPEALED TO JESUS to heal his paralyzed servant. We don't know how this military captain heard about Jesus or how he came to believe in him. Perhaps he had stood guard over a large crowd and listened to Jesus in the process. Nor do we know what observers thought about someone who represented the resented Roman presence appealing to one of their own for a miracle. But the centurion asked, Jesus answered, and this officer demonstrated remarkable faith in the process. He understood the parallels between human authority and spiritual authority.

We could learn some things from this military man. He saw himself as both under the authority of his superiors and in authority over his soldiers. He acknowledged a connection between those two perspectives—that unless you are the very highest in command, you don't exercise authority without also submitting to it. You fit somewhere in the middle, and if you don't follow well, you can't lead well. You don't have the option of leading and not being led. If you are part of the hierarchy at all, you have to understand how it works in both directions.

Many Christians make every effort to exercise spiritual authority without being nearly so diligent in submitting to it. That's a mistake, and it always results in futility. Our ability to speak words of faith like Jesus did and see people saved, healed, delivered, and profoundly moved depends quite a bit on our willingness to respond to his words and let them save, heal, deliver, and move us. Our effectiveness in ministry, prayer, and faith will usually flow from the ways we have received the ministry, prayers, and faith of others. The power of Jesus works through us to the degree that we have let it work in us. The world is blessed by those who move in the power of God because the power of God has moved in them.

God doesn't give kingdom authority to rebels.

ADRIAN ROGERS

According to His Will

If we ask anything according to his will he hears us. And if we know
that he hears us in whatever we ask, we know that we have the
requests that we have asked of him.   1 JOHN 5:14-15, ESV

MANY BELIEVERS ATTACH AN UNASSUMING PHRASE to their prayers:
"If it's your will, Lord." The thought is admirable; we don't want to make requests
that violate God's will. But sometimes this phrase is a reflection of our own insecurity
and uncertainty about his will and a ready-made justification for prayers that seem
not to accomplish anything. If God doesn't answer, this is as good a reason as any.

John assures us that we can have confidence toward God and be certain he has
heard us—and knowing he has heard us, we can be certain that he will fulfill our
requests. But this promise includes the phrase about his will, as opposed to Jesus' "anything you want" language (John 15:7). John's words apply to those requests that are
God's will, and they seem to provide that same caveat we add to many of our prayers.

We need to remember two things when we read this passage: (1) As a whole,
the New Testament does not give us the impression that God's will is hard to figure out or is somehow narrower than the work his Spirit is doing in our hearts.
(2) Grammatically this verse can just as easily mean, "If we ask anything, which is his
will"—meaning it's the *asking* that is his will. In other words, this promise does not
limit us to some specific will of God that we may or may not be able to figure out; it
refers to the fact that believers can know God's will (much of which has been revealed
in Scripture), and we are invited to pray with confidence for God to accomplish his
purposes in us, through us, and for us. He is eager to reveal himself and his purposes
to us, and he urges us to ask accordingly. That ought to be profoundly encouraging
and emboldening to those who pray. We are doing exactly what God wills and can
be confident he will answer.

No heart can conceive that treasury of mercies which lies in this one privilege . . .
to approach God at all times, according to his mind and will.

JOHN OWEN

God's Desires Within

It is God who works in you, both to will and to work
for his good pleasure.   **PHILIPPIANS 2:13**, ESV

LORD, I WOULD REALLY LIKE YOU TO ANSWER THIS PRAYER. But not my will, Lord; your will be done. Though I do hope your will is the same as mine. It's a running conversation in our minds whenever we strongly desire something but also want God's will to be done. Many of us think of our will and God's as two different things that occasionally overlap. And some of us assume that if we want something, it almost certainly can't be God's will and should therefore be denied. In any case, we search for God's will as if it's somewhere out there waiting to be discovered. Sometimes we have to be told to look within.

We are reminded of this in Scripture. The Holy Spirit is in those who believe, flowing out like rivers of living water (John 7:37-39). Jesus was so confident in the Spirit at work in the disciples' hearts and their union with him that he told them to ask "whatever" and "anything" (John 14:13; 15:7). And Paul told the Philippians that God was at work in them "to will." Their search-and-discover mission for God's mysteries was not only to be focused on the pages of his revealed Word but sought in the hearts and minds that had joined with him in spiritual union. As we believe and mature in that relationship, one of the ways we know God's will is by noticing the desires and ideas he has placed within us. If he is at work in us to will and to work for his good pleasure, then that's where we need to look for his will and pleasure: in us.

That doesn't mean everything you want is necessarily God's will. We have lots of desires that don't come from him. But his desires are to be found in us somewhere, and we can discern them through prayer, confirmations, and recognition of their nature and persistence within us. If you've ever wondered what to pray for, that's a great place to look for guidance. When he wants us to do something, he usually lays it on our hearts in the form of a strong desire or, at times, a conviction that stretches our desires in new ways. His voice is often clothed in our longings.

If ever desiring, then ever praying.

AUGUSTINE

Overcoming Unbelief

The father instantly cried out, "I do believe, but
help me overcome my unbelief!" **MARK 9:24**

SOME OF JESUS' DISCIPLES TRIED to cast an evil spirit out of a young boy, but nothing happened. Jesus made a remark about faithless people (Mark 9:19)—with no hint from the text whether he said this with an angry expression or a smile on his face—and asked them to bring the boy to him. The boy's father begged for mercy and asked Jesus to help if he could. "If I can?" Jesus remarked. "Anything is possible if a person believes." And the father responded with a statement almost every Christian can relate to: "I do believe, but help me overcome my unbelief!"

Yes, we have mixed measures of faith in our hearts. We believe—but we also wonder if what we believe is true. We declare things in faith and then grow anxious and fearful about the possibility of our faith going unrewarded. In this instance, the disciples had faith mixed with doubts; they wouldn't have been trying to deliver the boy from the evil spirit if they didn't believe it was possible. Yet Jesus called them "faithless." In other words, by his standards, the only faith that's real is pure faith. If it's mixed with doubt, it isn't truly faith.

Jesus did not rebuke the father who openly admitted his mixture of faith and doubt. God is merciful about such things. He knows our hearts and responds to faith the size of a mustard seed. But he wants our faith to be real. He continually urges us forward into the kind of faith that sees invisible things and will not be shaken by visible contradictions. He understands the journey we are on, and he applauds every step of faith we take, no matter how tentative. But he is pulling us, calling us, leading us into less tentative places. He is setting our spirit on more solid ground. He is conforming us to the image of Jesus, who absolutely insists that for those who believe—truly, purely believe—all things are possible.

Belief is a truth held in the mind. Faith is a fire in the heart.

JOSEPH FORT NEWTON

A Foundation of Love

This hope will not lead to disappointment. For we
know how dearly God loves us. ROMANS 5:5

PURE FAITH IS HARD TO COME BY. We grow up in a world of skepticism, and doubt is deeply ingrained in our thought patterns. The size of our faith may not be at stake, but the quality of it is. Scripture repeatedly calls us to the kind of faith that moves mountains and makes all things possible.

If you've had trouble maintaining faith, examine your foundation. Everything in the Christian life is to be built on a foundation of love, and for hearts that have been wounded by rejection and distorted love, that's a problem. We've been let down and disappointed and beaten up by a fallen world and all its dysfunctions. We've let key ingredients of faith and hope go missing, and it's impossible to have deep, overflowing, consistent faith without hope and anticipation. Likewise, it's impossible to have hope apart from the security and certainty of love. You have to know how loved you are.

Without that foundation of love, you will inevitably find yourself wondering if God's words to you are reliable, if he is guiding and shaping your thoughts and per-spectives faithfully, if he is going to hold you up throughout the trials and troubles of this faith journey, and—at the most fundamental level—if he is really good to you. Most of us know these things intellectually, but few of us hold them deeply in our hearts. Our wounds linger, and our perception of God is affected by them. Only when those wounds are thoroughly healed and redeemed by his love can we build a life of consistent hope and faith.

Love is your foundation, so make every effort to cultivate it and grow in it. Perfect love casts out fear (1 John 4:18), and fear is the enemy of faith. When you know you are loved, your faith grows purer and stronger. You rest in the security of your Father's assurances, and your heart is free to believe again. Your foundation can support a life of bold, unyielding, enduring faith.

The chains of love are stronger than the chains of fear.
WILLIAM GURNALL

Things That Last

Three things will last forever—faith, hope, and love—
and the greatest of these is love.   1 CORINTHIANS 13:13

IF YOU'VE SPENT MUCH TIME trying to muster up faith, you know how difficult it can be. It's like trying to will your garden to grow, watching and waiting for the first buds to emerge, wishing you could make them magically appear. But faith doesn't work that way. Sure, you can cultivate it by clearing away weeds and thorns—those doubts and fears that war against your confidence in the Father's goodness. And you can provide the right environment by surrounding yourself with worship, Scripture, and confident words of prayer (preferably out loud, since your mind responds to the sound of your own voice quite well). But most of all, you need to feed your faith for it to grow strong.

As we've seen, the most important food for your faith is love. Your loving relationship with the Father, in which you receive his love and become secure in it, and in which you express your love to him through praise and gratitude, is foundational. Knowing this love in your heart of hearts stirs up hope (not wishful thinking but confident expectation), and hope is essential for faith. But this love doesn't just fill up your spiritual reservoir; it overflows into the lives of others (1 John 4:19). It creates a climate in which the goodness of the Father is increasingly evident. A loving environment shared with others makes his presence tangible. It makes the soil of your faith rich with nutrients that will help it grow.

God's love for us and our love for him and others fuel our faith in remarkable ways. When we become saturated in the love of God, we are enabled to trust his goodness fully and be at rest in his purposes for us. That empowers faith in God's purposes for us. Then, being saturated in his love, we are free to love others and overflow with compassion for them. That empowers our faith in his purposes for them. We more strongly believe he will accomplish his will because our compassion insists that he must. Faith, hope, and love work together to bring his Kingdom into our lives and the world around us.

Real prayer comes not from gritting our teeth but from falling in love.

RICHARD FOSTER

The Atmosphere of Heaven

You are holy, enthroned on the praises of Israel.   **PSALM 22:3**

GOD IS ENTHRONED ON THE PRAISES of his people. And in them. And through them. The translations may differ—the old King James Version gives us the beautiful image of God inhabiting our praises. As is often the case in God-inspired words, an inclusive interpretation is the best way to capture the fullness of what he says. He is enthroned already, but our worship enthrones him in our hearts and the situations of our lives. He is everywhere already, but our praises make his presence manifest in our words and actions. He may have already answered our prayers in heaven, but our celebration of his goodness makes his answers tangible in our experiences. When we praise God, something happens.

It makes sense if we think about it. The atmosphere of God's throne room in heaven—where no evil, hardship, or obstacle dwells—is filled with songs and cries of worship. Isaiah told of seraphim constantly crying "holy!" because they could not turn their attention away from the glory of God (Isaiah 6:3). Revelation 4–5 shows us a powerful scene of worshipers declaring the beauty and glory of God and casting crowns before him. This is where God dwells already, and when he hears the echo of these praises from his people on earth, he enters in. He is already everywhere, of course, but his presence has manifested in different ways at different times throughout Scripture and the course of history. Our worship has something to do with how he manifests in our lives.

Praise brings the environment of heaven into earth, even into hellish situations. That is a powerful truth for praying people to cling to. We don't ever want to make worship a tool to be used, but the promise of his presence makes for a compelling reminder of where our hearts are meant to dwell. When we enter into the climate of the throne room, the climate of the throne room enters into us. Our words, songs, and spirit are filled with the presence of God, and he makes his presence known. The gap between heaven and earth is bridged, a highway is prepared for our King, and he moves in powerful ways.

In prayer we act like men; in praise we act like angels.

THOMAS WATSON

177

How to Enter In

Enter his gates with thanksgiving; go into his courts with praise.
Give thanks to him and praise his name.   PSALM 100:4

STORY AFTER STORY IS TOLD of situations changing once the atmosphere shifts from fear, dread, or sorrow to praise and worship. People experiencing hardship gather to praise God, turning their hearts away from the problem to the problem solver, and a solution comes. A marriage in crisis turns from argument to prayer and praise, and soon the tension dissolves. A horrible disease melts away when it is surrounded by worship of the healer. It isn't magic, it isn't a formula, and it isn't always instantaneous. Sometimes nothing but our perspective changes. But the stories and personal experiences are common enough and true enough to convince us. The power of heaven brings miracles when the presence of heaven fills our hearts and minds.

That's why it's so important to see passages like Psalm 100 and others that urge praise and thanksgiving as more than just an encouragement. Celebration, joy, praise, gratitude, adoration—these are life to us. In fact, it's entirely possible to read today's verse not merely as an encouragement to worship and give thanks to God but as instruction on how we are able to enter into his courts at all. In other words, we don't just enter his gates and courts *with* thanksgiving and praise; we enter *by* them. Worship and gratitude put us there. They embed us into the heavenly environment and, we can reasonably assume, embed the heavenly environment into our lives.

Praise and gratitude reflect reality far more clearly than our discouragement, regrets, fears, and problems do. And in reflecting the ultimate reality, they bring us to a place of breakthrough—of connection with God's heart, of awareness of his purposes and ways, of his supernatural wisdom, power, and love. They *are* the answer to our prayers, long before our prayers are specifically answered. They change the world within us and then change the world around us.

That's worthy of our focus every day. Entering his gates and courts is a life-transforming experience, and here's where it starts—with praise and thanks. Saturate your life in the environment of God and see how God changes your life.

Worship is not part of the Christian life; it is the Christian life.

GERALD VANN

Fuel for Our Faith

We know that God causes everything to work together for the good of
those who love God and are called according to his purpose for them.

ROMANS 8:28

THE LIVES OF THE PATRIARCHS—those stories of Abraham, Isaac, Jacob, and Jacob's sons—are filled with encouraging truths. They also reveal a really dysfunctional family lineage. We read of great faith and miraculous interventions but also of semi-legitimate children, stolen birthrights, competitive pregnancies, betrayal, rape, vengeance, and much more that we would not wish for in the context of our own families. Yet this is where the twelve tribes of Israel, the covenant God made with his people, and the promises of an everlasting Kingdom come from. We have no idea what the story would have been like if everyone had behaved well. We only know that God had already compensated for their dysfunction in advance. His plan, formed before the foundation of the world, already took the messiness of life into account.

That's really encouraging for those of us who struggle with deep regrets. It's also encouraging for those who pray for God's Kingdom to come in our lives and the lives of those around us. It means we can go ahead and praise God for everything, even the things we wish had never happened. We can worship from the middle of the mess rather than from an unreachable expectation beyond it. The praise and gratitude with which we enter his gates are not dependent on the level of dysfunction in our lives or the world around us. We can sing his praises at the top of our lungs, believing that he works everything together for the good of those who love him.

Knowing that God works all of life into his good purposes is empowering in faith and prayer and disempowering to bitterness, regret, and fear, which war against our faith and prayer. The problems and mistakes others might see as evidence against our worship can actually fuel it. We know who God is, and we know he is bigger than our past, present, and future. Our discouragement is undone, and our prayers—filled with praise and thanks—rise up in faith.

> Each time, before you intercede, be quiet first, and worship God
> in his glory. Think of what he can do, and how he delights
> to hear the prayers of his redeemed people.
>
> **ANDREW MURRAY**

Living in the Now

*Don't worry about tomorrow, for tomorrow will bring its own
worries. Today's trouble is enough for today.* **MATTHEW 6:34**

"YOUR HEAVENLY FATHER ALREADY KNOWS all your needs" (Matthew
6:32). With those words, Jesus urged his listeners to lay down their worries about
tomorrow and deal only with the issues at hand. After all, you do not have access to
past or future moments. You only have the "now." You can give thanks for the past
and plan for the future, but there's no point in worrying about either. You can live at
peace right now in this moment and deal patiently with the things in front of you.

That's a very simple concept and, for many of us, a very difficult practice. Fallen
human nature moves our eyes from the simplicity of trusting God to the problems
that need to be fixed or even to potential problems down the road. But worry is a
form of fear, and fear is a distorted form of faith—a belief that something bad will
happen. It's a perversion of the forward-looking vision God has given us. It turns our
focus on opportunities into a focus on possibilities for harm. It's a negative image
of faith.

For some people, though, worry is the only way they know how to prepare for
the worst. It assumes that God isn't going to be there when problems happen, which
is why Jesus anchored his command not to worry in the assurance that our Father
already knows what we need before we need it. He will be there. He will give enough
grace—and protection and provision and power—when the time comes. You don't
need to lie awake thinking about it. It's all in his hands.

Jesus lived with the understanding that God is in control and cares for us. Yes,
bad things can and do happen. But worry doesn't prevent that. Whatever happens,
God heals, delivers, and restores us, working all things into our redemptive story. He
is sovereign over our lives, and he will not allow us to be overcome, even when we are
having to endure. We are invited, even commanded, to live in peace.

Worries just don't matter. Things really are in a better hand than ours.
DIETRICH BONHOEFFER

The Gift of Peace

May they have abundant peace, both near and far.   ISAIAH 57:19

IF YOU KEEP AN EYE ON THE NEWS and watch the people around you, you will notice the swells of worry that pass through your world with remarkable predictability. They roll in like the waves of the ocean coming to shore, some merely creating mild concern and others inducing widespread panic. But those billowing fears affect only those whose hearts are focused on the rise and fall of circumstances. They are indicators of where attentions are fixed. They do not rattle those whose hearts are fixed on God because he does not rise and fall with the situations around us. He is absolutely secure against all storms, and he keeps his faithful ones sheltered within his unmoving arms.

God promises peace to those who trust in him, and Jesus assured his disciples that he would leave his peace with them—not the world's kind of peace, which shifts with every change in circumstances, but God's kind of peace, the *shalom* of his Kingdom (John 14:27). But there's a catch: We experience that peace only if we receive it, embrace it, and live as though it's true. When we nurture our fears by focusing on the potential threats headed our way or the waves of trouble rolling over the world, we will live in fear. But when we nurture our faith by anchoring our attention on God and his wisdom, power, and love, we will live in peace. The choice is ours. We have lasting peace when we feed our faith and starve our fears.

Too many people are feeding their fears. They ingest a steady stream of negative news from the media that thrive on such things. They guard against every rumor of hardship. They bow down to every threat that appears on the horizon. In seeking safety, they live in turmoil. They take on the pain of trouble before trouble ever comes.

The life of faith runs contrary to such thinking, securing our thoughts, expectations, and hopes on the goodness of God. We will weather the storms when they come, but for now, they are no concern of ours. Our eyes are always on our Father, and we freely receive the gift of peace that comes from him.

In his will is our peace.

DANTE ALIGHIERI

The Object of Faith

Jesus spoke to them at once. "Don't be afraid," he said.
"Take courage. I am here!" **MATTHEW 14:27**

FIXING OUR MENTAL GAZE ON GOD is a challenge for some of us. We know how to think *about* him, but many of those thoughts are speculative and hazy, maybe even a product of our own imaginations. We go to Scripture to find wonderful details and specific examples of God's presence, but until that presence becomes real in our own lives, we are engaging more in a theology than a gaze of the soul. And when our thoughts about God are just thoughts, our fears find ways of persisting. It's only when we really engage with God—when we realize he is in the room—that the conversation becomes real and our fears begin to subside.

That's the trajectory of Jesus' brief words when he walked toward his disciples on the water in the midst of heavy winds and waves. "Don't be afraid. . . . Take courage. I am here!" His presence is the key to ridding ourselves of fear and anxiety—and also regret, bitterness, guilt, shame, and every other distorted thought we have. When we're really in the presence of the one who is truth, we begin to think truth. And the truth is that we have nothing to fear. He is watching over our lives with care and compassion.

This is what the Incarnation is all about. A messianic prophecy told us of Immanuel, God with us (Isaiah 7:14; Matthew 1:23)—not a distant God, not merely a conceptual or theoretical God, but the real God, here and now with us wherever we are. In the grand, lifelong project of feeding our faith and starving everything that comes against it, this is ground zero, the front line, the key to victory. We don't gaze into the distant sky to encounter this God; we invite him in and let his presence cover us, fill us, and move us. We welcome him into the midst of our winds and waves, and he brings peace with him. We don't have to muster up trust in him. We simply trust. And when we do, we find courage rising up within us, our sense of his presence growing stronger, and our prayers of faith touching his heart.

It is not our trust that keeps us, but the God in whom we trust who keeps us.

OSWALD CHAMBERS

The Focus of Fear

When he saw the strong wind and the waves, he
was terrified and began to sink. **MATTHEW 14:30**

PETER DID EXACTLY THE RIGHT THING—at first. He "tested the spirit"—
that ghostly figure the disciples saw coming on the water—though the test put Peter
in a position of considerable risk. When Jesus invited Peter to join him, Peter stepped
out of the boat. Not only that, he walked on water, just like Jesus. He was entirely
successful and apparently confident as long as he kept his eyes on his Master.

But that all changed when the wind and waves caught his attention. Winds and
waves have a way of doing that; the storms of our lives keep positioning themselves
right in front of our faces and demanding that we look at them. It becomes really
difficult not to heed their demands. And when we do, we begin to sink in one way
or another. That's what happened to Peter, whose distracted focus undermined his
faith when he took his eyes off Jesus. He could not maintain the discipline of gazing
in faith without regard for the turmoil around him. The wind and waves did their
work well.

Peter's focus determined his experience. Ours will too. Focus is a function of
faith, and when we lose one, we begin to lose the other. Sheer determination can
take us only so far. The deeper issue in undoing our fear is knowing who we are and
whose we are. As we've seen, faith thrives in a climate of love. If you know how loved
you are, you don't start interpreting wind and waves as existential threats or evidence
that God is no longer on your side. You see them for what they are: distractions. They
are no statement on how he is treating you, no reason for fear.

Remember that, and you'll thrive in the midst of your storms. In those times,
don't make your dreams and vision smaller. Enlarge them. Turn your focus to the
source of miraculous power and follow him. Ask him to invite you to step out on
tumultuous waters. It's an opportunity to experience his power by keeping your eyes
on him.

The act of faith is more than a bare statement of belief;
it is a turning to the face of the living God.

CHRISTOPHER BRYANT

JULY 1

The Gaze of Faith

*I lift my eyes to you, O God, enthroned in heaven. We keep
looking to the Lord our God for his mercy, just as servants
keep their eyes on their master.* **PSALM 123:1-2**

FAITH IS A MATTER OF FOCUS and never a matter of looking at our circumstances. Peter discovered this when he stepped out of the boat onto the surface of
the water and walked toward Jesus, sinking only when he turned his eyes toward the
waves surrounding him (Matthew 14:28-33). The spies sent to Canaan discovered
this too when ten of them feared the strong people and walled cities in the land
and God rebuked them for spreading their fear—with a forty-year delay (Numbers
13–14). A focus on threatening circumstances produces fear.

But focusing on how much faith we have doesn't cause our faith to grow either.
That inward gaze is never satisfied; it is always aware of insufficiency and missing
the one thing that inspires our faith the most. Where looking at our circumstances
is a gaze sideways, looking at our own faith is a gaze in the opposite direction of its
true object. Faith grows when our eyes are fixed on him.

That's the truth behind the promise of peace in Isaiah 26:3 for those whose minds
are fixed on God, and it's the picture we see in 2 Chronicles 20:12 when Jehoshaphat
honestly declared he didn't know what to do when facing opposing armies but that
his eyes were on God. That's why worship and praise are so powerful in making us
aware of God's presence and cultivating our faith in him. Faith is not a theory or a
mechanism. It's belief in a person. When our vision of God grows, our faith grows too.

Whenever you are tempted to look within to find your faith, look instead to
God. Keep your attention on him, remembering and rehearsing his goodness and
faithfulness. Read of his mighty works in Scripture and recall his faithfulness in past
seasons of your own life. Fix your gaze on him like a servant watches his master, and
your faith will flourish in strength.

> You might as well shut your eyes and look inside, and see whether you have
> sight, as to look inside to discover whether you have faith.
>
> HANNAH WHITALL SMITH

The Feet of Faith

As soon as the feet of the priests who were carrying the Ark touched
the water at the river's edge, the water above that point began
backing up a great distance away. JOSHUA 3:15-16

WELSH MISSIONARY REES HOWELLS ONCE LEFT for his mission field without the funds even to catch the next train. He and his wife were headed to Africa in 1915, and they had been given money to get them to London, where they would receive more for the journey. But they had also been directed by God as a general policy to spend available funds on immediate expenses and trust him for later ones—"first need, first claim."[2] When an expense came up before his train trip to London, Howells followed his normal procedure. He emptied his pockets on the prior claim. He and his wife only had enough to get to the next station and wait.

So that's what they did. They traveled the first leg of the journey and then waited. Howells even stood in line at the ticket counter because, as he put it, God's promises were as good as money in his pocket. As the line moved forward, Howells wondered what he would say at that potentially awkward moment when he arrived at the counter without any money. But as that moment neared, a man in line got tired of waiting, inexplicably handed his fare to Howells, and walked away. God had provided as Howells stood expectantly in line, trusting in a promise.

That's often how God's provision works—in response to faith, and not a moment too soon. He also works in partnership with those who believe. Some step of faith, some indication that we are expecting an answer, some movement in the direction of our vision—like that first step of the priests into the Jordan *before* its waters parted—is enough to send the Father rushing toward us in response. Faith begins in the heart, but it does not remain there. Immobile faith is often a sign of no faith at all. Not every story ends exactly the way Howells's example did—God has a variety of responses to our trust—but many do. And one way or another, trust is always rewarded. Faith that banks on God's Word will always find him faithful.

Faith is the root of all good works. A root that produces nothing is dead.

THOMAS WILSON

The Mind of Faith

*Set your sights on the realities of heaven, where Christ sits
in the place of honor at God's right hand. Think about the things
of heaven, not the things of earth.* **COLOSSIANS 3:1-2**

KINGDOM FAITH REQUIRES a complete reorientation of our thinking. One of
the reasons John the Baptist and Jesus both begin their words in the Gospels with a
command to repent is that repentance—in Greek, changing one's mind or reorient-
ing one's vision—is necessary for seeing Kingdom realities. We can't see the truths
and possibilities of God's Kingdom with old thought processes, perceptions, and
assumptions. We have to renew our minds in order to look beyond the oppressive
realities of this world.

How? Paul tells us in Colossians. We are to fix our gaze and turn our minds
toward the things of heaven, where Jesus sits at God's right hand over all power and
authority. Earth presents one version of reality according to its own logic; God presents another. That's why his work in Scripture includes logic-defying events—seas
parting at a command, walls falling after a circular parade and a shout, ashes being
turned to beauty, water being turned to wine, death being turned to life. The list
could go on for pages, but the point is clear: God's ways are often counterintuitive
to human thinking. We are called to walk by faith, not by sight.

That isn't easy. Sight is relentless and often very convincing. Faith, on the other
hand, is the evidence of things not seen (Hebrews 11:1, NKJV). The contrast can be
frustrating, confusing, even excruciating. Yet it still demands a choice. Will we pray
and believe according to our natural eyes or our spiritual eyes? Will we honor the
voice of God or the arguments of human beings? Will we call the visible "reason"
and the invisible "a myth"? Or will we embrace truth as it has been quite reasonably
but often obscurely offered to us?

The mind of faith has to make its choice daily, and it begs our vision, feelings,
reasoning, and words to follow. When you set your sights on the realities of heaven
and not on the illusions of this world, they do.

> The great thing is to learn not to be disobedient to the vision,
> not to say that it cannot be attained.
>
> OSWALD CHAMBERS

Believers Believe

My righteous ones will live by faith. But I will take no
pleasure in anyone who turns away. **HEBREWS 10:38**

IN EVERY VISION, PROJECT, OR VENTURE OF FAITH there comes a time when choices must be made and steps must be taken. Some of those choices are deeply internal, affecting our moods and expectations. Others are external, involving practical decisions that depend on the vision being true. Subtly, deeply, superficially, practically, mentally, and emotionally, we are constantly living according to what we really believe. The question is whether what we really believe involves faith in God's words, promises, and purposes—or something else. If we feel hopeless, desperate, discouraged, or bitter, it's almost certainly something else.

Unbelief focuses on the situation as it appears right now and all the negative directions it could turn in the future. Faith refuses to look at the way things appear right now (at least as a true reflection of reality) and insists on envisioning God's goodness down the road. Unbelief sees a negative turn of events and worries or despairs. Faith looks at a negative turn of events and then looks to God for how he will do something awesome in it. Faith insists that it *will* turn out for the good of those who love him, that it *will* set up an opportunity for his kindness to be seen, that all the strategies of the enemy and the trials of the world *will* be turned to beauty, joy, and praise. The reality of these promises simply isn't a question for the believer. A believer believes.

When we are told to guard our hearts as the wellspring of life (Proverbs 4:23, ESV), this is why. Your heart will sometimes lie to you. It will make you think you believe when you don't. It will claim great faith while dragging you down in despair. It will weigh you down with discouraging thoughts even while you are praying for great victories. It will make you shrink back.

Don't let it. Faith and discouragement can't coexist. The focus of faith is hope—always. Live by it, walk by it, and never turn away. God will call your faith "righteous" and reward you for it. You are in a battle for your heart, and if you don't give up, you will win.

Discouragement is to be resisted just like sin.

J. O. FRASER

Living as Royalty

He has made us a Kingdom of priests for God his Father.
REVELATION 1:6

BELIEVERS STAND AT AN INTERSECTION of heavenly and earthly realms, serving as both kings and priests. We have been called to be priests (1 Peter 2:5)—representing God to humanity and humanity to God—and we have been called to rule with Christ. We have been given the keys of his Kingdom (Matthew 16:19), are seated at his heavenly throne (Ephesians 1:21-22; 2:6), and will rule with him on earth (Revelation 5:10). We have a more extraordinary calling than most of us understand.

Jesus spoke often about those who believe being able to see and inherit the Kingdom. Sometimes those verses have life-and-death, heaven-or-hell implications; sometimes they simply refer to the ability to experience Kingdom things. But in any case, they call us to see, think, pray, and believe like royalty and priests.

How do royal priests see, think, pray, and believe? We've looked at several of our characteristics already—walking by faith rather than sight, thinking about Kingdom-oriented possibilities, praying from victory rather than for it, and knowing who we are in Christ. We don't ask for the King's promises; he has already given them. We simply believe them. We don't try to become like Christ; we simply behave like him because we are his. We are citizens of heaven already, and we live like we know it—with all of heaven's values, virtues, and vision.

That's not a call to arrogance. Jesus is our model, and he never demonstrated pride. But he did carry himself like royalty. His kind of kingship involved servanthood, but always with authority. A royal priest in the Kingdom of God doesn't try to convince the kingdom of darkness of what's right; he or she simply says what is and isn't. Kings don't ask their realm to follow decrees; they expect decrees to be followed. We don't pray for God's promises to be true; we accept them as they are. We don't try to attain royal status; we have been born into the family. This is our identity, calling, and life-style. Live as a priest and a prince or princess. As a citizen of another realm, you are invited—even urged—to live with the authority Christ has given those who love him.

Power in complete subordination to love—that is something
like a definition of the kingdom of God.

WILLIAM TEMPLE

The Soil of Faith

Fix your thoughts on what is true, and honorable, and right,
and pure, and lovely, and admirable. Think about things that
are excellent and worthy of praise. **PHILIPPIANS 4:8**

FAITH CAN'T THRIVE IN ROCKY, SUN-SCORCHED SOIL. It can't grow when smothered by thorns, drenched with poison, or trampled underfoot. Yet many of us spend much of our lives saturating the soil of our minds with worries, fears, impurities, regrets, criticisms, skepticism, guilt, shame, and unworthiness. We haven't cultivated what is true, honorable, right, pure, and lovely. And minds that were designed for such things—to dwell on the spiritual realm and the beauty of God— have conversed instead with whatever is unholy, wretched, and corrosive. Then we wonder why faith feels so hard to come by.

Faith must be planted in good soil and watered and fertilized with the truths and perspectives of the Kingdom. That's why it's imperative to know Kingdom realities and dwell on them, to seek the Kingdom above all unrighteousness, to replace lies with truth, and to instill hope over despair. To do that, we have to let the Spirit search our hearts and minds.

If you really want to go deep in your faith, step back from your prayer requests for a moment and look at what's driving them. What is motivating your prayer for provision? A sense of insecurity, embarrassment, or unworthiness, or perhaps a lack of trust in God for your future? What drives your prayer for fruitfulness? An unaware-ness of how loved and valued you are and a desire to compensate for whatever short-comings you think you have? Why do you really want that miraculous answer? To satisfy a need or prove the skeptics wrong and increase your standing in their eyes? Our motives are complex, but God sees them all. The eyes of faith are content to let him.

Let him take you to those places so your faith can be rooted in pure, true, noble soil. God will meet you at every point of insecurity, shame, doubt, or pain, and your faith will become stronger in the long run. Let the King come into the depths of your thoughts; then fix them on Kingdom truths. You and your faith will be deeper, fuller, stronger, and radically transformed.

Let us learn to cast our hearts into God.

BERNARD OF CLAIRVAUX

A Model Balance

While Jesus was here on earth, he offered prayers and pleadings, with
a loud cry and tears, to the one who could rescue him from death.
And God heard his prayers because of his deep reverence for God.

HEBREWS 5:7

IN THE BEGINNING, Jesus (the Word) was with God, and he was God. This is
the staggering theological statement John makes at the beginning of his Gospel, and
the writer of Hebrews echoes it in the opening of his letter, calling Jesus the agent
of creation, the radiance of God's glory, the exact expression of God's character, and
the sustainer of everything (Hebrews 1:2-3). Yet this same writer emphasized Jesus'
humanness several pages later, describing how the Son learned obedience through
suffering (5:8). He also tells us that Jesus prayed with loud crying and tears—and was
heard because of his reverence for the Father, with whom he was "one" (John 10:30;
17:11). In other words, God's own Son prayed with godly fear.

We might think Jesus' conversations with the Father would be more familiar or
confident than this, but reverence does not contradict familiarity and confidence. As
a human being, he blazed this trail for us; he entered into the throne room of God
as a human with all the pains and turmoil that a human being would. He prayed
from the heart because God is full of emotion, as Scripture thoroughly attests, and
the Son, the exact representation of God, expressed emotion back to him. This balance of reverence and familiarity, emotion and maturity, and humanity and divinity
becomes a model for us. If this is how Jesus prayed, and we are called to pray in his
name and from his identity, then our prayers ought to look a lot like this.

Somehow, many Christians have the idea that we must choose between boldness
and reverence before God. Not so with Jesus. Many also have the idea that faith and
emotion are incompatible. Not so in Jesus. He is the image of God, and we are being
conformed to the image of Jesus—in keeping with our original design. This is what
prayer can look like. And in the Son of God, it was powerfully, eternally effective.

In that name, a man may draw near to God with boldness.

J. C. RYLE

Hearts Fully Trusting

Let us go right into the presence of God with sincere hearts fully trusting him. For our guilty consciences have been sprinkled with Christ's blood to make us clean, and our bodies have been washed with pure water. **HEBREWS 10:22**

THE WOUNDED HUMAN SOUL allows itself to be filled with all sorts of objections to God's goodness and love. It listens to the world's rationalizations and arguments about God's distance or nonexistence. It comes up with evidence and conditions that undermine God's promises. And most of its maneuverings are based on a very simple, subtle lie: that our sin has disqualified us from the ideal. God must handle our failures and shortcomings with restrictions.

That sentiment of unworthiness is based on truth as it would be if God had not redeemed and restored us. It is a Christless frame of mind, or at least a mind infected with Christless thoughts. The good news of our redemption and restoration is that God has made us absolutely clean, identified us with Christ, adopted us as his children, and lavished on us every spiritual blessing in heavenly places. There are no insufficiencies in us when we come to him, no legitimate faith-killing regrets, no sense that we are any less worthy than the name of Jesus we pray with. We come to God's throne clothed in the Son of God. That's what he sees. And it's glorious.

That means our hearts have been sprinkled clean, we've entered into the fellowship of the Trinity, and there is no blemish in us. We are not second-class members of the Kingdom, trying to grow to some unclear spiritual stature, earning our stripes in his army. We are there in the throne room with face-to-face fellowship and fully trusting hearts. There are no hindrances between us when we pray.

Few believers feel the emotions of that truth, especially when we recall a sin from years past, yesterday, or even a few minutes ago. Yet because our cleansing does not rise and fall with our feelings, neither should our confidence or our trust. We present every prayer to God *as if Jesus asked it himself.* That's what "in his name" means. Believe it. Celebrate it. Live it. And let your faith grow in the throne room of God.

Bold I approach the eternal throne, and claim the crown, through Christ my own.

CHARLES WESLEY

The Fellowship of Faith

You have come to Mount Zion, to the city of the living God,
the heavenly Jerusalem, and to countless thousands
of angels in a joyful gathering. **HEBREWS 12:22**

MAYBE YOU'VE FELT ALONE AT TIMES. Perhaps you've even wondered if God has abandoned you. But as we've seen, the life of faith is not based on visible experiences. It's based on a vision of truth. And the truth is that we are surrounded by a great cloud of witnesses encouraging us (Hebrews 12:1), we already have citizenship in heaven with access to the joys and celebrations of the city of God, and we have entered into a joyful gathering of saints and angels. We couldn't be alone if we wanted to—at least not in the sense of spiritual fellowship. We are fully integrated into the society of the eternal city.

We need that fellowship if we are going to persist in our faith. The writer of Hebrews has told us of the great men and women of faith who have filled history with their heroic perseverance. They felt alone sometimes too. As far as we know, no one but Abraham believed God for such outrageous promises in his time. Joseph sat alone in the bottom of a well and then in an Egyptian prison for years before faith became fruit. Rahab acted entirely against her culture and background in embracing Israel's chosenness. And not many people were standing up for the prophets who were persecuted and killed for telling the truth. The examples are numerous, but they all point to a similar truth: Genuine faith may be alienating at times, but it's rooted in a vast company of those who have believed. Our faith is bigger than we are.

If you are going to thrive, you will need to see yourself as part of this great company. Whatever you pray for in faith is not an isolated request. It is a piece of the whole. You can take great comfort in God's overall plan, and if you listen with the ears of the spirit, you may hear other participants cheering you on. You can run your race with endurance because you do not run alone.

The Bible knows nothing of solitary religion.

JOHN WESLEY

Unshakable Faith

Since we are receiving a Kingdom that is unshakable, let us be
thankful and please God by worshiping him with holy fear and awe.
For our God is a devouring fire. **HEBREWS 12:28-29**

THE LETTER TO THE HEBREWS is all about faith. When it speaks of running the race and inheriting God's promises, it means by faith. When it speaks of sin, it means unbelief. This letter was written to Jews who were questioning whether their initial faith in Christ was genuine and worth the persecution and problems they were facing because of it. So what was this writer's message to those who believe? You are receiving an unshakable Kingdom.

Faith is the currency of God's Kingdom. Whatever is given by grace through faith is therefore everlasting. The fruit of faith does not end; at the very least, it stands as an eternal testimony to the goodness and faithfulness of God. Even more, it likely results in genuine change to the hearts and lives of those affected by it—including yours. When you pray, believe, and receive, something happens in the eternal Kingdom.

Faith bears lasting fruit that cannot be shaken or destroyed. By contrast, whatever is born outside of faith is destined to wither away over time. That means our goals and dreams need to be centered on eternal realities, even if they have temporal implications. Our energy needs to be directed toward things that will last, even if it involves things that don't. And whatever the costs of our faith right now, the glory later will far outweigh them. Living in an unshakable Kingdom means having faith—and entire lives—that cannot be shaken.

Remember that as you press on toward the goal. Your perseverance matters because eternal fruitfulness is at stake. God never puts that kind of pressure on you, but he does motivate you to continue. Your faith is not just for this week's problems, next month's bills, or this lifetime's effectiveness. It is for an eternal testimony that he is at work in the lives of those who believe. He is calling us ever upward and onward in faith. Keep walking, and refuse to be shaken.

Faith is a living and unshakable confidence, a belief in the grace of God
so assured that a man would risk a thousand deaths for its sake.

MARTIN LUTHER

Shaken Faith

*Take your son, your only son—yes, Isaac, whom you love so much—
and go to the land of Moriah. Go and sacrifice him as a burnt offering
on one of the mountains, which I will show you.* **GENESIS 22:2**

ABRAHAM WAS GIVEN A PROMISE, and after years of waiting, stumbling, laughing, and waiting some more, the promise was fulfilled. Isaac, the son of laughter, was God's visible means for fulfilling his plan to bless the world with descendants of Abraham and Sarah. Yet one day, God told Abraham to sacrifice this one vessel of fulfillment. Abraham had a choice to make: God or the promise. The way the choice was presented to him, he couldn't have both.

We place our faith in unshakable things: God, his Kingdom, his character, his purposes for our lives, and that all that he tells us is true. But sometimes our faith itself is shaken. That jolt often happens when we are asked to surrender the very thing we are praying for. In Abraham's case, surrendering Isaac led to restoration of the promise. But our sacrifices would be meaningless if we assumed they were just a formality always leading to restoration. Sometimes the sacrifice is real—and extremely painful. But it's how God often works to bring us into a place of greater promise.

Our faith will be tested—sometimes by circumstances and challenges, sometimes by temptations or our own tumultuous minds, and sometimes by God himself. When the test comes from him—when it pits the object of our faith against its Fulfiller—we have to be willing to lay it down. We need to choose God over the very thing we are asking him for.

Never let your prayers of faith become bigger than the God you are praying to. He values a relationship of trust far more than an agenda for our lives. He promises abundance and fruitfulness, the joy of life in his Kingdom, but that joy begins with him. When we think our joy begins with the answer to our prayers, we need correcting, and the correction isn't easy. But it's always good. Choose him above all else. Lay down whatever rivals him and let your prayers flow from unshakable trust in him.

> For the first two or three years after my conversion,
> I used to ask for specific things. Now I ask for God.
>
> SUNDAR SINGH

Tested by Fire and Flood

*We went through fire and flood, but you brought
us to a place of great abundance.* **PSALM 66:12**

FOR CENTURIES, PSALMISTS AND PROPHETS celebrated Israel's deliverance from Egypt through the powerful intervention of God. They spoke and wrote of his great miracles, his victory over enemies, his provision and guidance in the wilderness, and his eventual gift of the Promised Land. But they never lost sight of the journey—the traumatic plagues that led to their deliverance; their times of testing in the wilderness; the turmoil within the camp and the enemies beyond it; and the knee-buckling, hair-raising crisis of passing between walls of water to get to the safe side of the sea. They understood that dramatic victories rarely ride in on easy roads; far more often they come to us through critical, faith-stretching experiences.

The good news is that when God takes us on a journey through fire and flood, abundance is on the other side. The idea that the Christian life is all pain and no glory as long as we are on earth is far too common. Yes, we experience ultimate victory on the other side of the grave, but we can also experience plenty of victories along the way. Though Old Testament heroes of faith "did not receive what was promised" and "saw it all from a distance" (Hebrews 11:13), they also experienced fulfillments in their time. Abraham's son really did come; Joseph really did become a ruler in Egypt; Joshua did enter the land of promise; faithful Caleb claimed his part of it; David ascended to the throne; Daniel was spared from the mouths of lions; Judah's captives really did return to their own land. These are not empty examples. They are given for our encouragement. God promises fulfillment, abundant joy, and rivers of living water now and in the age to come.

Refuse to defer all the good things to a later age. But do understand that God often leads you along a path of fire and flood on the way to them. We face afflictions and tribulations, but we are also rescued from them and overcome them (Psalm 34:19; John 16:33). Our faith carries us through into seasons and places of great abundance—now and forever.

If we are intended for great ends, we are called to great hazards.

JOHN HENRY NEWMAN

From Wilderness to Worship

[The LORD said,] "I am about to do something new. See, I have already begun! Do you not see it? I will make a pathway through the wilderness. I will create rivers in the dry wasteland." **ISAIAH 43:19**

IF YOU'VE LIVED THE LIFE OF FAITH for some time, you know by now that it isn't just about getting what you need, want, or dream about. It is God's means for partnering with his people to bring about his purposes in ways that satisfy their hearts. That certainly includes having our needs met, our God-given desires satisfied, and our Kingdom dreams fulfilled, but our faith doesn't begin and end with us. It begins and ends with God, passing through us as an invitation into his will and ways. This invitation to faith was on his mind before it was on ours.

So when God wants to begin something new, he starts to make streams in the desert. He meets us in the wilderness to walk with us into places of greater abundance. Most of us go through times that look completely barren spiritually, relationally, emotionally, and in the practical details of our lives, but barrenness is no obstacle to God. He calls the barren to sing and celebrate the fruitfulness that is coming (Isaiah 54:1). He urges us to go ahead and worship in our times of wilderness because we know they will not last forever. He promises to turn our wilderness experiences into rich, lush, blossoming gardens of joy—in his time.

One of the greatest acts of faith we can express is to worship in those dry seasons. It's easy to worship in times of abundance; even the immature can do that. But when God is stretching our muscles of faith and expanding our capacity to love and trust him, we rarely feel like worshiping. That's when worship means the most. It is the ultimate expression of love and trust because it has no props to lean on. It simply takes God at his word and appreciates him for who he is. The purposes and promises of God flow freely from such hearts. Streams, even rivers, begin to flow in the most unlikely places. And our deserts look like deserts no more.

All our difficulties are only platforms for the manifestation of his grace, power, and love.

HUDSON TAYLOR

Disciplined Faith

Wait patiently for the LORD. Be brave and courageous.
Yes, wait patiently for the LORD. **PSALM 27:14**

TIMES OF WAITING AND TESTING are no surprise to anyone with experience in the faith life. These trials of faith are common even (or especially) at the beginning. They are hallmarks of the faith journeys of heroes like Abraham, Joseph, David, Elijah, and many more. A promise is given and believed, but then time passes. And passes some more. And continues to pass while all sorts of opportunities to believe something different come along.

Faith is a discipline because it demands our focus even when we are faced with distractions, contradictions, diversions, temptations to unbelief, and much more. We wrestle with the balance between holding things loosely and standing firm. On the one hand, we know better than to be inflexible with God; on the other, we know better than to compromise the promises he has given. While we are waiting, we play out all sorts of scenarios in our minds about what God wants us to do, how we are to think, and whether the promise will come just as we envisioned. We also play out all sorts of emotions, guarding against disappointment while stirring up our confidence and joy. Sometimes it seems as if our waiting period is a brutal testing ground designed to try our faith.

It is—at least to some degree. God is not brutal, and he takes no pleasure in putting us through difficult circumstances. We can't blame him for such things, and the reasons for our waiting will always contain some element of mystery. But sometimes the delays are designed or at least used by him to serve as a training period. When we are forced to stand firm, refusing to be swayed, refusing to compromise mentally and emotionally with something other than God's will—you've probably experienced that dynamic of getting used to a less-than-ideal situation or accepting the "reality" of something you think is not right—we are either strengthened or weakened in faith. That's by design. We have to let the gap between promise and fulfillment do its work. Stand firm, remind yourself daily of God's faithfulness, and patiently believe. No matter what.

Patience means waiting without anxiety.

FRANCIS DE SALES

Contradictions or Confirmations?

Jesus soon saw a huge crowd of people coming to look for him. Turning to Philip, he asked, "Where can we buy bread to feed all these people?" He was testing Philip, for he already knew what he was going to do. JOHN 6:5-6

JESUS WAS ALREADY PLANNING to astonish his friends and feed thousands with just a few loaves of bread and some fish. Still, he framed the impossibility as a question to Philip: *How are we going to do this?* This seemingly playful question was loaded with more than just humor, however. It presented visible, tangible evidence as a direct contradiction to the coming reality. It put Philip in a mental dilemma that would later serve as a powerful object lesson: What we see isn't always the truth.

Our faith has matured when it has gotten to the point of seeing obstacles, challenges, and even contradictions to our prayers as confirmations rather than denials of them. Very often, the resistance we face is there to lift us up, not bring us down. For example, when you have been praying for someone's salvation or spiritual growth and that person makes an emphatic declaration against God's purposes; when you experience a financial setback just as you begin to pray for provision; when conditions worsen while you are praying for healing; when a conflict erupts just as you pray for a better relationship; do you see these as occasions to lament and assume your prayers are ineffective or do you see them as occasions to rejoice in the wonderful testimony that is coming? Immature faith defaults to the former, mature faith to the latter.

Just as Joseph voiced God-given dreams and then found himself in the bottom of a pit and David found himself in exile not long after being anointed, you will voice prayers that are followed by turns in the opposite direction of them. Is God opposed to your prayers? Has he said no? Not from that evidence alone. You are most likely experiencing the journey of faith in ways that allow you to grow, advance in God's purposes, and see great victories that result in greater testimonies.

Airplanes ascend best when taking off into headwinds. The resistance lifts them up. Let contradictions to your faith do the same. See them as opportunities to believe—and rise higher than ever before.

Endurance is not just the ability to bear a hard thing but to turn it into glory.

WILLIAM BARCLAY

A Turbulent Ascent

At this point many of his disciples turned away and deserted him.

JOHN 6:66

HEADWINDS ARE HELPS RATHER THAN HINDRANCES to the life of faith. Like a plane taking off into the wind, a believer of mature faith sees obstacles and contradictions to prayers as opportunities for faith to be lifted higher and evidence that God is setting the stage for a greater testimony. But a plane's journey is far from complete after its initial ascent. It must rise above the clouds to fly in clear skies. And those clouds can cause quite a bit of turbulence. If we didn't know better, we might think the resistance was a bad sign.

After Jesus fed thousands with a few loaves and fish, he engaged in a lengthy and contentious discussion with those who were offended by his metaphors—himself as the bread of heaven, his flesh and blood as true food and drink, and challenging words about his descent from and ascent back into heaven. Some listeners may have genuinely misunderstood these graphic metaphors; others simply rejected his claims. In any case, nearly everyone left him at this point. And the only reason his closest followers remained was, as Peter said, they had nowhere else to go, no other source for words of life (verse 68). Jesus' claims and the disciples' faith in them were being shaken and tested, and only the truest believers would remain.

You may go through turbulent times at various points in your journey of believing, and sometimes that turbulence comes right before the clearest and most beautiful views. It may come from the shift in circumstances that must occur before God's answers come, from the resistance of others who do not understand your faith, or from any other kind of spiritual opposition. But turbulence is a brief discomfort on a heavenward ascent, figuratively speaking, and it is never the right time to try to escape. Most of Jesus' listeners fled because they couldn't cope with the friction. Some stayed because they had focused their faith on him alone. As his words—his promises, encouragements, instructions, challenges, comforts, and plans—become more and more real in your life, they may demand more resolve from you. Cling to them, even when you are shaken. Clear skies are always ahead.

> Onward in faith—and leave the rest to heaven.
>
> ROBERT SOUTHEY

Faith for the Moment

Everyone who asks, receives. **MATTHEW 7:8**

GEORGE MÜLLER WAS TRAVELING across the Atlantic from England when his ship was slowed by dense fog. Müller was due for a ministry engagement in Quebec, and he did not believe this fog was God's means of preventing him from being there. After all, he believed God had called him to go. So when the captain told him they would not arrive at their port in time—the fog was just too dense—Müller informed him that God would find some other way. "My eye is not on the density of the fog but on the living God who controls every circumstance of my life."[3]

Müller prayed a very simple prayer and told the captain not to add anything to it because, as he explained, the captain didn't believe God would answer, and Müller believed he already had. The fog lifted almost immediately, and the ship arrived on time. Müller was able to keep his commitment. Why? Because faith overcomes fog—and anything else that would hinder it.

Müller was known for such prayers of immediacy. As the founder and leader of several orphanages and schools in England, he often had need of God's unusual provision. He had made a commitment early on to live by faith, dedicating all his resources to God and trusting him for the rest. So when lunch was needed for dozens of orphans but there was no food in the kitchen, he would pray, and a donation of food—or sometimes money to buy food—would arrive right on time, to the marvel of his peers. When he had to purchase land or buildings to expand his ministry and had no money in the bank, he got on his knees and asked God for provision, which almost invariably came by remarkable means. He understood what it meant to trust God for urgent situations and expect him to answer.

Sometimes our seeds of faith cannot wait for long-term fruit. We need God's timely provision, and we have to trust that he knows what time it is. He may reorient our definition of needs, but he always provides. He honors the prayers of those who believe he answers them plainly.

The reason why we obtain no more in prayer is because we expect no more.

RICHARD ALLEINE

Faith for a Lifetime

Keep on asking, and you will receive what you ask for.
Keep on seeking, and you will find. Keep on knocking,
and the door will be opened to you. **MATTHEW 7:7**

AS A YOUNG MAN, George Müller applied and planned to be a missionary through the London Missionary Society. Things never quite worked out—circumstances, timing, conviction, opposition from family members—and this German ended up living in England most of his life. Still, God had led him into tremendously fruitful ministry. He served faithfully for years, founding and operating orphanages and schools that had an enormous impact. But his desire to be a missionary—and his faith and prayers toward that end—seemed unfulfilled.

As we've seen, faith functions like a seed planted, and sometimes seeds take a very long time to grow to full maturity. Müller knew that dynamic well—his faith was rewarded quite often and tangibly over the years—and eventually those seeds sown early in his adulthood bore fruit much later. He traveled the world speaking about faith, going to places even beyond his early missionary dreams. God had opened and shut doors according to his timing, but he had not let Müller's faith fall pointlessly to the ground.

Many Christians live with disappointment for years, assuming faith in a particular area just didn't work out. Perhaps it didn't, and perhaps it never will in exactly the expected way. But that doesn't mean God won't honor it somehow. Disappointment is a middle-of-the-story phenomenon because it assumes an unhappy conclusion before we've gotten to the end of the story. That's especially true for believers, whose end-of-story prophecies and promises are remarkably gratifying. Yes, we may be disenchanted with the way things have worked out; many of us don't spend our lives walking out fulfilled dreams and expectations. But we still haven't seen what God is going to do with our faith. We have no business expecting disappointment in the end.

Don't walk away from the seeds of faith you've planted. You may have forgotten to tend to them. God hasn't. One way or another, they will bear fruit. You may have prayed in faith for a particular season, but God has applied it for a lifetime. And he is still writing a beautiful story with it.

Hope is patience with the lamp lit.
TERTULLIAN

Faith That Overflows

If your children ask for a loaf of bread, do you give them a stone instead? . . . How much more will your heavenly Father give good gifts to those who ask him. **MATTHEW 7:9, 11**

PEOPLE WHO KNEW GEORGE MÜLLER said his prayers sounded like a conversation between intimate friends. At its heart, that's what prayer really is—an intimate conversation between persons who know each other well. God already knows us in detail, of course, but the way we talk to him changes as we grow closer and know him better. Our prayers are not requisitions or purchase orders submitted to an accounting office. We are conversing with someone who loves us deeply, invites our love in return, and wants us to live out our relationship as his representatives on earth.

That kind of relationship doesn't remain secret forever. God's presence came through in Müller's prayers. There's a reason people said his prayers sounded like intimate conversations: They were witnesses to them. They recognized the familiarity between man and God and marveled at how it sounded—and what it accomplished.

God does not call us to flaunt our prayers (just the opposite, in fact), but he does urge us not to hide our light or become secret believers. At some point, whether or not anyone ever hears our prayers, people should recognize our relationship with our Father. We are not focused exclusively on what God wants us to do, like obedient servants, nor are we focused only on what we want him to give us. We are children of the King, and our words reflect that family relationship. The best way for people to know they can have that kind of relationship is to see it in real life.

When you have spent much time in prayer and are saturated in the Father's presence, you will be noticeably different—perhaps not to everyone, but to some. Confident, assured faith stands out. A relationship of trust with an unseen God appears delusional to some but inviting to others, especially when they see him answer. Your prayers may begin in the closet, but they have implications for the world. Let your life display a God who responds warmly to the hearts of his children.

> By prayer the Christian can open his heart to God, as to a friend, and obtain fresh testimony of God's friendship to him.
>
> **JOHN BUNYAN**

Heartfelt Beliefs

You must really believe it will happen and
have no doubt in your heart. **MARK 11:23**

THE HUMAN SOUL IS A COMPLEX MYSTERY. We have the ability to think one thing and feel another, have internal debates, be double-minded or half-hearted, change convictions, ride a wave of emotions, and second-guess just about everything. God knows this, of course; he created this complex mystery. But the fact that our minds and hearts are steeped in fallen nature and unable to fix themselves presents certain problems in the area of faith—namely, what does it really mean to believe? Is it an intellectual conviction, an emotion, a spiritual issue, or some combination thereof? If faith is the currency of God's Kingdom, this is something we really need to know.

Unfortunately—or fortunately, depending on your perspective—we'll probably never know all the mechanics of faith. But we don't have to. We simply need to learn to believe with everything in us. Jesus indicated as much when he gave the disciples very emphatic and strong promises about having faith, speaking to mountains, and praying with the expectation of receiving. In the midst of those extravagant promises, he issued a very revealing warning: We must really believe it will happen and not doubt in our hearts. In other words, we need to align all of the arenas of belief when we pray.

Most of us have had the experience, probably very often, of believing God for something in our minds while not quite sensing in our hearts that it's going to happen. That's not pure faith. The standard advice is to ignore those feelings and bank on what we know to be true, but that's not what Jesus said. He didn't tell the heart to be quiet. He didn't instruct us to set it aside as irrelevant. He told us to get rid of our doubts even there. Pushing our feelings away isn't enough. Our hearts need to align with the rest of us.

Only God can help us do that. Both our minds and our hearts—neither has proven very reliable—need to be brought under the influence of the Holy Spirit within us. Pray until that innermost place is transformed, and see what God does. Undivided faith is a powerful thing in the hands of God.

Only that prayer which comes from our heart can get to God's heart.

CHARLES SPURGEON

Harmonized Prayers

If two of you agree here on earth concerning anything you ask,
my Father in heaven will do it for you. MATTHEW 18:19

A FEW YEARS AGO, a friend endured an extremely long, intense season of prayer for a family member who was making bad decisions and harming the people she loved. But my friend knew at the outset that she would not be able to make this prayer journey alone. She knew she would need someone who could pray with her in faith nearly as intensely as she did. The well-wishes of friends and acquaintances who offered to lift up a prayer for her were helpful and kind, but she needed more—a partner interceding with her in a persistent, years-long petition to the Father. She needed someone who would build up her faith at certain weak moments and carry the weight of it in others.

God hears every prayer we present to him, but he seems especially drawn to those that are presented in unison. When we align in prayer with other believers—not just in the specifics of the request but with an urgency and intensity of heart with others who are as committed to believing as we are—we are expanding the conversation on earth with our holy intercessors in heaven, broadening the base of our faith, and confirming that the Holy Spirit is moving. An independent prayer may or may not be responding to the Spirit's prompts; two or more are less likely to go off in selfish directions. Like witnesses required for a legal testimony, two corroborating words are far more reliable than one. And when that corroboration is expanded even further to many other believers, the testimony of prayer grows stronger.

There is nothing in Scripture that says a request from someone alone in his or her prayer room is invalid. God does hear, and he responds to the secret petitions of our hearts. But there's a reason we seem to have an impulse to bring others into the circle of our praying, sharing our requests as widely as possible. The union of fellowship in prayer, even from different perspectives, is powerful. God attends to the pleas of his people when they reach his ear in perfect harmony.

Christians are not lone rangers.
CHUCK COLSON

As a Friend

The LORD would speak to Moses face to face,
as one speaks to a friend. **EXODUS 33:11**

WHEN THE HOLY SPIRIT FELL ON BELIEVERS at Pentecost, they were filled with boldness in their testimonies and prayers. That wasn't entirely new; a few prophets, priests, and kings were also bold in their words with people and God. But ever since the curtain in the Temple was torn, all who believe have been invited into the kind of relationship that was exceptional in Old Testament history. People like Abraham and Moses stood out for their friendship with God, while Jesus applied friendship to all who have been joined to him in life. And with that friendship comes an entrance into the throne room of God to have bold, personal, powerful conversations with him (Hebrews 4:16). By our union with Jesus, we are all now insiders.

This isn't just a conceptual issue. Most Christians who are steeped in Scripture could express the points above. But expressing a theology isn't the same as being on fire with the power of God. Why are we permitted to pray boldly as friends of the King? Because we've gazed into his eyes. We've heard his words. We've engaged in two-way conversations, not just one-way requests. We've spent time in his presence, grown deep in the relationship, and cultivated intimacy. When he speaks, we recognize his voice, and we acknowledge him as faithful and true. We don't even question whether something is possible for him, and we no longer fear his will because we know his heart. We have not so much entered into faith as faith has entered into us. Jesus is in us; what greater faith could we possibly need?

This is why prayer, faith, and a relationship with God can never end with intellectual concepts and theological positions. We may talk about cultivating faith, but the actual process is more a matter of being with God as a friend. Faith and boldness grow in those conversations, whether we're aware of it or not. Doubts fall by the wayside. Why? Because our hearts are his, and his heart is ours, and somewhere along the way the two have merged. We breathe the will of God in and then out again. Our hearts, fully alive and burning for him, have been transformed to believe.

> Prayer is the overflowing of the heart in the presence of God.
>
> MADAME GUYON

Zealous Intercession

We have not stopped praying for you. **COLOSSIANS 1:9**

JOHN HYDE, AN AMERICAN MISSIONARY TO INDIA in the early 1900s, constantly had profound prayers weighing on his heart—so much so that the bulk of his ministry was prayer, and his work was a matter of harvesting the answers. He prayed for fellow missionaries, unbelievers, cities, and more workers to be raised up for ministry. Those who knew him told stories about seeing the light come on in his room at 2 a.m., 4 a.m., and 5 a.m. because he just couldn't sleep without interceding for others. His evangelical outlook prompted far-reaching evangelical prayers, and God answered them.

That's an inconvenient prayer life, but it's also a powerful one. The God who never sleeps is certainly not opposed to our getting some rest, but Hyde was unusually sensitive to the burdens on his heart. His tears and persistence moved those around him. They seemed to move God, too. Using a wrestling term from which we get the word "agonize," Paul wrote of Epaphras praying earnestly for the Colossians (Colossians 4:12). He also told the church he agonized for them and the Laodiceans (Colossians 2:1). He made it clear in words and by example that no matter how familiar and intimate we are with the Father, Son, and Spirit, our prayers are more than a casual matter and can accomplish a lot in the spiritual realm. Some might think us strange to spend a night on our knees. God welcomes the fellowship and the petitions.

There will be times when you are called to press through to God with that kind of intensity—probably not to the same degree as Hyde, but with the same desire to see God work in the lives of those around you. The world desperately needs the things you will pray, and God longs to move in response to them. Fill heaven with the sounds, cries, tears, zeal, and persistence of your faith, and expect answers to come. God calls his people to pick up the mission of his Son, who prayed with loud crying and tears (Hebrews 5:7). Ask God to change the world through your requests as you lift up its gaping needs to him.

I know of no better thermometer to your spiritual temperature than this, the measure of the intensity of your prayer.

CHARLES SPURGEON

A Wide-Open Prayer

Open your mouth wide, and I will fill it with good things.

PSALM 81:10

"PRAYING HYDE" PLEADED PERSISTENTLY for God to answer the promise of Psalm 81:10—to fill the mouth wide open with answers to its requests. Hyde was thinking beyond food, of course. He saw the wide-open mouth as a sign of spiritual hunger and a vessel of bold requests. One year he prayed for at least one soul a day, and by the end of the year more than four hundred people had come to Christ through his ministry. The next year he doubled the request, and God answered. The year after, he doubled it again, and God answered again. Hyde saw no limit to the wide-open mouth. He was convinced that the wider a saint opens it, the more God is able to fill.

Sadly, too many of God's people live with closed mouths, closed hands, and limited expectations. God is good to us anyway; he meets our needs and fulfills many of our personal requests. But when we open our hearts and our expectations to fit the wideness of his mercy and the abundance of his Kingdom, we find extraordinary responses to our persistent faith. We become agents of a divine overflow, with heaven's graces pouring into the world through our prayers. The irreligious people of the world do not know such agents exist and will probably never recognize any validity to our prayers, but recognition is never the point. We serve God and respond to his ways. And his way is to reveal himself through the petitions of those who love him.

One of the greatest things you can do for this world, and one of the greatest marks on history you can make, is to devote yourself to the divine discourse in which God's people appeal to him and he accomplishes his will. We cannot do that with small expectations. We serve a big God. His agenda is enormous, and so are our prayers if we get a glimpse of his purposes. Open your mouth wide and see how God responds. Be persistent, and don't lose heart. The most effective place to be a world-changer is on your knees.

> Thou art coming to a king; large petitions with thee bring. For his grace and power are such, none can ever ask too much.
>
> JOHN NEWTON

Spirit-Directed Prayer

When the Spirit of truth comes, he will guide you into all truth.
He will not speak on his own but will tell you what he has heard.
He will tell you about the future. **JOHN 16:13**

IN HIS LAST LENGTHY CONVERSATION with his disciples, Jesus taught about the Holy Spirit, prayer, truth, love, and abiding in him. He was not speaking of these as individual topics but as part of a package, woven together in a comprehensive relationship that affects every area of our lives. So when Jesus said the Spirit of truth was coming to guide them into *all truth*, he was not only assuring future believers about the authenticity of Scripture and our ability to discern God's will. He was also referring to a powerful influence in our prayers of faith. The Holy Spirit is within us, guiding our requests, telling us what is being discussed and prayed in heavenly intercession (Romans 8:27, 34), and cuing us in to future directions. He is the inspiration for the things we pray.

If you've ever wondered what to pray for, that's great news. There will be times when the Holy Spirit turns our unspeakable desires, impulses, and groans into coherent petitions (Romans 8:26), but he will also fill our minds and hearts with vision, direction, and convictions about God's purposes. He will write his plans on the screen of our imagination—we know how to use our imagination in distorted ways, but it also has some very godly purposes—and move us to pray them into existence. As the Spirit of Jesus himself, he is the author and finisher, the champion and perfecter, of our faith (Hebrews 12:2), initiating what we believe at every level of our journey. We are not solitary petitioners. We are surrounded and filled with divine impulses and inspiration.

Learn to envision your prayers as a partnership with the Holy Spirit. You are not coming up with your own ideas and trying to twist the arm of your Father. If the Spirit is at work within you, shaping your desires and requests (Philippians 2:13), you are joining a holy conversation already in progress. Pray from that awareness and trust the Spirit's direction. You are being guided into a life of praying and receiving his will.

Prayer is none other but the revelation of the will or mind of God.

JOHN SALTMARSH

Granted Requests

*At that time you won't need to ask me for anything. I tell you
the truth, you will ask the Father directly, and he will grant
your request because you use my name.*   **JOHN 16:23**

THE DISCIPLES WERE BOTHERED about logistics. Jesus said he was going away. Then he said he would send the Holy Spirit to be with them and in them. Then he said they would not see him for a little while. Then he said they would see him again. The Spirit would take what is from Jesus and declare it to them but also speak truth from the Father. Meanwhile, they would carry his peace. It must have been very confusing.

That's why the disciples asked Jesus lots of questions during that long discussion the night before his crucifixion. It's also why Jesus told them plainly that a time was coming soon when the questions would stop. (The literal expression in John 16:23 suggests asking questions *of* him, not asking him *for* things.) Instead of trying to sort everything out and get straight answers from Jesus, they would enter into direct conversations with the Father and make requests in the name of Jesus, whose power and glory would then be clear. After Resurrection Sunday, their anxieties would fall away, and their spiritual position would become clear. They would have the same kinds of conversations with the Father that Jesus had been having.

That's an amazing privilege that comes with an amazing promise. We are sons and daughters of the King, and we can make requests of him in the name of the King's first Son. We enter into the heavenly conversation not on our own merits but on the credentials of Jesus, carrying petitions bearing his name. All of the shortcomings, insecurities, sins, and impulses of unworthiness we feel are no longer relevant because we are no longer praying in our own names. We have taken on the identity of the Son. As far as the Father is concerned, our requests might as well be coming from his mouth.

Pray with that assurance—and with the expectation that comes with being clothed in Jesus' identity. He has promised that requests will be granted, and we can believe him. The Son and the Spirit are with us when we pray.

The name of Jesus is a never-failing passport to our prayers.

J. C. RYLE

Lasting Fruit

*You didn't choose me. I chose you. I appointed you to go
and produce lasting fruit, so that the Father will give you
whatever you ask for, using my name.* **JOHN 15:16**

WHEN WE'RE CHILDREN, we simply want our needs met. But as we grow, we find ourselves in a lifelong search for significance. We want meaning and purpose. We want to do things that last. Why? Because we were designed for eternity.

There's nothing wrong with praying for our needs and even many of our wants. God loves to satisfy the desires of his people (Psalm 37:4; 145:16). But as we grow, we realize that's not enough. Our lives are not just about getting by, staying safe, and enjoying ourselves along the way. We begin to long for eternal fruitfulness, meaningful work, and fulfilling results. We crave the *shalom* of his Kingdom—that sense of wholeness, completeness, and peace—and begin to pray for ways to enter into it. Some of those ways are off target; the things we pray for aren't going to make everything just right and solve all our problems as we might hope. But the desire is good, and the Holy Spirit has likely stirred it up for a reason. He urges us to pray with an eternal perspective.

This is where God-sized dreams and Holy Spirit movements are born. We may think some of those dreams and goals are our own ideas, and perhaps our specific pictures of them are. But the art of envisioning is from God. He chose us for a purpose. He planted eternal desires within us. He created us for lasting fruit. We can only bear that kind of fruit through him, and one of the ways we accomplish it is by asking and receiving in Jesus' name—in his identity, with his righteousness, and for his purposes and glory. We become his agents in this world.

Don't narrow that down to a tight, stereotyped definition of the Great Commission. Our purpose most certainly includes that, but not all of us are extroverted evangelists. We bear fruit by demonstrating the Father's nature and drawing others into a lifelong relationship of joy, peace, and fulfillment with his Son. "Whatever you ask for" within that vision is enormously pleasing to him.

The Word of God represents all the possibilities
of God as at the disposal of true prayer.

A. T. PIERSON

Don't Let Go

I will not let you go unless you bless me.   **GENESIS 32:26**

JACOB WAS FACING AN UNKNOWN SITUATION that filled him with dread. Would the brother he had deceived so many years earlier come out to embrace him or kill him upon his return home? Time had either healed old wounds or allowed them to fester uncontrollably. And Jacob, returning to his homeland with wives and children and quite a bit of success, didn't know how Esau would respond.

The night before this potentially threatening reunion, Jacob had another mysterious encounter—this one with "a man" who appeared as a manifestation of God. They wrestled in the dark, just as Jacob had figuratively done with God for much of his life, and Jacob refused to let him go. This divine encounter is layered with profound and unsettling meanings, but at least one aspect of it is clear: God allowed and even invited human tenacity in his presence. Jacob insisted on a blessing, and God gave him one. It came at a cost, but it resulted in a new outlook on life and a new name. Jacob's identity was shaped by a stubborn refusal to let go of God.

That doesn't fit many people's definition of God, but God is used to defying definitions. Like an adult who gets down on the floor to wrestle with a child, he is willing to restrain his strength and let us "win" for the sake of a meaningful relationship. He is not content with slavish obedience and constant reminders of his unknowability, however justified they are in light of his majesty. He is eager to enter into a give-and-take relationship with lowly humans, even (or especially) those like Jacob who have a dysfunctional past, never disavowing his lordship but always inviting transformation. He rather enjoys the insistence of one who will not let him go until he or she is blessed.

Jesus encountered people like that (Matthew 15:21-28) and encouraged the same (Luke 18:1-8). While many are reluctant to pester God, God encourages and provokes pestering. Something happens to us in the process, even if the wrestling is uncomfortable. We may come out of it with a limp, but also with a new perspective and sense of identity—and the blessing of knowing our God.

> Storm the throne of grace and persevere therein, and mercy will come down.
> JOHN WESLEY

The Intercessor's Agenda

Remember your servants Abraham, Isaac, and Jacob. You
bound yourself with an oath to them. **EXODUS 32:13**

MOSES WAS PRESENTED WITH A DILEMMA. The people who had just followed him out of Egypt had also just fallen into idolatry by worshiping a golden calf. God told Moses he would destroy the Israelites and establish Moses as a new nation. But Moses reminded God of his promises, confessed their sin, and asked for his forgiveness, focusing his intercession on God's glory. He recognized the priority of God's purposes, and "the LORD changed his mind" (verse 14).

Did God really change his plans based on Moses' prayer? Perhaps in the sense that he let Moses' prayer shift the trajectory of the people's rebellion. But God had provoked that prayer in the first place with his daring proposal, and Moses didn't take the bait. He affirmed what God had wanted to do all along, refused to accept a self-serving alternative, and embraced solidarity with this flawed but chosen people—exactly the kind of responses God has always looked for in human leaders.

Our intercession should have the same characteristics. It should be rooted in God's stated plans and promises, identify with the people he has chosen and is calling into his purposes, resist the temptation for self-promotion, and be anchored in the ultimate purpose of glorifying God in his work and ways. God will often put praying people in situations that test these qualities, and he honors those who adhere to them with answers. He rewards intercessors when they are interceding with the right agenda.

We can't do that unless we know God's agenda. We have to understand something of his purposes in this world in order to pray for them. We need a broad awareness of the characteristics of his Kingdom in order to pray the big-picture prayers he is looking for. We must immerse ourselves in new ways of thinking if we are going to pray for his Kingdom to come. And we must root ourselves in his promises to have the faith that he will fulfill them. An intercessor's agenda isn't complicated, but it will stretch us. And it plays a significant role in God's work in this world.

We are never more like Christ than in prayers of intercession.

AUSTIN PHELPS

Hearing His Secrets

I was worshiping in the Spirit. Suddenly, I heard behind
me a loud voice like a trumpet blast. **REVELATION 1:10**

JESUS PREDICTED A BETRAYER IN THE DISCIPLES' MIDST, and only the betrayer himself knew who it was. But one disciple who was leaning against Jesus—the one who knew Jesus' love perhaps better than any other—got the inside information. He was positioned to hear the Lord's secrets. That same disciple was later worshiping while he was in exile, and "in the Spirit" he saw God's throne room and perspective on history unfold before him. In positioning himself once again to hear the Lord's secrets, John got a vision of staggering things to come.

God knows the language of our hearts, and he will speak to us in ways that reach us. He got Moses' attention with a burning bush. He confirmed his will for Gideon through dew on fleece. He sent Jeremiah to observe a potter so he could make a statement about starting over with his people. He showed Amos a basket of fruit, had Hosea live out a painful parable, gave visions to Daniel, and spoke to Elijah in a still, small voice. God knows the ways we hear, and he meets us there. He reveals his secrets to those who love him. And in revealing his secrets, he invites us to pray with wisdom and insight for the things he is planning to do. Sometimes he shows us what is to come (John 16:13), but most of all he interprets our situations and circumstances in light of his will. His heart opens before us when we love him, worship him, and pray in the power of his Spirit.

Pursue the merging of hearts that comes through your adoration of God and fellowship with his Spirit. This is where the power of God enters into the prayers of human beings in ways we can hardly understand. This is where we see things we did not know about and breathe in desires that transform us and our petitions. Our lives, already united with him, become intertwined in a unison of wills, and he shares his heart with us in greater measure. The language of our heart finds fulfillment in the expression of his love.

The life of man consists in beholding God.

IRENAEUS

Promises as Prompts

And now, may it please you to bless the house of your servant,
so that it may continue forever before you.   **2 SAMUEL 7:29**

GOD GAVE DAVID A STUNNING PROMISE—to make his dynasty everlasting and secure his throne forever. Naturally, David said "thank you." He marveled at the promise and praised God for his goodness. He recounted God's faithfulness to him and his people. And then he did something that hardly seems necessary in light of all that was just said: He prayed for God to do it—and even called it a bold prayer (verse 27).

If God had just promised to do something, why would David think it necessary or even appropriate to pray that promise back to God? Doesn't God keep his word? If God had said what he was going to do, why pray as though it were still up in the air? What was David thinking by repetitively asking God to confirm and fulfill the promise (verse 25), repeating its words as if God needed a reminder (verse 29)? Was David questioning God's integrity?

Of course not. David seemed to understand a fundamental truth about human responsibility to serve as stewards of God's plans. God expresses his will, and we agree with it by praying it, speaking it, and living it out. It's like a contract or a check that needs two signatures to be valid. God can do things unilaterally, but he almost always works out his purposes on earth through human agency. We are partners with him in whatever he wants to do.

We see this throughout Scripture, sometimes clearly and sometimes between the lines. God states his will and waits for a response. He warns of consequences and expects us to agree with his original intent. He speaks to prophets so they will declare what he has said and prompt listeners to agree in faith. He gives us examples of what is possible and then invites us to step into them ourselves. All of which means that your faith, prayers, words, and actions are clearly vital components of his plan. See them as means of partnering with him, and let his promises fill your petitions. They are given for just that response.

> When we find anything promised in the Word of God, we are not to neglect to seek it because it is promised; we are to pray for it on that very account.
>
> B. T. ROBERTS

A Model of Intercession

O Lord, please hear my prayer! Listen to the prayers of
those of us who delight in honoring you. Please grant me
success today by making the king favorable to me. Put it
into his heart to be kind to me.   NEHEMIAH 1:11

NEHEMIAH WAS A MODEL OF INTERCESSION. Upon hearing news from the exiles who had returned to Jerusalem that the city was still in disrepair, he confessed not only his own sins but also the sins of the people as if they were his own (verses 6-7) and then based his entire prayer on a promise God had given centuries earlier (verses 8-9). He was appropriately grieved but hopeful; appropriately humble but had a sense of ownership and responsibility; and appropriately confident but had an awareness that only God could put him in a position of helping. He saw himself as a leader of people and a servant of God far removed from the burden God had placed on his heart.

You'll find that the burdens on your heart are often prompts from the Holy Spirit to do something. Perhaps that "something" is intercessory prayer, advocating for the needs of human beings and pleading with God to intervene and provide. Or perhaps it's more—becoming an agent of change yourself. Even though Nehemiah was stationed in a distant Persian capital, he didn't just pray for the people in Jerusalem. He saw himself as part of the answer. He prayed knowing and even asking that God might rearrange circumstances to do a great work in his life.

You are called to great works too, some entirely on your knees as you petition your Father on behalf of this world and some through a calling to begin a movement, start a program, take the lead in a project, or mobilize others to action. Just as Nehemiah supervised the rebuilding of Jerusalem's walls and participated in its reconstruction of Temple worship, you have been given a mission of rebuilding lives and directing attention to God's goodness. How you do that depends on your particular calling; how that calling opens up before you depends on your prayers, faith, and availability. Those who ask God clearly receive his clear answers—and step into them as part of his plan.

When I say "hallowed be thy name; thy kingdom come,"
I should be adding in my mind the words "in and through me."

J. I. PACKER

Before You Ask

Before he had finished praying, he saw a young woman named
Rebekah coming out with her water jug on her shoulder.
GENESIS 24:15

ABRAHAM'S SERVANT WAS SENT BACK to the family homeland to find a bride for Isaac. When he finally arrived at the village well, he prayed for success and a very specific sign—that the right bride for Isaac would not only answer his request for a drink but offer to water his camels, too. Before he had finished praying, he saw a young woman on her way to the well. As it turned out, she was a relative of Abraham and very beautiful. The eager servant ran over to her to ask his test question, and she answered according to the sign he had prayed for. The prayer had been answered.

But the prayer had been answered well before the servant began praying. For Rebekah to make her way to the well in time to be seen by the servant just as he was concluding his prayer, she had to have gotten started before he even prayed. In fact, God had known about this servant's prayer long before a word of it was spoken. He had known about Isaac—the son he had promised Abraham decades before he was born—and he had known Rebekah was the right wife for him. Everything was already in the works. The prayer was a catalyst for God to do what was already in his heart to do.

That's how it works with our prayers too. We may not always see the answer forming before we finish praying—usually we don't—but the answer has already been in the works. God knows our prayers in advance (Matthew 6:8), and he knows the faith we will attach to them. Circumstances begin converging long before we pray. They have been orchestrated before the foundation of the world by the God who knows all our days in advance (Psalm 139:16). The prayer is simply the catalyst for receiving.

Pray with that awareness. Be encouraged that you aren't asking God to manufacture a situation he has never thought of. Expect his solutions to have already been shifting around your prayers. God has seen them—for years. And he is giving you the faith to pray them with confidence.

> The thing I ask when God leads me to pray
> begins in that same act to come my way.
> LETTIE COWMAN

When Heaven Moves

*Don't be afraid, Daniel. Since the first day you began to
pray for understanding and to humble yourself before your
God, your request has been heard in heaven. I have come
in answer to your prayer.* **DANIEL 10:12**

ABRAHAM'S SERVANT SAW THE ANSWER to his prayer coming his way
before he finished praying. Most of the time, we don't. That doesn't mean nothing
is happening in the spiritual realm; it just means we haven't seen anything change in
our visible world yet—and sometimes we won't for a very long time.

That was Daniel's experience when he prayed and fasted for three weeks for God
to deliver his people. Daniel knew the time was right; he had read Jeremiah's prophecy that the captivity would last seventy years. Like a good intercessor, he confessed
the sins of his people—he identified with them even though he was not responsible
for their sins—and based his prayers on a promise. As he embarked on his fast, he
saw no results. But a messenger from God came with a remarkable explanation of
what had been happening in heavenly realms. Daniel's prayer prompted action, but
a spiritual war was going on, and the messenger had been delayed. Only after the
assistance of the archangel Michael did Daniel receive a clear answer.

Sometimes we wonder if our prayers have been heard, usually because we've
seen nothing happen and don't know what to do with the silence. The testimony of
Daniel—and many others through Scripture and history—is that prayer is powerful
and effective, even when we see no results. The spiritual realm is busy with responses
that will not erupt into the natural world until the time is right. Our prayers are
instrumental in battles that we can only begin to imagine but would never discern
in the atmosphere around us without supernatural revelation. We are warriors in the
spirit, sometimes even when we are bored with our own words.

Enter into prayer with that awareness. Let your understanding of the supernatural realm fuel your faith. Make it a point to persist, even when it takes years for
visible answers rather than days. Your requests are being heard in heaven.

God is never defeated. Though he may be opposed, attacked, resisted,
still the ultimate outcome can never be in doubt.

BROTHER ANDREW

Beyond Questions

*Whom have I in heaven but you? I desire you
more than anything on earth.* **PSALM 73:25**

ASAPH HAD QUESTIONS, and he voiced some of them with a hint of accusa-tion, wondering why God would allow ungodly people to thrive while the righteous struggled. Faithful people seemed to be living under a curse while the unfaithful seemed blessed. That didn't fit his understanding of the goodness, truth, and love of God. It didn't even fit God's description of himself in Israel's Scripture. So Asaph expressed his laments, complaints, and bitter heart in a psalm.

But Asaph gained perspective when he went into God's sanctuary (verse 17). He realized that his glimpse of the world and limited time on earth were not the full picture, that the destiny of the righteous and the ungodly looked very different from what he was seeing with his eyes. He understood that he was torn up inside (verse 21) because of a distorted view of God and lack of spiritual vision. His encounter with God in the sanctuary reoriented his thinking, allowed him to let his questions go, and turned his attention to the privilege of knowing God. He replaced his questions with trust.

God is not afraid of our questions, and he doesn't mind when we ask them. But he does make it clear that our questions, complaints, and laments about the way things are in this world are usually not good fuel for our faith. In fact, they can interfere. When we're busy trying to solve all the mysteries, we are often neglecting our trust in God and casting doubt on his purposes. We are letting our desire for understanding supersede our need for worship. We are majoring on minor things.

Ask God all the questions you want, but don't get sidetracked with them or make them your priority. Get inside his sanctuary, and let an eternal perspective shape your worship, faith, and prayers. Keep your focus on him, your calling, and your mission. You can try to understand the world, but it's even more important to get on your knees to change it. A heart filled with God's wisdom, power, and love will pray powerfully toward that end.

I ought to spend the best hours of the day in communion with God.
It is my noblest and most fruitful employment.

ROBERT MURRAY M'CHEYNE

Bigger than Fears

When you go through deep waters, I will be with you.
When you go through rivers of difficulty, you will not drown.
When you walk through the fire of oppression, you will not be
burned up; the flames will not consume you.   **ISAIAH 43:2**

WHILE REGRETS EAT AWAY AT OUR SOUL, our fears, anxieties, and worries often paralyze it. These forward-looking thoughts are actually a form of faith but cast in negative terms. When we cultivate our anxieties—roll them over in our minds, think about them in the middle of the night, and live defensively to make sure nothing bad happens—we grow in our belief that a possible problem is a likely one. We have little trouble turning a subtle fear into a dreadful expectation and can often do so in a remarkably short period of time. If only we could accelerate and magnify our subtle hopes the same way and turn them into expectant faith.

We can, of course. It's the same dynamic. The difference is that our minds are well-trained in the art of turning bothersome molehills into intimidating mountains, even after we quote magnificent promises about faith being able to move mountains. That mental training takes us down frightful paths, where we rehearse the scenarios in our imagination and plan for ways around them. The result is a defensive, faithless life of self-protection that sometimes keeps us safe but rarely leads to us doing the things God has called us to do. If the heroic characters in Acts had embraced that thought life, they never would have changed the world.

God's promises cover every aspect of our future. They don't ensure that we will never face hardship; hardship is part of every life, even the self-protected ones. God's promises do ensure that he will be with us in any storm, providing ample grace for every moment, and leading us into extremely rewarding fruitfulness and joy. It's faith, not fear, that leads to great victories, and it's faith that aligns us with the heart of the Father and invokes his presence in every situation we encounter. Our worries and anxieties stunt our spiritual growth, while our faith accelerates and amplifies it. We have nothing to fear in the "rivers of difficulty" or the "fire of oppression." God overcomes all. In him, so do we.

God's promises are like the stars; the darker the night, the brighter they shine.

DAVID NICHOLAS

Bigger than Regrets

Return to your stronghold, O prisoners of hope; today I declare
that I will restore to you double. **ZECHARIAH 9:12**, ESV

REGRET IS CORROSIVE TO YOUR SOUL. You've probably noticed that. Along with its twin, disappointment, regret can eat away at your hope, undermine your expectations, and inhibit your faith. You may wish for God's powerful intervention while holding on to regret and disappointment, but you will find it very difficult to believe with any firm conviction that his goodness actually applies to you. When you allow your regrets to grow large, God's great works grow smaller and more distant in your eyes.

The problem with regret is that it lets past experiences dictate future possibilities. For example, regret focuses on those parenting mistakes that are now bearing fruit in an adult child's life and assumes it's too late to fix them. Faith remembers God's promise to teach our children himself and establish their peace (Isaiah 54:13). Regret focuses on those missed opportunities that, in retrospect, would have changed your life dramatically but are now lost forever. Faith remembers God's promises to restore the years the locusts have eaten (Joel 2:25, ESV) and give you double for your losses, even those that were your fault (Zechariah 9:12). Regret focuses on an embarrassing past and continues to carry the shame. Faith remembers God's promises that you will forget the shame of your past (Isaiah 54:4) and receive a double portion of honor (Isaiah 61:7). Regret keeps you looking backward, even as God's promises call you forward.

God's promises cover even our past. Many of his most extravagant promises of restoration in the prophetic books were given to people whose losses, disappointments, and shame were their own fault. He didn't promise only to restore what was unjustly taken from them; he promised to cover their mistakes, heal their self-inflicted wounds, and bless them doubly in return. That's an amazing gift. It turns every regret, disappointment, and loss into a victory.

Shun regret and disappointment as if they were diseases of your spirit. Choose the health of your soul. Leave the past behind and embrace God's extravagant promises of redemption and restoration. Your faith, hope, and prayers will soar with energy. Your past will look more beautiful, and your future brighter than ever.

When you feel that all is lost, sometimes the greatest gain is ready to be yours.

THOMAS À KEMPIS

Advancing on Your Knees

We always pray for you, and we give thanks to God. **COLOSSIANS 1:3**

PAUL WAS DRIVEN BY A VISION OF JESUS and a mission to reach the world with the gospel. He had an exceptional work ethic, was relentlessly evangelistic, and ceaselessly discipled believers and grew churches. He labored for years, enduring extreme hardship, persecution, and stress. He said he knew how to handle times of both abundance and need, but we get the impression that times of need were more frequent. If anyone could change the world through hard work, Paul could.

But hard work alone was not enough. He understood the balance and necessity of prayer. Praying without working is laziness, but working without praying is fruitless. So Paul prayed—a lot. He also requested prayers for his ministry. He recognized that the power of the gospel is not in persuasive words of wisdom but in demonstrations of a supernatural God (1 Corinthians 2:4). No amount of preaching, teaching, and persuading can change the human heart if the Holy Spirit hasn't first prepared it. Human effort and divine power go hand in hand, with divine power necessarily taking the lead. The most effective ministries, then, are those that proceed on their knees. So Paul prayed often and at length—with gratitude as the ever-present seasoning on his prayers—for the people and churches he had known, and he was never reluctant to tell them so.

That's our model for virtually everything we do. Jesus told his followers that without him, they could do nothing (John 15:5), so everything we do requires his motivation, involvement, and strength—attributes of the divine nature we can experience only through prayer. Though living faithfully and fruitfully requires frequent and repeated acts of our will, willpower is not enough. We have to walk in the power of the Holy Spirit. We need to live prayer-saturated lives.

Make that the highest priority every day. Yes, you likely have a long to-do list, but nothing meaningful and lasting can actually be done without the power of God. That's why great saints and servants of ages past have spent hours on their knees, literally or figuratively. You're called to join their company. Your prayers are essential for living with purpose and power.

> Prayer is striking the winning blow. . . . Service is gathering up the results.
>
> S. D. GORDON

Praying for Needs

This same God who takes care of me will supply all your needs from
his glorious riches, which have been given to us in Christ Jesus.
PHILIPPIANS 4:19

WHEN WE SATURATE OUR LIVES IN PRAYER, certain themes appear in our prayers again and again—physical and spiritual needs, protection and provision, healed and deepening relationships, growth and fruitfulness, and much, much more. In fact, there is hardly any limit to what we can pray for. And there is hardly any limit to God's promises. He covers every area of our lives with assurances of his care.

Of all of God's promises for provision, his promises to take care of our basic needs are perhaps easiest for us to understand and believe. Jesus told his followers not to worry because God cares for them like he cares for the lilies of the field and the birds of the air (Matthew 6:25-34). David said he had never seen the godly abandoned or their children begging for food (Psalm 37:25). There were times when God's people were living in rebellion and suffered extreme lack, but his promises to the faithful— and even the somewhat faithful—have always been emphatic. "Those who trust in the LORD will lack no good thing" (Psalm 34:10).

Still, we face job loss, market downturns, and other crises with trepidation. How are we going to pay our rent or mortgage? How will we feed ourselves? What if we're late with our bills? These questions linger and fester because most of us are well aware that we are living above subsistence level. Deep down, we know that maintaining our current lifestyle is a first world problem and that our survival needs are usually covered. Does God define our next-level concerns—*this* home, *this* neighborhood, *these* clothes—as needs? We hope so. But we aren't sure, and fear creeps in.

In certain situations, God's people have gone through the leanest of times and come out with testimonies of his provision. But his promises apply beyond the "just barely" provision of extreme circumstances. Though he doesn't guarantee a certain standard of living, he is gracious with our concerns and obligations. He defines *need* much more generously than our fears might assume. We can trust him in any situation. We can always pray with confidence for his provision.

You will never need more than God can supply.

J. I. PACKER

Praying for Wants

*Trust in the LORD and do good. Then you will live safely
in the land and prosper.* **PSALM 37:3**

"GOD WILL GIVE US WHAT WE NEED, not what we want." These words come out of many Christians' mouths as an automated response to the prosperity gospel and prayers of greed instead of need. At a most basic level, this is true. God has not promised to fulfill every single desire we ever have. And for those of us whose desires change almost daily, that's comforting. God is watching out for our best interests.

But does God really have a history of providing *only* what we need? Hardly. He opens his hand to satisfy desires (Psalm 145:16). He tells us that if we delight in him, he will give us the desires of our hearts (Psalm 37:4). He is the giver of all good gifts (James 1:17) and provides us everything richly to enjoy (1 Timothy 6:17). He has filled the lives of numerous saints with abundance. God is no hard master who demands that we eke out a minimal existence.

As important as warnings against a prosperity-only gospel are, they risk painting God as a miser—the father who only gives school clothes or the great-aunt who wraps up a pair of cheap socks for Christmas. Many Christians approach him as though he always insists on vegetables and never dessert. And while it's true that God does not obligate himself to satisfy our frivolous wants and demanding greed, he is much more extravagant with us than an austere master. His promises for spiritual, emotional, and even physical desires are enormously generous. Yes, most of them imply aligning ourselves with his character and nature and loving the things he loves, but in that context, he invites us to ask whatever we wish (John 14:13; 15:7). We can trust that in most times and places, he wants more for us than the bare minimum.

Ask freely with that in mind. Pray big prayers—not selfishly or greedily, but with an awareness of his generosity. Make it your purpose to freely receive so you can freely give with the same generosity your Father has. He is interested in your needs *and* your wants.

God is more anxious to bestow his blessings
on us than we are to receive them.

AUGUSTINE

Praying for Protection

*No weapon that is fashioned against you shall succeed, and you
shall refute every tongue that rises against you in judgment. This is
the heritage of the servants of the* LORD. **ISAIAH 54:17,** ESV

THE WORLD IS FULL OF DANGERS. We face numerous threats to our spiritual,
emotional, mental, relational, physical, and financial well-being. We are fed a constant
stream of headlines about crime, terrorism, health crises, social discord, leadership
abuses, international conflict, and local mischief. We face spiritual deception at every
turn and desperately want to protect our loved ones against it. We struggle with worries, fears, and anxieties deep in our hearts and minds. Inside and out, we are living in
the presence of potential harm.

Sounds frightening, doesn't it? Yet God is infinitely bigger than all of these concerns. He has given numerous promises about shepherding his sheep, caring for his
beloved, watching over our lives, and protecting us from harm. He tells us no weapon
formed against us will prosper, no evil will touch us, no plague will come near our
home, and we can rest in the shadow of his wings (Psalm 91). He is our rock, our
fortress, and our deliverer (Psalm 18:2). Yes, we will encounter tribulation in this
world. But Jesus has overcome the world, and therefore all the tribulation in it (John
16:33). We have nothing to fear.

That doesn't mean that no bad thing will ever happen to God's people. "Many
are the afflictions of the righteous" (Psalm 34:19, ESV). But we can be certain that
God is walking with us through every trial and tribulation, mediating the threats
that come against us, caring for us even in the valley of the shadow of death, and
zealously guarding our eternal well-being. In both practical and ultimate ways, he is
our guardian, shield, and protector. He has our back.

When we pray for protection, then, we are fully in line with the promises God
has given us. We can pray in confident faith for his loving care over us and our
families. We can base our prayers on his Word, knowing he will honor it for those
who respond to him in trust. We are always under the watchful eye of our Father,
and he will never let us down.

There is never a fear that has not a corresponding "Fear not."

AMY CARMICHAEL

Praying for Deliverance

Many are the afflictions of the righteous, but the Lord
delivers him out of them all. **PSALM 34:19**, esv

WE LONG FOR A TROUBLE-FREE LIFE. Many of us thought that's exactly what we would receive when we first became Christians. But it doesn't take long to realize that even though being a Christian delivers us from eternal trouble, it lands us in a whole new set of trials. We are promised the *shalom* of God's Kingdom—the wholeness, fullness, and completeness of his peace—and we can certainly have it but not in isolation, shielded from every hint of difficulty. For now, we have peace in the midst of chaos, and sometimes that chaos is threatening. As the psalmist said, many are the afflictions of the righteous.

As alarming as the first half of that verse is, the second half is profoundly comforting. God commits to delivering us from every single affliction. His definition of deliverance may differ from ours at times, but this is no ethereal promise that everything will be okay in eternity after we've gone through hell on earth. It is an eternal promise, to be sure, but it has practical implications now. It means that regardless of what we face, no matter how difficult and dreadful it feels, we can have rock-solid assurance that God will get us out of it or through it somehow. He is a deliverer at heart, and we can rest in the certainty that he will be true to his nature.

That's really the aim of the gospel, isn't it? God delivers. He frees us from sin and death, from guilt and shame, and from all the forces that have tried to deface his image within us. He goes before us and behind us and places his hand of blessing on our head (Psalm 139:5). He releases us from bondage of every kind. Even the things that seem to bind us now have no power over his Spirit within us. He promises that we will overcome. In a very real sense, we already have.

When you pray for deliverance, your prayers are in the center of God's will. Expect to experience immediate deliverance in your spirit and eventual deliverance in your circumstances. God is on an eternal rescue mission, and he has set his sights on your freedom.

My chains fell off, my heart was free. I rose, went forth, and followed thee.

CHARLES WESLEY

Praying for Relationships

He gave us this wonderful message of reconciliation.

2 CORINTHIANS 5:19

GOD IS A RECONCILER. He embodies perfect union in the fellowship of the Father, Son, and Holy Spirit (John 10:30; 17:11). He calls us to unity within that fellowship, with each other and with him (John 17:20-23). Though Jesus is a point of division even within families (Matthew 10:34-36), God's heart is for reconciliation (Malachi 4:6; 2 Corinthians 5:18-20). He defines himself as love (1 John 4:8, 16) and calls us to love each other with the same kind of love he has given us (1 Corinthians 13; 1 John 4:7-21). He is all about restored relationships.

That means when we pray for restored relationships, we never need to question whether we're praying in God's will. Yes, some relationships are only for a season, and some are best left in the past. But that doesn't mean they should be left with lingering bitterness and resentment, especially in our own hearts. We can pray for restoration in our attitudes, forgive others from the heart (Matthew 18:35), and cultivate love among those around us. We can pray for restored families, friendships, and fellowships not only for ourselves but for everyone we know. We can be ministers of reconciliation on our knees and in our words and actions. We have been given this mission, and it flows directly into us from the heart of the Father.

Our ministry of reconciliation begins with restoration of relationships with God. That's the context for Paul's words in 2 Corinthians 5. But reconciliation with God always has implications for relationships among human beings. That's why Jesus preached forgiveness so emphatically; as God has forgiven us, we are to forgive others (Luke 6:37-38; Ephesians 4:32). We are called to a ministry of magnanimous hearts, open arms, and welcoming gestures.

When you see discord among family and friends or in the workplace, community, or church, set your heart and mind on prayer. Base your prayers on the nature, character, and promises of the God who gave his Son to reconcile the world to himself and human beings to each other. Know that you are expressing his heart and ministering to others. You are praying his nature into your world.

There is no brotherhood of man without the fatherhood of God.

HENRY MARTYN FIELD

Praying for Children

I will teach all your children, and they will enjoy great peace.

ISAIAH 54:13

MANY BELIEVERS DO A WONDERFUL JOB of imparting faith and values to their children. Many others wonder where they went wrong. The difference is sometimes hard to explain; children have unique personalities, develop independent wills, and respond in individual ways. Good parenting is no guarantee of spiritual upbringing; bad parenting is never an insurmountable obstacle for God. The best we can do is our best, obviously—and then trust God with our children's hearts and the direction of their lives. But part of trust is praying diligently, persistently, and passionately for him to nurture them spiritually and guide them all of their days.

When we do, we are expressing the heart of the Father over his children. Perhaps better than any other experience, our love for our children reveals something of his nature. We bond with him in the joys and griefs of parenting, knowing that his love is far greater than ours. We are partners with him in his desire to impart truth, bless our sons and daughters, and see them grow as Kingdom citizens in this world. We long for them to know and love him even more than we do. He longs for that too.

We can be forever grateful that he gives wonderful, beautiful promises to our children. He pledges to teach them himself, even in areas where we've missed our opportunity to teach them well. He promises to rescue them from the forces that hold their hearts captive (Isaiah 49:25). He encourages us with proverbs about the wisdom and eventual maturity of our children (Proverbs 22:6) and makes his promises of salvation inclusive of entire households (Acts 16:31). He gives us everything we need to pray with confidence and expectation for our children.

Make that a priority, whether you have children or not. Pray for the next generation of believers. Ask God to raise up a generation of passionate believers who know and love him well and demonstrate his wisdom, power, and love throughout the world. Pray in complete faith that he would teach our children directly regardless of where we as parents may have fallen short. Ask that his Kingdom would come in their hearts, just as it is in heaven.

Your prayers for your children are the greatest legacy you can leave.

MARK BATTERSON

Praying for Wisdom

We understand these things, for we have the mind of Christ.

1 CORINTHIANS 2:16

WHENEVER WE'RE DRIVING SOMEWHERE we've never been before, we seek directions. We plug the address into an app and let the virtual voice guide us. When we miss a turn, our guide recalibrates and gives us the next best route. We depend on information beyond ourselves because we want to arrive at the right place.

We often approach God like a guidance system, asking him for specific directions, and he is happy to give them. He loves directing the steps of his children. He has assured us that wisdom is available to us simply for the asking (James 1:5), and he has provided his Word as a lamp to our feet (Psalm 119:105). He wants us to get to the right place too.

But while we are often looking for the next step or even the full route, God has bigger things in mind for us. He wants to impart an entire worldview, a heavenly perspective on earthly things, a mindset that guides us even when the next step isn't clear. He is far less interested in passing along information than he is in endowing us with his own mind. He wants us to be filled with his Spirit, think his thoughts, love what he loves, hate what he hates, and walk in his ways. He wants his values to become ours so that when we have to make a decision, it will come from a deep well of understanding. He wants us to live, think, dream, desire, and speak from a divine perspective.

So God has promised us more than wisdom and direction for the moment. He has given us the mind of his Son so we can change the way we see and think to the way he sees and thinks. We have access to the mind of Christ himself, the word of wisdom (*logos*) that laid the foundation of this world and sustains it in love. That's an astonishing gift that we can hardly claim as rightfully ours, but it's given to us anyway. Pray for its full revelation in you. Embrace the possibilities of heaven's perspective. Ask for wisdom and believe that he is working it into your thoughts daily.

> Common sense suits itself to the ways of the world.
> Wisdom tries to conform to the ways of heaven.
>
> JOSEPH JOUBERT

Praying for Forgiveness

He made him to be sin who knew no sin, so that in him we might become the righteousness of God.   **2 CORINTHIANS 5:21**, ESV

FOR MUCH OF CHRISTIAN HISTORY, forgiveness has been treated as a transaction. We sin, we ask for forgiveness, and we receive it. We sin again and ask again. And Jesus assures us we will be forgiven repeatedly, just as he tells us to forgive others with unending grace (Matthew 18:21-35). But while a transaction does take place when we confess our sins and receive God's forgiveness, he is much more thorough with us than a case-by-case remedy would suggest. He cleanses us from all unrighteousness (1 John 1:9). His Word declares that there is no condemnation for those who are in Christ (Romans 8:1). According to 2 Corinthians 5:21, he has made it possible for us not only to receive righteousness but to *become* the righteousness of God in Christ. He is absolutely thorough in his redemptive, restorative, cleansing work.

When you're praying for forgiveness, you will have plenty of evidence that contradicts this thorough cleansing. You will immediately be able to think of examples when you have not demonstrated the righteousness of Christ. No matter. You are basing your life on what God says, not on what your conscience says. Even when our own hearts condemn us, he is greater than our hearts (1 John 3:20, ESV). Paul goes to great lengths to convince us to see ourselves as God sees us, to consider ourselves dead to sin and alive to God (Romans 6). Why? Because the way we see ourselves will determine how we live. If we see ourselves as sinners, we will continue to sin. If we see ourselves as the righteousness of God in Christ, we will begin to act like it. Our forgiveness will be made manifest inwardly and outwardly.

When you are praying for forgiveness, refuse to water down the forgiveness God offers. He forgives *all* our sins (Psalm 103:3). He removes them as far as the east is from the west (Psalm 103:12). He has given us access to the divine nature (2 Peter 1:4). Our old nature was nailed to the cross with Jesus and left in his grave. Come out in faith and pray as the new creation you are.

When Christ's hands were nailed to the cross,
he also nailed your sins to the cross.

BERNARD OF CLAIRVAUX

Praying for Health

He forgives all my sins and heals all my diseases. **PSALM 103:3**

SOMEWHERE ALONG THE WAY, a belief that the gospel of salvation is "only spiritual" developed. Never mind that the prophets talked often about tangible justice, that Jesus healed physical diseases, and that New Testament writers and apostles cared a lot about material needs (Acts 6:1-7; James 2:16). The divergence in recent history between a "social gospel" that meets physical needs and evangelistic missions that focus exclusively on spiritual needs set up a false dichotomy that isn't visible in Jesus' ministry. He forgave sins and healed bodies even in the same scene (Mark 2:1-12). Why? Because God created whole beings and is concerned about whole lives.

Yes, our bodies eventually waste away, and spiritual salvation is the priority. But emphasis on an "only spiritual" salvation undermines our faith when we pray for health and healing. Many Christians forget that Jesus talked often about the Kingdom of God and demonstrated its comprehensive nature. Some have been led to interpret verses like Isaiah 53:5—"by His stripes we are healed" (NKJV)—exclusively as forgiveness of sin, even though Matthew applied it very physically (Matthew 8:17). Many have assigned the healing work of God to biblical times and decided, quite against the testimony of history, that it rarely applies today, even while we add sick people to our prayer lists and desperately pray for God to heal them. Numerous believers today have lost any sense of expectation that God might actually heal in response to our prayers.

He does, of course. Even when we can't explain the times he doesn't, we've been on the receiving end of his healing touch and heard ample testimonies of restored health. We have everything we need, through the witness of the Word and the healed, to have confidence when we pray. When we ask God for restored health in our bodies or others', we can pray in faith, passionately and persistently, trusting in his goodness for however he responds. We are encouraged to come boldly (Hebrews 4:16), pray with conviction (James 5:15), and press in with determination (Matthew 15:21-28; Luke 8:43-48; 18:1-8). God is far more willing to do great works than we are to expect them. Fuel your faith with anticipation of his healing power.

> The healing acts of Jesus were themselves a message
> that he had come to set men free.
>
> FRANCIS MACNUTT

Praying for Relief

Jesus said, "Come to me, all of you who are weary and carry
heavy burdens, and I will give you rest." **MATTHEW 11:28**

WHEN WE THINK OF PRAYING IN FAITH, we may envision a vigorous prayer life energized by God-given passion and persistence. But sometimes we have trouble even praying, much less pressing into our prayers with bold faith. Hope falters, arms hang, and knees feel too feeble to support a prayerful posture. We have a hard time praying when we're burned out.

God understands. He inspires our prayers with remarkable energy at times, but he also hears the cry of the weak and weary. Even then, he invites us to pray in faith— to lift up a simple request for refreshing, renewal, and restoration. After all, the entire biblical story is about redemption and restoration. If he can lift us out of death and the grave when we are helplessly bound in sin (Ephesians 2:5), he can certainly lift us out of discouragement, depression, and lethargy. In fact, he promises to do so. His Word is full of anticipation for seasons of refreshing and rest. He breathes life into weary souls.

God answers weak prayers and feeble faith. All we have to do is ask, and we can do so confidently based on the promises of his Word. He offers water when we are dry, restoring our strength and making us like an ever-flowing spring in a well-watered garden (Isaiah 58:11). He knows when we walk through painful valleys and promises refreshing springs of blessing on the other side (Psalm 84:6). He lifts the demands of oppressive religion and showers us instead with grace and new life. He assures us that his yoke is easy and his burden is light (Matthew 11:30). He leads us into green pastures and renews our strength (Psalm 23:2-3). In his Kingdom, burnout is simply a phase before rekindling.

Pray with the faith that God is not laying heavier burdens on you but instead is bringing you into places of rest. Understand the seasons of your life, especially that the difficult ones are temporary. Accept his promises of relief and rest. Your refreshing will come like the spring rains, and life will blossom again.

Jesus, I am resting, resting in the joy of what thou art. . . .
For by thy transforming power thou hast made me whole.

JEAN SOPHIA PIGOTT

Praying for Fruitfulness

They are like trees planted along the riverbank,
bearing fruit each season. **PSALM 1:3**

WE WERE CREATED FOR FRUITFULNESS. From the first command to be fruitful and multiply (Genesis 1:28) to the picture of Jesus as a vine that fills his branches with fruit (John 15:1-8), the Bible is clear that we are designed to mature and bear fruit in God's Kingdom. Jesus told parables of seeds and harvests (Matthew 13:3-23) and sent his followers out on the same mission the Father had given him (John 20:21). We were never called simply to make a living. We are called to bloom and grow.

Our concern is that we go through seasons of apparent fruitlessness. Bearing fruit "in season" implies not bearing fruit out of season. That can feel like a spiritual crisis, and sometimes we wonder if God has left us by the wayside or even uprooted us and moved on. After all, if we are created to bear fruit and aren't seeing any, isn't there a problem? Aren't we missing out on our original design? Has God decided he has no use for us?

Of course not. We have to understand the seasons of life. It's perfectly normal to go through times of preparation and then periodic journeys through the wilderness along our way. The key to Christian maturity is not insisting on constant fruitfulness but recognizing seasonal cycles. We have to learn to take advantage of unfruitful seasons to grow deeper roots and then take advantage of fruitful seasons to maximize the harvest. Both are necessary for a healthy spiritual life.

As you pray for God to do great and wonderful things in your life, don't get hung up on timing. Allow him to work for you, in you, and through you on his schedule. Cooperate with him, but don't force the issue. Just believe. His promises of fruitfulness are frequent and reassuring. He calls us not to manufacture results but to be patient and faithful to our calling. There's a time to sow and a time to reap and even a time to wonder what's going on. That's normal. Continue in faith, pray for abundance, and trust God with his timing. The seeds of faith will mature, and the harvest will be beautiful when it comes.

> It is said that in some countries, trees will grow but will
> bear no fruit because there is no winter there.
>
> **JOHN BUNYAN**

Praying for Spiritual Growth

*[Jesus said,] "Anyone who believes in me may come and
drink! For the Scriptures declare, 'Rivers of living water
will flow from his heart.'"* **JOHN 7:38**

JESUS WAS BLUNT ABOUT OUR ABILITIES: "Apart from me you can do nothing" (John 15:5). Even if we're offended by such a thought, we know it's true. We can accomplish a lot of things in our own strength, but none of them are lasting. They have no eternal consequence. We can't even grow spiritually without enormous grace and constant help. In terms of ultimate meaning, we really can do nothing.

In the power of the Holy Spirit, however, we can do virtually everything. Jesus said so himself, promising that his followers would do the works he did "and even greater works" in his footsteps (John 14:12). In our re-created, resurrected lives, we can walk in the power of the Spirit, receive the gifts of the Spirit, and bear the fruit of the Spirit. We are given "great and precious promises," everything we need for life and godliness, full access to the divine nature (2 Peter 1:3-4), even the life of Jesus himself within us (Galatians 2:20; Colossians 1:27). Our old lives were natural and fallen, but our new lives are supernatural and risen.

Jesus was clear about the Father's intention to give us the Holy Spirit. He told us to ask and keep on asking for his Spirit (Luke 11:9-13), suggesting much more than an initial experience at the moment of salvation. We are told to be filled with the Spirit continually as an alternative to counterfeit influences (Ephesians 5:18). Jesus assured us that all who believe will have rivers of living water flowing up from their innermost being (John 7:38). When we are praying for Holy Spirit power and dynamic, lasting spiritual growth, we are clearly asking in accordance with God's will.

Refuse to relegate the Holy Spirit to a past experience or just a subtle influence between the lines of your life. Pray daily to be filled with the Spirit's wisdom, power, and love. Learn to see your whole life in terms of being Spirit-empowered versus self-empowered, and always choose the former over the latter. God will back your prayers with a resounding "yes" and fill you with rushing waters of life.

> The Holy Spirit may be had for the asking.
>
> R. B. KUIPER

Praying for Others

I urge you, first of all, to pray for all people. Ask God to help them;
intercede on their behalf, and give thanks for them. **1 TIMOTHY 2:1**

REES HOWELLS WAS KNOWN FOR a ministry of intercession that began with prayers for individual lives and eventually led to powerful, moving requests for world events during World War II. He and his group of intercessors felt that the world had become their parish and praying for whole nations and generations was their responsibility. Though historians would never acknowledge a connection between prayer and headlines, the correlations were remarkable. His prayers affected spiritual battles as they played out in earthly realms and turned the tide of history.

Perhaps you look at headlines today, or even just the broken lives and relationships around you, and feel helpless. And perhaps you are, in terms of intervening in a tangible, material way. But as an advocate who has been invited to present petitions in the throne room of God, you are never helpless. Your requests are heard in the highest court and can be enforced by his agents in any earthly situation. It may take time to learn the ways of intercession, grow in the faith needed to support enormous requests, and develop the stubborn persistence of an advocate who knows God's will and refuses to let go of it, but your invitation is nevertheless waiting. You have been called to present your requests to God in order to change circumstances and shape history.

That invitation is repeated throughout Scripture by examples and exhortations. It's the template God gave us through Old Testament intercessors like Moses, Nehemiah, and Daniel; the mission Jesus embodied as God in the flesh, interceding then and now for his people and his Kingdom; and the pattern Paul used in growing believers and churches. It's represented in the golden censers in Revelation 5:8 and 8:4 and the many encouragements we are given to pray for each other and for the world.

Don't neglect that invitation. Leverage it for eternal purposes. Pray your heart out, knowing that God's hand is moved by the prayers and faith of his people. Your prayers can influence your family, church, community, city, nation, and world with the fruit that lasts forever.

To make intercession for men is the most powerful and
practical way in which we can express our love for them.

JOHN CALVIN

Earnest, Urgent Prayers

While Peter was in prison, the church prayed
very earnestly for him.   ACTS 12:5

A PERSECUTION OF CHRISTIANS BROKE OUT under Herod Agrippa's rule about a decade after Jesus' crucifixion, and James the apostle was executed. When the king saw his approval rating rise with James's death, he went a step further and imprisoned Peter. The entire church of Jerusalem felt threatened, of course, and dedicated themselves to prayer. Peter's life, along with their entire movement, seemed to be in danger as soon as Passover ended. They prayed "very earnestly" for God to intervene.

God did intervene, and a humorous story emerged from one of the New Testament's darkest crises. An angel woke Peter up, loosed his chains, and led him out into the streets, where he eventually realized his deliverance was much more than a vision. He went to the home where believers were gathered to pray, and the servant girl was so astonished to see him that she left him at the door to run to tell the others. They, too, were astonished and assumed she had seen Peter's angel, not Peter himself. They had been so desperately praying for his deliverance that they could only picture him in prison, not free in answer to their prayers. The effects of their own faith startled them.

Don't be surprised by answers to your earnest, urgent prayers. It's completely natural to pray for a desperate situation with the problem seeming much more likely than the solution, but we don't pray natural prayers. They are supernatural, and the God who sits above all earthly situations is listening to the petitions of his people. He may not always answer as we expect—Peter lived in this story, but James died tragically—but he does respond. The fervent prayers of his people matter to him very much.

Cultivate anticipation in your prayers to the point that you can see the answer without being astonished. Learn to expect the unexpected. Pray with the bold assumption that God is listening favorably and working out his purposes through the words you are praying. Envision all of heaven reacting to the petitions of believers on earth. The faith you have in your spirit profoundly affects the situations you will see with your eyes.

> The angel fetched Peter out of prison, but it was prayer that fetched the angel.
>
> THOMAS WATSON

"God Says"

Scripture cannot be broken.   JOHN 10:35, ESV

THE GAME "SIMON SAYS" trains children to listen carefully to the words being spoken. Whichever instructions are preceded by the phrase "Simon says" are to be followed; whichever ones are not are to be ignored. Young minds get confused in the midst of rapid-fire commands and react with a false step without Simon's authorization. But after a while, they learn to focus exclusively on that phrase. If they hear it, they tune in. If they don't, they tune out. Whoever does that the best wins the game.

That's a fabulous illustration of faith. When we base a prayer on a God-given promise or expression of his will, we are anchoring ourselves in truth. But we very often find ourselves growing discouraged the next day—or even the next hour—when we see evidence that contradicts the direction of our prayer. Is that evidence real? Only if prefaced by "God says." Otherwise, it's false evidence that fakes us out. If we are going to be consistent in our faith, we have to learn to tune in to every word that's preceded by "God says" and tune out to every word—or picture or hearsay or mood—that isn't.

That's how faith works. What God says matters. What other people say, do, think, or feel has no bearing on God's purposes. We jump when we see a negative shift in circumstances, a threatening situation, an unfortunate decision, or some other contradiction to our prayer. But if God didn't tell us to change our thinking, we are like children who jump instinctively at an unauthorized command. We have to learn the discipline of ignoring non-truth.

Whether in instructions, commands, promises, encouragements, prohibitions, freedoms, or any other inspired word, Scripture cannot be broken. We may wonder about correct interpretation, but we can never let our wondering undermine God's clear promises to us. We are never told to respond instinctively to the situations around us as though they are the truth about what God is doing. Only God's expressed intentions are the truth about what he is doing. That's where we anchor our faith and eventually win the "game."

> On these [promises] we are to build all our expectations from God; and in all temptations and trials, we have them to rest our souls upon.
>
> MATTHEW HENRY

Praying His Will

My sheep recognize my voice.   JOHN 10:27, TLB

IN THE LIFE OF FAITH, we are assaulted with doubts every step of the way. We want to pray according to God's will but question whether we understand it. We anchor our prayers in his promises but wonder whether we are interpreting them correctly. We seek confirmation from other sources—a convergence of internal and external voices that affirm what we think we've heard from God—but then wonder if these converging voices were a coincidence and ask for further confirmation. If we are ever going to arrive at a place of faith, we will have to trust that we have the ability to hear God's voice. Or to put it another way, we have to trust that his ability to speak to us is greater than our own ability to be deceived.

It isn't easy to get comfortable with that thought, but it's true. The world is full of voices, and all the while we have been hearing God's voice in the midst of them. The issue isn't whether we can hear him; it's whether we can recognize which voice is his. But over time, with practice and trial and error, we can learn to hear what he is saying to us. We don't have to offer up prayers that are like shots in the dark. We can ask him if a certain prayer is aligned with his will, hear his affirmation or redirection, and then pray accordingly.

Jesus understands our frustration and gave us an illustration of sheep recognizing the unique voice of their shepherd. It doesn't happen immediately; they have to grow accustomed to his or her distinctive sound. But when they do, all other voices become general noise. They are tuned to the shepherd's alone.

That's our goal when we pray. We want to isolate his voice, engage in conversation about the right and wrong things to pray, and then pray with confident faith. He assures us that we can, and when we hear his voice in our hearts—an application of a promise to a specific situation, a timely sermon or article, a Spirit-filled conversation that addresses our question—we can invest our faith there. And we can know we are praying according to his will.

It is essential that we acquire the habit of hearkening to his voice.

FRANÇOIS FÉNELON

Secrets Revealed

There is a God in heaven who reveals secrets, and he has shown King Nebuchadnezzar what will happen in the future. . . . God wants you to understand what was in your heart. **DANIEL 2:28, 30**

KING NEBUCHADNEZZAR WAS IN CRISIS over his dream, and the lives of Daniel and other court sages were on the line. The other sages feared the outcome, but Daniel did not. He knew God was greater than this situation and could reveal mysteries to his servants. So Daniel prayed for understanding and received it. He turned his prayers and faith toward the benefit of an ungodly kingdom.

We often seek God's will on our own behalf, asking for direction and guidance for our personal lives. Though he is certainly willing to guide and direct us, he often has a much larger picture in mind. He wants us to pray for things bigger than ourselves, including solutions to society's problems. Just as he cared about revealing his will to a pagan king in Babylon, he cares about revealing his will through his people to human governments, courts, schools, researchers, media, artists, entertainers, and more. When human need cries out for God's response, he doesn't withhold it to punish the nonbelieving world. He takes the opportunity to show his glory through his people. He accepts invitations into our crises.

The world needs Daniels who are bold enough to pray for solutions that would benefit "secular" society and then offer them freely as gifts from a loving God. That's what Daniel did in Nebuchadnezzar's court, and it brought glory to God and honor to Daniel, putting him in a position of greater influence. Through his example and others' in Scripture, we are invited to seek God's will and unveil his mysteries for people to see. We are to pray confidently and faithfully not only for our own lives and the work of Christian ministries around the world but for rulers, leaders, influencers, systems, and organizations. As agents of blessing with access to the revealer of mysteries, our prayers need to grow well beyond our immediate areas of need and influence. We are positioned in an unbelieving world to reveal, through prayer and faith, the goodness of our God.

To pray is to mount on eagle's wings above the clouds and get into the clear heaven where God dwells.

CHARLES SPURGEON

Promises as Weapons

Timothy, my son, here are my instructions for you, based on the prophetic words spoken about you earlier. May they help you fight well in the LORD's battles. **1 TIMOTHY 1:18**

WE DON'T KNOW WHAT PROPHETIC WORDS were given to Timothy or who said them. They weren't scriptural words, but they were an accurate expression of God's heart and his will for Timothy when they were given. They may have been spoken by Paul or one of his associates, the community of believers in Timothy's hometown, or any other combination of people listening for God's voice and declaring it. Regardless of the source, they were seen as authoritative and sufficient to fuel Timothy's calling and keep him focused.

God's words have that kind of power. When we hear them, whether directly in our spirits or through other believers, we have a divine invitation to cling to them and let them shape our focus. With all the distractions and obstacles that come against us, we need that. We won't stay on course in our prayers and faith if we're questioning the foundation we've put under them. We have a nearly limitless capacity to second-guess ourselves, and many of us constantly reconsider whether we're heading in the right direction. Confidence in what God has said gives us all the clarity we need.

Cling to what God has told you. You will have to go to battle with it later. When you pray, you will need to use his promises and instructions as weapons against doubt, compromise, and apathy, especially during long delays. Paul urged Timothy to fight with the words he had been given, recognizing that Timothy and those around him might begin to question his calling. Promises and prophecies that have fueled your faith in the past become an anchor when you begin to question your faith in confusing times. In God's Kingdom, when the going gets tough, the tough will use God's past words as weapons against every misleading thought, suggestion, distraction, and obstacle. You can use them to keep your prayers on course because his words remain valid until they are fulfilled. Whenever you begin to lose heart, look back to what he has told you, and pray it with unyielding resolve. His words yesterday are your key to victory today.

Prayer is the mightiest of all weapons that created natures can wield.

MARTIN LUTHER

A Limited Perspective

*When the Son of Man returns, how many will he find
on the earth who have faith?*   **LUKE 18:8**

IT ISN'T WORKING. That's the sentiment of numerous believers who have prayed
and then looked around to see whether anything is happening. Early in our life of faith,
that expectant survey may come just a day or two after we pray. But as we mature, we
know things can take a lot longer. Still, we all have a tendency to grow weary and discouraged when we haven't seen any fruit from our prayers over a long period of time.
We wonder if God is answering our prayers and sometimes assume he isn't.

But "it isn't working" isn't a valid observation. It would make sense if the prayer
of faith was a straight trajectory, an ever-upward line toward the goal. We could
measure progress and recognize when our efforts are futile. But if we charted a faith
endeavor—with all its twists and turns, ups and downs, and forward and backward steps that happen along the way—the graph would look extremely volatile and
unpredictable. Choosing a low point on that crooked line and saying "It isn't working" neglects the whole picture. It ignores the end. It's like choosing the moment of
the worst predicament in a novel and calling it a horrible story without reading any
further to see that it ends well.

God is working even when we don't see anything happening. We know that at
a theological level, but our hearts are slow to catch on. Yet many people have spent
decades praying for a loved one without seeing any results, only to witness a conversion in later years. Many have prayed for a promise sown long ago, only to see its first
shoots emerging from the soil after numerous painfully long winters. Jesus promised
that he would return again, and two millennia later we are still watching. Yet God is
not slow about his promises, counting millennia much differently than we do (2 Peter
3:8-9). Jesus' question to his followers still stands. Will he find faith on earth?

That's partly up to you. Make sure he does. Don't lose heart. Don't assume he
isn't working. The longer his promises take, the more magnificent they appear when
they come.

> There is no place for faith if we expect God
> to fulfill immediately what he promises.
>
> JOHN CALVIN

Your Winding Plotline

David was thirty years old when he began to reign. **2 SAMUEL 5:4**

DAVID WAS "ONLY A BOY" when Samuel anointed him as the next king (1 Samuel 16:11-12; 17:33), yet he didn't rule over all of Israel until he was thirty. In the years between, he was exiled by an emotionally volatile king, nearly killed on several occasions, forced to hide out in caves, rejected by his own men, and then at the center of civil wars after the reigning king had died. At numerous points along the way, God's plan for David looked impossible, as if Samuel had made a huge mistake in discerning God's voice all those years before. Yet David was one of many who had been given a promise or a vision only to endure long, winding, painful paths toward fulfillment. His story was neither a straight nor short plotline.

No good plotline is. Fiction writers are often taught to put their protagonist in an impossible situation and then, when things are almost unbearable, make it worse. Why? Because no one reads a novel or watches a movie for a modest victory over a few minor obstacles. Great victories come from great challenges. God is not writing fiction, of course, but he does have a flair for the dramatic. He is unveiling his nature, demonstrating his most stunning attributes over the course of history to a world that has forgotten who he is. You have both the privilege and the trauma of being one of his protagonists. The journey into your destiny is a winding road marked with extreme dangers. Your life of prayer and faith is not a cruise to the beach. It's going to involve some demanding turns and climbs.

Along the way, you will be asked to maintain faith and pray with conviction. You don't have to figure things out, but you do have to cling to trust. Even more, you will weather your journey well if you keep your eyes on the visions or promises God has given you and insist that they remain true. Faith rejoices over an answer even when it looks impossible. Like David and many before and since, you are moving toward a glorious resolution. Believe, and your time of fulfillment will come.

The Lord gets his best soldiers out of the highlands of affliction.

CHARLES SPURGEON

Until Faith Remains

Do you believe that I am able to do this? **MATTHEW 9:28,** ESV

WE HAVE A REMARKABLE ABILITY to believe something one day and then question it the next. Sometimes our questioning evolves into a near-certainty that the very thing we prayed for is not going to happen. A single word or circumstance can flip this switch in our minds, but no word or circumstance is even necessary for us to move from faith to discouragement. We can envision great outcomes in a challenging situation and then talk as if it is headed toward disaster without thinking. Jesus must confront us again and again with his pointed question: "Do you believe?"

When contrary thoughts throw you into a tailspin, take it as a sign that you weren't actually believing what you said you believed. Don't condemn yourself for it; this is good evidence to have. It means you're still growing in the process toward unshakable faith. But because you're still growing in that process, you will need to become aware of your mental vacillations and take charge of them. You will have to train yourself in the art of ignoring contrary indications and embracing God's perspective and promises again and again—until those black holes of faith are filled with abiding assurance. Like a parent training a child in a new habit, you may have to remind yourself to believe until you actually do.

You'll have plenty of opportunities. When you pray for someone to make good decisions and then hear of a bad one, your brain will want to slip into that sense of inevitability. Don't let it. When you pray for a door to open and see it shut the next day, you will be tempted to believe your prayers are futile. Don't fall for it. When you encounter difficulties and instinctively assume God is the one opposing you, don't be deceived. The ease or difficulty of a particular day or week is no statement on whether God is on your side. He has already said he is (Romans 8:31-32). That's enough. He has declared himself willing and able to respond to your prayers of faith. Give him that opportunity by praying them faithfully and consistently, and answer his pointed question with an emphatic yes.

Jesus promises his disciples three things: that they would be completely fearless, absurdly happy, and in constant trouble.

F. R. MALTBY

Decide Decisively

According to your faith be it done to you. MATTHEW 9:29, ESV

TWO BLIND MEN FOLLOWED JESUS, crying out for him to have mercy on them. When he finally gave them his attention, he asked the men if they believed he was able to heal them. We might wonder what would have happened if they had said no; in another situation, a candid confession of partial faith still resulted in healing (Mark 9:17-27). But these men wouldn't have cried out to him in the first place if they weren't convinced of his power. So he affirmed their faith and said they would receive in accordance with it. They got what they believed they would get.

We're reluctant to claim that much responsibility. We don't want God's work in this world to depend on whether we maintain our faith or not. On a grand scale, it doesn't, of course. He is still going to accomplish his purposes. But will he accomplish them in your life? Sometimes our faith is a necessary invitation for his work. There are things that will or will not happen based on whether we believe them. That's how his Kingdom works.

In every situation of praying in faith, then, we have to make a decision, and it can't be a tentative one. We have to decide whether we believe and then stick with that decision. That doesn't mean we harden our hearts and refuse to be redirected even by God himself. Sometimes we get it wrong and need to realign with his purposes. But when we base our prayers on his revealed will and attach our faith to his promises, we have to stick with them until he directs us otherwise. Circumstances, opposition, challenges, obstacles, and deceptive words have no bearing on our agreement with God. We have no business waffling on the things he has said he will do. If faith is the currency of his Kingdom and the key to answered prayer, then it's nonnegotiable. We have to pursue it relentlessly and rest in it when we have it.

When you pray, do you believe or not? Make that decision emphatically, purposefully, decisively. Then pray with conviction. According to your faith it will be done to you.

He does not believe that does not live according to his belief.

THOMAS FULLER

The Hindrance of Sin

*If I had cherished iniquity in my heart, the L*ORD
would not have listened. **PSALM 66:18,** ESV

DOUBT IS A HINDRANCE to the prayer of faith, for obvious reasons. We've seen that repeatedly throughout Scripture, in the words and lives of Old and New Testament saints, in the teachings of Jesus, and in our own lives. But Scripture mentions other hindrances too, and if we are serious about praying in faith persistently, passionately, and purposefully, we will need to be aware of them. One of the most significant is the presence of sin in our lives—not as an exception but as a welcomed, harbored, cherished companion. When we embrace sin, we release God's promises to the faithful.

It's important to remember that there is no condemnation in Christ (Romans 8:1). God removes our sin from us as far as the east is from the west (Psalm 103:12). When today's verse mentions the presence of sin as a hindrance to prayer, it needs to be balanced with the New Testament reality of Jesus' cleansing work for all who believe, even those who continue to struggle. In that context, this verse is not about people who struggle with sin or who fail frequently. People who fit that description generally hate their sin but are drawn to it from habit or to soothe their souls from unhealed wounds. No, this verse is about those who willfully and consistently push God to the margins of their lives until they need him and then plead for his help, wondering why he doesn't show up in their time of crisis. In his mercy, he does respond to these kinds of pleas at times. But he doesn't promise to. His promises apply to those whose hearts are tender toward him, even when they sin.

Resist the temptation to assume you are disqualified from answered prayer if you have sinned recently. That is not the testimony of Scripture. In Jesus, you are thoroughly, completely clean. But do take seriously the attitude you have toward sin. Do you cherish and nurture it? Do you push God away until you need him? Then confess, receive his forgiveness, and run back into his arms. He is waiting to welcome you and answer your prayers. He has dealt with your sin. Now let him respond to your confident faith.

Sin is a power in our life. Let us fairly understand
that it can only be met by another power.

HENRY DRUMMOND

AUGUST 31

The Hindrance of Selfishness

Even when you ask, you don't get it because your motives are
all wrong—you want only what will give you pleasure. JAMES 4:3

THERE'S NOTHING INHERENTLY WRONG with pleasure. God created it. He generously gives us all things to enjoy (1 Timothy 6:17). We are designed to celebrate God's good gifts and give thanks to him for all the joy and pleasure they bring. But fallen human nature turns pleasure into an end in itself and organizes life around that end. It prioritizes something that is secondary to God himself. Pleasure becomes an idol.

When we pray for our idols, we are outside of God's will. We have subverted the divine order in favor of the fallen natural order. We have deified ourselves and tried to make the rest of life serve the god we've enthroned in our hearts. That never works, at least not for long. Our motives are skewed, our pursuits are misdirected, and our victories are temporal. We have forsaken eternal fruit for temporary gain. It's never a good deal.

In his mercy, God rarely answers those prayers. If he does, it's only to show how futile they are. His greater purposes are for us to deny the centrality of ourselves and focus on him above all. Only then can we experience real pleasure, lasting fruit, and deep joy. Only then can we orient our lives around what truly matters. Only then can we expect God to answer our prayers according to his promises.

We are called to be Kingdom citizens who, when blessed with material blessings, understand them to be a means to bless others. We see whatever God has given us as an asset to further his Kingdom and demonstrate his kindness to others. We enjoy it, to be sure, but we don't seek his gifts only for our own enjoyment. We see ourselves as part of the whole, representatives of his nature, ambassadors for his purposes, and mediators of his goodness. That's a perspective that positions us to receive the fullness of his blessings. He can trust us with them when our desires are centered on him. We ask and receive according to his good pleasure—and, as a wonderful side benefit, according to ours.

The purpose of all prayer is to find God's will and make that will our prayer.
CATHERINE MARSHALL

245

The Hindrance of Ruptured Relationships

Treat her as you should so your prayers will not be hindered.

1 PETER 3:7

WE LIKE TO THINK OUR RELATIONSHIP WITH GOD is just between us—that if we're good with him, nothing else matters. But according to God's own Word, loving him involves loving others; fellowship with him implies fellowship with others; and being forgiven in a relationship of grace means forgiving others in a culture of grace. That's a major theme in John's first letter and Jesus' teachings. Our vertical relationship with our Father has quite a lot to do with our horizontal relationships with fellow human beings. And if those are out of sorts, something is wrong.

Conflicts and ruptures in human relationships can hinder our prayers. Jesus put forgiveness at the center of our relationship with God and other people, binding the horizontal and vertical into one coherent package (Matthew 5:23-24; 6:14-15; 18:21-35). If we aren't right with our brother or sister, we aren't entirely right with God. Redeemed and clean? Yes. Ready to proceed in a relationship of intimacy and grace? Not yet.

That has profound implications for our prayers. It isn't that God never answers the prayers of those who have conflict in their lives. Jesus experienced conflict all the time, and God clearly answered his prayers. But we need to pay attention to our role in conflicted relationships. If we can do something to resolve them, we should.

That is nowhere more important than in marriage. The relationship that best portrays the intimacy between Jesus and his beloved (Ephesians 5:25-33) is our highest priority for unity. It's true that friction is inevitable, and it's also true that one partner can be zealous about the spiritual implications of the relationship while the other ignores them. But neglect of this relationship implies a neglect of the nearest picture of Jesus and his bride. The ideal illustration of prayer and provision is undermined by a distorted portrayal of it. This has to change. When it does—or at least when we seek restoration—prayer is empowered and free, and God responds in love.

To live in prayer together is to walk in love together.

MARGARET MOORE JACOBS

The Hindrance of Bitterness

Look after each other so that none of you fails to receive the
grace of God. Watch out that no poisonous root of bitterness
grows up to trouble you, corrupting many. **HEBREWS 12:15**

JONATHAN GOFORTH, a Canadian missionary to China in the late nineteenth
and early twentieth centuries, was discouraged about his mission stations. "Cold and
fruitless,"[4] he called them. He planned to visit and try to revive them but felt an uneasi-
ness in his relationship with God—as if an issue first needed to be resolved. Goforth
prayed and soon realized the issue: He had a bad attitude toward another missionary
from an earlier conflict. The other man had been at fault and confessed with tears,
and Goforth had forgiven him. "But you still aren't loving each other as brothers," the
Lord impressed upon him. Goforth felt intense internal pressure to make things right.

Once when Goforth was preaching at the church at his home station, that pressure intensified. He felt an unbearable hindrance. In the middle of the message, he
thought, *Lord, as soon as this meeting is over, I'll go and make it right.* He said nothing about it in his message, and no one knew what was going on inside of him. But
the meeting immediately shifted with that decision. An unresponsive congregation
suddenly became engaged and attentive. At the end, people broke down weeping
in prayer. After having spent years of fruitless labor in the region, he began to see
lives transformed. Prayers that Goforth had prayed years before were suddenly being
answered. The tour to the mission stations was enormously fruitful. One simple
decision to love had prompted breakthrough.

Our unresolved internal issues can hinder the Holy Spirit's flow in our lives, and
our decisions to deal with them can release the flow again. If we want breakthrough
to come in our lives, this is a key—to be aware of our attitudes, attentive to God's
voice, and humble enough to respond. Our prayers and faith become uninhibited
and unhindered when we release the bitterness that constrains them. Our perspective
becomes more aligned with God and his mercy. There's no limit to what he can do
through vessels that have allowed him to cleanse them.

> If you hug to yourself any resentment against anybody else,
> you destroy the bridge by which God would come to you.
>
> PETER MARSHALL

The Hindrance of Neglect

God detests the prayers of a person who ignores the law.

PROVERBS 28:9

THE WORLD IS FULL OF NOMINAL CHRISTIANS—people who claim the name of Christ on a census form but pay hardly any attention to his teachings in daily life. They are natural by-products of cultural Christianity, a legacy of Christian history without the substance of meaningful worship and faith. In a pinch, they will turn to God in prayer and reclaim their religious affiliation. But for most other matters, they don't see him as very relevant.

Of course, no one knows the heart of each person brought up in a semi-Christian culture. And in his mercy, God answers the prayers of those who turn to him, regardless of their background. But those who have pointedly pushed him into the margins of their lives so they can follow their own plans are missing out on his promises for faithful believers. They may pray, but often without conviction. They may worship, but often without heart. And they may claim Jesus' name, but usually without his nature, power, or presence within. Their prayers are based on a wish and a hope rather than a changed heart and a covenant of love.

No one wants detestable prayers, but according to Proverbs, that's the nature of the prayers of those who are disinterested in God's will and ways. This passage refers not to those who aim to be faithful and are flawed in their devotion but rather to those who callously reject God as a real presence in their lives and then demand his attention when they are in need. Such self-serving prayers miss the heart of the Father. They are far beyond the scope of his commitments to the faithful.

Invest your life in the Word of God—not the law as the author of this verse understood it, necessarily, but the covenant of Jesus that fulfilled the law and works his purposes into our hearts. Let your life be saturated with his will. Your prayers will rise as pleasing incense in the presence of God, and he will honor your faithfulness with his provision. He delights to answer the prayers of those who love him.

Ask not for gifts but for the Giver of gifts; not for life but for the Giver of life.
Then life and the things needed for life will be added to you.

SUNDAR SINGH

The Hindrance of Prayerlessness

Far be it from me that I should sin against the LORD
by ceasing to pray for you. 1 SAMUEL 12:23, ESV

IT OUGHT TO GO WITHOUT SAYING: The most common hindrance to prayer is not praying. Yet as obvious as this seems, many believers assume that their desires have served as prayers and that unfulfilled desires constitute unanswered prayer. We can safely assume that unprayed prayers are guaranteed to remain unanswered, and prayed prayers are far more likely to be fulfilled. Even so, we often lament the unspoken—and therefore unanswered—pleas of our hearts.

Samuel considered prayerlessness a sin. He served as a prophet and priest, so his conviction is understandable. But in an age when every believer stands in Christ as a priest between heaven and earth, Samuel's words are pointed and profound. Our role as priests is to intercede between God and humanity, and our primary means of intercession is prayer. So what happens when we don't pray? Nothing. We miss an opportunity to connect heaven and earth with our requests. We let God's desires for his people and a world in need fall to the ground.

Think of the magnitude of this missed opportunity. On the one hand, we have the world's gaping needs, many of them staring us in the face in the lives and circumstances around us. On the other hand, we have God's extravagant promises, unfathomable mercy, and zealous desire to rescue the world with his love. What can bridge this gap? Jesus came to make a way; then he sent his followers into the world on his mission of reconciliation. That means that each believer stands between two realms with the authority, opportunity, and relationship necessary to invite the grace of God into the hearts, minds, circumstances, situations, communities, organizations, and systems we encounter. Meanwhile, we watch, criticize, lament, shake our heads, and walk away. Our moments of intercession fall away unfulfilled.

Refuse to miss those opportunities. Take up the calling to pray, intercede, plead, confess, and invite God's limitless provision into this world. Voice the requests of empty, wounded hearts and let God fill them with his love.

Do not let us fail one another in interest, care, and practical help; but supremely we must not fail one another in prayer.

MICHAEL BAUGHEN

Friendship with God

[Jesus said,] "I no longer call you slaves, because a master doesn't confide in his slaves. Now you are my friends, since I have told you everything the Father told me." JOHN 15:15

THE PRAYERS OF A SERVANT ought to be straightforward: "Your will be done." That's because servants exist for the sake of their master, and whatever the master wishes becomes the servant's business. That describes one aspect of our relationship with God, but that's not where the relationship ends. It grows into friendship. We do learn to serve, and God's will is always our highest priority, but Jesus invites us into a deeper level of companionship in which he shares his heart with us and we share ours. We learn to love what he loves, hate what he hates, grieve where he grieves, and rejoice where he rejoices. We receive inside information about his thoughts, and he welcomes ours. We think, see, and dream together.

This new kind of relationship shows up at times in Jesus' teaching, especially in the Gospel of John the night before his crucifixion. Jesus promises that he and the Father will come and make their home with us (John 14:23), that his Spirit will reveal deep truths about the future (John 16:13), and that we can freely ask what we wish (John 14:13-14; 15:7). But this kind of friendship with God isn't just a New Testament phenomenon. God told Amos that he does nothing without revealing it first to his prophets (Amos 3:7). He called Abraham a friend (Isaiah 41:8; James 2:23) and talked to Abraham about his plans and desires before acting on them (Genesis 15:1-6; 18:17-19). God will guide and encourage anyone who asks, but he seems to share secrets with those who have drawn particularly close to him. He invites us into a friendship in which he reveals his desires and openly receives ours.

Don't ignore that invitation. It's a remarkable opportunity to converse with the God of the universe in a way not many people do. He enjoys the fellowship, the give-and-take, and the heart-to-heart connection with those who have taken a step beyond servanthood. He builds his Kingdom through those who discuss plans, purposes, visions, and desires with him. He knows he can trust good friends with his—and their—dreams.

Some people pray just to pray, and some people pray to know God.
ANDREW MURRAY

Envisioning with God

I will certainly bless you. I will multiply your descendants beyond
number, like the stars in the sky and the sand on the seashore. Your
descendants will conquer the cities of their enemies. **GENESIS 22:17**

GOD LOVES TO SPEAK IN PICTURES. Some may think of the languages of
Scripture—Hebrew, Greek, and a dash of Aramaic—as his favorites, and others imagine him speaking in their own tongue. But even though his authoritative revelation is
written in words, those words are filled with images, parables, stories, metaphors, and
lots of other devices that bring pictures to our minds. In fact, he often gives his promises in scenic rather than contractual terms. He wants us to envision his purposes.

We've seen how God established that pattern early in his conversations with
Abraham. He told Abraham to look to the skies and try to count the stars as an
illustration of his numerous descendants (Genesis 15:5). He reiterated that scene
and added a picture of the sand on the seashore to emphasize the magnitude of his
promise after Abraham was willing to sacrifice it all in obedience. Abraham had
proven his obedience as a servant, but God wanted to lift him up into friendship and
expressed his thoughts, desires, and plans to Abraham through unforgettable images.

When we enter into that kind of friendship with God to hear what's on his heart
and express what's on ours, sharing dreams and desires with him to bring about his
purposes in this world, he imparts his visions to us. He gives us pictures to hold on
to because they sink much deeper into our memory and emotions than contractual
language does. We cling to the bare statements of a promise, but we're inspired by the
vistas he plants within our hearts of what those promises will look like when fulfilled.
He provokes our imagination so he can fill it with his desires.

Don't reject your imagination because of its potential to deceive. Give it to God
because of its potential to see the Kingdom playing out. Let God engrave his pictures
in your mind so you can pray them, believe them, and enter into them. He builds
his Kingdom through friends who are willing to see what he sees.

There is no vision but by faith.

WALTER CHALMERS SMITH

Always More

I am planning to go to Spain, and when I do, I will stop off in Rome.
And after I have enjoyed your fellowship for a little while,
you can provide for my journey. **ROMANS 15:24**

PAUL HAD PLANS. BIG ONES. He had learned the art of dreaming with God, and because he could envision great, eternal purposes, he was able to participate in them and advance them far beyond others' expectations. In a time when relatively few people pictured the spread of the gospel beyond Jerusalem, Samaria, and perhaps Antioch and Egypt, Paul and his friends could see much further in terms of time, geography, and the plans of God. So they went where few had gone before, driven by greater zeal than most had demonstrated, enduring and overcoming numerous obstacles to take the Good News of the Kingdom far and wide. Why? Because they had a vision.

Paul had a vision of Jesus that launched his initial calling (Acts 9:3-19), and then while worshiping was among several leaders to be given further direction into the Hellenistic world (Acts 13:2). We don't know if his plans to go to Spain by way of Rome ever materialized—by most accounts, he got to Rome under much different circumstances and died there—but that isn't the point. He had God-given longings (see also Romans 1:11-12, 15). His heart beat with God's; he could see down the road into God's global agenda, and he wanted to be part of it. And he was. He and a few other believers were instrumental in taking the gospel to distant lands because they had learned to desire, dream, envision, and walk with God.

When you think of yourself as God's friend, receive his desires and purposes, and begin dreaming and planning with him, you'll find that the desires of your heart grow much bigger than you are. You may wonder how you could ever possibly fulfill the things you would love to do, and you will be driven both to pray and act on the impulses and ambitions within you. Fulfilling them all is not the point; moving in the direction of them is what matters. You will pray, believe, and walk in step with the God who is always planning more and carrying out purposes that outlive you.

Vision encompasses vast vistas outside the realm of
the predictable, the safe, and the expected.

CHARLES SWINDOLL

Fearless Prayers

Now, O LORD, hear their threats, and give us, your servants, great
boldness in preaching your word. Stretch out your hand with healing
power; may miraculous signs and wonders be done through the
name of your holy servant Jesus. ACTS 4:29-30

PETER AND JOHN HAD JUST BEEN QUESTIONED, mistreated, and threatened by religious authorities to stop what they were doing. Their message was provocative, and people in charge rarely favor a disruption in the status quo. When Peter and John were released, they returned to a gathering of fellow believers and prayed—not for safety and protection or for God's vengeance on their adversaries but for more of the inflammatory effectiveness that got them in trouble in the first place. They asked for more power and greater boldness.

Why were Peter, John, and their friends willing to rock the boat even more? Because they recognized that God was doing something remarkable, advancing into hearts and minds by making a scene and turning social expectations and structures on their head to change lives. They discerned the difference between a time to play it safe and an opportunity to advance while hearts were open. They recognized the distinction between a threatening door and a closed one, and they wanted to enter into greater fruitfulness. They had faith that God couldn't be stopped.

Holy Spirit boldness does that to our prayers. When we get a picture of what God is doing in the world, we want to keep moving forward and maximize our participation in his plans. We don't want to sit on the sidelines and see how it plays out; we want to pray, believe, speak, and work in accordance with God's power and presence. We sense his movement and want to be part of it.

You will recognize a multitude of ways to be a part of what God is doing, and your involvement will depend on your particular gifts and interests. But the call to pray for a powerful advance of the gospel is universal. Pray for fearlessness in prayer—for the Holy Spirit to fill you with boldness to pray for earthshaking movements, explanation-defying demonstrations of power, and Jesus-glorifying works. Ask him for faith, then pray your faith assertively. The times are always ripe for his power.

Prayer obtains fresh and continued outpourings of the Spirit.

J. C. RYLE

Because of Faith

Daughter, your faith has made you well. Go in peace.
Your suffering is over. **MARK 5:34**

MANY OF US HAVE AN INNER THEOLOGIAN who demands precision and voices objections to people's statements about God and truth. That persistent voice bristles at passages like this. "No, Jesus," we want to say, "faith didn't make that lady well. You did." We want to take the emphasis off of a human response and make this healing glorify God rather than faith itself. And when Jesus disagrees with our inner theologian—when his own words defy our definitions of how God works—we have a bit of a problem.

Jesus' words created problems for a lot of theologians in his day too. If we entered into a discussion with him about this particular statement—how perhaps he should have worded it a little differently—he might even affirm some of our understanding about the priority of the power of God over the power of faith. Yet his words were no accident. He wanted to emphasize faith here. Why? Because it's a really big deal. How we respond to the power of God very often determines whether or not we will see it.

Does that seem like a lot of responsibility? It is. Yet this is how God has made his Kingdom to work. In heaven, where all things are seen plainly, faith in invisible realities doesn't apply. But here, where the human story began with a questioning of God's goodness and human hearts still have to make a decision about it, faith is essential. Can we see his wisdom, power, and love beyond the veil of this world? Or will we be blinded by the "reality" of finite circumstances, material limitations, and random processes? Will our hearts lean toward God or away from him? That's the question that faith always answers, and this world is the perfect environment for testing it.

Choose faith. Always. Insist on what your eyes do not see. Only then will you be able to prove to your eyes that invisible truth was greater and more real. God responds according to our faith because faith has chosen him above all appearances. And when he responds, appearances change and his power becomes clear.

Prayers are heard in heaven in proportion to our faith.

CHARLES SPURGEON

The Promise of Presence

*Do not be afraid or discouraged, for the LORD will personally
go ahead of you. He will be with you; he will neither
fail you nor abandon you.* **DEUTERONOMY 31:8**

ONE OF MOSES' BIGGEST FEARS at his burning-bush encounter with God
was the prospect of going back to the hostile environment of Egypt alone. He didn't
necessarily express that fear in those terms, but his uncertainty about how he would
be received in Egypt suggests visions of being out on a limb without a safety net. So
God gave him a different vision—the safety net of God's own name, his credentials,
and his power. Moses had little choice but to accept his mission.

Years later, when Moses was passing off leadership to Joshua, he recognized in
Joshua the same fears he once had and the need for assurance. With ample experience now under his belt, Moses was able to encourage Joshua that God would go
with him. No matter how things looked at certain moments—in the heat of battle
or in the midst of complaints—God would neither fail nor abandon him. He had
promised his presence to Moses and been faithful to keep his word; he would do the
same with the next generation. Joshua would never need to proceed in fear, wondering if he was out on a limb without a safety net.

We can take comfort in God's promises about his presence, not only to Moses and
Joshua but throughout Scripture. In fact, Jesus is called Immanuel, "God with us,"
for a reason. He is the emphatic statement that God's presence will always be with
those who believe. Jesus came to us in the flesh, and he sent his Spirit as a constant
companion and counselor not only to be with us but to live in us. We are never alone.

When you pray in faith about your future, don't let fears about going alone or
being let down creep in. God has promised to go with you. He has given you his
name, his credentials, and his power, just as he did with Moses. You can pray boldly
for whatever he wants to do in your life, knowing that if he has called, he will equip
and empower you. His presence removes the limitations of fear from your prayers.

> When Jesus is present, all is well, and nothing seems difficult.
>
> THOMAS À KEMPIS

The Promise of Success

Be strong and very courageous. Be careful to obey all the instructions
Moses gave you. Do not deviate from them, turning either to the right
or to the left. Then you will be successful in everything you do.

JOSHUA 1:7

DURING THE TIME OF MOSES, God established a covenant that would define Israel's relationship with him and measure its people's faithfulness. If they kept the law, they would receive blessings. If they didn't, they wouldn't (Deuteronomy 28). Over time, God's people would demonstrate the impossibility of living up to his standards in their own strength and the necessity of a Savior. But a principle had been established: Following God's will and his ways is the key to seeing his promises fulfilled.

Jesus fulfilled the law of Moses himself, and all of God's promises are now "yes and amen" in him (2 Corinthians 1:20). We can breathe a huge sigh of relief that our fortunes do not rise and fall with every act of obedience or disobedience. But even in the days of Joshua, God was more interested in the heart of the follower than the letter of the law. Then and now, he seeks hearts that are completely his, offering the full backing of his wisdom, power, and love to those who love him (2 Chronicles 16:9). Those who align with his ways in love receive the fullness of his blessings; those who don't, receive the correction and discipline they need. His desire is for each of us to walk in step with him.

That has enormous implications for every area of our lives, including our prayers. God isn't looking for rogue petitioners who want to receive his power and blessings and go their own way with them. He is looking for those who see his ways as their goal and the success as a by-product. He wants followers who align with his will not because they have to but because they love him. He wants to make us his friends.

Praying, believing, and walking in step with God is the key to success—not as a reward but as an inevitable outcome of embracing his wisdom. After all, he created everything and knows how the universe works. When we carefully invest our faith in the words he has said, it—and we—will be satisfied and fulfilled.

The faithful person lives constantly with God.

CLEMENT OF ALEXANDRIA

The Promise of Direction

Trust in the LORD with all your heart; do not depend on your own understanding. Seek his will in all you do, and he will show you which path to take. **PROVERBS 3:5-6**

GOD SEES EVERYTHING. He knows every detail about our circumstances. He sees the options we have and the paths we should take. He knows the obstacles and challenges we will face, the fruit that will come from our choices, and the purposes he wants us to fulfill. Like an eye in the sky looking down on the full parade, he sees the whole route, the front and back of the line, and all the participants and observers involved. He has no lack of understanding.

We do, of course. We see our little corner of the world, and even that is an incomplete picture. We try on different options to see how they feel, imagining this or that outcome, weighing our pros and cons, and figuring out which path to take. Our thought processes sometimes cause considerable anxiety, and sometimes they paralyze us in inaction. But we want to know. We need to take a step in one direction or another. We need the perspective of the one who sees it all.

God promises exactly that. We may not see everything he sees, but he does promise to guide us from his omniscient perspective. But we have to ask for guidance, and to do that requires humility. When we pray for his wisdom and understanding, we are confessing that we can't depend on ours. When we pray for direction, we are admitting we don't know which way to go. When we decide to trust God, we have to stop trusting ourselves. We embrace humility in order to receive all that he wants to give.

God honors that kind of humility. Throughout Scripture and history, he has resisted the proud and been drawn to the humble (James 4:6; 1 Peter 5:5). When his people give up their own wisdom and ask for his, he rushes in with his answers. Even when we don't see the right path to take, he directs our steps anyway (Proverbs 16:9). If we take a wrong step, he patiently puts us back on track. We can pray with extreme, unshakable confidence that he will always get us where we need to go.

Deep in your heart, it is not guidance you want so much as a guide.

JOHN WHITE

The Promise of Prayer

In those days when you pray, I will listen. **JEREMIAH 29:12**

GOD SPOKE SOME HARSH WORDS through his prophet Jeremiah, but the dark clouds of those prophecies were lined with rays of light. He promised to give his people a future and a hope, assuring them he was for them, not against them. Then he promised that he would listen to their prayers "in those days." They would enter into a time of favor, when God's ears were open to their requests and he would answer them in love. He promised a fruitful prayer life for his people.

We still live in those days. The time of restoration that God had declared happened long ago, and the coming of the Messiah centuries later ushered in a season of God's favor and life in the power of his Spirit. Though God had apparently shut his ears for a season of widespread rebellion—"in those days" implies a period of unanswered prayer beforehand—his ears are forever open to the redeemed. He had already promised to be close to those who call on him in truth (Psalm 145:18) and respond to the prayers of the destitute (Psalm 102:17). Through Jesus, we can go ahead and count on his "yes" (2 Corinthians 1:20). We are invited to participate in his divine nature (2 Peter 1:4). There is nothing that separates us from the love of God (Romans 8:38-39). He is forever "for us" and not against us, lavishing on us the blessings of his Son and much more (Romans 8:31-32). He eagerly listens to our prayers.

That's not what our consciences tell us when we sin, struggle to find words to pray, become discouraged, and wonder if our prayers are bouncing off the ceiling. If any hints of separation from God seep into your conscience that way, simply confess any hindrances and move on. Believe what he says about open ears and open heavens, regardless of what you feel or see. God has promised to listen, and only doubt can convince us that he doesn't. Release those doubts, embrace bold faith, and pray until your heart believes. God is welcoming you and your requests into his throne room and will advise, redirect, and answer with great pleasure in these days.

Be much in secret prayer. Converse less with man and more with God.

GEORGE WHITEFIELD

The Promise of Favor

*If God is for us, who can ever be against us? Since he did
not spare even his own Son but gave him up for us all,
won't he also give us everything else?* **ROMANS 8:31-32**

WHEN JESUS SPOKE AT THE SYNAGOGUE in Nazareth, he read a messianic prophecy from Isaiah that described his ministry but ended in the middle of a sentence. The first half of that sentence, which he quoted, declared a time of God's favor (Luke 4:19). The second half, which he did not read, declared a later day of judgment (Isaiah 61:2). In between those two phrases, we live in a season of God's ample, abundant, overflowing grace, when all who are willing can share in the life, love, joy, and inheritance of the Son.

That's an astonishing gift, and even many Christians aren't aware of its fullness. But as Paul and other New Testament writers would declare, God is on our side. We first decide that we are on his, of course, but then he comes alongside us as a Friend and lavishes his goodness on us. If we need correction or discipline, he addresses that need, but even then he is generous with his favor. He has lavished his love on us, brought us into the divine family, and given us everything included with that position.

There's a catch, though: We generally only get to experience the blessings we choose to see, decide to believe, and gratefully enjoy. If we're looking for evidence of his disfavor, life and circumstances will give us plenty of trials and obstacles to choose from. We can easily color our portrait of God in dark shades of negativity, seeing him as a hard and demanding master who puts us through the wringer as often as possible. But if we go through the same experiences with an understanding of who he really is, thanking him along the way for all the strength and joy he gives, we see a very different God. We experience the favor we have learned to expect from him.

Be careful how you paint your God. Pray with an overwhelming sense of his generosity and kindness. Learn to see him in dazzling light. According to your faith, the favor he offers will become your experience in the depths of your soul and beyond.

> God's gifts put man's best dreams to shame.
> ELIZABETH BARRETT BROWNING

A Child of Laughter

He who touches you touches the apple of his eye.   **ZECHARIAH 2:8**, ESV

IF YOU'RE LIKE MOST CHRISTIANS, you've experienced your fair share of difficulties in the life of faith. You may be accustomed to desperate prayers for help and pleas for change. Perhaps you've wondered how God sees you—if he really does delight in you, like certain biblical passages suggest, or if you're his problem child, as your conscience has tried to tell you. Sadly, the "problem child" syndrome is far too common among well-meaning believers. Many of us have a hard time seeing ourselves as the apple of God's eye.

Isaac was named the "son of laughter" because of the absurdity of Abraham and Sarah having a child in old age. The improbability of his birth made the fulfillment of the promise all the more joyful and worth celebrating. But we, too, are improbable children of God, his children of laughter, absurdly adopted into the divine family through no merit of our own but simply in fulfillment of a promise. God chose us before the foundation of the world (Ephesians 1:4), not because we were deemed worthy but because he wanted to. His love compelled him. He delighted in us before we were ever born. He knew about our faults and struggles in advance and chose us anyway. He welcomes us with open arms. He sings over us with delight (Zephaniah 3:17). No wonder John could marvel over the amazing love God has for his children (1 John 3:1). It's beautiful and unending.

You can't pray with much confidence if you don't believe this. No matter how uncomfortable you may be under the gaze of unbridled, overwhelming affection—many people do find it quite unsettling—you'll have to get used to it. Your Beloved adores you, delights in you, and invites you into his arms. If that doesn't change the tone of your prayers, nothing will. It gives you the freedom to pray your heart's desires, release those desires to him in trust, and know that he will make something wonderful of them. That expectation colors your faith brilliantly and makes any wait between the ask and the answer agreeable. No one doubts a promise born of this kind of love. It makes your faith burn brightly.

> God does not love us because we are valuable.
> We are valuable because God loves us.
>
> FULTON JOHN SHEEN

Breathing Faith

This is the work of God, that you believe in him whom he has sent.
JOHN 6:29, ESV

THE CROWDS SAW JESUS doing the works of God and wanted to know how they could do them too. Jesus' answer can be read with two different meanings: (1) believing in Jesus for salvation is a work of God in itself; or (2) believing in Jesus is the means of doing his works. Both are supported by other passages, even within John. No one comes to Jesus unless the Father draws him (John 6:44), and those who believe in Jesus will be able to do the same works he did (John 14:12). In spite of our tendency to emphasize faith for salvation and separate the Christian life into compartments, Jesus' answer is entirely reasonable when taken as a whole. Do you want to do the work of God? Then believe in Jesus, follow him, learn his ways, embrace his faith as your own, and the works of God will have already begun flowing through your life and will continue to do so. We do the works of God by fully identifying with Jesus.

Your faith is not divisible into salvation faith, prayer faith, promise faith, empowerment faith, works faith, and so on. Your entire experience with the Father, Son, and Holy Spirit is a *life* of faith, not a series of faith acts. Yes, there will be times when you respond to life with faith and other times when you don't, and you will likely have doubts along the way. But God is calling you into an identity, lifestyle, and way of seeing. By faith, you don't just enter into the Kingdom. You become a Kingdom citizen, live in Kingdom ways, and see Kingdom realities. And the way to do Kingdom works is to be clothed in the identity of the Son and filled with his Spirit.

Live, pray, and work with that understanding. You don't just believe in Jesus as the Savior. You live in Jesus like a branch on a vine or a new creation wearing new clothes. That comprehensive faith changes everything, and you don't have to muster it up when you pray. Your prayers flow from it naturally.

> You may as soon find a living man without
> breath as a living saint without prayer.
>
> MATTHEW HENRY

The Rest of Faith

Let us therefore strive to enter that rest. **HEBREWS 4:11, ESV**

FAITH IS A PARADOX. On the one hand, we struggle to believe, strive to arrive at a place of rest, and fight the good fight of faith (1 Timothy 6:12). On the other hand, genuine faith produces a calm assurance in our hearts and minds that God is going to do what he promised, and we can trust him with our lives. So do we fight for "the faith" (our set of beliefs and doctrines) and rest in "faith" (our attitude toward God)? Do we view the journey as a tumultuous process but the destination as a haven of rest? Is it really necessary to struggle to get to a place of peace? How do we balance striving and resting?

In a sense, all of the above approaches are true and have their place. But as we've seen, the life of faith is not so easily divided into components as we sometimes do when talking about it. There are times when we labor in prayer in order to get to a place of deep, enduring faith that can't be shaken, but that's more a matter of shaking off false attitudes to reveal real faith than trying to muster up faith ourselves. Because we have the Holy Spirit within us and have believed in the Son, faith is already there. The faith of Jesus is included in having the mind of Jesus (1 Corinthians 2:16). Our wrestling is not with faith itself but with its obstacles. Once we peel those back—often with considerable struggle—the faith we have been given stands clear. It's what we need to proceed, wait, act, speak, and wield as a down payment on God's promises. We can rest in it.

That's why we strive to enter in. We face a lot of obstacles within us and beyond us that would attack and undermine our faith. But it's there, and we can lean back into it whenever we choose. Entering in may require a bit of a fight, but abiding in it is effortless. The gift of faith is all we need to believe, receive, speak, live out, and celebrate God's promises.

> Quit sweating, quit wrestling. It is not *try* but *trust*.
>
> JOHN G. LAKE

To New Heights

*Those who trust in the LORD will find new strength. They will
soar high on wings like eagles. They will run and not grow weary.
They will walk and not faint.* **ISAIAH 40:31**

LONG DELAYS IN THE LIFE OF FAITH can wear us down. Our faith itself doesn't grow cold or heavy, but our assumptions and misperceptions about God's timing and means can seem to choke the faith out of us and leave us awfully disoriented. We long for resolution and fulfillment, and God's plans so often seem to stretch the process out. We become weak, tired, and powerless, wondering how long we can continue holding on.

God offers encouraging words to the weak, tired, and powerless. He promises new strength, soaring heights, and a spirit of endurance. He energizes our legs for the distance, revives our hearts with expectations, and reaffirms his purposes once again. Like a marathon runner who gets to that point of exhilaration where he or she forgets the pain and fatigue of the race, renewed faith takes us to new heights. We feel as if we could wait forever, though we hope we won't have to. The assurances of God give us patience and joy in the meantime.

How do we get to such heights? They are a gift for "those who trust in the LORD." The more we exercise trust—that place of rest in the spirit that comes when we lean back into his goodness—the more our strength and energy are renewed. We can't ascend to new heights by trying, and we can't give rest to our legs by stopping. But when we feel like we can't go back and can't go on, we can remember the kindness and faithfulness of the one we believe. We can reaffirm our trust in him and discover his strength for our need.

Whenever you find yourself in that awful, awkward place of not being able to move forward in faith and not being able to go back to the beginning—that sense of being stuck or suspended without any resolution in sight—reaffirm your trust. Tell God you need strength and ask him for encouragement. Soon enough, your energy will return, your wings will spread, and you will see from a higher perspective. Your faith will look different from above.

The principal part of faith is patience.

GEORGE MACDONALD

Audible Reminders

Faith comes by hearing, and hearing by the word of God.
ROMANS 10:17, NKJV

WE'D LIKE TO THINK THAT long periods of waiting would have no effect on our faith. God has given us his promises, we have believed them and based our prayers on them, and nothing has changed since. But the passing of time *is* change, at least in the way it alters our expectations, and sometimes our faith seems to be weakening. We ask God for encouragement in these moments, and he graciously provides. Still, we need frequent boosts to our faith. Sometimes we see movement toward an answer in our circumstances, and sometimes we don't. We have to remind ourselves of what we really believe.

One of the best ways to remember and stir up faith is to read God's promises out loud. Knowing the chapter-and-verse references for a few of them is fine for a quick lookup, but we don't always get the resounding effect from isolated verses. Sometimes God's voice thunders in our spirits, and sometimes it whispers far more softly than we'd like. We can amplify it greatly—or to be more accurate, tune our spirits to receive more clearly—by compiling a list of relevant promises and rehearsing them often. Reading them and listening to them back to back, again and again, is empowering. Faith that felt like a spark turns into a flame and then into a bonfire. Our passion is rekindled, our strength renewed, and we are soaring on the heights of certainty once again.

Try that next time you need to reignite your trust and revive your spirit. Faith comes by hearing God's Word. That's true not only in the salvation experience but, as we've seen, for the faith life as a whole. The faith that embraced the gospel is the same faith that enables us to see Kingdom realities. The more we immerse ourselves in God's repeated commitments and character throughout Scripture, the more our faith seems to grow. It strengthens, purifies, and sheds its encumbrances. Our minds are renewed to think in Kingdom ways. Our vision intensifies. And our efforts to honor God's promises make them seem to shine brighter than ever before.

What is more elevating and transporting than the generosity
of heart which risks everything on God's word?

JOHN HENRY NEWMAN

Faith Works

*Faith by itself isn't enough. Unless it produces good
deeds, it is dead and useless.* JAMES 2:17

IMAGINE A FARMER who expects his seeds to grow but never actually plants them or creates the right environment for them. Or imagine wanting to get in shape and envisioning how fit you will be but then never actually doing any exercise. Or imagine a builder who buys no materials. What does such inactivity tell us about the beliefs of these people? Either they don't understand the process or they never really believed in their goals to begin with. There's a disconnect between stated beliefs and actual experience, and nothing of importance will come of those beliefs.

That's James's argument about faith. Many have suggested that he and Paul disagree on the nature of faith, but Paul also understood that real faith produces certain responses (Galatians 5:6; Colossians 1:6; 1 Thessalonians 1:3). If real faith always has outward manifestations, then faith that does not work its way out in experience is not real. If we really believe what we say we believe, there will be some evidence of it in our lives. Works are no substitute for faith, but faith comes out in our words and actions. If it doesn't, it isn't faith.

It's pointless to separate faith for salvation from the rest of the faith life. It's the same entity; our belief in Jesus that brought us into the Kingdom also applies his promises and purposes to our lives thereafter. If we are praying in faith for God to do something in our lives and basing that prayer on some revelation of his will for us, we can expect that faith to affect our words and behavior in the meantime. In fact, it must. There are times when we should stand still and see the salvation of the Lord (Exodus 14:13), but faith will have brought us to that position in the first place. Almost always, we have to do something—even if it's a very small thing—not to earn God's response but to demonstrate that we actually believe it is coming. Faith that results in works is faith that works results.

Practice in life whatever you pray for,
and God will give it to you more abundantly.

E. B. PUSEY

Real Belief

*[Jesus said,] "Lazarus is dead. And for your sakes, I'm glad
I wasn't there, for now you will really believe."* JOHN 11:14-15

ONE OF THE MORE FAITH-STRETCHING EXPERIENCES of the New Testament began with Jesus learning of a good friend's life-threatening illness but then remaining where he was for two more days. The Savior who could heal with a touch or even just a word said and did nothing—at first. He even reassured his followers that his friend's illness would not end in death. So when Lazarus died, they had a crisis of faith. Was Jesus finally wrong about something? They couldn't imagine that death wasn't the end.

But Jesus was never out of control in this story or blind to the reality of the situation. In fact, he allowed the crisis to continue for a very specific reason: "So that the Son of God will receive glory from this" (verse 4). All of Mary's and Martha's tears, all of the pointed questions about why he had not come earlier, all of the strange looks he received when he requested that the stone be rolled away from the stench-filled tomb were orchestrated for one overriding purpose: for the disciples to "really believe." Jesus used a dark situation as a backdrop for his brilliance.

You'll find that same dynamic at work in your life. In the midst of dark situations, you'll wonder what went wrong, why God was late, and how he could possibly redeem a situation after its "end." Even when we don't understand, we can trust that God knows what he is doing and walks with us in our pain. But we can also take it a step further and actively exercise faith that God is eventually going to do something powerful and unusual. Just as Martha affirmed Jesus' statement that he is the resurrection and the life (verses 25–27), even though she didn't know what was coming, we can affirm that Jesus is who he says he is and has not lost control of the situation. We can expect him to continue working in ways we don't comprehend. We can see the light at the end. And as he intended, we can affirm that we "really believe."

Faith is like radar that sees through the fog.

CORRIE TEN BOOM

The Faith of Jesus

I have been crucified with Christ. It is no longer I who live,
but Christ who lives in me. And the life I now live in the flesh
I live by faith in the Son of God. **GALATIANS 2:20,** ESV

PAUL'S RELATIONSHIP WITH JESUS makes for fascinating study. He first
encountered the risen, living Jesus on a road to Damascus. He soon found his entire
identity in Jesus and lived exclusively for his purposes. But at some point, maybe
soon after his conversion or perhaps years later, he realized he wasn't just living for
Jesus but Jesus was living in and through him. This was more than a new identity. It
was a habitation of the divine glory within.

Paul never made an exclusive claim to this experience. Just the opposite, in fact.
He insisted that Jesus inhabits every believer, that we are living out the age-old mystery of God's plan: Christ in us, the hope of glory (Colossians 1:26-27). And if we
really let that truth settle in, we realize its enormous implications. We don't have to
strive for righteousness; we simply let his righteousness thrive in us. We don't have
to seek his wisdom, power, and love; we just put them on like new clothes. And we
don't have to try to muster up faith; Jesus' faith is operating within us. We believe
with the faith already given.

That fits with Jesus' statement in Mark 11:22, which can be translated as "have
the faith of God" as easily as "have faith in God." This is no command waiting for a
willfully obedient response. It's a supernatural gift, a power from outside of us now
planted within us. If it is truly Christ who lives in us rather than our old nature
struggling for its own new life, we can trust that Jesus brings his faith into our innermost being. We simply rely on what he has given us to enter into an attitude of pure,
rock-solid faith.

That takes all the stress out of biblical commands to have faith. This embracing
of what is already there may take some practice, but it isn't burdensome. Ask for
the insight and direction to step into that reality. It's wonderfully, powerfully yours.

> To believe in the God over us and around us and not in the God
> within us—that would be a powerless and fruitless faith.
>
> PHILLIPS BROOKS

Love and Faith as One

When we place our faith in Christ Jesus, there is no benefit in being circumcised or being uncircumcised. What is important is faith expressing itself in love. **GALATIANS 5:6**

PAUL WAS PERTURBED AT THE GALATIANS. Many of them had come to Christ by faith and then tried to live for him by their own works. Many have struggled to sort out the relationship between faith and works and discovered many nuances in how it plays out, but the Galatians had tilted far to one side, incorporating self-effort into their beliefs about salvation. Paul rebuked them sharply, always pointing to the power of the living Jesus within believers as the *source* of their works, not the *result* of them. And in order to correct their misunderstandings about law and grace, he described what faith really looks like. It isn't about external rituals. It's the faith of Jesus pouring out of us in love.

The relationship between faith and love is foundational. We can't believe without having an experience of God's love; we have to be aware of his kindness toward us and his delight in us if we are going to trust him with our lives. But it also works the other way around; we can't love well without having the faith of Christ within us. When we grasp both sides of that relationship—faith in the context of God's extravagant love, and God's extravagant love overflowing from us by faith—powerful things happen.

If you've ever tried to separate faith and love—to live by faith outside of the context of God's love working in you—you know how futile it is. We neither experience nor demonstrate God's love without faith, and we can neither experience nor demonstrate faith without God's love. If we don't see them as part of the same package— Jesus living within us—we'll fail at both. As Paul expressed it to the Galatians, only faith working through love counts for anything.

That thought is echoed elsewhere in Paul's writings (1 Corinthians 13:2, for example), which means it's not a peripheral thought. It's fundamental to our faith. Pursue it, embrace it, and live it out. You will believe only to the degree you love, and love to the degree you believe.

As soon as we are with God in faith and love, we are in prayer.

FRANÇOIS FÉNELON

Faith After Falling

I have pleaded in prayer for you, Simon, that
your faith should not fail.   LUKE 22:32

PETER FAILED. The bold disciple who declared his undying commitment to follow Jesus even into death backed down when the pressure was on. At crucial moments in Jesus' arrest and trial, Simon Peter denied even knowing the friend he loved most. And Jesus saw it coming. He told Peter about it in advance, giving him a generous heads-up so he wouldn't be caught off guard. But Peter was caught off guard anyway, and during his great opportunity to take a stand, he fell.

It's fascinating, then, that Jesus didn't pray for Peter to avoid this trial by not denying him in the first place. He plainly told Peter that Satan had asked to sift him like wheat (verse 31). But then he skipped straight to the aftermath: "when you have repented" (verse 32). As the Son of God with all authority in heaven and on earth, he could have said no to Satan's request. He could have asked the Holy Spirit to strengthen Peter in this critical time and give him the courage to identify with his Lord. Instead, he prayed for Peter in the aftermath of his fall because he knew it would become a catalytic moment in his faith that would stick with him the rest of his life.

Our failures do not define us, but our responses to failure can shape us forever. Your sin does not destroy your faith; God is quite ready to forgive you and move on. But guilt and shame can eat away at you, nagging at you about your unworthiness and weakness, convincing you that you will never be strong in faith or overcome the world of temptations and sins, mocking you for not being like those heroes of faith you've read about. Your conscience and the accuser's voice will try to convince you that you're disqualified from that kind of life and will never experience such miraculous answers to prayer. For those inner conflicts, Jesus' words to you are the same as his words to Peter: "I have prayed for you."

It's true, you know. He is interceding for you even now (Romans 8:34). Receive restoration and believe the promises he has given you. Rise up in faith, boldness, and power and overcome.

> I think that if God forgives us, we must forgive ourselves.
>
> C. S. LEWIS

Faith That Overcomes

This is the victory that has overcome the world—our faith.

1 JOHN 5:4, ESV

THE NIGHT BEFORE HIS CRUCIFIXION, Jesus made two remarkable, back-to-back statements. He warned the disciples who were expecting great victories that they would encounter trials and tribulations in this world, and he promised them that he had overcome the world (John 16:33). This juxtaposition of apparent defeats and ultimate victory is a little disorienting. How can we overcome the world while it's beating us up? What kind of victory looks so traumatic?

This same tension between trials in the world and victory over it continues throughout the New Testament. Late in the first century, John wrote that our faith is the victory that overcomes the world. We don't overcome just by surviving. We overcome by winning faith-filled victories.

That happens in two ways. Our faith in Jesus overcomes the world by bringing us into God's eternal Kingdom. But it also overcomes the world by enabling us to participate in Jesus' transcendent life, which he demonstrated by calming storms, healing diseases, and being raised from the dead. We may feel limited by our world, but Jesus can overcome limitations through prayer and faith. We are not bound in a finite existence like philosophers have imagined. Faith lifts us above it.

That means we can look at every hardship as temporary and every victory as eternal (Romans 8:18; 2 Corinthians 4:17). We can face every problem with a plea for divine solutions (2 Chronicles 20:12). We can present our requests to God with gratitude and experience transcendent peace (Philippians 4:6-7). By faith, we overcome every attack, accusation, deception, hardship, failure, regret, and problem even while we are feeling the weight and pain of them. If God is for us, who can be against us (Romans 8:31)? No one of consequence. We are more than conquerors in Christ (Romans 8:37). Whatever comes against us is momentary. Our overcoming in Jesus is already certain and everlasting. We can live, speak, rest, and pray with that assurance. In him, by faith, we will—and already have—overcome the world.

A person who wholly follows the Lord is one who believes that the promises of God are trustworthy, that he is with his people, and that they are well able to overcome.

WATCHMAN NEE

Strengthen Your Heart

Make sure that your own hearts are not evil and unbelieving,
turning you away from the living God.   HEBREWS 3:12

MANY JEWISH CHRISTIANS IN THE FIRST CENTURY were turning away from their belief in Jesus because of hardship and persecution. They had started out well but encountered resistance. Some of their peers rejected them. They found themselves at social and economic disadvantages. The path was harder than they expected. Some began recanting their faith and turning back to their traditions.

The writer of Hebrews reminded these believers of their history—how many complained, lost faith, and missed out on the promise on the way to the Promised Land. He unsympathetically referred to this turning away as "evil" and "unbelief." He reminded them that faith has always been challenging, and only the persistent and patient will receive what has been promised. All the rest have traded God's best gifts for more immediate comforts and conveniences.

That's harsh, but it's true. Hardship and pain generally drive people in one of two directions: deeper into faith or further away from it. Trials have a way of separating those who truly believe from those who don't. Those who have the vision to see what lies at the end of the road will endure with faith and patience. Those who don't, won't. In the process, God reveals the hearts that are truly his.

Many people turn away from God's promises because believing them feels too difficult, there are too many obstacles to overcome and too many temptations to walk away, and waiting for fulfillment can seem to take much too long. But when God works an eternal perspective into our hearts, we see the big picture. We grow strong and stay the course. We become willing to endure the problems at hand in exchange for the glory to come. We recognize the difference between what lasts and what is passing away.

Pray and believe with that perspective. When you grow weary, ask for encouragement. When you encounter trials, ask for strength. Above all, don't develop an unbelieving heart. Hardly any of God's promises come with an expiration date. Hang on to them in patient, resilient faith.

> You never know how much you really believe anything until its truth
> or falsehood becomes a matter of life and death to you.
>
> C. S. LEWIS

271

Inside Information

The Spirit helps us in our weakness. For we do not know what to pray for as we ought, but the Spirit himself intercedes for us with groanings too deep for words. ROMANS 8:26, ESV

IMAGINE ASKING GOD WHAT HE WANTS TO DO, hearing his voice with precision, and then praying perfectly in accordance with his will. How many of your prayers do you think he might answer with that approach? All of them. Sometimes the only gap between what he wants to do and what he actually does is a prayer that hasn't invited him to do it yet.

In our limited vision, we don't always know what to pray for. But the Holy Spirit who intercedes in heaven, along with the interceding Son and the Father who expresses his will, knows divine intentions. This heavenly conversation completely captures God's purposes and invites us into the discussion. Though we don't know how to pray as we ought, we can find out. The Holy Spirit can impress it on our hearts when we ask to see his purposes. Even when our words and longings don't come out the right way, he knows how to take them and adapt them to his purposes. We are not alone in our requests. We are given an opportunity to cooperate with God to bring his purposes into our situations on earth.

The Holy Spirit knows what he wants to do for us, and he prays it. He doesn't just pray for us; he helps us pray the right things. He turns our groans into prayers, he fills our mouths with words that hit the mark. Instead of our searching for an answer, he is putting the answer within us to pray it back to the Father. In this process, we aren't trying to get God to do something he doesn't want to do. We are agreeing with him on what he does want to do.

That's a different approach to prayer for many, and it requires us to develop some listening skills. But Jesus promised that we can hear his voice (John 10:27), he gave the Spirit to guide us (John 14:26), and he resides within us (Galatians 2:20). If we ask to hear, he will teach us. And his Spirit will transform our disoriented prayers into precise requests that God wants to fulfill.

The best prayers have often more groans than words.

JOHN BUNYAN

Unchanging Promises

God is not a man, so he does not lie. He is not human, so he does not change his mind. Has he ever spoken and failed to act? Has he ever promised and not carried it through?   **NUMBERS 23:19**

WHAT IF GOD DIDN'T MEAN what I thought he meant? What if this promise applied then but not anymore? What if I've been disqualified for a lack of faith, a sinful mistake, a gross misunderstanding? What if times have changed? What if . . . In the long process of believing God for an answer to prayer, we have no shortage of questions. We entertain doubts; possible exceptions, conditions, and caveats; fine print between the lines of biblical claims; and so many more uncertainties. Our faith can rise and fall at the slightest hints in an overheard conversation, a circumstantial change, a pointed sermon, an ambiguous sign, or a discouraging mood. We may admire unchanging faith, but as we're learning what that entails, we just don't know how to have it.

God is not a con artist. He doesn't fill Scripture with fine print and unattainable conditions. In spite of the many sermons we've heard and books we've read that major on what a promise doesn't mean rather than what it does mean, we don't have to condition our theology with so many disclaimers. God means what he says. He doesn't lie. If we misunderstand, we can ask him for understanding. He isn't playing games with us; he wants us to believe.

That's a hard concept to grasp in a world of fake news, legal maneuvering, policies and warranties that are filled with exceptions, equivocal politicians, sly winks, and crossed fingers. But while God is hidden to untrained eyes, he doesn't want to remain obscure to our faithful gaze. After all, the Bible and the Incarnation are *revelations* of himself. He wants to be known. He says so clearly. And he wants his words and his will to be known too.

Trust your unchanging God. He has no interest in deceiving you. He will never jerk the rug out from under you. You may go through trials—even surprising ones— but not without his guiding, comforting hand. And his words to you will forever remain true.

Though men are false, God is faithful.

MATTHEW HENRY

World-Changing Prayer

If my people who are called by my name will humble themselves and
pray and seek my face and turn from their wicked ways, I will hear
from heaven and will forgive their sins and restore their land.

2 CHRONICLES 7:14

WHEN SOLOMON FINISHED BUILDING THE TEMPLE, he and the whole kingdom celebrated with a dedication ceremony. Solomon prayed magnificent, sweeping prayers for God's presence and power in that place, pledging the devotion of his people and asking for their prayers to be answered. The glory of God filled the Temple, so much that priests and observers couldn't enter in and fell to the ground in worship. Then God made a promise based on the certainty that the people would sometimes fail to keep the covenant and reap the consequences. He told them that if they turned to him in humility, rejected evil, and sought his face, he would forgive and restore. He would heal the land—and, we can assume, the hearts of the people in it.

That's a comforting promise, and it's recalled often at national, denominational, and organizational prayer initiatives. But we don't have to wait for big events to claim it. We can pray it now—for our communities, cities, nations, and world. We can even pray it for ourselves, our families, and our churches. Though it was given to a specific kingdom in covenant with God, it expresses his heart toward everyone who is in covenant with him. It captures his side of the relationship—his reluctance to bless those who have strayed far from his character and would only abuse and distort his blessings, but also his eagerness to bless those who align their hearts with his and reject old, ungodly ways. It stands as an open invitation for all believers at all times.

Accepting this invitation is a tremendous opportunity, and it would be tragic to miss out on its promise. From where we sit at this moment, we can sow faith into the direction of history and bend it toward God's purposes. In fact, he has called us to do so (1 Timothy 2:1-8). The course of history is not in the hands of the ungodly. It's in ours. Never neglect that privilege.

> God has no greater controversy with his people today than this,
> that with boundless promises to believing prayer, there are
> so few who actually give themselves to intercession.
>
> A. T. PIERSON

Evangelism by Prayer

This is good and pleases God our Savior, who wants everyone to
be saved and to understand the truth. **1 TIMOTHY 2:3-4**

WILLIAM CAREY, OFTEN CONSIDERED "the father of modern missions," had a vision for taking the gospel to people in distant lands who had never heard the Good News. At one point, he was told bluntly to mind his own business—that God would convert the heathen if he wanted to—but Carey persisted. Hudson Taylor grieved over "China's millions" who had never known of Jesus. John Hyde prayed boldly for one soul a day in India, then two, then four, each year receiving the numbers he asked for. Amy Carmichael served in India for fifty-five years without a furlough, calling missionary service "a chance to die." History is filled with sacrificial hearts that have eagerly surrendered to God's rescue mission in this world. People who get close to him know his desire to share his goodness and glory across this planet.

Most of us have heard appeals to give to missions, pray for missions, and consider becoming missionaries. Scripture is clear that God longs for people to be saved and know the truth. Theologically, most Christians are on board with that mission, even though it has long been under attack for cultural imperialism and alleged intolerance of other faiths. But even though we agree with it in our hearts, we tend to neglect it in our prayers. Why? Perhaps because we don't know how to pray for those who don't believe, or our culturally diverse society emphasizes the value of all perspectives, or our hearts have just grown cold. But we can love and value people of other faiths while praying for them to know the magnificence of salvation in Jesus. In fact, we are called to do so. God wants all to know him personally.

When we pray evangelistically, we do not have to wonder if we are praying in God's will. We can ask that the gospel would be taught more sensitively, more compellingly, and more winsomely than at times in the past, but we still must pray that it would spread far and wide. God still loves the world, and Jesus still calls for faith. Prayer stands in the gap between him and needy souls.

To know the will of God, we need an open Bible and an open map.

WILLIAM CAREY

An Unlimited Asset

You can pray for anything, and if you have faith, you will receive it.
MATTHEW 21:22

IMAGINE BEING ON A SCOUT TEAM sent from the front lines into enemy territory to find people and places held captive. You are told that the enemy employs a variety of tactics, and you should expect to recommend different solutions for each situation. But you are to seek out areas of need relentlessly and report them to home base. You are promised unlimited provision to address each situation, whether immediately or in follow-up operations. But none of your observations and requests will go unheeded. After all, you were given authority to recommend and requisition anything that would help. Your role is critical, and your requests are the key to freeing hostages, providing for needs, and restoring life. Headquarters has promised to back you up.

Sounds exhilarating, doesn't it? A little dangerous perhaps, but it's an irresistible opportunity to win battles and make a difference in a war-torn world. With the assurances you've been given, there's no reason not to proceed. Yes, you may encounter resistance, but you'll also overcome it. And many lives will be helped and saved in the process.

That's essentially what Jesus promised his disciples. He told them to pray for anything—no limits other than an implied adherence to Kingdom values—and it would be done for them. They would have to pray with the expectation of answers—that's faith—and with Jesus' purposes in mind. But other than that, they were free to go about doing good, walking in spiritual power, preaching and teaching the Good News of the Kingdom, and setting souls free. His promise assured them of a constant link with headquarters and its unlimited resources.

We may need to grow in our understanding of that promise, but it still applies. Jesus didn't mean it only for his closest followers in that generation. He meant it for all who would follow him in the centuries to come. Many people ignore this promise because they've tried it out and thought it "didn't work." But for those who keep pressing in, it does. God will teach us if we let him. And our prayers of faith will become powerful Kingdom assets in the undoing of powers of darkness.

Prayer is a shield to the soul, a sacrifice to God, and a scourge to Satan.

JOHN BUNYAN

Release the Weight

Give your burdens to the LORD, and he will take care of you.
He will not permit the godly to slip and fall.   **PSALM 55:22**

IF YOU REALLY TOOK THE NEEDS OF THE WORLD upon yourself to pray for them thoughtfully and earnestly, they would overwhelm you—especially when added to the pressures of daily life, with all of its responsibilities and complicated relationships. Even our own to-do lists for this week can feel like a crushing weight. The call to influence the world by prayer and advance God's Kingdom by faith, personally and corporately, is more than we can handle.

God knows that. He enlarges the capacity of our hearts, but he doesn't expect us to carry the weight of the world's problems. He doesn't even expect us to carry the weight of our own pressing concerns. He offers to take responsibility for the outcomes of all of our issues if we let him—not to remove us from stewarding them, but to lift the burden of them off our shoulders. Jesus promised us deep peace and an easy yoke, and he meant it. He didn't deliver us from the weight of guilt and shame only to place us under the weight of false responsibility. He promised freedom. And one of the ways he gives it to us is by carrying the load himself.

We have to cooperate with that offer in order to experience its benefits. Biblical instructions to cast our burdens on him (1 Peter 5:7)—literally translated, to throw them off as if we want nothing to do with them—are not just encouragements. If we take them seriously, they aren't even strong recommendations. They are commands. God knows the only way we can handle life is to trust him with it.

Release the weight of your concerns to God and refuse to pick them back up again. Trust that he is going to do the heavy lifting for you. You will still have to walk through your responsibilities, but the outcomes are on him. The life of faith is too great a responsibility to handle yourself; God-sized compassion is too big for one finite heart. Feel his love and concern but let him handle the pressure of it. The weight of the world is on his shoulders, not yours.

Trust involves letting go and knowing God will catch you.

JAMES DOBSON

The Symptoms of Your Heart

My heart is confident in you, O God; my heart is confident.
No wonder I can sing your praises! **PSALM 57:7**

IF YOU'VE EVER WONDERED how fully you believe something, how settled you are in your faith that God will answer your prayers, you can tell from the lightness of your step and the praises on your lips. When your heart is truly confident in him, it is at rest. When your heart is filled with doubts and uncertainty, it isn't. The peace within tells you a lot about the faith you're carrying.

With that in mind, become very familiar with the symptoms of your heart. Notice when you are unsettled and investigate why. If gratitude and praise aren't coming naturally, ask yourself what you aren't seeing correctly. If you've prayed for something important and feel hopeless about it, be honest enough with yourself and God to ask why it's difficult for you to believe. Your attitudes and moods are reliable reflections of your inner beliefs.

One exercise that might help is to envision yourself in the throne room of heaven, where praise and gratitude flow freely. There, where your vision is clear and God's power and love are undeniable, you'll see no fear, discouragement, or insecurity. Whatever God says is unquestionably true; whatever he does is unquestionably good. Now bring that vision into your present circumstance. What in the situation around you overshadows that glorious environment? Whatever it is, your heart is making too much of it. That's where your perspective is off and your confidence is under assault. That's where you can begin to reorient your thoughts toward truth.

Discouragement is almost always based on a lie, a misperception about God's purposes and promises, a skewed perspective on your circumstances, a lack of trust or faith in what God intends for you. Once you replace those lies and misperceptions with truth and a heavenly perspective, you will find your confidence in God growing and your praises flowing. You will begin to see through the lenses of his wisdom, power, and love, and all contradictions will begin to fade away. Your heart will return to the peace and freedom it is meant to have, and your faith will revive once again.

A little faith will bring your soul to heaven,
but a lot of faith will bring heaven to your soul.

D. L. MOODY

Prayers of Love

I love the LORD because he hears my voice and my prayer for mercy.

PSALM 116:1

IMAGINE A PARENT-CHILD RELATIONSHIP in which the child makes frequent requests but the parent rarely answers them. The child is supplied with the most basic needs of shelter, clothing, nourishment, and instruction, but anything beyond necessity is conspicuously withheld. It's perhaps a functional relationship, but it hardly seems a loving one. There's not much affection in calculated, minimal provision.

Now imagine a parent-child relationship in which the child receives answers to requests and even nice surprises, too—not enough to spoil the child with gifts beyond his or her level of maturity, but enough to communicate affection. Basic needs are covered, to be sure, but so are many of the heart's desires. This is a relationship of warm and nourishing love.

Many Christians see their relationship with God resembling the first paragraph more than the second. Perhaps they come from a background of austerity, firm warnings against greed and pride, or overcompensation for abuses like a prosperity-only gospel or selfish faith. But does that kind of relationship really capture the love of the Father? Does it fit Jesus' statement about the Father's good gifts (Matthew 7:11)? No. Somewhere along the way, traditional Christian teaching has distorted the biblical view of God.

The context for prayer is a loving relationship with God. The more attentive he is to our pleas, the more we love him; and the more we love him, the more attentive he is to our pleas. Unfortunately, the converse is true. The less we perceive his love, the less attentive he seems to our pleas because we don't actually believe he will answer them. And the less attentive he seems, the harder it is to love him. Somehow, we have to place extravagant, affectionate love back at the center of the relationship.

You will always underestimate God's love for you, but make it a point to underestimate it less and less each day. Assume that he adores you and wants to give you his best. Your prayers and faith will grow into that assumption—and ever closer to truth.

> We should speak to God from our own hearts
> and talk to him as a child talks to his father.
>
> CHARLES SPURGEON

Never Stop Asking

Because he bends down to listen, I will pray as long as I have breath!
PSALM 116:2

IMAGINE BEING INVITED TO BRING any need or desire you can imagine—for yourself and anyone else —into the court of a king. You have caught the attention of His Majesty, and he wants to hear what's on your heart. He wants to know your needs and wants, along with the needs and wants of those beyond the palace. He's interested in your opinions on what he can do to make his kingdom as bright and beautiful as possible. Would you come with a short list or have trouble thinking of things to say? Would you want to limit your requests out of respect or turn down his generosity because it just seems like too much? Probably not. You'd go in with everything you've got.

There are some flaws in that example, of course. God doesn't exactly promise to give us everything we could ever want. But he does want to hear it, and he also wants us to bring the needs and desires of others to him too. He places no limits on what we can talk to him about. Some things are ripe for his action; others may take a while or need to be redirected into a more reasonable or beneficial request. But he invites us into an inexhaustible conversation to bring his Kingdom into our lives and the world around us—on earth as it is in heaven. It's an astonishing invitation.

There's no sense in imposing limits on a conversation he has made limitless. There's no reason to hold back. As we learn what he is like and how he wants to work, we may adapt our prayers to fit his nature, character, and purposes. But even then, will we ever run out of things to say? Not likely. Prayers unprayed are prayers unanswered. That's so unnecessary.

God will not answer every prayer with a yes, but he will never stop listening to them if our hearts are inclined toward him. We have nothing to lose and everything to gain by continuing the conversation. We need his intervention in our lives. The world desperately needs it too. Never stop asking for it as long as you have breath.

> You know the value of prayer; it is precious
> beyond all price. Never, never neglect it.
>
> **THOMAS BUXTON**

A Fruitful Promise

[The LORD said,] "I am with you, and no one will attack and harm you, for many people in this city belong to me." **ACTS 18:10**

FOREIGNERS WERE NOT WELL RECEIVED in some regions of China in the late 1800s, but when missionary Jonathan Goforth was led through north Henan by a guide, he felt led to pray that God would give him that region as his field of ministry. He sensed assurance that this prayer was granted, but over the next six years, entry into the area seemed impossible. One of the main cities of the province was hostile toward missionaries, and Goforth and his colleagues were mobbed and threatened at times when they visited. But he never lost sight of the promise and never questioned whether it would come to pass. After six years and periods of intense prayer, Goforth was able to secure a piece of property—a site he had earlier prayed to receive as an ideal location—and the area began to open up. He and his family received constant visitors inquiring about the Christian faith. It became a very fruitful field of ministry.

The Goforths understood the power and purpose of a prayer of faith—they greatly advanced God's Kingdom in China through asking and receiving from God—and demonstrated the life of faith through frequent hardships, dangers, and delays. When many other foreigners were killed in the Boxer Rebellion, the Goforths survived by clinging to the promise from Isaiah 54:17 that no weapon turned toward them would succeed and by the prayers of many Christians back home in Canada. They lived out the promise of Psalm 34:19—that "many are the afflictions of the righteous, but the LORD delivers him out of them all" (NKJV)—by facing down disease, attacks, injuries, rejection, and the death of several children. In the end, they wrote and spoke of numerous testimonies of God's faithfulness in spite of the losses they suffered.

God's promises don't always come without a cost. But they are given for a purpose, and when we exercise faith in them—for six years or even much longer—they eventually come to pass. Through them, he wants us to persist in the direction of his calling and our God-given desires, to learn of his faithfulness in the process, and to advance his Kingdom in this world.

> During all those years, my husband never once lost sight
> of God's promise to him nor failed to believe it.
>
> ROSALIND GOFORTH

Following a Vision

I was not disobedient to the heavenly vision. **ACTS 26:19,** ESV

CAMERON TOWNSEND, THE FOUNDER of Wycliffe Bible Translators and its associated organizations, had a vision of people throughout the world reading the Bible in their own language. In Latin America, where Wycliffe got its start, that meant translating Scripture into indigenous languages, even though most people could read Spanish. He believed that a national administrative language doesn't always speak to the heart—that having the Bible in one's mother tongue is the greatest missionary in the world because it never goes on furlough and is never considered a foreigner. So Wycliffe spent his life following that vision of reaching linguistic minorities in their own language. He even started learning a new language at the age of seventy-two to extend his mission as long as he could.

When God gives a vision that will advance his Kingdom in this world, a promise is implied in it. He doesn't give visions for entertainment; a response of faith is required. That response may launch a new movement, as Townsend's did, or it may simply align us with a mission, ministry, or career field where we can bear Kingdom fruit. The size of the vision isn't the issue, and neither is its nature or arena. The dynamics are almost always the same. God implants dreams, pictures, ambitions, goals, and desires in our hearts, and we are meant to follow them once we discern they are truly from him. And when we begin following them, we can be sure that God intends to back us every step of the way.

That doesn't mean there will be no obstacles. Paul faced many, even though he was certain God had called him to spread the gospel among Gentiles throughout the Greek and Roman world. Townsend faced plenty, even though God blessed him with fruitfulness and resources throughout his ministry. God-given visions can draw criticism, slander, resistance, opposition, and hardship, but they can also bring remarkable breakthrough and fruitfulness in regions, systems, organizations, and individual lives. Only the eyes of faith can persevere through the obstacles to carry out the mission. In one way or another, faith brings vision into reality.

The vision must be followed by the venture. It is not enough to stare up the steps—we must step up the stairs.

VANCE HAVNER

Following Desire

Commit everything you do to the LORD.
Trust him, and he will help you. **PSALM 37:5**

AMY CARMICHAEL WAS BORN IN NORTHERN IRELAND and did mission work in Japan and Sri Lanka (Ceylon then), but she spent fifty-five years of her life in India, most of them rescuing children from temple prostitution and slavery. Her work infuriated temple authorities, she endured accusations and legal prosecution, and she had to overcome the resistance of other missionaries who thought she was wasting her time or becoming too focused on what they saw as a relatively minor issue. But Carmichael knew what happened behind temple doors—she had stained her skin with teabags, covered herself in a sari, and entered in at times—and had a passion for the children who had been dedicated to temple priests by their parents or otherwise been drawn into captivity. By faith, she simply went where she was led, ministered where her heart was drawn, and fulfilled the vision and desires God had given her. The ministry she began in the early 1900s continues today.

Carmichael wasn't driven by an overarching vision, at least not at first. She had sensed a call to missions in general and worked at several ministry fields, but she followed God's leading step-by-step into the type of ministry she was eventually known for. She responded to needs, those responses built certain interests and desires in her heart, and she pursued the passions she had been given by faith in order to help a segment of the population that had few, if any, advocates. She understood the workings of God in her heart and wrote about them prolifically. She dedicated her life to the moment-by-moment calling God had given her.

Sometimes God fills our hearts with faith for a big vision or specific calling. Sometimes he only unfolds the vision a day or a season at a time. He knows when we need the whole blueprint or when it's better to have it in stages, and usually our faith involves elements of both. But no matter how big and coherent the vision seems, the response of faith is always today. Faith embraces God-given desires and the next step toward them.

It is a safe thing to trust him to fulfill the desire that he creates.

AMY CARMICHAEL

Kept in Peace

You will keep in perfect peace all who trust in you,
all whose thoughts are fixed on you! ISAIAH 26:3

SOME PHILOSOPHIES TEACH THAT the key to peace is emptying our minds of all anxieties and fears—that we arrive at peace by avoiding the things that unsettle it. But empty minds are easily filled again, and if we haven't replaced anxieties and fears with something much greater, they return with a vengeance. The effort to sweep the mind of negative thoughts can be as exhausting as trying to keep a leaky boat from filling up with water. It's a never-ending process, and for many people, a futile one.

Scripture gives us a much more satisfying alternative. Our minds are kept in perfect peace by filling them with the one who is above all anxieties, fears, worries, conflicts, threats, dangers, and whatever else the world throws at us. We have no shortage of fear-inducers—a dreaded diagnosis, a financial setback, a volatile relationship, a rejection letter, and so much more. These carriers of potentially harmful information present unwanted facts. But God is never subject to "facts." He is reality, and every fact we perceive has to submit to his definition of truth. Faith sees beyond immediate situations and into the heart of the Father above them.

That's why we can remain in peace. We don't deny circumstances, close our eyes, and try to shut out anxieties. All of those responses are still, in one way or another, a focus on the problem. We focus instead on the solution, the God who has authority over all circumstances and can change them. When our minds are riveted on him and filled with his goodness, we receive the peace that passes understanding. We remain constantly in the eye of the storm, where calmness reigns regardless of the winds swirling around it. In the center of his promises, we aren't rattled by circumstances. We are able to trust in him.

That kind of trusting peace opens our hearts to all kinds of blessings and answers to prayer. It builds faith that refuses to bend to visible demands. We see beyond the visible into the revelation and receive what God wants to give. Most of all, he wants to give himself. Focused there, our hearts and minds are at rest.

If the basis of peace is God, the secret of peace is trust.

J. N. FIGGIS

Quiet, Confident Faith

In quietness and confidence is your strength.   ISAIAH 30:15

SOME PEOPLE THINK THEIR STRENGTH is their work ethic. Others think it's their ingenuity, talents, personality, or social skills. While all of those can be wonderful assets for succeeding in the working world—and even in the Kingdom of God—they are no substitutes for the strength of God that comes through faith. Though diligence is important, none of our busyness will bring us to a place of complete security. None of the character traits we rely on can move mountains, calm storms, and invite the supernatural work of God into our lives. Only faith can do that, and faith operates best in a climate of quietness and confidence. In fact, it helps create that climate. We are strongest when we are resting in the Lord.

That's because no matter how industrious or ingenious we think we are, his strength is greater than ours. When we're surrounded by problems bigger than ourselves, attacked by forces more relentless and intimidating than we are, or trapped in habits or influences that have proven to be stronger than us, we need outside help. We need to be able to access the power of God. And the only way to do that is by faith.

As we've seen, we can cultivate an atmosphere in which faith thrives by our worship—celebrating God's goodness, resting in his strength and promises, and simply trusting him to deliver. In that atmosphere, prayer flows naturally and freely, and we see his faithfulness and promises more clearly. Like Jehoshaphat when Jerusalem was surrounded by three armies in 2 Chronicles 20, we can turn our gaze to him, declare that we don't know what to do, listen to his voice, and send up the songs while he fights the battle. That response goes against all of our natural instincts, but it's spiritually wise. It recognizes our utter dependence on him, his unrivaled power, and his desire to save. It wins through quietness and confidence.

Train yourself in that mental, emotional, and spiritual posture until it becomes your first response to a crisis. Base it on unwavering trust in God's goodness and words. When you learn to rest in faith, you win victories that no amount of effort can accomplish.

O God, make us children of quietness, and heirs of peace.

CLEMENT OF ROME

OCTOBER 11

Everything

With God everything is possible.   MATTHEW 19:26

ASK ANY BELIEVER if anything is impossible for God, and the answer will quickly come: *No, of course not.* Ask any believer to pray for something impossible, and the reluctance is palpable. Our theology says one thing; our faith says another. And nowhere in Scripture does God promise to honor our theology, as important as it may be. He does, however, promise to honor our faith. We generally don't receive what we wish for or think about. We receive what we believe.

The problem is that even though we know God *can* do the impossible, we are rarely confident that he wants to. Some things seem too unrealistic, too outside-the-box, perhaps even too frivolous. When Jesus told his followers that everything was possible with God, he was likely speaking in hyperbole about salvation for those who are most often blind to their need for it. *Ah*, we might think, *he's using "impossible" for something very common, very doable from my experience.* After all, people with money and spiritual blindness are saved quite often and go on to use their material resources very faithfully. How impossible does that really seem? Yet Jesus also calmed storms, made the lame walk, fed multitudes with a small bag of food, cleansed lepers, turned water into wine, and raised the dead. *Impossible* takes on all sorts of meanings when we survey the scope of his ministry beyond this passage.

Much of the life of faith is a stretching exercise in filling the gap between our theology and our actual expectations. One of the best ways to do that is to recall all that God has done. If, for example, we believe he can create an entire universe out of nothing, the rest is easy. Resurrections, parted waters, and healed diseases are a piece of cake. Faith-building involves seeing the impossible as doable—consistently—and then stepping into it even if first efforts to do so end in failure. Over time, if we are persistent, our definition of *impossible* becomes more realistic and our definition of *realistic* grows larger. We begin to believe in greater measure. And things that were once impossible become common.

The miracles of Jesus were the ordinary works of his Father.

GEORGE MACDONALD

286

When God Doesn't Answer

The LORD's arm is not too weak to save you,
nor is his ear too deaf to hear you call. **ISAIAH 59:1**

IT'S A LAUGHABLE THOUGHT—God having weak arms and deaf ears. Even the most hardened hearts in Israel and Judah would have known from their own traditions that Yahweh was, at least in theory, able to save. After all, their kingdom was built on remembrances of the Exodus and the Promised Land. Those foundational stories were rehearsed often, even in times when the law had been forgotten. Yet something in the attitudes and behavior of Isaiah's day suggested people were underestimating this God. They had forgotten that their Savior could actually save.

Isaiah's passage addresses the problem of people's prayers not being answered. In his day, their sins had turned God away from them, and he refused to listen. How this plays out in our post–New Testament lives is debatable—our sin has been forever covered by Jesus, though ongoing rebellion surely distorts our prayers and desires—but God's ability remains unquestioned. He is not a weak God with short arms and limited opportunities. He is no one's pushover. He is never in a position to be bullied, never at a loss for words, always wielding the upper hand. He is never short of wisdom about what to do, and never short of the means to do it. He sits above all and does what he pleases.

So when we wonder today about unanswered prayers, what thoughts about God go through our minds? Do we wonder if he's far off or uncaring? Do we relegate all his greatest works to the distant past of the Bible or the distant future of Jesus' return? Do we beat ourselves up for being unworthy of his wonderful works and assume that only the super-spiritual can experience them? Have we forgotten that the idea of being super-spiritual is mostly a matter of faith?

God is not too weak to save, and he still responds to audacious, persistent faith. If you wonder whether sin might be in the way, confess it, ask forgiveness, and move on. He calls for you to believe him. And when you call for him, he is more than willing and able to hear.

> What is impossible to God? Not that which is difficult to his power but that which is contrary to his nature.
>
> AMBROSE OF MILAN

The Power of Testimony

Give thanks to the LORD and proclaim his greatness. Let the whole world know what he has done. **1 CHRONICLES 16:8**

FANS OF SPORTS DYNASTIES love to talk about their team's great victories and lasting dominance. They boast about winning seasons, "miracle" plays, star athletes, come-from-behind wins, record-setting performances, and pennants on display. They wear their team's brand on their clothes and cars. They exhaust others with trash talk and their team's exploits—exploits they had nothing to do with, by the way—but they carry on anyway. There's glory in victory, even a vicarious one.

God has an awesome track record, but his people—like sports fans of mediocre or losing teams—often bring a what-have-you-done-for-me-lately attitude into the relationship. We would never phrase it that way, and when asked to identify what we're grateful to God for—often around Thanksgiving—we usually have no problem coming up with some standard and meaningful answers. But do we brag on him? Recount his amazing exploits? Talk about his astonishing abilities? Hang his pennants from the rafters of our own minds and conversations? Perhaps sometimes, but not often enough. Talking about God can be even more provocative than talking about sports and politics. We often refrain from being too vocal.

But testimonies about God carry power and stir up faith. When we get specific about answered prayers, miraculous provision, or the joy and beauty of his blessings, we cultivate an environment of faith for them to happen again and again. There's no need to force those conversations on people; when we're really grateful, they overflow from our hearts and mouths. Even when we recall the testimonies of ages past—not only from the Bible but from the lives of people who have experienced his presence and power—his presence and power come alive in our minds. We adopt a heavenly perspective and realize just how far his victories extend.

Practice the power of testimony. Bring God's track record into today's memories and conversations. Let your heart be filled with faith again and again. Praise him for what he has done—and expect him to do it again.

> Be not afraid of saying too much in the praises of God; all the danger is of saying too little.
>
> MATTHEW HENRY

True Security

The LORD is your security. He will keep your foot
from being caught in a trap. **PROVERBS 3:26**

CONCEPTUALLY, WE DON'T HESITATE to place our security in the Lord. Emotionally, we find lots of other forces at work. We trust God but buy plenty of insurance and alarm systems. We pray in faith but guard our hearts against disappointment. And we sometimes hedge our bets with fallback applications, opportunities, and, for some people, even relationships. There may be nothing wrong with some of those positions; sometimes insurance plans, alarm systems, and secondary applications are part of God's provision for us. But mentally, where are we really placing our trust? The lines between God as our security and people, resources, and things as our security can get pretty blurred.

Our hearts give us good indications, though. When you place faith in circumstances—when you attribute power to chance, possible dangers, unfortunate accidents, or malicious threats—you have every reason to be unsettled. Your mind will tell you that anything can happen, good things happen to bad people, and God may not be in control. But when you place your faith in God as your security, you find yourself at rest. You can lie down and sleep soundly (Proverbs 3:24). You can be confident that whatever happens, God is overseeing it and working out everything for your good. When he is your security, the burden of your well-being is on him.

Be diligent about attributing power to God not only at a head level but also at a heart level. There's no need to abandon all sources of human security plans, but learn to see them—and make decisions about them—in the context of God's sovereign, zealous concern for you and the things you care about. Your prayer life should serve as a consistent, repeated statement of shifting your trust from the things of the world and the rationalizations of the heart to the doting provision and protection of your Father. He is your first recourse for safety and security; everything else falls in place at his direction. Your life, your family, and all of your concerns are solidly and completely in his hands.

> The saints in heaven are happier but no more secure
> than are true believers here in this world.
>
> LORAINE BOETTNER

A Wall of Fire

I will be to her a wall of fire all around, declares the LORD,
and I will be the glory in her midst. **ZECHARIAH 2:5,** ESV

MARIE MONSEN WAS A NORWEGIAN MISSIONARY in China in the early 1900s who, though single and often unaccompanied by any trustworthy men, traveled dangerous roads from town to town under God's protection. One night early in her ministry, Monsen woke up from what she thought were blows to her shoulder and was immediately terrified, thinking she was under attack from robbers. Instead, she saw a momentary picture of a wall of fire around her and felt immediate peace. Zechariah 2:5 came to mind, and she carried that vision and promise with her the rest of her life. She told stories of bandits running toward her transport cart and then suddenly being unable to find it; groups of brigands surrounding her Bible study meetings and then inexplicably walking away without attacking; and even a pirate who pointed a gun at her but couldn't pull the trigger because she told him God wouldn't let him. She lived in the safety of God's presence, even as dangerous and malicious threats raged around her.

God's promise to be a wall of fire around Jerusalem and the glory in its midst is a wonderfully encouraging promise to grasp by faith and remember in trying times. It also makes an awesome prayer for the people you love. It gives us a picture of enormous flames standing guard around those we pray for and of the fire of the Holy Spirit burning within them. It's a spiritual, physical, relational, circumstantial, and emotional promise applicable to a multitude of experiences we might face.

We know God encourages us to practice the art of envisioning because he gives us such visual reminders of his wisdom, presence, power, and love. Such pictures fuel our faith and give us a way to express it that captivates our attention far quicker than words ever could. When we pray those images back to God, we feel them coming alive in our spirit and trust him to carry them out. We sense his presence in them and rest comfortably in his faithfulness.

It was as though the roof was lifted off the house and I saw that
I was surrounded by fire, a high, impenetrable wall of fire.

MARIE MONSEN

Shields of Prayer

The angel of the LORD encamps around those who
fear him, and delivers them.   **PSALM 34:7**, ESV

JONATHAN AND ROSALIND GOFORTH tell of God miraculously coming through to meet their pressing needs, finding out only much later (in the days of slow communication) that a church had felt led to pray earnestly for them at exactly that moment. Marie Monsen told of sensing special protection when pirates took over the steamer she was on and held her and the other passengers captive for days. Missionaries often share stories of breakthrough moments with God and connect them to praying friends and churches back home. The stories of God impressing people to pray at crucial moments are too numerous and too dramatic to dismiss.

We need to become spiritually sensitive to those impressions—alerts about people who might be undergoing exceptional temptations or dangers. These may come as sudden remembrances seemingly out of the blue or as someone weighing on your mind persistently without any discernible reason. Pray for these people—the trials they may be going through; the spiritual, physical, relational, mental, emotional, or circumstantial dangers they may be facing; the accusations or misunderstandings that may be coming against them; or whatever the Holy Spirit impresses upon you. Don't ignore these alerts. They are opportunities to pray diligently for God to intervene in the lives of people you know, whether these people come from your distant past, live in distant places, or are among your close circle of friends, coworkers, and neighbors. You can even pray through the daily news this way. The world is in desperate need of intercession.

As you pray, believe that God surrounds those who love and worship him with angelic protection that keeps evil from doing its worst in their lives. You can also trust him to open doors of opportunity, turn the tables from adversity to advantage, cause breakthroughs, and establish fruitfulness and peace. There are plenty of other promises to support your faith in your prayers. But those mental impressions and alerts very often have to do with impending threats and potential harm. In those moments, God is calling his praying people to intercede for his protection over those who serve him. Your prayers can make an enormous difference in their lives.

The world may doubt the power of prayer, but the saints know better.

GILBERT SHAW

Our Prayer Guide

Your word is a lamp to guide my feet and a light for my path.

PSALM 119:105

PAUL WAS RIGHT ABOUT US NOT KNOWING what to pray for—and about the Holy Spirit being happy to help, interceding for us according to the Father's will (Romans 8:26-27). But if we want a more tangible, black-and-white (and sometimes red-lettered) guide, we have a wealth of source material in the words the same Holy Spirit inspired. God's Word gives us plenty of direction for life and decision-making, but it also gives us plenty of direction for prayer. Anything he has promised, any of his revealed purposes, any examples that he has worked through the lives of his people are invitations for us to pray and believe.

We pray powerfully and according to God's will when we pray his Word back to him. The easiest ways to do that involve the prayers his people have prayed; we've looked at some of Paul's prayers for the Ephesians in particular (Ephesians 1:15-23; 3:14-21). The intercession of Moses (Exodus 32:9-14, 30-34), Nehemiah (Nehemiah 1:4-11), Daniel (Daniel 9:1-19), David (Psalms), and others are powerful examples too, as are the prayers of gratitude from people like Hannah (1 Samuel 2:1-10) and Mary (Luke 1:46-55). We can pray these prayers almost word for word, adapting them to our situations as needed, with confidence. But the prophecies and promises God has given us and the clarity of his purposes are inspired words too, designed not only for the situations in which they were first given but also for us today. Context is important for specific understanding, but it should never obscure God's character, principles, purposes, and heart, all revealed for general application. God's words are rarely a one-off experience. They are fulfilled again and again.

Let them be fulfilled again and again in your life too. Use Scripture as a prayer prompt daily, even hourly. God is the same yesterday, today, and forever. His words are everlasting. Apply them freely, boldly, and creatively to your life, weaving them in and out of your prayers, reaffirming his truth as the basis for your faith. Your life—and your prayers—will be guided well.

I have found in the Bible words for my inmost thoughts, songs for my joy, utterances for my hidden griefs and pleadings for my shame and feebleness.

SAMUEL TAYLOR COLERIDGE

Pray the Precedents

God's way is perfect. All the LORD's promises prove true.

PSALM 18:30

PSALM 18 IS THE ULTIMATE ANSWER TO PRAYER. It begins with a moment of worship and recounts a desperate plea for help followed by a fiery, thunderous response from heaven. Not only is David rescued; he is *resoundingly* rescued as enemies are routed and humiliated in defeat. It's the kind of heavenly response we long for whenever we are in a crisis, yet our urgent prayers are hardly ever filled with such glorious expectation. We'd love to have that psalm as our frequent experience.

Yet in the midst of a crisis, we fumble around for words. We struggle to articulate our specific requests because we aren't sure exactly how we want God to answer. We want him to show up, to be sure, but when we can't see a clear way out, we don't quite know how to ask him for one. We forget that he has numerous possible solutions even when we can't think of any. All he asks of us is to ask of him. Our trusting, believing cry for help is all that's needed. A testimony that stirs up and builds our faith might be helpful too.

Why not pray this psalm or another like it? Many psalms begin in crisis and end in worship, with God's deliverance, protection, and provision in between. Reading or reciting that trajectory back to God prayerfully—whether word for word or the gist of it—honors his testimonies and applies them to our lives. You'll find prayers for all kinds of crises, including unfair accusations, secret plots, societies under siege, spiritual apathy, the heart's deepest longings, confessions of sin and pleas for forgiveness, and much, much more. Whenever you feel under siege, plotted against (by real people or spiritual forces), weighed down, surrounded or overwhelmed, guilty and ashamed, or simply longing for something more, certain psalms are waiting for you. They are there for more than your encouragement. They are precedents waiting to be prayed, in faith, with conviction and expectation, for your life today. Envision God's responses for you just as you read them in the lives of those who wrote them. He is tipping you off to his intentions through age-old words.

> I find that the psalms are like a mirror in which one can see oneself and the movements of one's own heart.
>
> ATHANASIUS

A Mighty Fortress

You hide them in the shelter of your presence, safe from
those who conspire against them. **PSALM 31:20**

DAVID WAS USED TO CONSPIRACIES. For years he lived in exile while a mentally and emotionally unstable king sought to kill him. He found himself at the center of civil war as he ascended to the throne of Judah and then all of Israel. One of his own sons rebelled and fostered an uprising. And David died with enough ambiguity in his succession plan that his son Solomon had to forcefully claim the throne. As a king, he was well acquainted with political plots and maneuverings. On a personal level, we can hardly relate to such conspiracies.

Or can we? We live in a world filled with deception at nearly every level. Most of us have endured seasons in which the odds seemed to be stacked against us and things went from bad to worse. In our struggle to get ahead, many of us keep hitting ceilings, glass or otherwise, that effectively keep us in our place, even though we know our place in God's purposes is higher and better than our station in this world. These limitations and challenges seem awfully orchestrated at times, as if life and circumstances were coordinating a vast conspiracy against us. Whether such a plot is imagined or not, we long for that place of shelter in God's presence, where those who conspire against us cannot touch us.

God gives us free license to pray for that. It's a promise in his Word, a desire of his heart, a repeated offer that we have every right to enter into by faith. He describes himself as a shield, a rock, a fortress, a protective angel or great bird inviting us into the shadow of his wings. He knows how to manage our reputation, vindicate us when we have been mischaracterized, misdirect enemy plots and even cause them to backfire, and protect us from every kind of harm. In a world of spiritual darkness, confused beliefs and arguments, hidden agendas, and animosity toward God's people, we find David's words startlingly relevant. They are God's promise to us, in all ages, that he is standing vigilantly between us and dangerous elements. We can pray it back to him with conviction.

A mighty fortress is our God, a bulwark never failing.

MARTIN LUTHER

First Love

The eyes of the LORD watch over those who do right;
his ears are open to their cries for help.   **PSALM 34:15**

IN THE OLD TESTAMENT, God answers the prayers of those whose hearts are his and want to do the right thing. In the New Testament, God answers the prayers of those who believe in Jesus. Is there a difference? Perhaps in theological nuances, there is. But practically, those who believe in Jesus are also those whose hearts are his and want to live righteously. It goes against the Christian grain to live independently of his love and desires. In the Old Testament and the New, faithfulness and faith are inextricably linked.

Religious systems have often turned this into a reward system—those who behave get their prayers answered. And while Scripture mentions rewards, it's never in the context of earning merit or God's favor. Prayers are answered when we align our hearts with God, believe his words, and seek his face in all our pursuits. If there were ever a formula for prayer (though there isn't), that would come close to it. It's true in any age.

Far too many Christians have tried to seek God's favor without also seeking his face. We've aimed for the blessings over the Blesser, the gifts over the Giver, the goods over the highest Good. We've sought presents more than presence, and that's a problem. Prayer is meant to be part of a deep, abiding relationship that also includes adoration, confession, gratitude, heart-to-heart talks, conversations about meaning and purpose, and desires to serve well. If we pray without love for God, we risk trying to use him for our own purposes. Even then, he sometimes answers. But he doesn't promise to. He saves his promises for those who have gone deeper than asking for favors.

Set your heart on God above all. Ask freely, but make asking the smaller portion of your prayers rather than the beginning, middle, and end of your conversations with him. Let your love for him show up in your words, attitudes, and actions. His ears and heart will be open to your cries for help—and just about anything else you want to ask.

> Let us make God the beginning and end of our love, for he is the fountain from which all good things flow and into him alone they flow back.
>
> RICHARD ROLLE

The Rescue Mission

The LORD hears his people when they call to him for help.
He rescues them from all their troubles. **PSALM 34:17**

GOD IS ON A RESCUE MISSION. We see glimpses of it in the Old Testament, when he promised his people an everlasting Kingdom and vast influence, delivered them from captivity and oppression, led them to pleasant places, intervened miraculously throughout their history, and established prophets, priests, and kings to care for them and guide them. We see a full expression of it in the New Testament, when Jesus said that the Father loved this world so deeply that he sent his own Son to redeem and restore it. Early on, Scripture sets the stage with a fallen existence; the rest of the story tells of a great rescue and a glorious end. He is able to save completely.

We are called to fit into that rescue mission somehow. As those who have been rescued (and are still being rescued in many ways), we join God in his global operation to redeem and restore lives. We each have a different part in that plan—telling the Good News in certain places, training those who have been rescued to be rescuers, leading others in worship of the Rescuer, and living out our many other gifts and callings. But we are all given the assignment and the opportunity to pray for the mission daily. We pray for our own part in it, we pray for those who need to be rescued, and we pray for the global efforts as a whole. We have entered into a comprehensive plan to grow God's Kingdom on earth until the King returns.

In our prayer agenda, it's important to learn to see people in new ways. While some divide humanity into those who are rescued and those who are not—the people of God versus the world—we need to see humanity as those who are already God's children and those who are potentially God's children. In other words, our prayers for people need to be filled not only with faith but with kindness, generosity, and undiscriminating love. The rescuing God builds his mission on such prayers, and his people will carry it out in power as he answers.

The Spirit of Christ is the spirit of missions, and the nearer we get
to him the more intensely missionary we must become.

HENRY MARTYN

A Very Present Help

God is our refuge and strength, a very present help in trouble.

PSALM 46:1, ESV

A PLOW VIOLENTLY TILLS THE GROUND, the planter sows seeds into it, and over time, often with quite a bit of care in the process, a harvest comes. The fruits of long growing seasons are always pleasant, but the means for arriving at them rarely are. Some aspects go more smoothly than others, but the first—the plowing of the ground—is the roughest. It involves a deep rupture of the hardened surface in order to put something valuable beneath it.

That's how crises work in our lives. They violently open our hearts to the seeds God wants to plant in them. He doesn't necessarily author those crises, but he does know what to do with them. They become the fertile ground of some of our most authentic prayers, and if we keep coming to him in faith, we are drawn closer to him in the process. Eventually, we see the fruit of that tumultuous season, and it's wonderful to taste. But we know it didn't come easy.

God promises to be "a very present help" in all of our troubles, and our cries to him in the midst of a crisis are as raw and real as they are instinctual. But think about what we would know of him if we didn't have those moments of need. We would never know his mercy, deliverance, healing, and comfort, all of which imply problems to address. We could not know him as Defender, Rescuer, and Strength. Our darkest trials become the backdrop for his most brilliant work, and they reveal his character to us and to anyone who happens to be watching. They are the stage that presents his nature.

That's why our best prayers for help are not laments, complaints, or desperate pleas—though he gladly hears them all—but faith-filled requests for him to show himself strong on our behalf and expectant questions about how he wants to do it. He is drawn to hearts that trust in him not only to meet their own needs but also to display his glory in the process. He is very present when our lives are plowed by the brutal instruments of life, and he eagerly sows seeds for a magnificent harvest into them.

When I am in the cellar of affliction, I look for the Lord's choicest wines.

SAMUEL RUTHERFORD

From Weeping to Joy

*When they walk through the Valley of Weeping,
it will become a place of refreshing springs.* **PSALM 84:6**

IF YOU'VE EVER GONE THROUGH a wilderness season—and virtually every believer does—you know how frustrating it can be. When you experience losses, feel stuck, long for greater fruitfulness in a spiritually dry and barren land, or are desperate for opportunities to come along, you may have a hard time even praying at all, much less praying in faith. Even so, God has encouraging promises for you to cling to. He will turn your valleys of weeping into places of refreshing springs.

God doesn't insist on bold, unshakable faith in promises like these. He understands the challenges of faith and the dynamics of dry and painful seasons. But even clinging to such promises with a feeble grip can be powerful. We can be confident that "those who plant in tears will harvest with shouts of joy," and even though "they weep as they go to plant their seed," they will come back singing in the end (Psalm 126:5-6). There is an unmistakable relationship in Scripture between painful seasons of sowing and joyful seasons of reaping. Seeing that relationship operate in real life requires patience, insistence on his goodness regardless of what you might see, and at least a desire for faith, even when faith is hard to come by. But the God who cannot lie promises that your valleys of weeping will turn into pleasant oases in time.

The best response to a desert is to lean into God and ask him to make it fruitful, at least eventually. There's nothing wrong with asking him for that fruitfulness soon, as long as you understand that his *soon* is not always the same as yours. But he does know your limits, values your dependence on him, honors your trust, and sees the end of your story even before it starts. He does not withhold good gifts forever for those who trust in him. He cultivates faith, sows good seed into the plowed ground of our lives, and tenderly, patiently oversees the growing process. Open doors of opportunity, restoration for losses, and refreshing springs of abundant life are part of your inheritance as a believer. Your times of joyful singing are coming.

God has a bottle and a book for his people's tears. . . .
What was sown as a tear will come up as a pearl.

MATTHEW HENRY

No Good Thing

The LORD God is our sun and our shield. He gives us grace
and glory. The LORD will withhold no good thing
from those who do what is right. **PSALM 84:11**

IT'S A WONDERFULLY ENCOURAGING PROMISE—God as our light and warmth, our protection and shelter, the giver of grace and glory. He withholds nothing good from us, lavishing on us the beauties and joys of creation. Still, our hearts fall when we read "those who do what is right," or, in other translations, "those who walk uprightly" or "those whose walk is blameless." These are hard words. We *try* to do what is right, but we aren't perfect. We aren't blameless on all counts. And we begin to wonder if this promise applies to us.

It *does*, and we can believe it enthusiastically. For one thing, the Bible's words are never directed to those who are completely blameless because it is emphatic that no one except Jesus is. It addresses the general tenor of our hearts—whether we are growing in maturity and committed to following God's ways. If we're running toward him, his promises for the righteous apply.

Even more important, though, is the opportunity in promises like these to base our prayers not on what we've done but on what Jesus has accomplished for us. Remember, we don't pray in our own name. We pray in his. Our petitions are backed by his righteousness, worthiness, and standing with the Father. It's still important to align our hearts with him in every way, but the basis of our prayers isn't our own perfection. It's his. The Lord will withhold no good thing from those who find their identity in the worthy, perfect Son.

That's worth pursuing in passionate faith and embracing without reservation. We can think of a lot of "good things" we want to receive from God, most of which we can be confident are good in his eyes too. He is rich in mercy, creative in his works, generous with his blessings, and always willing to lead us into the best he has for us. That may not be a smooth journey, but it's always good. And we can take him at his word and pray emphatically in his name.

My hope is built on nothing less than Jesus' blood and righteousness.

EDWARD MOTE

An Open Invitation

What do you want? Ask, and I will give it to you! **1 KINGS 3:5**

BEFORE SOLOMON BUILT THE TEMPLE, many of the people of Israel worshiped at local altars and shrines. Early in his reign, Solomon went to one of them to make his offerings, and God appeared to him there in a dream and extended an extraordinary invitation. He told Solomon to ask whatever he wanted, and it would be given to him.

Like us, Solomon could probably think of a lot of possibilities in that situation. It's the closest we see God come to our fantasies of a genie in the bottle, though he does not subject himself to the whims of untrustworthy people. And Solomon, at least at this point in his life, was trustworthy. He prayed a good prayer, asking for wisdom to govern God's people well.

Because of this noble prayer, God promised to give Solomon not only the wisdom he asked for but much more. Solomon would accumulate enormous wisdom, power, and wealth, and for much of his life, he brought glory to God. He understood God's priorities and asked according to his will, and in the process he received more than he could have hoped for.

We could hardly ask for a better illustration of New Testament promises for God's people. Jesus said that if we "seek the Kingdom of God above all else," all else would be added to us (Matthew 6:33). He told his followers to ask "whatever you wish," and it would be done for them, as long as they were rooted in him (John 15:7, ESV). God extended this sort of invitation to very few people in the Old Testament, and explicitly only with Solomon. Yet he extends it today to a Kingdom of priests, members of the royal family who are united with his Son.

Don't let this offer fall to the ground. Take God up on it—again and again. Don't be flippant with it; think it through as a steward of his riches and an ambassador of his Kingdom. But with those priorities in mind, ask extravagantly. Look at the needs around you and envision God's unlimited resources. Talk with your Father, the King, and recognize what he wants to do. Then hear his voice: "What do you want?"

Nothing is too great and nothing too small to commit into the hands of the Lord.

A. W. PINK

Kingdom Values

Give me an understanding heart so that I can govern your people well
and know the difference between right and wrong.   1 KINGS 3:9

IN ASKING FOR WISDOM, Solomon demonstrated that he already had some wisdom. He took the seeds of what had been given to him and asked for more of it. An unwise request would have sought superficialities above substance—outward things that might be assumed to satisfy a hungry heart rather than an understanding heart. Solomon asked for what he knew to be God's priorities based on the godly calling he had been given. After all, God had demonstrated that he wanted kings after his own heart (1 Samuel 13:14), so Solomon essentially asked to become one. He discerned God's purposes even before he asked for discernment.

When you answer God's open invitation to ask what you want, pay attention to the persistent, godly desires he has already put within you and perhaps even begun to fulfill. Ask on the basis of those gifts, trusting that they are signs of his ultimate intentions for you. Almost always, he has begun a work in you before ever inviting you to ask for its fulfillment. Your asking is meant to further the purposes he has planted from the start.

That doesn't mean God is playing games with you—that he only says to "ask whatever you wish" as long as you wish within tight limitations. That's double-talk, overtly saying one thing while secretly meaning another, and God doesn't engage in such tricks. No, he really does mean to give you more than you ask for. But he also urges you to embrace Kingdom priorities. As a parent who wants to raise responsible children *and* give them enjoyable things, he knows which is more important. And he means for our prayers to recognize the same values. He doesn't want us to place the perks of this world above the treasures of eternity.

Pray noble prayers above all. Don't be so afraid of the fun and frivolous that you assume he has nothing to do with them. But fit them within the big picture. Pray with an eternal perspective. Pray for what you can give as well as what you can get.

The chief purpose of prayer is that God may be glorified in the answer.

R. A. TORREY

Faith That Multiplies

"Bring them here," he said.   **MATTHEW 14:18**

THE CROWDS SWARMED WITH SPIRITUAL HUNGER to a remote area to hear Jesus' teaching and experience God's power. Now they were physically hungry, and no supplies were in sight. Rather than sending them away, Jesus told the disciples to feed them. But the only food the disciples knew of was five small loaves of bread and two fish. For Jesus, that was enough. He told them to bring what was available as a launching point for making more available.

That visual example is a great illustration of the description of faith in Hebrews 11:1. The bread and fish really were the "substance" or "evidence" of things hoped for yet still unseen. They were a taste of the bigger picture, the down payment of a miracle, the seed that would grow into a great harvest. The same is true of our faith. From a sample we get an abundance—if we know how to sow it into the ground as seeds for the coming fruitfulness. We take what we have and give it to Jesus, just as the disciples did. But we also hear from Jesus the promise that we can do the same. The Lord who said, "You feed them" (verse 16), is the Lord who hands us the raw materials of a miracle and tells us to believe.

When you find yourself in an overwhelming situation, with a need far greater than current provision, don't dismiss that provision. Take it to Jesus. Tell him what you have and hand it over. By faith, embrace the assignment to make much out of a little, to sow seeds of need and desire into the soil of his Kingdom and insist that they grow. Where physical sight sees physical limitations, faith sees Kingdom realities, where all things are abundant and promises are available for the taking. By faith, refuse to leave them in the storehouse of heaven. Become a distributor of Kingdom gifts, feed multitudes, and satisfy the hunger of your world. You get to enjoy the meal too—without restraint. And all who eat will be filled with the goodness of God.

One of the words very frequently used of these miracles in the Gospels is the ordinary term "works." They were the natural and necessary outcome of his life.

GRIFFITH THOMAS

OCTOBER 28

Seeing Ahead

Only I can tell you the future before it even happens. Everything I plan will come to pass, for I do whatever I wish. **ISAIAH 46:10**

FROM THE TOP OF A SKYSCRAPER, you can see things happening for miles around—the traffic jam that cars speeding down the highway will soon be stuck in; clouds on the horizon that will soon determine the weather in your city; the end of the route in a parade or marathon, even as some participants are just getting started. You know a lot simply because of your lofty perspective.

God sees everything—the beginning of the story and the end of it, possibilities and problems, participants and observers, all at the same time. He knows the future before it happens, and he allows nothing that will interfere with his ultimate plans. He is never caught off guard, and he is completely at peace even as the story progresses. His lofty perspective puts him above whatever causes us anxiety, stress, and strain.

Faith is meant to lift us from an earthly to a heavenly perspective. Whether or not God has revealed his specific intentions—sometimes he gives us that privilege—we can trust in his purposes and outcomes. We can rest completely in peace as the story progresses because we know nothing will ultimately thwart his plans for us. We can embrace a skyscraper point of view with an eye on coming events, potential problems, and available solutions because we know the one who is over them all. We have no need to question the end of the race. It is already seen from above.

That doesn't mean God will show us every detail of the trials and processes we are going through, but he does allow us to enter into the emotions and hope of his perspective. If we seek him, he shows us enough of what we need to know. Regardless of how clearly we see, standing at the beginning and seeing the end is part of the vision of faith. The prayer of faith calls into the present what has not yet come to pass. It puts us in a place of lofty, hopeful expectations. It gives us peace no matter where we are along the way.

> Those who keep speaking about the sun while walking under a cloudy sky are messengers of hope, the true saints of our day.
>
> HENRI NOUWEN

Praying the Past

*Every day of my life was recorded in your book. Every moment
was laid out before a single day had passed.* **PSALM 139:16**

IMAGINE GOING BACK IN TIME and being an invisible observer to the
moment of your worst mistake. You can't stop what is about to happen, but you can
talk to God about it. What would you say? How would you pray for the outcome of
this unfortunate event? What would you want God to do in the aftermath? On the
flip side, imagine observing the moments of your best decisions. What would you
ask God to do with them? How would you want them to shape the future?

If God is outside of time, can we pray to change the past? Perhaps not, but we
can certainly pray for the effect those moments had. We can be assured that God
knew then of our prayers now. He was an observer too, and he looked ahead to our
conversations with him today. We can pray for the outcomes of horrible events to be
minimized and the outcomes of great works to be magnified—bringing healing and
fruitfulness for ourselves or others. We don't stand outside of time as God does, but
our prayers just might. He has known them in advance. If he is not bound by the
limitations of time and space, neither are the prayers he has already heard, including
those that have yet to be prayed.

This is no New Age, out-of-body projection, of course. God never invites us to
engage in such things. See it instead as a spiritual exercise that acknowledges God's
authority over time and space. God gave Ezekiel the ability to see an alternate version of Jerusalem in the Spirit, transported Philip geographically, and opened the
eyes of prophets to see events beyond their time. He can certainly apply our prayers
to past, present, and future, just as he applies them in our homes, across nations,
and beyond seas. We can pray across history, bringing past events and works into
greater (or lesser) effectiveness today, envisioning the God who stands outside of time
massaging its movements for his purposes. He had perfect foresight then and has
perfect hindsight now. Your times—and all times—are in his hands.

In God, time and eternity are one and the same thing.

HENRY SUSO

Praying in Power

You will receive power when the Holy Spirit comes upon you.

ACTS 1:8

JESUS TOLD HIS FOLLOWERS to ask and keep asking for the Holy Spirit (Luke 11:9-13). Regardless of our various beliefs about the Holy Spirit's work, Jesus' words urge us to move beyond a onetime experience into an ongoing empowerment. He told the disciples about the Holy Spirit before his crucifixion (John 14–16), breathed his Spirit into them after his resurrection when he sent them out to continue his mission (John 20:21-22), and told them right before his ascension to wait in Jerusalem until they received power (Acts 1:4-5, 8), which came upon them in a dramatic experience on the day of Pentecost (Acts 2). Long afterward, Paul urged his readers to keep being filled with the Spirit as a central aspect of their lives and worship (Ephesians 5:18). Some men were considered to demonstrate more evidence of being "full of the Spirit" than others (Acts 6:3). The Bible's teaching on our relationship with the Holy Spirit suggests a dynamic, repeatable, nuanced, diverse experience.

We need the Holy Spirit's power for a lot of things, including faith and prayer. Scripture mentions his ministry in the context of faithfulness, fruitfulness, testimony, strength, wisdom, and worship, but also as the means of and result of powerful prayers (Acts 4:23-31; Romans 8:26; Ephesians 6:18; Jude 1:20). God hears prayers of all kinds, but those inspired and empowered by the Holy Spirit were already generated by his heart, and they provoke a resounding response from him. Spirit-influenced prayer comes from God, through him, and to him.

Seek to pray *for* this power and *in* this power. If you don't know how, ask. If nothing happens, ask persistently, just as Jesus said, trusting that he is answering. Keep pressing in. Make it a lifelong endeavor—not to arrive at some magical event but to grow in the power that has been given in ever-increasing measure. Your prayers of faith have already been influenced by the Holy Spirit and will continue to be shaped and empowered by him more and more as you pursue his ways. You will hear his voice, grow in his wisdom, speak his words, pray in his strength, believe with his certainty, and experience his answers according to his glorious purposes for you.

Prayer is the secret of power.

EVAN ROBERTS

As He Prays

As He is, so are we in this world.   1 JOHN 4:17, NKJV

JESUS' DISCIPLES ASKED HIM to teach them to pray (Luke 11:1), and he answered with a model prayer. He followed it with a humorous illustration of perseverance; instructions about asking, seeking, and knocking until we receive, find, and enter open doors; and some reassuring words about the good intentions of our very kind and generous Father. It's a marvelous section of Scripture that packs a lot of prayer principles and truths into a short conversation. It gives us a lot to go on.

But Jesus didn't just teach about prayer. He modeled it. He withdrew to be alone so he could talk to the Father without interruption. He thanked God for the people who opened their hearts to his message. He told people he only said what he heard the Father saying and did what he saw the Father doing, suggesting some pretty vivid divine conversations. He prayed for people's forgiveness, blessed food, spoke miracles into being, interceded for wavering disciples, and much more. If anyone had a powerful, fruitful, effective prayer life, it was Jesus.

If only we were like him, we might think. Yet that's our calling—to be just like him, to be conformed to his image, to be "as he is" in this world. In other words, we are the spitting image of our Master, invited to do his works, speak his words, experience his power, be filled with his Spirit, walk in his ways, and bear his fruit. If Jesus had a remarkably powerful prayer life, so can we. That's our calling. We should never settle for anything less.

That means that when we experience less—and we so often do—we should make it a point to pursue more, draw closer to him, submit ourselves to his purposes, pray for his power, and keep growing into his image until we experience the kinds of intercession and answers he experienced. We should read the Gospels eagerly and expectantly to discover the keys to a Spirit-saturated life like the one Jesus showed us. We should hunger and be filled again and again, just as with our physical meals. He will guide us as we learn. As he prays, so can we pray in this world.

A Christian should be a striking likeness of Jesus Christ.

CHARLES SPURGEON

Influence Your World

The harvest is great, but the workers are few. So pray to
the LORD who is in charge of the harvest; ask him to send
more workers into his fields. MATTHEW 9:37-38

AS JESUS TRAVELED THROUGHOUT THE VILLAGES and towns of Galilee, he had compassion on the crowds and ministered to them. Like sheep without a shepherd, they flocked to him for healing, deliverance, words of wisdom, and a touch from God. At one point, Jesus turned to his disciples and told them the harvest was plentiful. But he didn't ask for more opportunities or more efficient ministry. He told them to pray for more workers to be sent into the harvest.

Was he appealing for a larger group of disciples to follow him as he went into the fields? Perhaps. In the next passage and another, he sends the twelve and then the seventy followers out on their own ministry trips as the beginnings of something more. But his instruction to pray for laborers stands as a timeless appeal for believers not just to go but to *pray for more goers*—to be engaged in his mission in all places and at all times, even on our knees. If the harvest was ripe then, we can trust that it is still ripe today. And the only way to deal with a vast harvest is to recruit more workers to handle it. Great crops are labor-intensive.

This then becomes a major focus of our prayers. When people hear of prayer meetings or groups, they often imagine faint results and perhaps nothing more productive than nice wishes. But prayer is a ministry in itself, a key component of advancing God's Kingdom in this world. It's a weighty calling.

Ask God to send not only more workers but diverse, sensitive, knowledgeable, creative, winsome, Spirit-empowered workers. Be ready to become an answer to your own prayer; God often involves us in his responses one way or another—in this case, by supporting, going, and/or getting involved where we are. Even if you are limited in your opportunities, you can have a powerful, lasting influence on people, cultures, nations, institutions, families, churches, and much more. Touching the world through prayer is a calling you can fulfill anytime and anywhere.

> You can influence more people for God and have a greater role
> in advancing Christ's cause by prayer than in any other way.
>
> WESLEY DUEWEL

Ever Interceding

He is able, once and forever, to save those who come to God through him. He lives forever to intercede with God on their behalf.

HEBREWS 7:25

JESUS CAME AS A PROPHET, lives to intercede as a priest, and will come again as the King. As our Savior, he is able to save completely—spiritually, to be sure, but as he demonstrated in his earthly ministry, salvation is much more comprehensive than many of us have made it out to be. He came to bring the fullness of the Kingdom to us—beginning when we believe and growing and continuing until the consummation of the Kingdom at his return. Or as some translations of this verse say, he is able to save "to the uttermost." And part of his saving work continues right now at the throne of God as he intercedes with God on behalf of all who believe.

Jesus intercedes for us by applying his sacrifice, his righteousness, and his strength to our lives. His priestly ministry is ongoing. But he also invites us to join him in that ministry, becoming priests to one another and to the world as a whole (1 Peter 2:5-9). By faith, we can therefore apply his sacrifice, righteousness, and strength to those who need him. We can pray for salvation "to the uttermost" for those around us. We cooperate with his ministry when we join our prayers to his intercession for other believers.

That's a much more satisfying approach than complaining about people's flaws and mistakes or verbally jousting with them. Using Jesus' great intercessory prayer in John 17 as a model, we can pray for believers' protection (17:11, 15); their unity and intimate fellowship with each other and with the Father and Son (verses 11, 21-23); their joy (verse 13); their grounding in his Word (verse 17); their holiness, or being set apart to him (verse 19); their experiences of glory (verses 22, 24); their love (verse 26); and his manifest presence in their lives to empower, encourage, and inspire them (verse 26). In an age when Christians regularly lash out at each other over doctrinal preferences and worship practices, that's a refreshingly constructive approach. We are called and blessed to pray for each other—in faith and love—always.

> When we pray for each other on earth, we do so believing that all things are given to us through Christ alone.
>
> **HULDRYCH ZWINGLI**

Ministers with God

You will be called priests of the LORD, ministers of our God.
ISAIAH 61:6

WHEN JESUS RETURNED TO HIS HOME SYNAGOGUE in Nazareth, he declared his messianic manifesto—a quote from Isaiah about his mission (Luke 4:16-21). In the original passage, Isaiah calls his hearers, the people of God, priests of the Lord. That means we can continue whatever our great High Priest did through his power working within us. We, too, are called to bring good news to the poor, bind up the brokenhearted, proclaim freedom for captives, and declare the Lord's favor (Isaiah 61:1-2). We, too, can offer beauty instead of ashes, blessing and gladness in the place of mourning, and "festive praise instead of despair" (verse 3). By faith, we build up ancient ruins, repair destroyed cities, and revive lives and societies (verse 4). We are not just nominal priests. We actually do things that matter.

But all the priestly things we do must be backed by priestly prayers of faith. In the realm of the spirit, we join in partnership with God at any moment for any need anywhere in the world through such prayers. There is no limit to our ministry. We pray especially powerfully in areas of our particular knowledge and relationships, but the entire world is our field. Why? Because the entire world is Jesus' field, and we are in him and he in us. We are priests because we are as one with the great High Priest (John 17:22, 26; Galatians 2:20). We haven't just believed in him as our Savior. We've joined with him in his mission.

If your prayers have focused on your own needs or circles of relationships, lift up your eyes to the horizons of the world and see fields that are white for harvest. Recognize your astonishing position to shape history, influence cultures, and bless individual lives by praying *with* him, not just *to* him. Learn to see the news as your cues to pray God's purposes into this world. Learn to see people's frailties and foibles as opportunities to pray God's presence and power into their redemption and restoration. Become a missionary in the spirit through prayers that are prompted by, filled with, and answered in faith. You are a priest, a minister of your God.

> Next to the wonder of seeing my Savior will be, I think,
> the wonder that I made so little use of the power of prayer.
>
> **D. L. MOODY**

Praying in New Clothes

All who have been united with Christ in baptism have put on
Christ, like putting on new clothes. **GALATIANS 3:27**

PEOPLE WHO SPEND ENOUGH TIME in a different culture begin to reflect its ways. They think, talk, eat, dress, and behave like the people of that culture. Missionaries sometimes demonstrate this when they return home to speak; they dress in the style of their new culture in order to represent it to their old. As citizens adopted into the Kingdom of God, we take on its culture as our own to an even greater degree. We become like the King in order to represent his Kingdom to the world we came out of.

That's essentially what Paul told his readers. By believing in Jesus, we don't have to stress and strain to become like Jesus in our own strength. We simply put him on. We wear him around because his Spirit is in us and we are in him. We clothe ourselves in Jesus and then live out the part. Over time, this new life becomes as natural as being immersed in a new culture. His nature is available to us not just one day in the future but now, where we are.

That has profound implications not only for the ways we think and live but also for how we pray. In our prayers for our own spiritual growth, it means that we can go ahead and step into the new nature we've been praying for. It may be instinctual to pray, "God, please do this . . . ," but much of the gospel is an emphatic statement of what God has already done. We need not ask him to give things that have already been given. We just receive them and wear them around like new clothes.

In our prayers for what God hasn't done yet, whether in our lives or in the lives of others, it means that we enter into the heavenly conversation already happening. Remember that we are praying *with* the Father, Son, and Spirit, not just *to* them. Jesus and the Holy Spirit are interceding. When we learn to listen to God's voice, we discover what to pray in advance. We bring our requests to him, clothed in Christ. And he always hears the voice of his Son.

> The essence of prayer does not consist in asking God for
> something but in opening our hearts to God, speaking with Him,
> and living with Him in perpetual communion.
>
> SUNDAR SINGH

Everything by Faith

By faith these people overthrew kingdoms, ruled with justice,
and received what God had promised them. **HEBREWS 11:33**

HISTORY IS FILLED WITH POWER-HUNGRY CONQUERORS who overthrew governments, built vast empires, and made a name for themselves. History is also filled with Kingdom-minded servants who have influenced empires, established justice, and called God's promises into earthly experience merely because they prayed and lived by faith. Those two very different descriptions aren't always easy to discern. Some who claimed the name of Christ fit the first description much better than the second. But people who are powerful in God's Kingdom are often unknown in the wider world because they are rarely self-promoting. They trust in the wisdom and power of God to accomplish his purposes and simply see themselves as participants in his plan.

Still, the works of faith recounted in Hebrews 11 are impressive. While people like Alexander the Great, Genghis Khan, Napoleon, and other conquerors built kingdoms or imposed cultures that lasted a few decades or centuries, works of faith contribute to an eternal Kingdom that never fades or diminishes. They do more than exert power; they establish the character and purpose of God's Kingdom on earth. They don't just shift circumstances; they bring hearts and lives into alignment with the love and goodness of God. They accomplish things that matter forever.

We are invited into that vast, sweeping movement of God's Kingdom on earth. But no one prays with history-changing faith without history-changing vision. Those who pray small prayers do so because they have small vision. Those are the only kinds of prayers they can pray. But when we ask God to expand our vision, increase the capacity of our hearts, and fill us with God-sized faith, we begin to see greater possibilities, the enormity of our calling, and the possibility of eternal returns on our momentary investments. We recognize the potential to have greater influence than the great conquerors, reap greater rewards than the sharpest investors, and pray justice into the most unjust, oppressive, intractable situations. We need no large army, ingenious conspiracy, or influential faction. We just need God. And by faith, we bring his Kingdom into lives, cities, and nations of the world.

God does nothing but by prayer, and everything with it.

JOHN WESLEY

From Weakness to Strength

They shut the mouths of lions, quenched the flames of fire,
and escaped death by the edge of the sword. Their weakness
was turned to strength. They became strong in battle
and put whole armies to flight. **HEBREWS 11:33-34**

DANIEL SURVIVED A LION'S DEN BY FAITH. His friends survived a furnace by faith. The Israelites brought down the walls of Jericho by faith. Gideon put armies to flight by faith, Jehoshaphat set armies against each other by faith, and Elisha relied on vast heavenly armies by faith. The examples of what faith has accomplished—not only in Scripture but throughout history as God's people have turned to him in trust—could go on and on. It would take forever to recount them all. Fortunately, we'll have forever to celebrate them.

Meanwhile, many of God's children today feel stuck in circumstances, victimized by their trials, bound by addictions and habits, and limited by the weight of debt, sickness, or decisions of other people. There is glory just beyond the veil of their sight, but they haven't yet learned how to access it. God has given promises that address virtually every situation they can encounter, but many of them seem beyond their grasp. It's true that God gives us the faith to only endure at times, but eventually he gives us the faith to break through into a new season. The problem is that when we've experienced enough setbacks, we cease to believe in the breakthroughs. We forget that God is not defined or limited by our past, temporary experiences.

God was behind all of those great events mentioned in the book of Hebrews and experienced by his people throughout history, of course. But faith is what set the stage for his intervention in all of them. We don't know what he would have done in the lives of Daniel, his friends, Gideon, Jehoshaphat, or any number of other people if they hadn't believed, but we do know they are commended for their faith, and God's response is tied to it. That ought to encourage us to believe, seek greater and purer faith, rest in God's faithfulness, and patiently persist in our prayers. Great things happen when God's people believe. Weakness is turned to strength, and strength breaks through in our lives.

What can be hoped for which is not believed?

AUGUSTINE

When He Waits

*Therefore the LORD waits to be gracious to you, and therefore he
exalts himself to show mercy to you. For the LORD is a God of justice;
blessed are all those who wait for him.* **ISAIAH 30:18, ESV**

WRITING TO REBELLIOUS PEOPLE, Isaiah expressed God's desire to be gracious and show mercy, justice, and blessing. Though they needed God's intervention and had been waiting for answers, God wasn't the problem. They were. They had turned away from him in independence and then turned toward him when they had a need. They were trying to play their relationship with him both ways. So God waited.

Andrew Murray wrote that there are two hearts in every prayer: our heart with small expectations for our immediate need and God's heart with infinite, divine intention to bless us.[5] Those two hearts have different perspectives, assumptions, and timelines. They also have a different understanding of the dynamics involved and the purpose behind the prayer. We often see nothing more than our need to have God show up in our lives in tangible ways. But God sees the entire relationship—his showing up in our lives, to be sure, but in the context of love, closeness, and a united purpose. Whether he waits to respond is not a matter of a carrot-and-stick reward system. It's an invitation to come closer.

God's heart is the true one, of course. He understands our limited vision of the dynamics of prayer, but our limited vision is supposed to be temporary. He reveals his heart every step of the way if we have eyes to see it. Prayer and faith are meant to draw us deeper into the relationship, to be the vehicle of his revelation in our lives in which we seek him in love and he responds to us in love. His apparent silence is hardly ever a "no." It's a call to come closer, seek more eagerly, adjust our thinking and vision, and press in to his presence. He wants us to hear his heartbeat. When we do, we find him entering into our petitions and fulfilling them with pleasure. We discover that those who wait for him—and cultivate the relationship in their waiting—really are blessed, as he promised.

> Bow before him, waiting on him until your soul envisions that
> you are in the hands of a powerful, wonder-working God.
>
> ANDREW MURRAY

Called to Rest

My dear Martha, you are worried and upset over all these details!
There is only one thing worth being concerned about. **LUKE 10:41-42**

MARTHA WAS BOTHERED that Mary wasn't as worried as she was. Work needed to be done, and Mary was listening to Jesus rather than being a good hostess and helping out. Martha's literal complaint to Jesus began with "Do you not care?" (verse 40, ESV). It sounds awfully similar to the words the disciples once spoke to Jesus when the waves of a storm were crashing into their boat (Mark 4:38). On that occasion, Jesus had been resting in his Father's love even as the storm raged. Here, Mary is resting in Jesus' love even while her sister storms about. Apparently, resting in God can look a lot like not caring.

We see that all around us, don't we? When people are completely stressed out about a pandemic, a rumor of war, or a threatening political or social trend, they tend to look at those who are calmly trusting their Father as uncaring, insensitive, even irresponsible. That's because internal peace can look remarkably similar to apathy at times. Since many people seem to believe that worry is the best motivator for action, they see a lack of it as evidence of inaction—even when the peaceful heart has taken all necessary precautions or preparations.

The heart of faith, however, refuses to get upset over the details that other people may think are necessary. We want to be responsible and do our part, and we certainly want to serve as Jesus called us to serve. But we don't want to panic when the rest of the world is panicking. We are called to believe, trust, rest, and be patient. Those are difficult postures for alarmists to observe, and they are difficult for us to maintain in the face of criticism. But the life of faith compels us. If we are in the center of God's will, all is well, even when it isn't well by human standards. Only one thing is worth being concerned about: clinging to the words and will of the Savior.

> The beginning of anxiety is the end of faith,
> and the beginning of true faith is the end of anxiety.
> GEORGE MÜLLER

Faithful Prayers

*I made you, and I will care for you. I will carry
you along and save you.* **ISAIAH 46:4**

ISAIAH SAW PEOPLE OF ISRAEL AND JUDAH falling for Babylonian gods
and being carried away with them into captivity. Whether this was a vision of the
future or an observation of current practices, it grieved the heart of God and the
prophet, and God spoke tender words calling them back to himself. He reminded
the people that he was the one who made them. He was there when they were born
and would carry them through their old age. Those false gods that had so captivated
the people's attention—perhaps because they promised benefits without demanding the commitment of a relationship—were unworthy trinkets, empty hopes, and
intruders in the divine plan. They represented frivolous dalliances interrupting
true love.

Few people today bow down to actual carved idols like those of Babylon, but we
engage in plenty of frivolous dalliances with things that distract from our relationship with God. Perhaps like the people of Isaiah's time, we like the idea of benefits
without the commitment of a relationship. But true prayer and genuine faith are not
casual affairs. They cannot be had in a frivolous relationship that offers gifts without
love. When we confuse the dynamics of real prayers of faith with the dynamics of a
divine friend with benefits, we are missing the whole point. We are praying a form
of self-love centered only on our own agendas while distancing ourselves from the
heart of God.

God promises to carry us from birth to death, to care for us the entire span of
our lives, tenderly and generously providing, protecting, nurturing, encouraging,
and even lavishing us with gifts of his favor. It's a wonderful offer, but it can't be had
casually. We can't flirt with his rivals and still claim to treasure him in our hearts.
We can't bow before the gods that satisfy our whims and still love and believe in the
God who fulfills our deepest desires. We have to choose, and there's really only one
choice that makes sense in the long run. We commit to love, know, and trust him
for a lifetime, and he carries us all the days of our lives in return.

God did not call us to be successful but to be faithful.

MOTHER TERESA

Keep Pressing Through

*I don't concern myself with matters too great or
too awesome for me to grasp.* **PSALM 131:1**

MOST PEOPLE OF FAITH have gotten mired in the deep questions and mysteries of prayer somewhere along the way. We've read the promises of Scripture and found them not to "work" quite as they seem. We've cried out to God and been left waiting, longing, begging for an answer. And when it's delayed, we've turned to our analytical brains to sort things out and to our gut emotions to complain about how unfair things seem to be. We sink deeper into the mysteries and rail against their heartlessness. Like infants who have suddenly decided we need to know how the universe works, we concern ourselves with matters too great and awesome for us to grasp.

Resist the temptation to "figure out" prayer—to know why, when, and how prayers will or will not be answered; to find the formula; to learn how to work the system. Such efforts will lead only to confusion, stress, and frustration. Do be diligent about discovering what God says about prayer—how you can align yourself with his purposes in it and receive what he wants to give—but don't get caught up in fruitless questions whenever something doesn't seem to make sense. Whenever you find yourself thinking, *It's not working*, pull back and remember that this is a relationship. It isn't meant to be "worked." It's meant to be enjoyed, explored, appreciated, and developed. Prayer and faith are products of that relationship, not tools to exploit.

David said he did not concern himself with things too weighty to understand. He had learned the futility of being burdened with God-sized mysteries. Far from advocating ignorance, he had made a conscious decision to choose trust. His choice, inspired by the Holy Spirit and incorporated into our Scripture, is an invitation for us to do the same.

In your life of prayer, you will find evidence against it at times, that it doesn't seem to make sense. Let your faith press through the contradictions. You are under no obligation to explain them. Simply believe. In time, your trust will be answered far more clearly than your questions are.

> Trust God where you cannot trace him. . . .
> The mystery is God's; the promise is yours.
>
> JOHN R. MACDUFF

Hearts at Rest

*I have calmed and quieted myself, like a weaned child
who no longer cries for its mother's milk.* **PSALM 131:2**

BABIES COMMUNICATE THEIR NEEDS by crying. It's the only way their hungry hearts and stomachs find expression. They remain unsettled until they are soothed. But over time, children learn to speak, express their needs, and wait without panic. Their parents' track record of providing for and nourishing them is enough to calm their nerves and instill patience. Children who have been cared for well don't wonder if they will be cared for in the future. They can rest in the assurance that help is coming soon.

When we are young in our faith and encounter needs, crises, and urgent situations, we cry out to God, sometimes in a panic, screaming for the problem to be addressed as soon as possible. We haven't had enough experience with the God who shows up in good time to calm our fears and soothe our anxious hearts. But over time, we learn to express our needs to him with confidence, wait for his answers to come, and be content in the time between the request and fulfillment. Why? Because we've learned something about him. We've seen him at work. We can rest in the assurance that help is coming soon.

Some believers learn that lesson early; others never do. But as we dwell in his presence, drink in his Word, immerse ourselves in his goodness, and follow the leading of his Spirit, we soon grow out of that state of panic so instinctual to infants, become trusting children, and then mature into patient adults. We recognize the movements of God and understand what a lack of movement might mean. We see the bigger picture and fix our gaze more on eternity than on time. Our hearts return to rest.

Make that your testimony. God understands our urgent pleas, and he addresses them urgently when he wants to. But sometimes he allows our needs to stretch us, expand our vision, and train us to rest in him. We mature into a life of calm assurance, where our prayers are uttered with confidence and our hearts are at peace. Instead of growing weaker over time, our faith grows stronger—and refuses to be moved.

> Stayed upon Jehovah, hearts are fully blest, finding,
> as he promised, perfect peace and rest.
>
> FRANCES RIDLEY HAVERGAL

New Hope Always

The story sounded like nonsense to the men, so they didn't believe it.
However, Peter jumped up and ran to the tomb to look. **LUKE 24:11-12**

ON THE MORNING OF THE RESURRECTION, several women went to Jesus' tomb only to find it empty. They were first confused, then informed by an angelic visitor that Jesus was no longer there, and then reminded that Jesus had foretold this event, albeit at a time when he had said many cryptic things they didn't understand. So they ran to tell the disciples, who had also heard Jesus' words about rising again, and most of them promptly rejected the report. In the short time between his death and resurrection, the disciples had allowed their expectations to be colored by disappointment and skepticism rather than hope and faith.

We do that too. We may begin with naive hopes and faith-filled anticipation, but many of us become disillusioned by the ways of God—those crosses that fill our lives with dark and disturbing evidence. But as it turns out, our naive hopes were on the right track. We may not have understood the path toward their fulfillment then, but we weren't wrong. Over time, if we continue living in expectant faith, we discover that our brushes with disappointment and skepticism discolor our vision of Jesus. We rediscover our hope.

In Luke's account of the Resurrection morning, the disciples' unwillingness to embrace a testimony of a miracle is remarkable. Perhaps this miracle seemed too far-fetched or too far removed from Jesus' many other miracles. But what does it say of our faith when we reject a testimony because it doesn't seem appropriate to our times, doctrine, or experiences? What is going on inside us when we hear glorious news and reject it because we didn't see it ourselves? It means we have lost the innocent optimism of newfound faith—and that we have to recapture it.

Don't become jaded. Yes, some reports of miracles are false, but many others are true. Believe them, embrace them, even choose to be naive about them, knowing you will sometimes be wrong. Your heart will be right, and your faith will be gloriously resurrected.

> I never have difficulty believing in miracles, since I experienced
> the miracle of a change in my own heart.
>
> AUGUSTINE

Forever Faithful

If we are unfaithful, he remains faithful,
for he cannot deny who he is.   **2 TIMOTHY 2:13**

GOD IS FAITHFUL. Unfortunately, we aren't—at least not always. We may be faithful to varying degrees and for certain lengths of time, but we aren't perfect. Our hearts are not yet fully mature, we have not yet fully removed every hindrance to the faith he has put within us, and we haven't yet lost the ability to sin. Even so, as Paul assured Timothy, God remains faithful. He can't deny who he is.

That doesn't mean God answers our prayers whether or not we believe his promises or that he continues to feed willful rebellion with his blessings. It does, however, mean that we base our faith on his nature, not ours—that we trust him because he is trustworthy, rest in his promises because of his integrity, and invest our entire selves in his commitment to us. We may stumble at times, perhaps even going through periods of questioning and holding weakly to our faith. But he remains faithful throughout. He is patient and kind because he is love, and love is always patient and kind (1 Corinthians 13:4). He walks with us throughout our journey of faith and carries us when we falter.

We therefore don't have to feel the pressure of developing perfect faith in order to receive God's good and perfect gifts. We can grow into it, knowing that our faith rests not in our own wavering spiritual maturity but in his constant character. He is always calling us forward in faith, so we are never to use his promise of faithfulness as an excuse to be faithless. But he is far more interested in the direction of our hearts than their perfection. Our inconsistencies have no effect on his unchanging covenant of love.

Pursue faith and faithfulness with all your heart, but give yourself the grace to pursue and believe imperfectly. God gives you that grace, and you are rightly agreeing with him when you apply it. Just as you can't force a tree to bear fruit, you can't force your faith to grow. You can only nurture it with the right conditions, and it will soon become all God intends it to be.

> What more powerful consideration can be thought on to make
> us true to God than the faithfulness and truth of God to us?
>
> WILLIAM GURNALL

Believing for Others to See

Jesus asked, "Will you never believe in me unless
you see miraculous signs and wonders?" **JOHN 4:48**

CRITERIA FOR FAITH make frequent appearances throughout the Gospel of John. Some people believe because of Jesus' miraculous signs, others refuse to believe in spite of them, some believe in order to receive them but then don't follow any further, and eventually some believe without seeing. That last response wins Jesus' highest praise (John 20:29), but he also accepts those who believe because they have seen. He understands that people often need demonstrations of power in order to recognize supernatural realities. But seeing is not the priority. Belief has to come first.

Skeptics say, "I'll believe it when I see it." The testimony of Scripture for those who already believe is that we will see it when we believe it. For us, seeing does come, but faith is very often the prerequisite, the key that unlocks the door of heaven, the human acknowledgment of who God is that prompts him to demonstrate the truth of our belief. Many unbelievers will never believe the logic of Christian apologetics or the heartfelt testimony of a changed life, but they will respond to a demonstration of God's supernatural power. Meanwhile, those who already believe are called to invest their faith on what remains unseen for now, knowing that their faith can be the catalyst for God's demonstrations. We do not depend on evidence to overcome our skepticism because our faith has already overcome. We become the testimony we want others to see.

Understand the role of unexplainable works in your life and in the lives of others. You do not need God to prove himself to you, but someone who doesn't know who he is just might. Let your faith in the unseen become a vehicle for their faith in the seen. Go out on a limb to pray for people's healing, provision, protection, and more. Don't be afraid that they will reject God if your prayers seem unanswered. They already don't believe; your prayers of faith may be the key that unlocks their heart. Pray for God's powerful works to demonstrate his kindness to those who don't know him and trust him to answer. In Jesus, he revealed his nature by responding to people's needs. Through your prayers, he still does.

Miracles are the great bell of the universe, which draws men to God's sermon.

JOHN FOSTER

"Even If He Doesn't . . ."

If we are thrown into the blazing furnace, the God whom we
serve is able to save us. He will rescue us from your power,
Your Majesty. But even if he doesn't . . . **DANIEL 3:17-18**

THREE JEWISH ADMINISTRATORS IN BABYLON refused to bow down to Nebuchadnezzar's golden statue. Shadrach, Meshach, and Abednego were threatened with their lives for not worshiping the king's image, but just as they could not eat foreign foods that violated God's commands (Daniel 1:6-16), they could not honor a foreign god—or a king who wanted to be honored as one. So they made their stand and took their chances with the king's threats.

These three men displayed a well-rounded faith—the kind that simultaneously holds belief in a certain outcome and trust in case of a different one. They boldly stated that God was able to save them and expected that he would. Yet they knew they had not been given a clear promise about surviving, and they trusted God anyway. Was this their time to be a testimony of salvation or of unwavering conviction even in death? Either way, their faith was a testimony, and either way, they knew God would take care of them. They believed he would save them but were prepared not to be saved.

That might seem like double-minded faith to us—like believing without really believing. But far from watering down their faith or hedging their bets, they were able to declare their absolute confidence in God while also trusting him regardless of the consequences. They added trust to their faith, insisting on believing in his goodness regardless of what happened.

When God gives you a specific promise with a clear outcome, it's important to believe what he said. That becomes the substance of a faith that doesn't hedge its bets. But when you are thrown into a situation without clear direction about what God wants to do, declare your faith anyway—faith for him to save, protect, deliver, heal, or whatever the situation demands, but also trust for him not to. Either way, you become a powerful testimony, and you can rest in the center of his will.

> All God's giants have been weak men who did great things
> for God because they believed God would be with them.
>
> **HUDSON TAYLOR**

Great Expectations

Daniel answered the king, "Keep your gifts or give them to someone else, but I will tell you what the writing means." **DANIEL 5:17**

DANIEL DIDN'T LACK CONFIDENCE. But his confidence wasn't in himself. He had a track record with God, past experiences that had convinced him that God would come through in times of need and reveal what he needed to know. Early on, after Daniel and his friends had demonstrated their faithfulness, God had given Daniel the ability to interpret visions and dreams (Daniel 1:17). That gift had proven reliable in interpreting Nebuchadnezzar's strange dreams, so Daniel knew it would apply when Belshazzar saw strange writing on the wall. It was a message of judgment, and Daniel wasn't afraid to declare it.

Joseph also had that confidence in interpreting dreams for Pharaoh (Genesis 41:16). David was sure he would see God's goodness in the land of the living (Psalm 27:13). A bleeding woman boldly pressed through crowds because she was convinced Jesus could heal (Mark 5:25-34). A Canaanite woman confidently pestered Jesus until he responded with a miracle (Matthew 15:21-28). A paralytic's friends were persistent enough to lower him through a ceiling to be blessed by Jesus (Mark 2:1-12). Peter insisted on a hope that cannot perish (1 Peter 1:4), and on and on the examples of holy resolve continue. Even people like Gideon who began in fear ended up with bold faith after God trained them in the art of believing by giving them experiences of answered faith. A mark of a true believer is the assurance that God is at work in his or her life and will certainly come through one way or another. Faith would sound like arrogance if it were based on self instead of God.

Your faith may begin tentatively and stay that way for years, but you can make a decision at any point to keep stepping forward in it until it becomes a bold assurance. Don't be afraid to trust God's leading or his promises. Let his words sink deep into your heart, develop a track record with him, and allow your experience to back your boldness. He does not waver in his commitments to you. Become unwavering in your beliefs about him.

> Assurance grows by repeated conflict, by our repeated experimental proof of the Lord's power and goodness to save.
>
> JOHN NEWTON

Complete Dependence

"It is beyond my power to do this," Joseph replied. "But God can tell you what it means and set you at ease." **GENESIS 41:16**

MOST OF US ARE AFRAID to stick our necks out—or, in this case, to stick God's neck out—like Joseph did after Pharaoh asked him to interpret his troubling dreams. But Joseph humbly disavowed any special ability of his own and put God's reputation on the line. If Joseph wasn't able to interpret the dreams, God would take the blame, and an opportunity to prove him in a foreign land would be missed. But Joseph had apparently come to understand his purpose in Egypt and why he had suffered all the adversity his brothers' betrayal brought to him. He remembered his earlier years, when God had given him audacious dreams and promises. If Joseph had spent his years in slavery and prison assuming those dreams were just a misunderstanding, he never would have been able to promise an interpretation to Pharaoh. But he believed that his times and purposes were still in God's hands.

The journey of faith will involve many more ups and downs than it already does if we spend much time wondering if we've gotten off track. God is sovereign over our circumstances and the path we've taken even if we think we missed key steps along the way. We don't have to come to him with a sterling record of listening for direction, innate abilities to do great works, or even a solid understanding of the gifts he has given us. We simply need to come with an understanding that wherever we are, he wants to use us in that place and in that moment to reveal something of who he is to the people around us. We can have the faith that he will show up if we defer completely to him and offer ourselves in his service.

Self-confidence is not an attribute of faith. Dependence is. Our greatest moments of faith come when we recognize God at work in our lives and say yes. We don't need to bring anything into that situation other than our willingness and confidence in him. He steps in to change lives, circumstances, and even nations.

> Complete weakness and dependence will always be the occasion for the Spirit of God to manifest his power.
>
> OSWALD CHAMBERS

Everything Until . . .

The one thing I ask of the LORD—the thing I seek most—is to live in the house of the LORD all the days of my life, delighting in the LORD's perfections and meditating in his Temple. **PSALM 27:4**

DAVID'S "ONE THING," his deep desire, is Exhibit A in the case that he was a man after God's own heart. He wanted to live in God's house for all his days, delighting in God's perfections and meditating in his Temple. It's a beautiful expression of worship and an example for God's people to follow. Our highest goal is to enjoy his presence.

Often missed in sermons and reflections on this verse is the fact that the Temple did not yet exist. David had wanted to build it, but God deferred it to the next generation. David's son Solomon would be the one to build and dedicate this monumental house of God, yet David still set his heart on meditating in it. The promise may have been deferred, but it was still his. He wrote a psalm of dedication for it (Psalm 30), gathered up materials, collected offerings, designed the blueprints, called the nation to pray for it, and offered God praise for it (2 Chronicles 29). He did everything he could do up to the point of stacking the first stones. Even though God had said yes to this prayer but no to its fulfillment in David's lifetime, David still insisted that he would see God's goodness in his lifetime (Psalm 27:13). Regardless of God's response to his deepest desire, he would not allow his vision of God to be clouded by disappointment.

Whatever your deepest desire is, your faith will pursue it as far as possible, whether God has said yes to it in your time or in his, now or in eternity. God values that response. He loves it when his people refuse an all-or-nothing approach to his answers and persist in what he has allowed. Faith may ask for the stars, but it still accepts crumbs from the Master's table, though he offers much more than that. Hearts of faith are grateful for his goodness in whatever form it comes. Focused not on his gifts but on him, they are therefore satisfied.

God denies a Christian nothing but with a design to give him something better.

RICHARD CECIL

Expecting Great Things

God raised Jesus Christ from the dead. Now we
live with great expectation.   **1 PETER 1:3**

PETER WROTE TO BELIEVERS dispersed throughout Asia Minor, challenging and encouraging them to live out their calling in trying times. He began with praises to God and superlatives about the salvation and inheritance we've been given, but tucked away in this glowing description of the glories of our faith is a brief comment, almost a passing phrase, about our response. It's preceded by a mention of the most trying time of all—the death of the Son. Because God raised him from the dead, we can now "live with great expectation." In other words, regardless of what is happening in your life and world, no matter how much destruction and death seem to hover as a threat, no matter what persecution and adversity you face, God has ultimate answers. The power of the Resurrection is still ours.

Peter should know. He denied Jesus during that unjust trial and fled before the Crucifixion, abandoning the Lord he had promised to die with, if necessary. In the darkest moments between the Crucifixion and the Resurrection, he had surely wondered if all hope was lost, if his years of following this amazing Master had been pointless, if he had chosen the wrong side of history. In later years, he would be beaten, threatened, and imprisoned, and he would follow the steps of Jesus to a cross. But if God could overcome everything Peter had experienced with a resurrection, what can't he overcome? What problem is too heavy? What nights are too dark? God raised Jesus from the dead; now we live expectantly because we know what he can do.

In fact, Peter knew from Pentecost onward the power of God at work in his people through the Holy Spirit. He had prayed prayers of faith and received their benefits on more occasions than he could count. He had seen God overcome unruly authorities and save Gentiles. God had given him every reason to live with expectation. He has given us every reason too. The life of faith is one of constant anticipation that we will see the goodness of God at work in our lives and our world. We live—and pray—in resurrection power.

Seek this power, expect this power, yearn for this power.
And when this power comes, yield to him.

MARTYN LLOYD-JONES

Restoring Thanks

Give thanks for everything to God the Father in the name of our LORD Jesus Christ. **EPHESIANS 5:20**

CORRIE AND BETSIE TEN BOOM WONDERED how they would survive the awful conditions of a concentration camp. But after reading Paul's instructions about giving thanks in everything, they realized that gratitude was a God-given tool. So they began thanking God for each other, for the fact that they still had a Bible, for other Christians in the camp, and for the cramped conditions that would allow more women to hear the Good News when they read from their Bible. But when Betsie thanked God even for the fleas, Corrie objected. She couldn't see how fleas could possibly be redeemable, how they could be a gift from God.

Much later, they realized why the room where they gathered and had the freedom to talk was not closely watched. The guards didn't want to go in because of the fleas. What looked like an unfortunate curse turned out to be a divine blessing. Many women had come to believe in Jesus in their barracks because the guards stayed away from the fleas.

God never tells us that we have to enjoy every aspect of life. He does tell us, however, that every circumstance can be turned around to serve his purposes and bless his people when we have enough faith and trust to thank him for them. He makes all things work together for the good of those who love him and are called according to his purposes (Romans 8:28), and those with thankful hearts can see that promise unfold in real time. Something significant happens in the spiritual realm when God's people devote themselves to thanks and praise. Dreadful circumstances become less dreadful. Sometimes they even change dramatically.

Devote yourself to gratitude and praise. You have nothing to lose and everything to gain. Negative perspectives discard the lenses of faith for less worthy views. Worship and thanksgiving restore them. For lives fruitful in prayer, this becomes not a season of the year but a lifestyle forever. And it delights God's heart and opens us to receive all the insight, fullness, and answers he wants to give.

One act of thanksgiving when things go wrong with us is worth a thousand thanks when things are agreeable.

JOHN OF ÁVILA

An Atmosphere of Thanks

*Sing psalms and hymns and spiritual songs to God with thankful
hearts. And whatever you do or say, do it as a representative of the
Lord Jesus, giving thanks through him to God the Father.*

COLOSSIANS 3:16-17

FOR MANY PEOPLE, gratitude seems like an afterthought, a reaction to something good rather than a prediction of it. Someone gives us a gift or does something
nice, and we say thank you in response. But as is often the case, the Kingdom of
God switches our expected order around. In the Kingdom, gratitude is meant to be a
continual attitude of the heart and the natural environment we live in. We don't just
say thank you for what God has done. We say thank you for who he is—all the time.

Sometimes we do thank God in advance because we know he is faithful and keeps
his word. Perhaps this is why Paul told the Philippians to fill their requests with
gratitude (Philippians 4:6). It may come as a surprise, but we're much more likely to
receive blessings of fulfillment from God by thanking him than we are by asking for
them. He invites our prayer requests, of course, but the climate of the heart is critical to what those prayers accomplish. If we're able to thank God ahead of time for
what he is going to do—even if we don't know exactly what that will look like—we
have come to a place of trust that delights him. And his delight provokes all sorts of
wonderful, encouraging responses.

Whatever it takes, cultivate gratitude. Let your days be filled with breaths of gratitude to God for whatever he has given you. If you have trouble thinking of things to
be thankful for, begin with the fact that you are breathing, with the beauty around
you, with the forgiveness he offers, and let your list build from there. Choose to focus
on blessings, privileges, and even the basics of life. The world is permeated with his
goodness, if you have eyes to see it. So is your life. Choose which eyes to see with, and
let gratitude become your constant environment. God fills that environment—and
our prayers—with his presence.

> Gratitude is not only the memory but the homage
> of the heart—rendered to God for his goodness.
>
> NATHANIEL PARKER WILLIS

The Faith of a Friend

Seeing their faith, Jesus said to the paralyzed man,
"My child, your sins are forgiven." **MARK 2:5**

WHEN YOU PRAY FOR SOMEONE, whose faith matters? Yours as the one who prays or that of the person who will receive the benefits of the answer? The answer in Scripture and history is varied. There have been times when ungodly kings or priests have prayed for people who believed God would answer, and their faith resulted in healing. There have been times when very godly, faith-filled people have prayed for unbelievers and miracles happened. In almost any situation we can think of involving the faith (or lack thereof) of the one praying and the one prayed for, we can find contradictory examples. Even Jesus seemed limited by the faithlessness of people in his hometown (Mark 6:5).

Scripture is clear that faith matters, and someone involved in the prayer must have it. But in the case of the paralyzed man whose friends brought him and lowered him through the roof to see Jesus, the focus is on neither Jesus' faith nor the paralytic's faith. It's on the faith of the four men who carried his mat and so audaciously found a way to get him in front of Jesus. That faith prompted divine forgiveness for the paralytic, an important and contentious discussion of Jesus' authority to forgive and to heal, and then the paralytic's actual healing. Spiritual and physical needs were addressed, an example of great faith was evident to all, and bad theology was corrected. All in all, it was a breakthrough moment for Jesus' ministry and certainly for this man's life.

But the friends who brought him got to see it all. They clearly believed Jesus could heal, and they went away even more convinced that Jesus could heal and forgive. They didn't sit back and assume that if God wanted to heal, he would open a way to Jesus. They were desperate enough on their friend's behalf to find whatever way they could. The walk home must have been an exuberant experience for all five of them. They worked hard to put their faith in a position to work, and they received the answer they were looking for and more.

> Faith is to prayer what the feather is to the arrow;
> without faith it will not hit the mark.
>
> J. C. RYLE

Increasing Faith

You faithless people! How long must I be with you?   **MARK 9:19**

A FATHER BROUGHT HIS SON TO JESUS and, in the Master's absence, asked some of his disciples if they could deal with the boy's affliction. Though the disciples tried to cast out the spirit, they couldn't. Jesus arrived at the scene, having come from a mountaintop where the veil of heaven was pulled back to reveal his glory and Moses and Elijah too, and the contrast between heavenly realities and earthly problems was stark. Jesus remarked sharply about the disciples' lack of faith and proceeded to evict the afflicting spirit from the boy. Then he told the disciples that this kind of spirit could only be cast out by prayer and (according to some manuscripts) fasting.

Whether Jesus was genuinely angry or playfully teasing his disciples for their feeble faith is impossible to discern in a written text, though the latter seems more in keeping with his patience and love. But regardless of his demeanor, his point was clear. The situation called for faith and prayer, and the disciples, though they had already seen plenty of signs and wonders and been sent to the villages and towns on a mission of miracles (Mark 6:7-13), weren't approaching it right. Apparently, they were surprised that they were unsuccessful too. Something in their faith, prayer, or resolve was lacking.

We might wonder, then, what Jesus would say to us about our faith. Having believed in his teachings, miracles, and promises, and having been "with" him in the power of his Holy Spirit ever since we believed, would he consider us "faithless" as he did the disciples? Would he display indignation, feigned or otherwise, over our feeble prayers and faltering faith? Would he marvel at how many problems, diseases, crises, and broken relationships we allow to remain around us? We hope not. But we suspect he might.

We know he loves us, of course. And we know he is still teaching us the ways of faith. But we also have to know that the things he taught the disciples also apply to us—that he did not suggest that prayers of faith were good for his times but not thereafter. So we press in, we believe, and we pray, "Lord, strengthen our faith."

The prayer of faith is rooted in the life of faith.

ANDREW MURRAY

Faith after Fear

Don't be afraid. Just have faith. **MARK 5:36**

THE LEADER OF A SYNAGOGUE pleaded with Jesus to come heal his daughter. But before Jesus could arrive, messengers came with word that the girl was already dead. Jesus calmly told Jairus, the father, not to be afraid but to have faith. Then he prohibited the surrounding crowds from following any further. Once at Jairus's home, he forcefully told hired mourners and skeptical crowds to leave, insisting that the girl was only asleep, not dead (Matthew 9:24-25). Only Peter, James, John, and the girl's parents were allowed in the room with him, and then Jesus raised the girl back to life.

Why did Jesus leave the first crowd behind and then evict the crowds that were gathered at Jairus's home? Why did he empty the room of mourners but allow his three closest disciples to go in with him? Did he simply want to work privately—a condition rarely duplicated at any other point in his ministry, when he was used to healing and delivering in front of multitudes? Or was something else at stake in limiting the audience for this particular miracle?

Perhaps Jesus wanted to remove skeptics and hired mourners because they contribute nothing to an atmosphere of faith. Maybe he wanted to work in front of people who could believe, who had seen his wonders before. Perhaps he wanted the girl to open her eyes to love rather than gawking spectators and mourners who now had no reason to keep working. Whatever the case, Jesus considered it important to shape the environment around him as he prayed, believed, and spoke life back into this girl.

Part of shaping that environment involved telling Jairus not to be afraid and sparking a hint of hope. The man had believed in Jesus enough to go find him but then had been disappointed enough to despair. Now he was being invited to see a great miracle and have his fears banished and faith restored. After a crushing loss, such a miracle might restore his hope forever—surely Jesus' goal for him, and for us, too. In your darkest moments, do not be afraid. Just believe.

> Faith given back to us after a night of doubt is a stronger thing, and far more valuable to us than faith that has never been tested.
>
> ELIZABETH GOUDGE

Open Records

She thought to herself, "If I can just touch his robe, I will be healed."
MARK 5:28

THE HEMORRHAGING WOMAN was apparently past her fears. For years, she had bled uncontrollably, and no doctors had been able to help. Her condition made her ritually unclean for Temple worship and offerings and likely resulted in some degree of social marginalization. Technically, she shouldn't have been touching other people, but she pressed through the crowds to get to Jesus, certain that if she could just touch the hem of his garment—likely the tassels of his prayer shawl, popularly called wings—she would be healed. *This really must be the Sun of Righteousness with healing in his wings* (Malachi 4:2), she must have thought. This was her chance to receive a touch from God.

She did receive a touch from God, and Jesus felt it. He could sense the power going out from him (Mark 5:30). He immediately wanted to know who had touched him, and the woman's fear returned. She pleaded for mercy and received it. Jesus blessed her and told her that her faith had made her well.

The story of the hemorrhaging woman is fascinating for many reasons, including the interplay between this woman's fearless faith and then fearful confrontation with Jesus. She thought her faith would be kept secret—that she would be healed without anyone noticing and then go on her way with a new life. But Jesus had something else in mind. Her story became an eternal testimony of his kindness, as well as an intriguing example of how his power works. Yes, faith had made her well, but so had the tassels she had touched and the power that flowed out from the Son of God. Her bold but secret faith turned into a spectacle that still encourages us today.

If you've ever wanted to have secret dealings with God in the realm of faith, you may need to prepare for alternate plans. He may be discreet with you, but he may turn his provision for your need into a testimony for others to see and hear. Our faith not only receives his works; it amplifies them for a wider audience. Faith begets faith as others see the invitation implied in it and respond. And many more receive the power of God.

Fear looks; faith jumps!
SMITH WIGGLESWORTH

Beyond Unbelief

*Because of their unbelief, he couldn't do any miracles among
them except to place his hands on a few sick people and heal them.
And he was amazed at their unbelief.* MARK 6:5-6

JESUS DEMONSTRATED AUTHORITY OVER NATURE by calming storms
and multiplying food. He demonstrated authority over diseases by healing the sick
with his words. He commanded demons to flee and, as he informed his disciples
and accusers, could have commanded legions of angels to come to his defense if he
wanted to. He saw into people's hearts, declared the future, and interpreted history as
something leading up to him. He walked in unison with the Father by doing whatever the Father did and saying whatever the Father said. He thoroughly demonstrated
that he was God incarnate visiting us in person.

Yet, according to this passage, he couldn't do many miracles in his hometown. It
wasn't because he didn't have authority or power or because he didn't want to. It was
because the people in Nazareth didn't believe. Theoretically, God incarnate could
overrule the faith of human beings and act autonomously. But whether by the terms
of his covenant with human beings or by his consistent preference to work in accordance with human faith, he generally doesn't do miracles on earth that no one asks
for or believes. Scripture is one long testimony of God revealing his will, prompting
human beings to ask for it, and then accomplishing it according to their requests
and faith. And that day in Nazareth, not many people were asking or believing. He
only did a few "ordinary" miracles, if there is such a thing. And he was amazed that
people didn't come to him asking and believing for more.

If that doesn't stir us to ask and keep asking prayers of faith, nothing will. The
idea that God is going to do whatever he wants to do regardless of our thoughts,
desires, prayers, and beliefs is undone in this passage. God has not put us on auto-
pilot to receive whatever he plans to give. When we wonder why he hasn't done what
we need, it's probably because we haven't asked or believed with persistence. So ask
and believe. Invite and expect his works. If he is amazed at unbelief, he is certainly
satisfied with faith.

> Thank God one day we will be done forever with unbelief.
>
> A. W. PINK

Simple Faith

Why do you have so little faith? MATTHEW 6:30

FRANCIS OF ASSISI WAS SAID to have preached to birds on occasion. He told them how they had the freedom to fly, were covered with layers of feathers to keep them warm, never had to sow and reap, and had an endless supply to eat and drink from the fields and rivers around them. He talked to them about the love the Father has shown them and warned them against the sin of ingratitude. He essentially turned Jesus' sermon about worry back toward them and showed how they and the wildflowers are clearly cared for by the God who watches over them. In so doing, he emphasized Jesus' point: that if such relatively minor figures in creation are cared for so well, why wouldn't we assume that human beings made in God's image are under his even greater care?

Still, many of us grow anxious when funds get tight, jobs are lost, the economy turns downward, unexpected expenses hit, and savings dwindle. In our biggest prayers, we ask God to give us huge gifts, grant great breakthroughs, bear substantial fruit, and open significant doors. But in trying times, our prayers grow small, almost as if we wonder whether he will help us survive without too much pain. Yet the psalmist said he had never seen the godly abandoned or their children begging for bread (Psalm 37:25), and Jesus pointed to birds and lilies as case studies in God's provision. We may go through trying times, but we have nothing to worry about.

In your prayers of faith for big things, don't forget to trust God for the little things too. Thank him for everything—each meal, each gust of a refreshing breeze, every beautiful scene, every gentle smile from a loved one, and anything else you can think of. Your practice of gratitude will remind you constantly that God has been with you every step of the way and filled your life with his touch. And your prayers for daily bread will touch his heart as profoundly as your prayers for the spiritual welfare of entire nations do. Learn to rest, trust, embrace peace, and live in freedom from anxiety. Your Father can be trusted and responds to your faith with love.

> He who gives you the day will also give you the things necessary for the day.
>
> GREGORY OF NYSSA

The Higher Will

I want your will to be done, not mine.   **LUKE 22:42**

JESUS TOLD US TO ASK FOR ANYTHING we want (John 15:7). Then he went out to a garden that same night and demonstrated a different kind of prayer: He prayed for what the Father wants. Actually, he *did* ask for what he wanted, but he followed it up with a submissive prayer to the higher will, the plans he already knew to be true. He sacrificed his preferences for God's purposes.

Submissive prayer is clearly not a sign of doubt or unbelief. It presents the Lord with a preference but also recognizes that our preference might not be the right one. Asking God for something specific when his will is already known is not a name-it-claim-it approach, as some people charge, nor is asking for the things we desire, which Jesus encouraged us to do. But submission is the background to all our prayers. If we ask anything that misses God's purposes, anything that is contrary to his will or his best for us, we submit to the better purpose. We pray for our desires, trusting that God has put them in our hearts, but we hold them loosely enough for God to redirect us if he wants. And when we don't know his will—or we have another preference and want to ask "if it's possible," as Jesus did—we simply say, "Your will be done."

At their core, our prayers of faith are meant to represent an alignment of our hearts with God's. Those who argue that our prayers are strictly a conformity to his narrow purposes, with no possibility of moving his heart, are missing his generosity in the relationship and denying both Jesus' words and biblical examples. Those who argue that our prayers of faith are all about our desires—that we simply name whatever we want and claim it by faith—are missing the transformation he offers and discernment between self-generated and God-given desires. Somewhere between, we align with his heart and he is drawn to ours, and we ask whatever we want with a desire to submit to his will above all else. We hold his promises tightly in faith and loosely in submission, both at the same time.

Our satisfaction lies in submission to the divine embrace.

JAN VAN RUYSBROECK

Be Specific

What do you want me to do for you? **MARK 10:51**

A BLIND BEGGAR SITTING by the side of the road was shouting at Jesus, and the crowd kept telling him to be quiet. But when people are desperate for help, they don't exactly listen to crowds. So Bartimaeus kept making a scene, more interested in his healing than his dignity. Eventually, Jesus turned his attention to the noisemaker and asked him a pointed question: "What do you want me to do?"

Jesus, who often saw clearly into people's hearts, asked a question anyone in the crowd could have answered. When a blind man is screaming for mercy, he obviously wants to receive his sight. Jesus wasn't blind to Bartimaeus's blindness, but he still wanted the prayer to be voiced. Bartimaeus had to make a request more specific than "Have mercy."

A principle of prayer is that faith comes before sight. With Bartimaeus, this was literally true. But a specific request had to come first. This passage from Mark teaches us a lot about prayer, including another lesson on the validity of being bold in our requests just as we've seen elsewhere in Scripture—earnest pleas, pushing through crowds, abandoning decorum, not taking no for an answer when we know our desire is within Jesus' power and will to answer, and "bothering" him with our shameless persistence. But we also learn that Jesus wants us to articulate our desires. He wants our prayers to be specific questions aimed at a specific response. He gets much more glory from fulfilling a particular desire than from showing general mercy in response to a general request. He wants us to recognize what he has done.

We don't always know what kind of answers to expect from God, when they will come, or how he will go about fulfilling our petitions. But when we have something specific in mind, he wants us to express it. Desire is not enough. It's a prompt, not a request. Hope is not enough. It's the expectancy we have in the process, not the means to an end. Prayer involves asking, and asking involves having an idea of what we want to happen. We submit that to God's will, but we still expect good things. If we want him to answer specifically, we have to ask specifically.

Many things are lost for want of asking.

ENGLISH PROVERB

The Fears Below

Would you like to get well? JOHN 5:6

THE MAN HAD BEEN LAME FOR THIRTY-EIGHT YEARS and, like many other sick people, was at the pool of Bethesda to be healed. Its waters were said to be especially effective when stirred, presumably at the touch of an angel. Yet this man was never able to get to the water first; in a rush for healing, the lame are at a competitive disadvantage. However long he had been positioning himself at the water's edge, he could never touch it at the right time. So Jesus asked if he wanted to get well.

Whenever Jesus asks an obvious question, we can assume he sees beyond the obvious. Clearly a paralyzed man at a pool known for healing waters would want to be able to walk again. So Jesus' question and this man's avoidance of giving an answer are revealing. The man had been waiting for healing but not close enough to the water to touch it. He was going through the motions of getting a miracle without expecting one. Though he wanted to get well, perhaps he was afraid of the radical change it would bring to his life.

The human heart often longs for change while being strangely attached to the status quo. We want something new but cling to the familiar because at least we know how to manage it. We tell God we want a radical difference but are intimidated by the possibility that he might actually answer. The consequences could be challenging. It's one of the reasons some people remain in abusive or oppressive situations. This is what they know.

It's important to look beneath the surface to whatever wounds and scars might be undermining our prayers of faith. If we have never known real freedom, healing, and joy—if our old identity still controls us—we will inch toward the new without genuinely seeking it. We might put ourselves in position for a miracle but never quite take the step or have the faith to get it.

Don't be afraid of the radical change Jesus offers you. Refuse to be stuck in the familiar. Wherever he leads, even into the unknown, is good. By faith, go there with him without fear.

> The best answer to fear is to have a firm grasp of
> what it means to be accepted by God.
>
> JOHN GUNSTONE

With New Eyes

"Please, sir," the woman said, "give me this water! Then I'll never
be thirsty again, and I won't have to come here to get water."
JOHN 4:15

JESUS HAD A FASCINATING CONVERSATION with a woman at a well in Samaria. At several points, he presented her with timeless truth, and each time, she brought the conversation back to immediate questions and needs. She was caught up in the novelty of a Jewish man speaking to her—a marginalized Samaritan woman—against all cultural protocol. Then she turned an obvious metaphor into a literal observation, then marveled at his prophetic insight, and took the opportunity to ask a controversial question that divided her people from his. Still, Jesus kept bringing her back to his true identity as an answer to her false one.

That false sense of identity—as a sinner, a lowly woman, a rival to Jews—blinded her until the piercing nature of Jesus' words broke through. That's often our story too. We see ourselves as stuck in sin, though we've been freed from its power and consequences; as weak in faith, though we have the presence and power of Christ within us; as flawed and tainted, though we've been resurrected to new life with Jesus. The examples could continue, but the point is the same: We have a hard time seeing past our old identity and embracing the new, just like the Samaritan woman did.

As a result, we often seek answers to the wrong questions, just as she did. We often talk to God from a limited sense of identity, just as she did. We often fail to see the enormity of his promises—things like living water and pure, true worship—as too far beyond us to grasp, and we bring them back down to our level, just as she did. But if our old identity continues to shape our faith and prayers, we have not fully embraced our new identity. Only when we radically change the way we see can we experience radically new faith—just as she did.

I have seen the hidden things of God.

CATHERINE OF SIENA

Praying from Above

He raised us from the dead along with Christ and seated us with him
in the heavenly realms because we are united with Christ Jesus.

EPHESIANS 2:6

BELIEVERS IN JESUS are citizens of heaven (Philippians 3:20). We have been raised up into new life with Jesus and are seated with him in heavenly realms—at God's right hand, far above all rulers, authority, and powers (Ephesians 1:20-21). This exalted position with him is not a far-off aspiration; we are in it already. In a very real sense, we walk in two realms simultaneously, living out our material lives on earth while spiritually inhabiting a supernatural Kingdom.

When we pray, then, why do we most often see ourselves as praying from earth to heaven rather than the other way around? Why do we envision ourselves speaking upward to God, asking him to pour the blessings of heaven into our earthly realm? Perhaps it's because we follow the instincts of virtually every religion, which almost always divides the universe into above and below, ourselves being below until we die. But if God has brought our citizenship in heaven forward—if we can go ahead and live from the reality of heaven long before our physical bodies die—we have the opportunity to envision, access, and pray for heaven's blessings with an eye on earth rather than praying as earthly citizens with an eye toward heaven.

What's the difference? That vision of our citizenship in heaven changes our perspective. We no longer see ourselves as reaching for something not quite attainable. We see it within arm's length, available for us not only to claim for our own lives but also to minister to earthly needs around us. Paul told us to fix our minds on things above, where Christ is, which is also where we are (Colossians 3:1-2), which means we can see ourselves as ministers of heaven's realities in earthly realms. In other words, we are no longer beggars; we are benefactors. And we are invited to pray with that authority as stewards of the great King. When we see ourselves for who we are, we pray with the faith of those who have already received and have plenty to share. And that changes everything.

> We talk about heaven being so far away. It is within
> speaking distance of those who belong there.
>
> D. L. MOODY

Guided in Prayer

Stand still and watch the LORD rescue you today. . . .
Tell the people to get moving! **EXODUS 14:13, 15**

AFTER MOSES LED THE ISRAELITES out of their captivity in Egypt and down a very unexpected path to the edge of a sea, many began to complain. They thought they were hopelessly trapped, but Moses boldly told them to be still and watch God work. Two verses later, God told Moses to tell the people to go forward.

The more we think about each of those instructions—the commands to be still in faith and to move ahead in faith—the more we realize how biblical both of them are. God often tells his people they will not have to fight a battle because he will fight it for them; all they need to do is stand firm. And he often tells his people to go forward, press ahead, take some kind of action in faith and watch circumstances bend to his purposes. There are even plenty of situations that involve in-between instructions—Gideon paring his army down to a mere three hundred to go into battle in faith, or people marching around walls as though everything depended on their marching but then standing back to watch the walls crumble as though everything depended on God. If we're looking for a formula for when faith involves standing still and when it involves advancing, we could get awfully confused.

That's why it's so important to be able to hear God's voice or sense his leading when we pray. We can't just rely on "the biblical approach" when several approaches are biblical. We have to learn to sense God's timing and direction to follow the scriptural approach he wants us to take—to know when to keep praying, rest in what we've already prayed, press in for more faith, or trust that our faith is already sufficient. There are times to wait for God to work and times to pray, speak, and act on what we believe.

Prayer is a dialogue, not a monologue, and we have to learn to listen. Ask God for that sensitivity, learn from him, and acquaint yourself with the movement of his Spirit. He will guide your learning and speak when you need to hear. Your prayers will align with his purposes in the moment.

Prayer is conversation with God.

CLEMENT OF ALEXANDRIA

In His Hands

The LORD himself will fight for you. Just stay calm. **EXODUS 14:14**

YOU HAVE CERTAINLY FOUGHT BATTLES, and you will likely fight them again. You may even be in the middle of one now. If so, you know how easy it is to feel isolated, abandoned, overwhelmed, and hopeless. Yet *hopeless* is not part of our inheritance. Neither are those feelings of isolation and abandonment. Yes, you may be overwhelmed with things too enormous for you to carry, but you don't have to carry them. God is infinitely larger than anything you are facing. Your battles are in his hands.

That theme comes up again and again in Scripture, and it is presented as a promise for those who have come to God in faith. We see it in many of Israel's battles, in the lives of its judges and kings, in the ministries of its prophets, and in the work of apostles and believers everywhere. Sometimes God requires his people to take a strategic position or a few steps forward. Other times he requires a choir of worshipers or a period of waiting. But it always involves faith. We don't see his presence in our battles and enjoy great victories by crossing our fingers and hoping he shows up. We see him and enjoy his victories by asking him to intervene and believing that he will. Then we ride out the chaos with peace and calm inside.

That isn't easy to do. The idea of God fighting our battles may sound easy, but it takes a lot of fortitude to trust that he is at work even when we don't see evidence of him. The Israelites at the Red Sea had not yet learned that lesson, and many were even willing to return to slavery instead of falling in defeat. Yet defeat was never in God's mind for them. And it's never in his mind for you. By faith, he is leading you onward into pleasant places.

God never tells us we will avoid all battles and experience no setbacks. He tells us that he is with us in the midst of those battles and setbacks to deliver us, defend us, and restore us. Don't assume he'll do magic tricks in your crisis, but do expect him to show himself strong on your behalf. Your heart can rest in his promise to fight for you.

Be still, my soul: your best, your heav'nly Friend
through thorny ways leads to a joyful end.
KATHARINA VON SCHLEGEL

Beyond Disappointment

We can rejoice, too, when we run into problems and trials,
for we know that they help us develop endurance. . . .
Hope will not lead to disappointment. **ROMANS 5:3, 5**

IN ENGLISH, *HOPE* HAS A BROAD MEANING. We hope our team wins, hope for great weather, and say, "I hope so," while shaking our heads in a gesture that indicates anything but hope. But, as we've seen, biblical hope is an expectation of what is certain to come in the future, an anticipation of what God has already placed on the timeline ahead of us, even as we wait to get there. Yet even with this kind of hope, when we believe God will do something but then discover he won't or is still holding it for long past the time we would like, we get discouraged. We wonder what went wrong. Our hopes end in disappointment.

How do we handle disappointment? We can't blame God—or at least in the depths of our souls, we know we shouldn't. Sometimes we blame others, resenting them for getting in the way. But mostly we blame ourselves, beating ourselves up for misunderstanding the dynamics of faith and sometimes vowing never to put our hearts out there like that again. Disappointment is a brutal kind of pain, and if we let it linger, we eventually have to numb our souls to its effects. We shut down our expectations and go through life without much joy.

We can trust God absolutely that, in the big picture, the hope he has given us will not disappoint. His promises of salvation, redemption, restoration, and ultimate joy are clear and unchanging. In that context, temporary disappointments along the way become much more manageable, especially when we use them for growth, endurance, and an opportunity to hope again. Like David, we can spend our lives preparing for the fulfilled promise, even though it may come to the next generation (see devotional reading for November 18). Like the disciples, we can go fishing until Jesus shows up again (John 21)—and we know he will. Whatever it takes, we lift our gaze and expect good things because God brings resurrection out of death, and his mercies endure forever. In his Kingdom, disappointment is temporary and hope lasts forever.

We must accept finite disappointment, but we must never lose infinite hope.

MARTIN LUTHER KING JR.

Remember

*The grass withers and the flower fades. But the word
of the LORD remains forever.* **1 PETER 1:24-25**

REMEMBER. That word represents a crucial foundation for faith. Through Isaiah, God told his people to remember the rock they were cut from—their ancestor Abraham, the promises God had given him, and the faith he lived by. Through psalmists and chroniclers, Israel was reminded again and again of the miracles God had employed to deliver them from Egypt, lead them victoriously into the Promised Land, and build their kingdom generation after generation. Through the writer to the Hebrews, Jewish believers in Jesus were reminded to look over their history and consider how faith had always involved patience and endurance. God's people have always been told to remember his works, his promises, and his faithfulness. Why this emphasis on remembering? Because if we don't remember, we have little to base our faith on. We need to look to the future with an eye on what God has already done.

Peter told his readers that their new life would last forever because it was based on God's Word, which unlike the grass and flowers will never fade away. Modern Christians often read promises about "new life" in terms of a salvation experience that gets us to heaven, but those promises involve an entirely new, holistic way of living—a new mode of existence, the way life plays out here and now, the dynamics of things like faith, patience, godliness, wisdom, power, and love *in this age*. The gospel of the Kingdom includes everything we need from God and all his purposes for us. Anything he says relating to Kingdom life and any promises he has made don't expire. The promises he gave the disciples are good today. The words inspired through the prophets have forever applications. The mission Jesus declared in Nazareth is still true. The "good news that was preached" to us (verse 25) covers a lot of territory.

Don't narrow God's words about salvation, eternity, faith, his mighty works, or anything else to a particular era, a specific sphere of life, or a certain kind of people. His words reveal his character, and his character applies always. His promises show us his purposes, and his purposes are still playing out. The stronger we want to believe, the more we will need to remember.

People need to be reminded more often than they need to be instructed.
SAMUEL JOHNSON

The Life of Faith

The righteous shall live by faith. ROMANS 1:17, ESV

PERHAPS THE MOST FOUNDATIONAL and oft-quoted verse of the Reformation can look quite different in its various iterations in Scripture. Depending on the translation, Romans 1:17 can mean that those who are righteous live by faith; that those who by faith are righteous will live; or that those who have faith will live righteously (or be counted as righteous). The order of the words can emphasize either faith, righteousness, or living, and in the various places in Scripture—Habakkuk 2:4, Galatians 3:11, Hebrews 10:38, and here in Romans 1:17—we suspect that God has in mind an entire way of life. Righteousness, faith, and life are all part of the same package.

The New Testament speaks of faith as our big-picture entrance into the Kingdom of God and our day-to-day relationship with God concerning guidance, prayer, promises, and responding to trials and temptations. We can be sure that God means for us to begin in faith, continue in faith, and be consummated in faith, with every aspect of our eternal hope and daily lives saturated with our belief that he is present, powerful, wise, loving, and always working for us, in us, and through us. In other words, no matter how much is going on in this verse and its interpretations, regardless of whether we are applying it to big-picture salvation or today's needs, faith is not just an attitude. It's a lifestyle.

A lifestyle of believing is continuous. We don't take breaks from faith. We have it at home with our families or friends, take it with us to school or to work, carry it along on vacation, apply it in the community, see the world through its lenses, incorporate it into our speech, and allow it to infiltrate every aspect of our lives. Faith is not something we do or say. It becomes who we are. It's why we call ourselves *believers*. We believe.

In all our talk in Christian circles about faith, it's easy to see it as a commodity. Resist that urge. Make it part of every breath, every thankful thought, every longing, every relationship, every word. In so doing, you will be righteous. And you will truly live.

> There is no more blessed way of living than the
> life of faith upon a covenant-keeping God.
>
> CHARLES SPURGEON

Find Rest

His faithful promises are your armor and protection. **PSALM 91:4**

AFTER THE FALL OF COMMUNISM in eastern Europe, many Christian believers came forward with stories of God's protection. They did not deny the severe abuses or extremely lean times they went through. But in spite of their troubles, they testified that God either sheltered them from the worst of offenses or gave them the strength to endure. He gave them faith *from* adversity or faith *in the midst of* adversity. He buffered them from the strategies of evil and, like good armor, absorbed the worst blows.

Times of adversity seem to come in waves, whether personally or on a large scale. We go through long seasons of relative peace and contentment punctuated with volatile seasons of social unrest, economic stress, wars and rumors of war, personal crises, political animosity, relational conflict, and more. At times we lament the turmoil swirling around us. At other times, it shakes us to our core, and we feel threatened and afraid.

The same was true in biblical times, when cities prospered for decades but then fell to a conquering tribe or empire. Families and communities were separated, sold into slavery, abused, exploited, or simply killed. Diseases appeared suddenly and spread quickly, devastating regions and generations. Yet even in that ever-threatening climate, God spoke words of comfort. He is faithful to his promises, and we can use them as our armor and protection.

Psalm 91 begins with one of those promises—those who live in the shelter of the Most High find rest in his shadow—and continues with encouraging words about God's protection all the way through. These are not just words of comfort to cheer us up. They are words of commitment from the God who watches over us. Yes, he may define *protection* a bit differently from our expectations, but the promise does not lose its meaning in the process. He means what he says. We can have faith even in the worst of times. His promises are still true. Believe them, invest your heart in them, and find your rest in them. His faithfulness never ends.

Be thou a bright flame before me . . . a guiding star above me . . . a smooth path beneath me . . . a kindly shepherd behind me, today and evermore.

SAINT COLUMBA

Sight Unseen

Jesus told him, "You believe because you have seen me. Blessed are those who believe without seeing me." **JOHN 20:29**

A FRIEND TELLS OF A LONG SEASON of believing God for something specific and, at several points, crying out in frustration to see the answer come. But God's soft voice always came back with a gentle reminder that this gap between promise and fulfillment is what faith is all about—the assurance of things not yet seen. Of course, if answers remained forever unseen, there would hardly be any point. A time of fulfillment *does* actually come. But until it does—and that can take a really long time in some journeys of faith—we have to remember the conditions of faith. We rarely see the answer with natural eyes until we have "seen" with spiritual eyes. Just imagining the end is not enough; actively envisioning the answer as a certainty before it comes (assuming God has guided us into it) cultivates the faith we need to see it in the spirit before we see it in the flesh.

Thomas refused to believe in Jesus' resurrection until he saw Jesus and his wounds with his own eyes. Jesus' response to him became a call to believe for every generation after (with some exceptions, as in the case of Paul, who actually saw Jesus with his own eyes). This passage refers primarily to big-picture faith in the resurrection of Jesus as the Son of God and the salvation that comes through him. But as we've seen, faith is not separable into faith for salvation and faith for other things. It's all part of the same package. Though we haven't seen Jesus' resurrected body walking around on earth giving sight to the blind, cleansing lepers, and raising the dead, we can still believe all of it. That's the point of faith. It's the assurance of things hoped for and evidence of things not yet seen (Hebrews 11:1). We see Kingdom realities with eyes that are learning to envision in new ways.

You will spend the rest of your life honing this sense of spiritual vision. That's expected. But it's also essential. You cannot live the life of faith without it. You can hope for things and trust God vaguely, both of which are significant. But deep, lasting faith comes with the art of envisioning. Unlike Thomas, choose to believe without seeing, but *see* with your believing. Jesus blesses those who do.

Detachment from visible things is to open your eyes to the invisible.

JOHN CLIMACUS

Sanctuary of the Heart

*Guard your heart above all else, for it determines
the course of your life.* **PROVERBS 4:23**

THE WRITER OF HEBREWS repeatedly warned his readers not to turn back
from the faith they had once embraced. He was speaking of the Christian faith as a
whole, of course, but he made reference to the Israelites in the wilderness, a generation of God-followers who complained about their hardship and missed out on the
promises God had given them. The writer consistently contrasted the disappointments and devastations of unbelief with the mighty works and glories of belief, citing
numerous Old Testament heroes as examples of how to persist in faith regardless of
the adversity that comes against it. His words are a case study in how to saturate our
minds in the language of promise.

The proverb tells us to guard our heart above all else because it will determine the
course of our lives. That is nowhere truer than in the area of faith. If we entertain all
the reasons we shouldn't believe, we will end up not believing. If we carefully cultivate
the seeds of faith that have been planted within us, we will end up with the fruit
of faith. It's actually a choice, not a destiny. Unbelief doesn't just happen to us. We
choose it moment by moment, word by word, day after day. It is up to us to reverse
that trend and choose a better path.

Are you taking in thoughts of unbelief? Staring at evidence that is contrary to
your faith? Drinking in the arguments of "common sense" that weigh against the
unexpected goodness of God? Then you are allowing dirty water into your heart,
and it is not a good mix for the rivers of living water God brings up from within
you. Your vision of faith will likely become corrupted and confused. If you take in a
steady diet of spiritual junk food, your spiritual health—and your pure faith—will
be compromised. There's nothing wrong with being reasonable, as long as reason
doesn't corrupt the words God has given you. But reason together with him (Isaiah
1:18, ESV). Let him inform your faith. Fertilize those seeds and give them room to
grow. Guard your heart as a sanctuary of genuine faith, and genuine faith will reap
its harvest in your life in due time.

The heart has eyes that the brain knows nothing of.

CHARLES HENRY PARKHURST

Guided by Faith

They headed north for the province of Bithynia, but again the Spirit of Jesus did not allow them to go there. **ACTS 16:7**

AMY CARMICHAEL FIRST GAINED ministry experience in the slums of Belfast. Then she applied to the China Inland Mission but was denied because of her health. She then enlisted in the Church Missionary Society, which sent her to Japan, but after a time, her health forced her to return to England, where she almost decided she was never meant to be a long-term missionary. But an invitation to Ceylon (now Sri Lanka) and then to southern continental India began a fifty-five-year career in life-transforming, society-changing service. God had shut doors and opened them to get her to the place where she would have her most fruitful service.

Paul and his companions were twice redirected from the route they had planned to go—we don't know specifically how, only that it was a matter of the Holy Spirit's direction—and soon found themselves entering an open door to European regions they had not yet considered. Whether they felt frustrated at the time isn't clear. But they ended up being grateful for God's leading. Their new direction shaped history in ways they could hardly have imagined.

As much as we want clear direction from God telling us where to go and when—and he does give us that at times—he often uses the process of shutting and opening doors to direct us. It can be a frustrating experience if we don't trust him in the process, but when we do, we find ourselves serving in the most fruitful, rewarding places. By faith, we take the next step—and the next and the next. We may long for the entire road map, but in his wisdom, God often gives us only the next turn, and then sometimes only after we think it's too late. If we ever take a moment to look back, we realize that he has always been leading us, even when we weren't aware. Our faith at times has resembled vague trust, but he has responded to it just as well. Believing he is the Lord of our steps, we find they turn out to be well-directed.

> I know not the way God leads me, but well do I know my Guide.
> MARTIN LUTHER

347

Worship as Faith

Around midnight Paul and Silas were praying and singing hymns to God, and the other prisoners were listening. ACTS 16:25

IT TAKES A LOT OF FAITH to worship when you've been unjustly accused, attacked, beaten, bound, and left to contemplate your offenses in jail. But that's what Paul and Silas did. We don't know if they were praying for deliverance (no hint of that sort of petition is mentioned), but we do know they were not concerned for their deliverance. They understood that God was in control. After all, he had beckoned them into Macedonia through a vision, given them a reception in Philippi with God-fearing women gathered at the stream, and worked his power through their ministry, declarations, and demonstrations of deliverance for spiritual captives. What could possibly go wrong in that day's riot and that night's imprisonment? Through eyes of faith—nothing. So Paul and Silas worshiped at the top of their lungs.

God honored their faith with a dramatic release, the conversion of a jailer and his family, and a citywide testimony that vindicated them and their cause. They still had to leave town—nobody under the watch of Rome likes a riot—but their point was made and a church was established. By shifting their focus from their own problems to the glory and majesty of God, they remained at peace in their hearts above their circumstances. They brought heaven's environment into their earthly surroundings, and God worked mightily through them. They insisted on the character and nature of God regardless of what their eyes—and their bruises and broken bones—told them.

If every believer approached their trials with the same response, the world would be radically transformed. That's because the church would be radically transformed, and observers would be amazed. Not everyone would be converted, to be sure; many reject even the most obvious testimonies. But faith would do its work by inviting God into the world's worst offenses. And anyone with half a heart to believe would be moved to embrace the God who invades the lives of his people.

To believe God is to worship God.

MARTIN LUTHER

Beaten, Bruised Faith

Though he slay me, I will hope in him. JOB 13:15, ESV

JOB THOUGHT HE HAD BEEN beaten up by God. From all appearances, the hand of the Almighty was against him. He didn't see the divine controversy behind the scenes that provoked his time of testing, but even if he had, he might have said the same thing. After all, the vagaries of circumstance and the strategies of spiritual adversaries still have to answer to a sovereign God. If Job hadn't been beaten up by God, he had been beaten up by forces that God had allowed. Regardless of the cause, he saw himself on the Creator's bad side.

That's easy to do. When we encounter spiritual resistance, circumstantial misfortune, pointed opposition, or what the world calls plain bad luck, we start to feel as if God is no longer on our side. Even when we remain on his side—though we can all think of times we've failed—we start to wonder if his promises for those who believe still apply to people like us, who believe only weakly at times. A round of illness, a season of conflict, a string of setbacks, a few days of bad moods or bad weather—literally or figuratively—can throw us into an existential crisis. We wonder what we've done wrong. And if we can't think of anything important enough to provoke this kind of divine response, we wonder if God has abandoned us.

He hasn't, of course. Faith sees through this kind of fog, even when it sees only vaguely. Job went on to say that he would argue his case before God—a statement no human can make without trust in the Almighty's character, mercy, and love. We cannot proceed into this courtroom without confidence in who God is. We have to know he is on the side of justice and love—and forgiveness for when things go wrong.

That's faith. Even when the world is crumbling around us, we can trust and believe in the God who loves us. Even when nothing makes sense, we can envision mercy and restoration in times to come. The prayer of faith banks on such things; the heart depends on them as life itself. And God responds—in time—with abundant blessings and grace.

> All our difficulties are only platforms for the
> manifestation of his grace, power, and love.
>
> HUDSON TAYLOR

Life Restored

*Speak a prophetic message to these bones and say, "Dry bones, listen
to the word of the LORD! This is what the Sovereign LORD says: Look!
I am going to put breath into you and make you live again!"*
EZEKIEL 37:4-5

SOMETIMES WE LOOK ACROSS THE LANDSCAPE of our past and wonder
if God can bring it to life again. And sometimes we hope he doesn't. The idea of our
past revisiting us is just too painful. But God is all about restoration, and he promises
to restore lives, rebuild city walls, renew minds, and redeem mistakes. He makes *all*
things work together for the good of those who love him (Romans 8:28). He is the
God of resurrection.

Ezekiel looked across Israel and Judah's past and was commanded to declare the
restoring, life-giving breath of God into it. Dry bones would get up and grow flesh
again. The raw materials of life would become new. He was then told to speak to the
winds to fill those restored bodies with breath and movement and power. The Spirit
of God came in power and initiated a new genesis. Life itself became new. What
seemed to be dead really wasn't. What seemed to be lost was made even better than
before. That's the nature—and the promise—of our God.

What losses litter the landscape of your life? Don't give them up as losses. At
any point in your life of faith—and, if you are willing, in many—you can ask God
to breathe on the prayers and service you have already given. What looked like the
ruins of futility might grow into new structures and forms. What seemed fruitless in
the past may be latent seed that can still grow up and produce a great harvest. What
seemed to be missed opportunities may appear again as open doors in front of you.
Again, that's the nature—and the promise—of our God.

The life of faith never leaves death in the past and moves on. It never counts bad
mistakes and misguided beliefs as wasted time. It doesn't write off its losses or forget
its tears. It looks to the God who breathes new life into old promises and says, "Live."
And it is rewarded with continual, satisfying restoration.

The house of my soul . . . is in ruins. Restore it.

AUGUSTINE

Ready to Receive

If you are untrustworthy about worldly wealth, who will
trust you with the true riches of heaven?   **LUKE 16:11**

IMAGINE A FATHER WHO WANTS TO GIVE his son everything he desires but then observes his son mishandling almost everything he is given. No wise father would continue pouring out such generosity and wealth—not because he loves his son less, but because his son needs to learn a few good lessons. Responsibility managed well results in greater responsibility. Responsibility managed poorly results in less responsibility.

If you've ever wondered why God seems to be withholding his most generous blessings, consider this possibility. It applies in spiritual, material, and relational areas of life. If you've mismanaged whatever worldly goods you have, why would the Father pour answers to your prayers into your life, knowing you have no means for dealing with them? He wouldn't. He will spend some time—as much as needed—training you for better things to come.

Many undisciplined souls have asked God for blessings that require disciplined stewardship. As much as God wants to answer your faith, he doesn't want to ruin your life. Prayers for relationships depend on stewardship of your relationships; prayers for material goods depend on stewardship of your material goods; prayers for fruitfulness and meaning depend on your handling of fruitfulness and meaning. And your greater prayers for deep spiritual blessings? They depend on all of the above. A good steward can expect more; a bad steward has some growing up to do. The Father still wants to give, but he is a master of timing.

As you pray in faith, also pray with a sense of responsibility. Make any adjustments necessary to demonstrate your readiness for more. God is on your side. But that also means he guards your weaknesses. Strengthen them, grow in faith, and receive in the wisdom of his timing.

> The most important thought I ever had was
> that of my individual responsibility to God.
>
> DANIEL WEBSTER

The God Who Gives

God is the one who provides seed for the farmer and then bread to eat.
In the same way, he will provide and increase your resources and then
produce a great harvest of generosity in you. 2 CORINTHIANS 9:10

"YOU CAN'T OUTGIVE GOD." It's a common saying among those who have increased their giving over time. They have found that the more they inch up their donations to Kingdom-oriented ministries, the more God inches up—or pours out—his abundance on them. This is no formula, of course; otherwise, people would be giving in order to get. But it is a biblical principle that generally proves true. The cycle of giving begins with God's generosity, which results in ours, which prompts a response from God in increasing measure, which prompts a response on our end in increasing measure, and on and on it goes.

It makes sense, doesn't it? This is how planting and harvests work on the farm. It's also how we become apples who haven't fallen far from the tree, the image of our generous Father who wants us to give in the same spirit that he gives—cheerfully. Paul wrote that God loves a cheerful giver (verse 7), and he used the same word we get *hilarious* from. God loves those who laugh because of their overwhelming joy when they give. We join in his cycle of generosity when we take what he has given and spread it to others with the same generosity of spirit he has shown us. God gives more to those who give more.

The same principle is true in the realm of prayer. Answered prayer comes more readily to those who will do something fruitful with the answers. If you are known as a sower, you can expect an increase to your seed. If you pray for opportunities for fruitfulness, you will need to be fruitful in them to benefit yourself and others. If you pray for more financial resources, you need to be the kind of person who handles financial resources in God's ways. If you pray for lasting, eternal value, invest it lastingly and eternally. God provides seed and growth and abundance for those who sow in generosity and faith and gratitude.

A man there was, though some did count him mad;
the more he cast away, the more he had.

JOHN BUNYAN

Above the Details

The LORD said to Moses, "How long will these people treat me with contempt? Will they never believe me, even after all the miraculous signs I have done among them?" NUMBERS 14:11

THE ISRAELITES DELIVERED FROM EGYPT knew they were headed to a land God had promised. They followed God's guidance because they believed, though slowly and with some miraculous convincing. They received his laws, won decisive victories, were fed with bread from heaven, and envisioned the joy of living in their own land. But they didn't know the details of entering the land. So when scouts came back with a report that the land was inhabited by strong people, most of the Israelites forgot all about the promise and instead focused on the difficulty. Their vision of defeat became bigger than their vision of fulfillment.

Anyone who has clung to a promise from God knows that temptation. When we start to look at the details, we start to lose faith. We get caught up in the *how* of God's purposes and begin to lose faith that he will accomplish them. If we don't train ourselves to focus on the promise and the Promiser rather than the details of arriving where he has called us, we will most likely give up before we ever arrive.

When you see the beginnings of an answer from God, resist the tendency to notice what is still left to be done. Those details are much less important than the fact that God is already at work. Go overboard in giving thanks for the portions of the answer you have already seen. As when Jesus gave thanks for the loaves and fishes before multiplying them, our gratitude magnifies the progress we have experienced, just as our complaints or laments magnify the progress not yet made.

When you see any hint of an answer from God, refuse to give him more step-by-step instructions. Cover that partial answer with gratitude. Bless it, gaze at it in awe, and rejoice that things are happening. A focus on what God has done rather than what he hasn't done reorients our vision. It's part of the process of receiving by faith. It trains us emotionally to steward the small gifts well so we can steward the large gifts well too. It undoes our worries and increases our faith. And it honors the promise God has given.

Worries just don't matter. Things really are in better hands than ours.

DIETRICH BONHOEFFER

Holy Confidence

*My heart is confident in you, O God; no wonder I can sing
your praises with all my heart!* **PSALM 108:1**

JIM ELLIOT, ONE OF THE MISSIONARIES killed in the 1950s after making
land contact with the Huaorani people of Ecuador, made a profound statement
that continues to inspire many: "He is no fool who gives what he cannot keep to
gain that which he cannot lose." This statement gained even more impact after his
and his colleagues' deaths. They knew their mission was risky but were willing to
make the ultimate sacrifice for it. No one says such a thing—or backs it up with his
life—without supreme confidence in God, his ability to protect and deliver, and his
promises for eternity. Only someone who trusts God implicitly can sing his praises
in the face of such danger.

Confidence in God is part of the inheritance of all who believe in him. Paul
demonstrated this throughout his ministry. He got up and walked back into a city
immediately after being dragged out of it, stoned, and left for dead (Acts 14:19-20).
He told the Philippians he was confident that God would complete his work in
them (Philippians 1:6). And he told Timothy that in spite of suffering in prison, he
knew the one he trusted and was confident God would guard his work to the end
(2 Timothy 1:12). He understood that we don't just believe in God for the things he
can give us. We invest our hearts in his eternal purposes. We trust him with our lives.

Live with that inheritance in mind. Don't hold back in the life of faith. You've
been bought with a price (1 Corinthians 6:20), and you've been given multiple
assurances that God is watching over you, guiding you, listening to your longings
and prayers, protecting you from ruin, and teaching you through all of life's ups and
downs. All that's left is to have confidence in him and sing his praises. Even your
hardest experiences will soften when you do, and the joy of being his beloved child
and friend will keep coming irrepressibly to the surface. You will live with confidence
when you've placed your trust in him.

> Wherever you are, be all there! Live to the hilt every
> situation you believe to be the will of God.
>
> **JIM ELLIOT**

Holy Stubbornness

Let's not get tired of doing what is good. At just the right time we will reap a harvest of blessing if we don't give up. **GALATIANS 6:9**

WHEN SINGLE WOMEN BEGAN APPLYING for missionary service in the 1800s, many men who led mission organizations were reluctant to accept them. Over time, they did, but single women were often resisted at mission stations on the field. The attributes that qualified them for service—persistence, assertiveness, outspokenness, and an adventurous and independent spirit—were apparently the same attributes that rubbed fellow missionaries the wrong way. Maude Cary was often called prideful in her early years in Morocco.[6] Lottie Moon repeatedly felt the need to insist on equality in the work assigned to her in China.[7] Isobel Kuhn was at first considered "likely to be a troublemaker."[8] Women like these felt it necessary to pray persistently and faithfully on two fronts: that God would use them to reach people with the gospel and that they would be accepted by fellow believers.

Those prayers were eventually answered on both fronts. These single women missionaries became fruitful in their ministries, sometimes after years of hard work in difficult fields, and were eventually accepted as significant, even indispensable colleagues. At certain times—during the world wars, for example—they were the only missionaries "manning" the stations and keeping the work alive. What had begun as a slow and controversial practice in missionary recruitment developed into a mainstay of missionary service. God backed them up with his presence and power, even in those early years when he may have seemed far away.

If we want not only to pray with faith but also to dedicate our lives as offerings of faith, we will need a holy stubbornness to continue the work God has given us and to believe in spite of contrary and adverse situations. God never promises easy roads for those who follow him, and sometimes the difficulties come within our own camp. But he does promise to be the Lord of the harvest, and in time, our faithfulness reaps its rewards. We bring to him our weakness; he gives us his strength. And one way or another, his work in us proves fruitful.

It is indeed a wonderful story. . . . We began in weakness, we stand in power.

HELEN BARRETT MONTGOMERY

A Living Sacrifice

I plead with you to give your bodies to God because of all he has done
for you. Let them be a living and holy sacrifice—the kind he will find
acceptable. This is truly the way to worship him. **ROMANS 12:1**

JOHANNA VEENSTRA LEFT the "bright lights and gay life" of New York City in 1919 to serve at a mission station in Nigeria, where she encountered swarms of white ants and bothersome rats and bicycled across rough terrain from village to village. But this service was an answer to her prayers of faith, and she successfully preached, did medical work, and started schools for training evangelists. Today, a seminary in Nigeria is named in her honor. She gave herself for a God and a people she loved.⁹

Veenstra's friends back home and her biographer marveled at this life of sacrifice, as friends and biographers tend to do. But for a person who trusts God to fulfill his calling and watch over those he loves, such sacrifices hardly seem sacrificial at all. Paul urged Roman believers to offer themselves to God as a living sacrifice and a continuing act of worship. The life of faith will not say no to that offering, especially in light of the offering God has given us in the sacrifice of his Son. When we come to him in faith, it is not because we want to do him a favor. It's because he is our source of life, our faithful friend, our gentle and powerful Lord, and the lover of our souls. What kind of sacrifice is that? It's actually a pleasure to give.

It's essential to make the offering of our lives to him the context for our prayers of faith. We do not come to God to attempt to make him our servant. We come as his servants, as well as his children, followers, friends, and beloved companions who have given our hearts to him. Our prayers themselves become sacrifices of worship; we join our desires with his to further his purposes in our lives and world. They are a pleasing aroma (2 Corinthians 2:15; Revelation 5:8) and represent a longing to fit ourselves into his plans. And he works his gifts and blessings into the lives we have offered.

> There has been no sacrifice, because the Lord Jesus
> himself is my constant companion.
>
> JOHANNA VEENSTRA

Faith from the Depths

Deep calls to deep at the roar of your waterfalls; all your
breakers and your waves have gone over me. **PSALM 42:7**, ESV

JONAH WAS THROWN INTO THE SEA by people who were certain he was the cause of the storm. While in the belly of a fish, he cried out to God for rescue. He had been resistant to the mission God had given him, and even after carrying it out, he was confused and resentful about its outcome. Yet in this terribly disorienting time, when little seemed to make sense, Jonah offered God the faith he had and was used for God's gracious purposes.

The psalmists capture those times of distress and the disconcerting ways of God. Prayers of faith are not nearly so confident in those seasons of life. Sometimes all we have to offer him are sobs of hope and pleas for mercy. Yet even in our distress, we can know he hasn't abandoned us. We can take comfort in the stories of Jonah, Joseph, Job, David, and many other psalmists and prophets of God. Like Peter, Paul, Silas, and others who were in prison, we can lift up our praises in spite of our circumstances rather than because of them. In the depths of our souls, we can return to our knowledge of who God is and trust that his plans for us are good.

Even so, there will be times when we feel as if all of God's waves have pulled us under, and all we can do is cry out from our depths into the depths of his bottomless love and mysterious ways. There's no shame in that. Sometimes the hints of faith in those moments are more honoring to him than the shouts of faith in less troubling times. Though the next verse of this psalm doesn't completely pull us back to the surface, it does give us a lifeline to cling to: "By day the LORD commands his steadfast love, and at night his song is with me, a prayer to the God of my life." No matter how deep we've gone, we can know he is with us. Whatever faith we have, we give to him. Whatever prayer we call out, he hears it. And whatever season we're in, he answers.

Faith is the subtle chain which binds us to the infinite.
ELIZABETH OAKES SMITH

Enduring Well

Because of the joy awaiting him, he endured the cross, disregarding
its shame. Now he is seated in the place of honor beside God's throne.
HEBREWS 12:2

ATHLETES ENDURE LONG YEARS of early-morning training, intense work-
outs, and seemingly endless exercise repetitions for a shot at a championship or
Olympic medal. People trying to get in shape submit to rigorous diets and exercise
programs for the health and look they want. Scholars spend years in arduous research
for the great discovery or paradigm-shifting publication they have set their hearts on.
We understand the need for sacrifice in order to reach a greater and higher good. It's
built into our nature.

Jesus willingly suffered the torture, humiliation, and separation of the Cross in
order to experience the endless honor and glory to follow. It's true that he sought
another way in his fervent prayer the night before, but the emotion of joy at the
end of the journey outweighed the emotion of fear at the front of it. The writer of
Hebrews used that focus as an example for Christians who were entertaining second
thoughts about the faith they had initially embraced. Jesus kept his gaze on the prize,
and that was enough for him to run the race with endurance.

In our prayers of faith, some of which can take years and involve confusing and
challenging turns, we will need the same focus—not just on the answer itself but on
the joy and satisfaction of the answer. The journey can be demanding, but the end
is exhilarating. The more we can emotionally, mentally, expectantly put ourselves
in the place of having already received—celebrating, laughing, rejoicing, and giving
thanks for the fulfillment—the more we will be able to persist in faith. It's part of our
Kingdom vision. We can endure a lot when we are focused on the prize.

Just as God told barren women to rejoice over their coming children (Isaiah 54:1)
and invited a celebration of beauty and praise instead of ashes and mourning (Isaiah
61:3), he tells us to fix our vision by faith on the joy set before us—in the grand
scheme of eternity and the prayers of our passing lives. All faith in him ends in glory
and is very much worth the journey.

You can fight with confidence where you are sure of victory.
BERNARD OF CLAIRVAUX

Prayers of Blessing

*May the LORD bless you and protect you. May the Lord smile on
you and be gracious to you. May the Lord show you his favor
and give you his peace.* **NUMBERS 6:24-26**

EVERY DAY, WHETHER IN PERSON or through an audiovisual medium, you
encounter hundreds, perhaps thousands of people who need a touch from God. You
may not know the troubles and questions beneath the surface—the traumas a person
is carrying or the disappointments he or she has suffered—but you can assume they
are there. Everyone has them. Some deal with them in the context of their relationship with God. Others don't even know if God exists. All of them need his touch.

Through prayers of blessing, you have an opportunity to give it to them—to set
them up for some kind of divine encounter, whether subtle in the depths of their
spirit or dramatic in the circumstances and messages they hear. History is full of stories of those who have suddenly sensed his presence, completely changed their minds
about him at a word, or woken up in the middle of the night knowing a change
of direction in their lives is needed. In most cases—probably all of them—such
encounters have come because someone prayed. When God's people bless others in
their prayers, things happen.

That's why God instructed Aaron to bless the people of Israel in his name and
promised to honor the blessing. We aren't limited to these words when we pray for
God to bless people, but they make a good start. Sometimes such words are best
spoken directly to the people we want to bless; more often, they are conversations
between us and God about filling lives with his goodness. If his kindness leads to
repentance (Romans 2:4), why wouldn't we want everyone to experience it, even
(or especially) those who are thorns in our side? If we bless indiscriminately, many
people will.

That's our calling, even with people who are least worthy of a blessing (Romans
12:14). Our words and prayers are the means by which his grace is applied in the
hearts and lives of other human beings. It's a golden opportunity, and many people
miss it. By faith, we can pick it up and change the world.

Until we meet again, may God hold you in the palm of his hand.

IRISH BLESSING

Jesus the "Yes"

The Holy Spirit was upon him and had revealed to him that he would not die until he had seen the LORD'S Messiah.   **LUKE 2:25-26**

SIMEON HAD RECEIVED A PROMISE FROM GOD that he would not die until he had seen the Messiah. So when the Holy Spirit led him one day to the Temple in Jerusalem, he knew to keep his eyes open. There he saw a young couple presenting their first child to God and was drawn to them. He held the child in his arms and blessed him. He knew he was holding the salvation of Israel and a light to the Gentiles. He thanked God for fulfilling the promise and said he was ready to die in peace.

A prophetess named Anna was also there. She was always there, worshiping in the Temple through the many years since her husband's death. When she saw Simeon with Joseph, Mary, and Jesus, she recognized what was happening and praised God too. She then went around telling everybody that this was the promised child. She and Simeon were both "prisoners of hope" (Zechariah 9:12, NIV), heirs to a promise, people of faith who saw into the spiritual realm and recognized God's purposes. And their faith was rewarded in his due time.

Simeon and Anna are wonderful representatives of the dynamics of faith, one holding to a personal promise he had been given, the other focusing on a promise given to the people of God as a whole. Their faith in God's words found fulfillment in the child of Bethlehem who had been brought to the Temple. Because all of God's promises are "yes" in Jesus (2 Corinthians 1:20)—he has won the full inheritance of the Kingdom for all of us to share—our faith in God's words finds fulfillment in him too. He is the centerpiece of God's faithfulness, the evidence that God keeps his word, the embodiment of the character and nature of the God we have placed our trust in. If we ever wondered whether God fulfills his purposes even after extraordinarily long and trying waits, Jesus confirms it. Just as God spoke through the faith of an old man and a prophetess, so will he speak through ours and carry out what he has said.

Jesus is the yes to every promise of God.

WILLIAM BARCLAY

In the Fullness of Time

When the fullness of time had come, God sent forth his Son.
GALATIANS 4:4, ESV

WHILE OUR SENSE OF TIME IS SHAPED BY our limited life spans, our impatience, our plans and agendas, our biological clocks, and the schedules imposed on us by others, God's sense of time is impeccable. Sometimes we wish he'd hurry up, and other times we think he's already too late. But God knows when the harvest is ripe and ready, and because our faith harvests more than we think—it involves other people, occasions for testimony, and ongoing ripple effects in peripheral facets of our lives—he waits until it has the maximum fruit for the greatest number of people. For us, that's hard to handle. For him, it's the fullness of time.

The long-awaited Messiah is the prime example. God's people surely thought many earlier moments would have been perfect for the deliverer to come, but God worked for centuries for the intersection of cultures, the expectations of his people, and the religious climate of an empire to come together in just the right ways. In the minds of his people, this was long overdue. In the mind of God, the timing was perfect.

There are hints of pregnancy and labor in today's verse—an appropriate metaphor for the seeds of faith that have been planted within us. God puts a promise deep within the soil of our hearts, and we wait until the time of labor for its birth to come. That wait can seem uncomfortably and even painfully long. So can the labor pains we experience at the time of fulfillment; his promises often come forth with a bit of trauma. But while we wait, we nourish those seeds, watch over them, and create the right climate for them to grow. We are pregnant with the promises he has given.

God is teaching us the way of faith, so we rarely experience immediate answers to our asking. But that doesn't mean nothing is happening. Seasons shift, plans develop, conditions ripen, and the harvest is never late. God—the master gardener, the fulfiller of divine purposes, the giver of life—is at work. And when the time is right, life comes forth. And it is always worth the wait.

The birth of Jesus is the sunrise in the Bible.

HENRY VAN DYKE

Loud and Joyful Faith

Sing, O childless woman, you who have never given birth!
ISAIAH 54:1

IN THE LATER CHAPTERS OF ISAIAH—those poetic and prophetic passages filled with hints of messianic ministry, the cost of redemption, and ultimate restoration—the prophet makes a startling statement: He tells barren women to sing. Why? Not because barrenness is worth celebrating; not because their shame is unwarranted (though it is); not because it's better to be childless in difficult times; but because they are about to have numerous children. The very things they are ashamed about, their deep disappointments of the past, are going to be undone.

These are not just words of a prophet, of course. They are words of God put into the mouth of Isaiah, who boldly says this is a divine decree. It's remarkable for numerous reasons, not the least of which is the fact that the barren are going to be fruitful. But just as remarkable is the command to go ahead and sing. By faith, the "barren"—literally and figuratively—are supposed to have a joyful celebration based on nothing other than the fact that God has foretold something. They don't see any evidence yet—their prayers have not yet been answered in any visible way—but the answer has been given. And that calls for a party.

Why does God tell people who have been repeatedly disappointed to go ahead and sing "loud and joyful" songs? Because faith expresses itself. When we hold back our celebration and our words to see if God is going to do something, we aren't yet convinced that he will. Faith doesn't say *if*; it says *when*. It goes ahead and counts on the fact that God has something good in store, and the rejoicing begins. Faith knows that the promise of God outweighs past disappointments and shame and celebrates the victory.

Don't rest in your faith until you get to that point. Don't let past disappointments color future expectations. Let your words, songs, dancing, and celebrations erupt in the assurance of his voice. Fruitfulness is coming. Let your faith—and your songs of joy—rise up in your heart.

Faith is the bird that sings while it is yet dark.

MAX LUCADO

Making Room for a Promise

*Enlarge your house; build an addition. Spread out
your home, and spare no expense!* ISAIAH 54:2

THE PROPHETIC WORDS OF ISAIAH told the barren to go ahead and sing because a season of fruitfulness was coming. Their disappointments would turn into praise. Their lack would turn into gain. Their pain would give way to rejoicing. No matter that there were no signs of this coming fruitfulness yet, no evidence of pregnant promises. The word was true. It was a done deal. The time for celebrating had already begun, even though the answer was not yet seen.

But the prophetic word doesn't end there. Faith not only sings and celebrates the promise of God. It does much more than anticipate. It prepares. The "barren" and "childless"—again, literally and figuratively—were not simply to wait for the appearance of God's answer. They were to go ahead and enlarge their houses. They needed to make room for the promise in advance.

That's how faith works. Passive, sofa-sitting faith is not the way God normally partners with his people. When we really believe God is going to do something, we prepare for it. We make room. We take a step in that direction. Like Noah building his ark, we have to get ready for the day of fulfillment. Otherwise we won't be able to handle the fulfillment when it comes. God calls us to be equipped to carry the weight of the promise when he gives it.

This is how God works, not just with barren women and captive people in Isaiah's era, but at all times—especially in an age of redemption and restoration, the year of God's favor Jesus inaugurated. It doesn't mean we can simply presume upon God to fill up any empty vessels or empty rooms we've prepared. We have to hear and receive his promise first. But once it's given, we are to partner with him, at least in some degree. We affirm with our words and do something, no matter how small, to suggest that we actually believe. It is never up to us to bring his promise about. But it is up to us not to be caught off guard by its fulfillment. We do that by putting feet to our faith, even as we sing and celebrate his faithfulness.

Action springs not from thought but from a readiness for responsibility.

DIETRICH BONHOEFFER

All Things New

*Fear not; you will no longer live in shame. Don't be
afraid; there is no more disgrace for you.*   ISAIAH 54:4

"THINGS NEVER WORK OUT FOR ME." "It's just always out of my reach."
"My time never seems to come." Heavy hearts say or think such things, usually with
complete conviction. But hearts have selective memories and skewed perspectives.
The truth is that God has already blessed us with every spiritual blessing in heavenly
places, promised to make all things work together for our good, and given us everything we need pertaining to life and godliness, including great and precious promises
that enable us to participate in the divine nature. None of that sounds like things not
working out for us or being just out of reach. Our time has already come. We just
need to know how to believe it.

But hearts that are well-acquainted with disappointment have trouble believing
the best, and God's promises are always the best. So we prophesy disappointment
over ourselves to protect our hearts from experiencing it once again. But in the
Kingdom of God, that's a problem. It's a false prophecy, a negative expectation, a lack
of faith—or actually faith in the reverse of God's will. When we assume his goodness
doesn't apply to us, that we just aren't going to have the same fulfilling experiences
other people have, we are suggesting that there is favoritism with God after all, contrary to his assurances that there isn't (Acts 10:34; Romans 2:11). We are letting our
shame, discouragement, and hopelessness dictate our faith.

There is only one solution: Stop. Your past disappointments do not apply to the
present or the future. No matter how tempted you are to guard your heart by not
getting your hopes up, it is imperative to get your hopes up about the things God
has clearly spoken. If you need to protect yourself from wishful thinking, go ahead.
But if you're trying to protect yourself from God's Word, you're undermining his
will for your life. The things-never-work-out-for-me syndrome is a spiritual disease,
and faith is the only cure. Embrace God's promises, sing about them, prepare for
them, and don't give up, no matter how much contrary evidence you think you see.
Breakthrough is surely, mercifully, resoundingly on its way.

The best is yet to be.

JOHN WESLEY

An Eternal Testimony

"The mountains may move and the hills disappear, but even then my faithful love for you will remain. My covenant of blessing will never be broken," says the LORD, who has mercy on you. **ISAIAH 54:10**

ULTIMATELY, OUR FAITH RESTS IN GOD'S FAITHFULNESS, and his faithfulness reflects his love. Prayer is not a technique, and faith is not a means to get what we want—though it eventually results in the fullness of life that we want. Prayer and faith are relational; the primary emphasis of both in our lives is to embrace the goodness of God, knowing that he will not let us down, even in the devastating moments when we may think he has. Faith looks to the end, sees the whole story— even when all the details aren't known—and says, "Yes." It embraces the faithfulness of God because that's the foundation of history and the anchor of our souls.

We see that in all of his promises—his zeal in telling the barren to sing; his extravagance in giving us every spiritual blessing; his encouragements along every step of the way; his assurances that all things, no matter how confusing, will ultimately work together for our good because we love him and are called according to his purposes. From the beginnings of Abraham's journey, across the vast vistas of redemption's story, through the ups and downs of covenant life and long seasons of frustration punctuated with great victories and joy, into the excruciating but glorious birth of new life into this world and the power God has given those who believe, we see his heart. His purposes are filled with his love. And that's the point.

In our journey of faith, we talk about God's promises, the mechanics and psychology of believing, the attitudes and actions we embrace along the way, and what life in his Kingdom is all about. But none of these are anything outside of a covenant of love with someone who is absolutely, irrevocably, unequivocally faithful. If our faith and prayers don't begin and end here, we've missed the whole purpose. We are redeemed and restored for our sake, to be sure, but also for a larger purpose. The journey of our lives is an eternal testimony of his heart.

I believe the promises of God enough to venture an eternity on them.

ISAAC WATTS

Always There

Be sure of this: I am with you always, even to the end of the age.
MATTHEW 28:20

DAVID LIVINGSTONE HAD HIS FLAWS, but he also had his faith. He was thoroughly convinced of his calling to go to regions where no missionary had ever been. He endured a mauling by a lion, the deaths of his wife and two of his children, the wrath of his mother-in-law, and resistance from other missionaries who did not get along with him. He vehemently opposed slavery and opened the eyes of many Europeans to Africa's needs. The reporter-explorer who found him in the depths of Africa—and who is said to have greeted him with the famous words "Dr. Livingstone, I presume"—described his faith as constant, earnest, sincere, quiet, and practical. It was also brash and stubborn at times, but it was never in question. Livingstone had staked his life on the promise that Jesus would always go with those who carried out his mission.[10]

Of all God's promises, this one is perhaps the most comprehensive and encouraging. Moses refused to continue on his mission unless God committed to go with him (Exodus 33:12-17). God promised Joshua on numerous occasions that he would be with him in his battles (Deuteronomy 31:6; Joshua 1:5, 9). The writer of Hebrews reminded his readers that God had promised never to leave, fail, or forsake them (Hebrews 13:5). And Jesus famously told his followers that he would be with them even to the end of the age (Matthew 28:20). As much as we look to God's promises, it's even better to know that the Promiser is with us. Faith fills our hearts and minds when we remember and rest in God's presence.

Wherever you find yourself on the journey of faith, remember this. Refuse to see faith as a commodity or a tool rather than as a product of God's presence in your life. Make every effort to align your prayers with the mission of Jesus and the nature of his Kingdom, knowing that you are speaking to someone in the room who has very definite plans for them. Rest in the confidence that you cannot stray beyond his reach or pray effectively beyond his love. He is both our safety and our strength, and he is with us to the end of the age—and beyond.

On these words I staked everything, and they never failed.
DAVID LIVINGSTONE

Mysterious Ways

*Now we see things imperfectly, like puzzling reflections in a mirror, but
then we will see everything with perfect clarity.* **1 CORINTHIANS 13:12**

NO ONE MASTERS GOD'S WAYS. They originate in an infinite mind and
cover an infinite range of possibilities and situations. He graciously shares with us
a revelation of his ways in Scripture, but as Scripture itself admits in several places,
there is far more that could be written and much more we will see in the end. As
the psalmist said, God's knowledge is too wonderful, too great to understand (Psalm
139:6). For now, we see through a glass darkly, waiting for the day when everything
appears with perfect clarity. Faith grasps some of that clarity now, but sight will one
day far outshine it.

In the meantime, you will continue to have some mysteries in your life, prayers
you thought God would answer a certain way but didn't. You might chalk them up
to misunderstanding his will or promises, and even so, you will have received far
more in your journey of faith than if you had started out questioning, doubting, and
praying tentatively. Continue in that same spirit of belief. Don't focus on anything
God hasn't done, but instead celebrate what he *has* done and press forward in faith.
If you fix your gaze on what you think remains missing, it will grow larger in your
own mind. If you set it on what God has done, that will grow larger, and you will
be filled with gratitude.

That's ultimately where the journey of faith ends—with gratitude. No one fin-
ishes this journey disappointed, at least not after reaching the other side of the
veil. When we look back from that place, we will see every yes, every no, and every
season of waiting as pure love. We will realize that the temporary pains of the world
could never outweigh the glories of the Kingdom, no matter how difficult they were
to bear. Disappointments will fade into nothing; fulfillment will seem even more
monumental than it first appeared. Faith will become sight, hope will be rewarded,
and love will remain the greatest of these.

> Deep in unsearchable mines of never-failing skill, he
> treasures up his bright designs and works his sovereign will.
>
> WILLIAM COWPER

Notes

1. Janet and Geoff Benge, *Isobel Kuhn: On the Roof of the World* (Seattle: YWAM Publishing, 2010).
2. Norman Grubb, *Rees Howells, Intercessor* (Port Washington, PA: CLC Publications, 1952), chap. 22.
3. Adapted from L. B. Cowman (Mrs. Charles E. Cowman), *Streams in the Desert* (Grand Rapids, MI: Zondervan, 1996), devotional reading for August 17.
4. Jonathan Goforth, *By My Spirit* (Toronto: Evangelical Publishers, 1929), 26.
5. Andrew Murray, *Waiting on God* (Minneapolis: Bethany House Publishers, 2001), 64.
6. Ruth A. Tucker, *From Jerusalem to Irian Jaya: A Biographical History of Christian Missions*, 2nd ed. (Grand Rapids, MI: Zondervan, 1983, 2004), 249–51.
7. Tucker, *From Jerusalem to Irian Jaya*, 296.
8. Tucker, *From Jerusalem to Irian Jaya*, 251.
9. Tucker, *From Jerusalem to Irian Jaya*, 304. See also Chris Meehan, "Nigerians Honor 'Spiritual Mother,'" *Banner*, January 18, 2011, https://www.thebanner.org/together/2011/01/nigerians-honor-spiritual-mother.
10. Tucker, *From Jerusalem to Irian Jaya*, 155–63.

Scripture Index

About the Author

Insightful and thought-provoking, **CHRIS TIEGREEN** has inspired thousands of people through his popular One Year devotionals, including *The One Year Walk with God Devotional*, *The One Year At His Feet Devotional*, *The One Year Hearing His Voice Devotional*, and *The One Year Experiencing God's Presence Devotional*. He is also the author of the devotionals *The Wonder of Advent* and *The Promise of Lent* as well as *Unburdened* and numerous other books that have been translated into more than thirty languages. Tiegreen's experiences in ministry, journalism, and higher education bring a unique perspective to his writing.

Devotionals by Chris Tiegreen

The One Year At His Feet Devotional

The One Year Experiencing God's Presence Devotional

The One Year God with Us Devotional

The One Year Hearing His Voice Devotional

The One Year Heaven on Earth Devotional

The One Year Praying in Faith Devotional

The One Year Shine Your Light Devotional

The One Year Walk with God Devotional

The One Year Worship the King Devotional

The Promise of Lent Devotional

The Wonder of Advent Devotional

CP1707